Chickens, Turkeys, Eggs

and Other Fowl Business;

a Poultry Memoir

by

Peter Hunton

D1692830

<u>Chickens, Turkeys, Eggs and other Fowl Business :</u>
<u>A Poultry Memoir</u>
<u>by: Peter Hunton</u>

published 2022
ISBN 978-1-77835-149-5
ISBN 978-1-77835-063-4 ebook

author: Peter Hunton, Ph.D
206-127 Blair Road,
Cambridge,
ON N2J 2S2
CANADA
email: peter.hunton@rogers.com

front cover design by David Gee

rear cover; the author at the XXI World's Poultry Congress,
Montreal, 2000

TABLE OF CONTENTS page

This book is dedicated to the worldwide community of poultry farmers, large and small, to those who supply their needs, and those who help them succeed.

Prologue

The motivation to prepare this memoir was entirely selfish. After a long career which involved a lot of writing about poultry came to an end, I very much missed the activity of putting words on a page. I had kept a daily journal throughout my life, and here, I thought, was an opportunity to put it to use. At first, I thought I would concentrate entirely on the poultry aspect of my life, since that was what put a roof over our heads and kept bread and wine on the table. But it became clear to me that separating the poultry from the personal would not be representative of my life as a whole, and so domestic matters became an important part of the composition.

The poultry industry has evolved quite remarkably over the time I have been a part of it, and I would not be so vain as to believe that anything I write now might possibly influence its future. It has been said that those who ignore the mistakes of the past are bound to repeat them; there have been plenty of mistakes in the poultry business but in the main, industry has had to take corrective action very quickly and this has been a part of its evolution.

As I point out early in the memoir, my entry into the poultry sphere resulted not from any burning predisposition, but more because it seemed to be an open field. That, of course, was an error on my part. I soon found that many others had already entered the field, but they were a welcoming bunch, and I have always been grateful to the people I have worked with for their cooperation and good will. I have a huge respect for the industry and all of the business and academic institutions that have supported it over the past sixty years.

We in poultry are a relatively small part of the food world. I still find people who say "What on earth do you do?" when I tell them I am a poultry scientist. I hope this memoir will provide a thoughtful answer.

Chapter I

My Early Life, and First Steps Into The Field Of Poultry.

I was born on June 12th, 1936 in Jesmond, a district of Newcastle on Tyne. My father, Stanley Hunton, was a clerk in a shipping office on Newcastle's quayside. My mother Esther Hunton, never worked but diligently kept house for the family. She was also a keen gardener and a student of natural history with a special interest in Alpine plants.

At the beginning of World War II, the family moved to Ponteland, about 10 miles out of the city, to avoid possible bombing of our urban house. Bombs did in fact fall close enough to the old house to shatter some windows. The bungalow we moved to was at first rented, but eventually was put up for sale and my parents bought it for £1250. This was a huge leap for my father, who was not from a moneyed family, but he got a mortgage and eventually owned it outright – I am not sure when. His father, Thomas Alfred Hunton had been a corn (i.e. wheat) trader and had not done well. In fact he and his wife Elizabeth had no home; in the winter they rented accommodation in Bridlington, a seaside town in Yorkshire, and in summer circulated among his three daughters and us. My mother's family was more well to do. Her father, Spencer Hume, worked as a stockbroker and accumulated some wealth. Her mother Kitty, from whom my Jewish heritage arose, died when I was three years old and I don't remember her at all. Interestingly, the Jewish angle was suppressed to the extent that my mother only told me about it when I was about forty years old!

When I was growing up in Ponteland, I wanted to be a farmer. So I got to know the folks who ran the local dairy farm, the Straughan family led by brothers Jack and King, and I helped with the cows. At that time, the farmstead was in the village but the grazing and crop land was a half mile or so away and each day we had to drive the cows along a main road to and from their pasture, and damn the traffic; the cows had priority. These were Ayrshires, about 15 of them, and they had their own bull, named Hebron Golden Future, who stayed in his pen at the home farm until needed. He was typically bullish, and once cornered Jack Straughan in his pen while being fed, and gave him a nasty fright. The Straughans cooled and bottled their own milk, unpasteurized, and delivered it house to house in an old Ford van.

To encourage my interest, the herdsman, Harry Thompson, helped me groom a calf and exhibit it at the local Agricultural Show. I learned the basics of livestock judging and how to parade the calf in front of judges.

The only reason I can remember chickens at this farm is because a weasel got into the coop one night and killed about half of them.

At that time the local Young Farmers Club was very active and I joined. They provided good training in livestock judging, many aspects of farming and agriculture and particularly public speaking. I moved into their public speaking competitions and was quite successful, and this has been extremely useful in my subsequent career. The ability to hold an audience, to respond to questions and indulge in intelligent conversations in public has been of tremendous value.

But the longer I was involved in the Young Farmers, the more I came to recognize that the ambition to become a farmer was unlikely to be realized; the need for a large initial capital outlay was obvious, and our family circumstances would not come close to providing it. One of the other factors highlighting this realization was the experience of Harry, the herdsman at the Straughan farm. He by now had married the dairymaid, and left to start his own farm, a fifty acre holding established by the local government to rent to beginning farmers. I could see the impossibility of making a decent living from such a business. I believe he was better off financially, even if less independent, as a herdsman.

This realization was only confirmed during my time at the Kings College Department of Agriculture where I went to study for my Honours Degree. This covered the period from September, 1955 until June 1958. At that time, the College was part of the University of Durham. It is now the University of Newcastle. The College had a fine reputation and an excellent faculty. Head of the Department was Prof. M. McG. Cooper, an agricultural scientist originally from New Zealand.

After an initial year of general studies, students specialized in either crop or animal husbandry, and I chose the latter. The College owned two large active farms in the County of Northumberland. Nafferton Farm had a large dairy herd and several hundred acres of crop land, while Cockle Park ran beef, grazing and cash crops. At the time Cockle Park was famous for it's pasture seed mixture. It also housed an experimental chicken flock.

In their final year prior to graduation, Honours students had to undertake a small research project. Most of the other animal production students opted for large animals. But the Lecturer in Genetics and Statistics, Dr. M. Rex Patchell, suggested to me that I undertake "A Study of Some Factors Affecting Fertility in Poultry", and so for the first time, I became interested in chickens. Part of the reason for my decision was that the poultry field appeared to be practically empty; why join the competition in the large animal field, when I could apparently have poultry all to myself? And so began a lifelong interest, nay, fascination, with the chicken and indeed the other domesticated poultry species. For this, I am extremely grateful to Dr. Patchell. His statistics lectures were incomprehensible to me until after I took a similar course later, but he was a pleasant and helpful supervisor. He later returned to New Zealand and enjoyed a long and successful career at Massey Agricultural College (now an important part of Massey University).

My study of fertility in chickens really did begin at "square one". I knew absolutely nothing about the anatomy, physiology or behaviour of birds in general or chickens specifically. So I read some text books and reviewed the current literature. This was made more difficult by the fact that the University Library did not subscribe to any poultry journals; I eventually traced some in the local Ministry of Agriculture, Fisheries and Food library, and received special permission to use it. Even there, they did not carry the Worlds Poultry Science Journal, but the local Poultry Adviser allowed me to borrow his copies!

In collaboration with Patchell, I then planned a basic experimental program. For the observations of mating behaviour, I set up a platform overlooking four single-male pens in the converted barn where the birds were housed. Each pen contained one male and twelve females. Inevitably, I became known to all and sundry as "the cock-watcher"! I sat up there with a set of binoculars on Fridays from 7.00 am to 9.00 pm. with breaks for meals and relaxation. After 3 weeks, by which time the daily pattern of matings had been established, I commenced observations at 3.00 pm. Most eggs were laid prior to noon. Everyone knows now that matings prior to this time may be less successful because of the chance that a hard shelled egg may be present in the hen's oviduct, thus obstructing the passage of sperm up the oviduct to storage glands in the infundibulum.

Like most other species that practice sexual reproduction, the system in poultry is extremely wasteful. Following a single successful mating, female chickens produced fertile eggs for about a week. With turkeys it is closer to two weeks. At each natural mating, literally millions of spermatozoa were transferred from male to female, yet only one was needed to fertilize each egg. The cockerels I watched mated an average of 10 times daily but there were large differences between them. In one pen, the cockerel mated an average of 12 times daily, while another averaged only 6. However, there was no difference in the fertility of the eggs gathered from these four pens.

When I was undertaking this study, artificial insemination (AI) was well established in cattle, and was beginning to replace natural mating on a large

9

commercial scale. Probably the Straughans would have gotten rid of Hebron Golden Future by then! But in poultry, AI was still in its infancy. Although a technique had been reported almost twenty years previously, nobody had found a way to preserve or dilute poultry semen and still yield acceptable fertility. So as a commercial technique it had limited application (although as we will find later, primary breeders came to use it extensively). However, we decided as part of my study, to look at semen quality in a dozen Rhode Island Red and Light Sussex cockerels.

I had to learn the technique of semen acquisition from cockerels from scratch. The birds were kept together in a pen, not in cages. As I later discovered, this was not in my best interest as a novice experimenter! However, I managed to get semen from the majority of the birds, and looked at it under the microscope. It would be true to say that I learned nothing that was not already published, but the experience was a valuable asset.

Six of us were involved in the Honours Animal Production program. We had our own study room, called "the Honours Hut" and we became good friends over the 9 months we were together. In the end, two received First Class Honours. One of these was Mike Leyburn, who had completed Military Service before coming to university. Mike was a brilliant student and I think he went on to a successful career with the Milk Marketing Board, which was involved with a large scale Artificial Insemination program. I got a Second Class, Upper Division Honours Degree with which I was quite satisfied. But I still had no idea for a future career. I had, however developed an ongoing interest in poultry. My decision to enter this apparently empty field had led to the discovery that it was not entirely empty, but that there were many interesting avenues that awaited exploration. And so I looked for an opportunity to further my education in the science of poultry.

When I discovered that Wye College, a part of the University of London, was offering a newly established course leading to a M.Sc. Degree in Poultry Science, I became extremely interested.

Chapter 2

Wye College and Continuing My Interest in Poultry.

Because I lived only a few miles from Newcastle, and had a motor cycle, it was easy to live at home while studying for my first degree. It was also very cost-effective.

Going to Wye would be a different matter. Acceptance there was not a problem but I needed a scholarship to fund tuition and accommodation. These were available from the Ministry of Agriculture, Fisheries and Food (MAFF) at the level of £400 *per annum*. I applied for one of these grants, took the interview during my first ever visit to London, and was successful. With vacation work, this would see me through the two-year course in reasonable shape.

My social life in Ponteland had revolved around the Blackbird Inn, which is still in business in 2021. It was a very old stone building, actually an ancient castle, with a narrow spiral staircase to my favourite bar. It was walking distance from home. In addition to my regular attendance at the upstairs bar, a group of us played music on Sunday nights in the music room. This began as a "Skiffle Group" with guitars and singing, but later evolved into a drop in of all kinds of musicians and a jazz flavour. The landlord, Willy Holmes, provided us each with a pint for the evening, which was a great deal for him, as we drank and paid for several more and the room was packed to capacity most nights. My paternal grandfather did a very good watercolour painting of the pub, which I still have. I was very sorry to leave this part of life behind!

I missed the Blackbird, but soon discovered many wonderful pubs near my new home in Kent.

At the end of September, 1958, I started in the M.Sc program at Wye College. Although part of the University of London, Wye is located about 60 miles east of the city of London, between Ashford and Canterbury. I decided to live in the Postgraduate Residence, "Squires", as I had no idea what other choices there might be. There were 10 of us enrolled in this inaugural course, 8 men and 2 women. Not surprisingly, we became a fairly close-knit group within the College.

The Principal at the time, Dunstan Skillbeck, was a typical Oxbridge type, and attempted, quite successfully, to make Wye like a small version of an Oxford college. We wore gowns for dinner in "Hall" and the Senior Common Room was a smoke-filled chamber where Port and Sherry were served at appropriate times. Students attended "handshakes" with the

Principal at the end of each term (semester). Several of us poultry students lived in Squires, including Rodney 'Dan' Durrant, who became one of my lifelong friends. (He died in 2015). Pat Howe and Janice Coppock lived in Withersdane Hall, the women's residence. Martyn Sharpe, the son of a commercial poultry breeder in Yorkshire, lived in Squires, as did Noel Holt and Joe Byng. Two of the other men, Peter Thompson and Mike Festing were married and lived off-campus, as did Philip Lee, one of the wildest characters I have ever met. Philip knew all the pubs, all the girls and pretty much everything a student needed. His father was the Canon of Southend in Essex!

Our leader and mentor was Eric Maddison, a Cambridge graduate in Statistics, who developed, promoted and led the Poultry Science M.Sc program. Eric had become interested in genetics, and had started a selection program for increased egg production in two flocks, one Rhode Island Red (R.I.R.) which had been closed for 10 years and one Light Sussex (closed for five years). He was an enormously likable and generous man, and a huge asset to us and the College in general. In the early days, he would join us in The George pub, which quickly became the haunt of the Poultry group.

In addition to Eric, the other faculty member in the Department of Poultry Science was a Scottish woman called Ann Murray. Ann had a M.S. in Poultry Science from Ohio State University and taught Poultry Management. She also undoubtedly had a hand in designing the course, based on her experience in Ohio, and led most of the field trips.

The M.Sc. program took two years. The first year involved only taught courses and field trips. The taught courses covered a complete range of subjects: Nutrition, Zoology, Economics, Statistics and Genetics. At the end of the second year, we had an intense 3-week program on Poultry Health and Diseases, with two weeks in London at the Royal Veterinary College and one week at the Houghton Grange Poultry Research Centre. Also in the second year, each student was assigned a free-standing research project and prepared a thesis describing it, plus of course a defense with an external examiner.

The College Poultry Department farm housed Eric Maddison's selection populations and included, at the time, free range rearing facilities (replete with exposure to foxes) and loose-housed (deep litter) laying facilities with trap-nests for individual record keeping. The Farm Manager was a Yorkshireman called Charles Day, and he supervised a staff of about 10 people. The farm had its own feed mill and incubator.

Wye College comprised the University of London's faculties of Agriculture and Horticulture. So, in addition to the poultry farm, the College also owned and operated several other farming facilities and a large Horticulture Department. There was a Department of Hop Research, as its location in Kent placed it in one of the two major hop growing areas in England.

An important part of the poultry course involved visits to commercial farms and also attendance at industry functions. At the time, each county in England had a MAFF Poultry Adviser, and they set up useful meetings with a variety of speakers. The Poultry Adviser for Kent was Tom Crocker, who became a personal friend during my time there.

Many of the farms we visited were using a bewildering array of non-agricultural buildings to house laying hens. One 17th century mansion housed birds in many separate rooms, and at another location, a disused swimming pool was used. The poultry industry was slow to recover following World War II, as the priority use for the limited supply of grain was for human food. The poultry meat industry was almost non-existent; chicken and turkey were luxuries. However, during my time at Wye, a few pioneers, led by the indomitable Geoffrey Sykes, investigated the US broiler industry and began to emulate it. One of the pioneering companies, Buxted Chicken, processed 16,000 birds/day. Few may remember this, but when the first broiler growers in the UK started, they had a choice between growing cockerels that were the brothers of the brown-egg laying hens, or the scarce and much more expensive specialized meat chickens hatched from breeding stock imported from the United States.

Laying hens were all loose housed, as cages were only just being introduced in the US and British farms were much more familiar with floor management.

Student life was busy but fun. We had our lectures, farm and industry visits, and regular reviews of activity at the College farm. Our social life was chiefly at The George, and in addition, a variety of lovely local pubs in the Kent countryside. One favourite, which was quite a distance from Wye, near Harrietsham, was the 16th century Ringlestone Inn. This was presided over by two women, mother and daughter, and we nicknamed it "Dirty Dora's". We would show up, to be met by these two, dressed in ankle length gowns, and the welcoming cry of "Gentlemen of Wye College – How nice to see you!". We then proceeded to sink many pints, and sing the most raucous rugby songs imaginable. Dorah would respond with equally riské stories. {I recently (May 2017) googled Ringlestone Inn. Today Christina and Kevin will serve you a Steak and Ale pie (no doubt microwaved from the freezer) for £14.95}

Each M.Sc. student spent a week working at the Poultry Department, which included trapnesting, sorting hatching eggs (which were sold to a commercial hatchery), record maintenance, feeding the flocks and other routine chores.

At the end of my first term, I traveled home by motor cycle. I chose a route avoiding London, going by way of the Gravesend-Tilbury ferry, then wending my way through the countryside and finally to the main A1 road north. It took 11 hours! During the second year, I bought, for £25, a 1931 MG model A. The first time I drove it home took more than 13 hours! Much later in my time at Wye, after the construction of the Dartford Tunnel and some ring roads and motorways, the journey took about 10 hours, and by then I was driving my first Morris Mini Minor.

For December-January, 1958-59, a vacation job had been arranged for me at the Fairbairn hatchery in Carlisle and this provided useful practical experience. It was managed at the time by George Fairbairn. Of course, the hatchery business was then still quite labour-intensive, with manual setting of eggs, candling by hand at 18 days, transferring eggs to the hatchers and finally pulling, grading and sexing chicks. Most sexing was by the Japanese method, but some varieties used down-colour sexing, as in the Rhode Island Red x Light Sussex, which was very popular at the time. I commuted to Carlisle by motor-bike, staying in a boarding house through the week and going home on the weekends.

I returned to Wye in early January, 1959; it was good to be back! Our lectures, seminars and farm visits continued, as did our social life in various pubs. I also began to attend live theatre in Canterbury, at the lovely old Marlowe Theatre. Although I had been to live theatre in the Memorial Hall in Ponteland, and a few shows at the Playhouse in Jesmond, I really began to seek it out in Kent. Thus began a lifelong pursuit, and as will be detailed later, diversions from audience to participant! When we were in London at the end of the second year, on our course at the Royal Vet. College, I went to see *The Mousetrap*, then in its 13th year, at the Courthouse Theatre.

Our little community at Squires contained not only poultry postgraduates, but a variety of others, mostly from overseas. One of these, Reg Appadurai from Ceylon (now Sri Lanka) was in residence for a year before being joined by his wife, when he moved out into rental accommodation. Reg taught me how to cook curry; and incidentally, dahl and boiled rice. We had these delicacies especially on Sundays, when the meal "in hall" was a very basic "cold meat and salad". Along with two other students from Sudan, we cooked up some very hot dishes; they had hot pepper spice sent from home! I still enjoy these from time to time.

We as poultry students attended all the local industry meetings and became familiar with local and national developments, as well as meeting some of the participants. We also enjoyed a visit from Dr. Rupert Coles, Chief Poultry Adviser to the Minister of Agriculture. Rupert was quite a character; always wearing a bow tie and a carnation buttonhole. When he visited, all the students wore similar garb! I never knew quite how much Dr. Coles knew about poultry, but he was a great spokesman for the industry when it really needed one, and was able to maintain a very high profile advisory service for a number of years. No doubt he also helped secure scholarships for several of the Poultry M.Sc students, including me.

Towards the end of this first year at Wye, I determined the subject for my research project to occupy the second year. This was to build on the topic of fertility that I studied at Cockle Park, extending it to embrace hatchability, with specific reference to genetic control. To this end, I began to monitor the hatchability of the R.I.R and Light Sussex flocks at the Poultry Department, which involved breaking out all unhatched eggs to determine fertility and/or time of embryonic mortality. In the course of this work, I identified dead embryos from a few specific families in the Light Sussex flock that showed symptoms of a lethal gene, which I successfully found in the literature. This was called "Talpid" because the embryos had a superficial resemblance to a mole, and was the subject of my first scientific publication. We called it "talpid^{3}" since two previous publications had described it, and we had no way of knowing whether this was identical, or a unique mutation. But as a result of the discovery, we quickly removed the families carrying the lethal gene from the pedigree flock.

At the end of the year, Eric Maddison arranged a trip to The Netherlands to see some of their poultry industry and research. Even then, as now, that country was a poultry powerhouse, not particularly for primary production, but for many of the supplies industry relied on. Incubators, processing equipment, feed additives, primary breeders, and many others were based there and had huge international businesses.

We had two Volkswagen buses, that we picked up in Arnhem, after travelling by ferry to Ostend, and by train *via* Brussels, Antwerp, Roosendaal and Nijmegen. We stayed in a Hostel with communal bedrooms and ate out. We visited commercial hatcheries and breeding farms, the Reform Incubator Company (now Pas-Reform) and the University of Wageningen. We met Prof. Romijn, a world renowned embryologist and incubation specialist (he advised Reform). We saw duck growing and processing, egg production and packing, and the Poultry Testing Station at Putten. The Poultry Research Station at Beekbergen was particularly impressive, as it encompassed many aspects of poultry research at a single location.

We did the tourist things in Amsterdam, and saw the polders and land reclaimed from the sea. Quite the trip in a mere 7 days!

Soon after our return, I started my summer job in Yorkshire, with the conglomerate then owned by the Reed brothers, Eric and Guy. They hatched, grew and processed broiler chickens and turkeys. This later became part of the Buxted/Western Chicken group and eventually Ross Poultry, but in 1959 was still independent. My boss was a wonderful man called Jim Richards. Jim was determined that I should see and do everything. So I worked in breeder houses, chicken houses, turkey houses, hatcheries, the whole nine yards. For the final two weeks, I was seconded to the company's chicken barbecue shop in Harrogate, called Barbec. I was told this was to fill in for the manager while he was on holiday, but when I arrived, I found that he either quit or was fired, and I was his replacement! I also had to train his and my successor. So I quickly learned how an electric rotisserie worked, how to mount the chickens on spits, and how to operate the cash register. At this time there was no Kentucky Fried Chicken, no McDonald's, in fact very little fast food at all. We sold a lot of chickens! The downside for me was the pervasive smell of hot chicken fat, which followed me home at night, and on weekends, and I couldn't face eating chicken for several weeks after I left. The new manageress, Dorothy was very attractive and we had a brief relationship before she took up with company whiz Guy Reed. I don't know what became of that, but of course, I was totally outclassed!

For the second half of the summer vacation, I worked with a crew from Wye running a hop picking machine in rural Sussex. This was the third or fourth year that Wye had supplied the crew, and one of the poultry postgraduates, Peter Thompson, was the Manager. Philip Lee and Dan Durrant were also part of the group. One of the Wye undergraduates, Peter Gooch, of whom more later, was another member. We lived, about ten of us, in a farm cottage built to hold a small family, while the one female member of the crew lived in a house trailer in the yard. She cooked for us. We got up early every morning and our job was to bring in, on trailers pulled by farm tractors, the entire hop vines which were cut off at ground level and pulled on to the trailers. These were then hung on a conveyor and the leaves and flowers stripped by rotating fingers (not unlike a poultry defeathering machine!). A fan operating near the stripping machine blew many of the leaves off, leaving the heavier flowers, which fell on to a conveyor, and a crew of women removed by hand the remaining leaves. We then filled loose sacks (called "pokes") with the flowers and took them for drying.

Our job ended when the requisite bulk of hop flowers was harvested, and loaded into the familiar conical oast houses for drying. So we had a few hours to eat, and visit one of the lovely Sussex pubs for the evening. This was usually the 14th century Peacock Inn, near Goudhurst. The Peacock is still there, but with a full dining menu as well as beer, cider and a large wine list. We wouldn't have dared to mention wine in 1959!

The hop picking machine we worked on probably replaced about fifty hand pickers, but the majority of hops were still picked by hand, with the pickers being Londoners who came in droves as a holiday. So there were huge numbers of "out-of-town" people around, to the extent that many of the nicer pubs posted signs saying "No hop pickers"! But we "gentlemen from Wye College" were kindly exempted and had a wonderful time. Late in the evening, whenever the hops were dry, a few of us would be employed in the oast house taking out the hops and packing them in "pockets", huge sacks about ten feet tall full of compressed hops, but still easily carried by one man. The oast house contained a barrel of "Mild ale" which was free to workers, but at the ambient temperature of the oast house (probably about 23°C this wasn't anybody's favourite drink. Especially after several pints of best bitter in the pub.

Hop picking lasted only about three weeks, after which we were offered apple picking on a piece work basis. After two days, I found that I wasn't even making enough to pay board and lodging, so I quit and went home for the remaining few days of the summer vacation.

For our second year, we had some lectures but mostly worked on our research project, and at the end of the year we had exams in all subjects, plus of course presentation and defence of our theses. My thesis was entitled: "A Study of some factors affecting the hatchability of chicken eggs, with special reference to genetic control."

When the exam results were published it turned out Dan Durrant and one of the girls, Janice Coppock, had failed. In Dan's case I was sure that this resulted from an incorrect estimate of how little work he could do and still pass. It didn't stop him from securing a very good job with Western Chicken, which led to a successful career, ending up as a nutritionist for the Buxted Group, of which Western became a part. Some time late in the 1960's, the University contacted him with the news that if he didn't re-sit the exams, he would become permanently ineligible for the degree. So he swotted furiously and based on this and his subsequent experience, passed. Bravo!

Chapter 3

A Taste Of Research and Teaching.   Wye College, 1960-66

The subject of hatchability in poultry proved of great interest to me. Already in print was a textbook from 1949 and a monograph published in 1951, both by American authors. I reviewed the subsequent literature, again mostly American, and became familiar with the names of scientists working in the field.   One, Peter Lake, was a specialist in artificial insemination (AI) and worked at the Poultry Research Centre in Edinburgh. Although we used natural mating for all the stocks at Wye, I had become familiar with AI while working at Cockle Park, and its use would become widespread as more and more commercial and research flocks were housed in cages. I got to know Peter quite well in subsequent years.

Most of the literature on hatchability suggested mostly environmental, rather than genetic influences. Of course, lethal genes like Talpid provided exceptions.

I became increasingly adept at analyzing unhatched eggs. This too was to prove useful in later life. The ability to distinguish infertile eggs from those with very early dead embryos has quite a substantial commercial application when investigating breeder flock and hatchery performance. Fertility is clearly a function of the breeder flock, but embryo mortality may result from egg mis-handling, incubator problems, or a combination of causes.

I analyzed all of the unhatched eggs from both the R.I.R and L.S. flocks during the reproduction of the lines in 1959. The analysis was consistent with published data, showing the majority of embryo deaths occurring either in the first 3 days or the last 3 days of the 21 day incubation period. The exception was the Talpid embryos, which tended to survive up to 10 or 12 days of incubation.

My estimates of the heritability of hatchability were generally higher than the few literature values previously published.

All of the statistical analyses were conducted using the then state-of-the-art Facit calculator. It was only a year or two later that a Ferranti computer came on stream at the University and Eric Maddison quickly succumbed to what was then called "infatuation with computers syndrome". Similarly, the thesis of ~ 8,000 words was roughly typed by me on an old upright typewriter which I had acquired and learned to use, and then a fair copy, with two carbons, typed by Mary Skinner, the College Principal's secretary. For this she was, not very handsomely, paid.

Mary had a nice room in what was known as the Lepper Colony, a very large old house owned by Dennis and Grace Lepper. They lived in part of the house and the rest was divided up and rented. Mary's was the largest and nicest of the rented rooms. Many of us went to her place for coffee after a night at the pub. How she put up with this, I will never know.

The Leppers had one son and two very attractive daughters one of whom, Liz, was employed for a time at the College. I dated her once or twice, but she eventually married one of the Poultry Postgraduates, Jim Parlour. I have kept in touch with them on and off ever since. After receiving his M.Sc., Jim did a Ph.D at Oregon State, worked for a while in Winnipeg and returned to the UK. They ran a small hotel, Jim worked teaching at a community college and bought and sold antiques. They had a daughter in Calgary, and visited us in Cambridge once, *en route* to Calgary

During the Spring of 1960 I was in discussions with Eric Maddison regarding my future. He hoped to establish another poultry position, which I would occupy as Assistant Lecturer. (This was roughly comparable to Assistant Professor in N. America). In addition, I applied for a job back in Newcastle, also at the Assistant Lecturer level. I had an interview but the job eventually went to Maurice Bichard. It is interesting, but maybe unprofitable, to speculate as to my subsequent life and career if I had been appointed to that position!

In early June, I was offered, by the Principal, a Postgraduate Research Fellowship paying £700/*annum*. I had been hoping for Assistant Lecturer at £900. After some negotiation by Eric Maddison and both of us present in the Principal's office, the offer was changed, and everybody seemed happy.

Later in June, on the way home, I stopped in to visit Jim Richards in Dalton, mainly to say "Hello", but he offered me a job as Personal Assistant, and in charge of Turkey Breeding. Of course, by this time I had accepted the job in Wye, but it was nice to feel wanted. In the event, I became Consultant to the Yorkshire Turkey Breeders program, which gave me a nice foot in the door of commercial breeding. I worked this consultancy for the next six years, in collaboration with Jim's subsequently appointed Personal Assistant, Tony Dewhirst. This involved visits to Yorkshire several times a year, and we developed some useful turkey strains. I stayed in nice hotels and indulged in very good eating and drinking!

In the summer break prior to starting work at Wye, I took a job with Yorkshire Turkey Producers, and lived in the Company hostel with a couple of others. One of them was Jack Harrison, newly appointed advertising/PR person for the Group. We had lots of late night talks about the industry and our place in it, mostly in some of east Yorkshire's excellent pubs.

My first official activity for Yorkshire Turkey Producers was to visit the University of Edinburgh to talk to people about turkey breeding. George Clayton at the Institute of Animal Genetics was for many years a consultant to British United Turkeys (B.U.T) so he was a bit circumspect, but as an academic person, was obliged to listen to my questions. I also met Ranald McIver, lecturer in genetics at the University. The following week, Jim Richards and I visited Brian Dale, who was breeding and growing some 300,000 turkeys annually. George Clayton was consulting here as well as B.U.T. Jim tried to buy some of his male line but he declined, and I can't say I blamed him.

So we essentially started our male lines from scratch. Jim had "acquired" a strain of small turkeys from the Wrolstadt company in the US, developed from the Beltsville Small White, which we began to develop as a female line, but their small size was limiting and we eventually had to look elsewhere. We got some Broad Breasted Whites from a company called Spiller (no relation to the feed company of the same name). During that summer at Yorkshire Turkey, I put together a breeding program which after some tweaking, became the blueprint for the following years. It was an interesting time and I thoroughly enjoyed it. I visited several times each year for two or three days and the program worked very well.

One innovation for us was to house the female lines in cages, for ease of recording egg production. Little did we know that by doing this, we suppressed the expression of broodiness. This trait had afairly strong genetic basis and when subsequent generations were bred in floor pens, we had high levels of broodiness. One lives and learns.

Social life as always centred on pubs. Jack Harrison, Keith George (nutritionist for the associated feed company, Nitrovit) and others met most nights in one of many, with a wonderful range of names; the Horsebreakers Arms, the Shoulder of Mutton, the Golden Fleece, the Jolly Farmers, the Three Tuns, among them. And a few, which we knew well, stayed open after regular hours (10.30 closing on weekdays) and we were not always in bed by midnight. At home on weekends, I spent time with parents and friends, often traveling Northumberland and the border countryside in my car, or grandfather Hume's. The parents never owned a car, although my mother bought one following my father's death in 1968. Evenings, however, were spent with old friends in the Blackbird and other local pubs.

I returned to Wye at the beginning of September, 1960, to start my job as Assistant Lecturer. For the first while, I rented a bedroom on a local council housing estate and ate meals at the Wye Hill Café. But after a while, when Mary Skinner left, I got her place in the Lepper Colony, where I could cook my own meals.

I stayed there until I bought a small bungalow in Stelling Minnis, about 8 Miles from Wye. I am not sure why I chose Stelling Minnis, but the local pub, the Rose and Crown with a Geordie landlord, may have had something to do with it.

My first job at Wye was to help with the new (third) intake of Poultry M.Sc. students, in terms of arranging farm visits etc.

I was also to register for my Ph.D. degree, as in those days one could do this while employed as a lecturer. For this, I planned to extend further my studies of hatchability and to look at its relationships with other traits like egg production rate and egg weight. All of this, of course, using the College flocks of R.I.R. and L.S. While Eric Maddison was still there and very much in charge, he had an aversion to writing up the long-term results of the selection work and I became interested in this as well as my thesis topic. By this time, the University of London computer was on stream; a Ferranti Mercury, it occupied a 3 story townhouse in Russell Square and it had to be booked several days in advance. As I remember it, the computer occupied the ground floor, a refrigeration and air conditioning unit in the basement, and peripherals upstairs. Eric Maddison was writing software programs and he was the main user from Wye, but the only time he could get to test them was overnight. We sometimes went together, leaving Wye about 9.00 pm by train, working in Russell Square until about 4.00 am and returning to Wye in time for morning lectures! Input to these computers was *via* punched paper tape, so we had a punch machine and operator (Mrs. Askew) at Wye who became quite adept with this technology. Mercury was soon replaced by Atlas, and so on until I left.

Eric wrote programs to calculate heritabilities, correlations, and inbreeding coefficients, among other things. He eventually created a program that calculated heritabilities, using data from a given flock, then undertook index selection for a single trait based on its calculations. This made a good start for both experimental and commercial populations, although I soon found that one needed to apply other parameters in practice when using this in a commercial context.

Social life continued to be concentrated in pubs, with The George as home base. But we also traveled into the many small villages in the Kent downs and surrounding countryside. The pub names certainly rivaled those in Yorkshire: The Bonny Cravat, The Six Bells, The Compasses, The Lord Nelson, The Red Lion, The Bowl, The Old Flying Horse, The New Flying Horse, The White Horse, The Duck, The Woodman's Arms, The Rose, The Rose and Crown, The Wagon and Horses. The Wheel, The Woolpack, The Timber Batts and many more.

Besides tutoring students, developing some lectures on turkeys and working on the records from the Wye selected populations, I also attended industry conferences, including the British Poultry Breeders Roundtable, held in Oxford in 1960 and Bournemouth in 1961. This was modeled on an American conference of the same name, but the British version was sponsored by one of the breeders each year and so moved around the country. Many years later while I was working for Ross, we sponsored the meeting near Edinburgh. The meetings involved formal papers from professional geneticists and other specialists relevant to poultry breeding, and lots of time for what later became known as "networking" among the industry and academic geneticists.

I also visited many commercial operations including Western Chicken, where Dan Durrant was working. This enabled me to see first hand how the newly emerging broiler industry worked. Along with Buxted Chicken in Sussex, this was a highly integrated company with its own hatchery, breeder farms and processing plant, and growers on contract to produce live chickens for processing. The Managing Director of Western Chicken at the time was Dr. Toby Carter, a scientist who previously worked at the Atomic Research Centre at Aldermaston, and later became Director of the ARC (Agricultural Research Council) Poultry Research Centre in Edinburgh.

We hosted visiting speakers for our poultry students, including the world famous geneticist Alan Robertson from Edinburgh, Bill Weekes, a highly opinionated economist from my old Kings College, Peter Higinbotham from Buxted, Sid Fox and Trevor Morris from the University of Reading and several others. For its time, the Poultry M.Sc. gave students an excellent mix of academic and practical knowledge.

In January, 1961, I learned that my colleague Ann Murray was leaving at the end of April, to take up an industry position with a company called W.D. Evans, who marketed a layer known as Evans' Maxilay. This was one of the many breeders that emerged and disappeared within a relatively brief period. Ann was a victim of this after only a short time, and she never returned to the poultry field.

The result of her leaving was that I was asked to take on her teaching load in addition to the farm visits which I had already begun to organize. She taught poultry management to the M.Sc. students, and also gave a few lectures on poultry science to the undergraduates, so my teaching commitment more than doubled overnight. However, it also provided some degree of security, as we were now down to two faculty for a very considerable amount of work with two groups of M.Sc. students on stream at any given time, whose numbers were not diminishing. I had until September to prepare for these new responsibilities.

However, this change paled in comparison with Eric Maddison's announcement, in February 1961, that he was leaving to take up a position as Agricultural Director with Buxted Chicken, and would I please prepare to take up his teaching duties with respect to Genetics. This was an entirely different kettle of fish! Of course, the College would be appointing another Head of Department but there was no assurance that this person would be a geneticist, and in fact he turned out to be a physiologist.

Although granted my M.Sc. soon after the 1960 academic year ended, the formal ceremony only took place in March, 1961, at the Albert Hall in London, where I received the degree from Queen Elizabeth, the Queen Mother. She was, at that time, Chancellor of the University. A most gracious lady, she may have been at least partly responsible for my lifelong support and admiration of the British Monarchy.

Another event of note in the spring of 1961 was meeting my father in London to attend the Calcutta Cup rugby match between England and Scotland at Twickenham. Dad made a point of attending this match every year, alternating between Twickenham and Edinburgh. He and I were never particularly close but this time was memorable. I drove to London on Saturday morning and met him at the Ambassador Hotel, where he spent the night. We took the train to Twickenham, watched England win 6 – 0, then had dinner at the Angus Steak House in Leicester Square. Finally we saw *West Side Story* at Her Majesty's Theatre before I drove us both back to Wye, where he stayed at The George for a couple of days, before returning to Newcastle.

In late June, the College appointed Dr. Alan Sykes as the new Head of the Poultry Department. He hailed from the University of Liverpool and specialized in physiology. First impressions were favourable, and in fact we established a good relationship which continued and survived long after we both left Wye. This was pretty important in a Department with only two faculty members.

At the end of the academic year, I took myself home by air, the first of what turned out to be many, many, flights. This was in a Vickers Viscount turboprop, owned by BKS Air Transport. Newcastle Airport was just a ten minute drive from Ponteland so very handy for pick-up, and later, for my mother to use in occasional visits to me.

At this time I visited Edinburgh again, to talk to Dr. Alan Robertson about the future of our poultry breeding program at Wye, and to George Clayton to talk turkey.

Most of the summer was spent in Wye, preparing my lectures for the next year, receiving visitors (Alan Sykes was not yet in residence) at the Poultry Department and generally getting my act together for a much enlarged academic presence. I did manage a couple of weeks in and around Ponteland at the end of July.

Social life in Wye continued to centre mainly at The George, and particularly with David Martin, a postgraduate in the Hops Department. David later became a poultry person and our paths met in a number of ways, of which much more later. During this summer, Mary Skinner left her job as Principal's secretary, and I moved in to her room in the Lepper Colony on Upper Bridge Street. It had a tiny "kitchen" with basically a single ring electric burner, but with this, a kettle, and a coffee maker, one could survive. It remained the "go-to" place for coffee many evenings when the pubs closed. I had to do the washing up in the (shared) bathroom! The room also boasted a fireplace, which I used occasionally, mainly with logs acquired from local sources.

Another newcomer to the Colony was Patricia Mulvihill, an American girl doing a "tour" of Europe. She and I spent a lot of time together the summer of 1961, but it was strictly platonic (though not for want of ambition to change that on my part!). I got her some part time work at the Poultry Department and, much later, met up with her again in the United States.

One of the new intake of postgraduate poultry students in 1961 was Geoff Fairhurst. He had graduated from the University of Wales at Aberystwith, and became a very good friend. We both enjoyed beer and darts. I think he was the better darts player but we were about equal in beer capacity. Geoff had serious back problems all his life and spent a good part of his first year in Canterbury Hospital. We double dated two of the nurses and I remember his description of the one he took out: Black hair, blue eyes, gorgeous and Irish!

Pubs were a major part of life. Remembering this now, when just one or two drinks will get you in jail if caught, it is amazing that we often "crawled" by car to five or six pubs in the course of an evening, with at least a pint in each, before ending up at either the George or the Bowl, and then driving home! The longest "crawl" recorded included ten pubs. David Martin, Geoff Fairhurst and I also helped behind the bar in the George from time to time, to give Liz Hogg, the landlady, a chance to get out for an hour or two. Liz was a great lady. When we first went to the George, it was run by her and her husband David, but he died within a year or two, and she continued alone, although later helped by a partner, Brian Little, who also headed a local dance band. Liz had two drop-dead gorgeous daughters, who visited from time to time. They fitted in perfectly to pub life and the regulars loved them.

About this time, I began to use the Bowl at Hastingleigh as my "local" instead of the George. This was primarily because the George installed a one-armed-bandit (also known as a fruit machine) It wasn't long before all the pubs had one, but the Bowl also turned out to be on my way home when I eventually moved to the house in Stelling Minnis. The landlady, Peggy Newport (Husband George died shortly after I first went there) was a lovely person. And after she retired, Len and Brenda Nuttall took over and became good friends. Len was a retired R.A.F. officer; Brenda was much younger and quite glamorous. The locals loved her, and so did some of the other regular customers.

In September, 1963, just before the students arrived, Alan Sykes and I attended the inaugural meeting of the Kent Poultry Discussion Group, formed by the local Poultry Advisory Officer, Tom Crocker and I joined its committee. I also joined the organizing committee for the Kent Egg Producers Association.

This was a busy time what with two groups of poultry students and associated lectures and farm visits, my ongoing consultancies with Yorkshire Turkey Breeders and with two egg layer programs in Kent and Surrey previously overseen by Eric Maddison. All that and being on darts teams at the George and the Bowl. Never a dull moment or bed before midnight most nights. But at the age of 25 it seemed just fine.

The consultancy inherited from Eric involved N.R.B Farms, a joint venture led by Hugh Finn, who owned a large acreage near Canterbury, and Peter Nugent, who owned Blacknest Farm, a breeding farm in Dunsfold, Surrey. It was typical of the time: independent breeders who didn't want to leave the business, and thought they might survive with some extra scientific input. In this case, the science was probably appropriate, but the marketing skills needed to compete with the larger, national and international breeders was lacking. Many similar initiatives lasted but a few years, before competition drove them out. Whether their stocks were competitive was largely irrelevant. Hugh Finn was an aristocrat and during our brief business relationship, he gave me lunch at London's Athenaeum Club, and at the Strangers Dining Room in the House of Commons!

The lectures in Poultry Husbandry and Management, and Animal and Poultry Genetics to both postgraduate and undergraduate students went relatively well. I slavishly followed the notes I had taken from Eric Maddison's genetics course, and these, along with careful reading of Douglas Falconer's book *Introduction to Quantitative Genetics* got me through. Math had never been my strong suit and I had to be absolutely certain that the notes were correct and defensible. I probably didn't have to worry as much as I did, since it was likely that none of the students was any more accomplished at math than I was. The Management courses were easier, as I had constant exposure to farm practice through visits, my consulting and various meetings, and so was able to provide real-life examples as well as regular updating as the commercial industry evolved. As the years progressed, I became more confident. I eventually began to enjoy the process of teaching.

After Eric Maddison left, he was replaced as Statistics Lecturer by Reg Wimble, who was strictly statistics and not the least interested in poultry. But he was a good statistician and shortly after he arrived, was visited on a consulting basis by John Archibald, geneticist for Chunky Chicks. Chunky was based in Scotland and had imported pure line broiler stock from Nichols in New Hampshire. This was my first meeting with John, of whom much more later.

Eric did in fact return to give a few lectures on his new area of work, "Operations Research", which he was using in his role as Agricultural Manager in Buxted's integrated broiler production enterprise.

October 1962 saw the enlargement of the department academic staff once more; David Hodges, a zoologist with no poultry background, joined and restored us to three. However, I remained the only "agriculturalist" and thus retained the largest teaching and mentoring role.

In November, 1962, I had an exciting telephone call from a contact of Keith George, nutritionist at Nitrovit, the feed company in Yorkshire supplying all the turkey and chicken production. Would I be available to visit Chris Pantall in South Africa, to consult on breeding with his chicken production company there? No question there; just send me the ticket! At that time, one needed a battery of vaccinations to visit anywhere in Africa; I had a smallpox shot from the local doctor in Wye, then two weeks later a series of three typhoid A and B plus cholera which caused huge reaction, and finally, courtesy of BOAC, a yellow fever shot.

I flew home for Christmas, then on December 27, flew back to Heathrow and in the evening joined a South African Airways Boeing 707 for the flight to Johannesburg. These were the days of limited range and we stopped in Zurich, Rome, Nairobi and Salisbury (now Harare) before arrival in Jo'burg at 1.15 pm the following day. Mid-summer; I had the sense to buy some lightweight clothes but couldn't find a bathing suit in London in December! I was met by Chris's wife Ann, in a Bentley, and driven directly to the Sunnyside Poultry Farms office to meet Chris. I lived in a guest cottage in the grounds of the Pantall residence in a very upscale suburb of Jo'burg. This was a time when apartheid was well entrenched and unquestioned. I still couldn't bring myself to confidently stand outside the cottage and shout "Boy!" when I needed something.

I visited the whole operation of Sunnyside, which included breeding farms, a hatchery, broiler production farms and a processing plant. Some pure line breeding stock had been smuggled in from the US and it was this, plus some existing commercial meat chickens, that they planned to use for the company breeding program. I put together a program that they could probably follow without too much difficulty. At this point in time, all that was needed was to weigh birds at killing age and select the heaviest. Later we would divide into male and female lines and pay some attention to reproductive efficiency, but this would be expensive and require resources not available at the time. Any attempt at pedigree breeding and wingbanding identification would have been out of the question. The following year, they appointed a Breeding Manager, Alan Hazel, but I have no idea how long the program continued. I would very much like to have visited again, but never did.

Besides the work, Chris and Ann gave me a wonderful time with theatre, movies, a visit to the Voortrekker Monument, and the seamy side of South Africa, with a visit to one of the black townships.   I drove myself to Pretoria one day, to meet Ann Duff, one of Liz Lepper's friends, and dined with her and her family. I stayed with the Pantalls two weeks and thoroughly enjoyed it.

I returned to London in an East African Airways Comet, with stops in Nairobi, Benghazi and Rome, arriving at 8.15 am on January 13, with snow still on the ground over most of England. Perhaps that is how I came to love the opportunity for some sunshine and warmth between Christmas and Easter. The snow lasted until late February.

Sunnyside Poultry continued to prosper for a few years but eventually, I heard that the Pantalls sold up and returned to England.

Besides my responsibilities at Wye, I began to speak at industry meetings at various levels. Early 1963, this included the British Turkey Federation at Eastbourne, the Worshipful Company of Farmers Farm Business Management course in Folkestone, and a conference sponsored by Glaxo in Weston-Super-Mare. I also began to write articles for some of the poultry industry magazines. This was in addition to preparing scholarly papers for publication in peer-reviewed Journals. I enjoyed writing and will devote a separate chapter in this memoir to that topic. (See Chapter 9)

The first group of M.Sc. students, of which I was one, believed we were something special, and determined to have a reunion. We decided that one of us would organize it each year in a different location, and also invite an industry personality to join us for dinner and discussion. I think the first one was organized by Dan Durrant, in Devizes, with Geoffrey Sykes as the guest. Geoffrey, with his brother Frank, owned F.& G. Sykes Ltd. breeders of the Sykes Hybrid 3 layer. But Geoffrey was also a bit of a visionary and an excellent dinner guest. Another reunion was arranged by Joe Byng with Cyril Thornber as guest. Thornbers was for several years the dominant breeder of commercial layers in the UK market. One reunion took place in Northampton, with guests Jock Cooper and Ian Parkin, who worked for W.D.Evans, one of the breeders that emerged and disappeared quite quickly. We called the group the "Two Feathers" club and even had a tie made – brown woolen tie with two white feathers in a V shape at the bottom. However, the momentum soon evaporated as we dispersed to various remote places, got married, had children etc. etc.

Our own group, and most of the succeeding ones, all found good jobs in the industry. Several joined Thornber Hatcheries, others went to a variety of breeding companies, integrated egg, chicken and turkey production companies, feed companies, etc. Several emigrated to Australia. One of our year, Mike Festing, went to Canada to Shaver Poultry Breeding Farms, but did not survive long. He subsequently left the poultry field but became well established as an academic geneticist. Dick Wells, one of the second group, went to Harper Adams College, where a Diploma in Poultry Husbandry was offered, and eventually succeeded the long term and justly famous Harold Temperton.

In May, 1963, I first met Henry Bayley, who joined the college later in the year as Assistant Lecturer in Nutrition. Henry was finishing his Ph.D. at

Nottingham and would become a lifelong friend. While at Wye, we would often share meals, coffee, and outings to various pubs and restaurants. He stayed at Wye for only two years, before moving to the University of Guelph. When I emigrated to Canada, Henry met me off the plane.

For holidays from Wye, I tended to return to Ponteland and the family, but in the summer of 1963, I flew to Jersey with Mike Bertram (ex Royal Grammar School, and resident of Ponteland before joining the Merchant Navy). There we met Ken Hughes and Judy Wilson, two other Ponteland expatriates. A pleasant trip to a nice little island.

On another occasion, I met up with my parents in the Lake District, which had always been their favourite holiday destination, and enjoyed the lakes and mountains. The affinity for mountains intensified and has persisted for the rest of my life. I think it came primarily from my father. He read avidly about mountaineering and when he died, I think he owned most of the books written about Mount Everest, but of course never saw it. In fact his only experience of overseas travel was to the front lines in France during World War I. I am fortunate to have actually seen Mount Everest, as well as many other more accessible mountain ranges like the Rockies and other mountains in British Columbia.

Wye College continued to emerge as a centre for poultry knowledge and we began to receive visits from some of the famous North American poultry scientists like George Jaap (Ohio State Univ.), Rob Gowe (Agriculture Canada) and Hans Abplanalp (Univ. California, Davis). These were always welcome and gave us a new perspective on the poultry field. We also entertained Ben Bohren (Purdue Univ.) and Ed Merritt (Agriculture Canada) during this time.

By 1964, the laying flocks under selection had all been moved to single cages, making recording much easier, but necessitating Artificial Insemination for the reproductive phase. So the experience gained during my project at Cockle Park finally came into use. We also divided the Rhode Island Red flock in two: one population continued to be selected for egg numbers, while the other was selected solely for egg weight. Results here happened quickly; while slow progress in egg numbers continued in the first line, rapid progress in egg weight, and significant reduction in egg numbers, occurred in the second group. There were also unexpected side effects. In the line selected for egg numbers, the birds progressively lost their feathers, and ended up almost naked at the end of the laying year. In floor management conditions, this may have led to increased mortality from cannibalism, but with the birds in cages, they were protected. In the line selected for egg weight, not only did this increase, but the shell colour became progressively darker with each generation. Once this was noted, we began to measure egg shell colour on samples of eggs from all the flocks, using equipment similar to that seen in use by Michael Quick at Sterling Poultry Products. I published a paper later, showing heritability of this trait to be in the medium range.

Publication of other results from the selection program were slow and sporadic. Eric Maddison was notorious for his reluctance to write up results. Several of the M.Sc. students wrote up parts of the data as their thesis, and a few of these were later published, but the overall results were never written up. One of the challenges to interpreting the results of this program was the lack of an unselected control population. This meant that year-to-year changes in performance were a combination of environmental variation and genetic progress.

In late October 1964, I traveled to Norwich for Geoff Fairhurst's wedding to Chris. This was a morning affair and after a pleasant lunch, I drove south again to Dan Durrant's place in Framfield, Sussex. (Dan and his wife Margaret were at this time living with Dan's mother). On arrival, I received and urgent message to phone Wye, and discovered that my father had died suddenly the previous day. So after a restless night, I drove back to Wye and then immediately left for Ponteland.

Dad had returned from a night out (a rare occasion for him) and in the morning, went to do something in the garden and fell dead in his tracks. Of course, the shock was tremendous, but even my mother, once she came to terms with it, had to agree that it was a merciful way to end his life. He was just 68 and had been retired less than 3 years. I stayed home for the rest of the week before returning to Wye.

In the autumn of 1964, I began to think about moving. A bed-sit was OK but it seemed a good time to buy a house, and my then bank manager agreed. The timing coincided with my first meeting with Peter Bomford, a new staff member teaching Agricultural Engineering. Peter would need a place to live and I could use a tenant if and when I became a home-owner. I eventually bought a small bungalow under construction in Stelling Minnis, a ten minute drive from Wye, with The Bowl at Hastingleigh *en route* and The Rose and Crown within a stone's throw. Also in the same village lived Julie Bailey and her mother. I dated Julie on and off for a couple of years, and after that ended, remained good friends with her mother Marjorie. The bungalow took for ever to complete. I moved out of the Lepper colony in January 1965 and lived for a while at The Bowl, finally moving in to the bungalow, with Peter Bomford as tenant, in early April, 1965. I called the bungalow "Simonside" after the hill we often visited in Northumberland. The move was not without problems; it took me a long time to master the solid fuel boiler that heated water, and part of the house. In the first couple of days I succeeded in blowing the electrical circuits and had to get help from the utility company to get power restored.

Perversely, at about the same time as moving in to my own house (with a mortgage of course) I began looking at other jobs, The first, which for me, turned out to be a non-starter, was with Cherry Valley Farms, an international breeder of meat ducks. I spent all day at an interview but didn't feel comfortable about the company and especially about the man for whom I would be working, so I did not go further with the application. The job eventually went to John Powell, who had been working at Thornbers; he stayed until retirement and made a great success of the opportunity.

In October 1965 I received a very tempting offer from a breeder in South Africa (not Sunnyside, where I consulted in 1963) to work in Cape Town. But it wasn't tempting enough, and I did not pursue it.

Around this time, Peter Bomford and I were dating, respectively, the College Registrar's secretary, Janice and the Principal's secretary Judy. Peter and Janice were married in September, 1965. My relationship with Judy was not so successful. She left Wye in the summer of 1965 to spend a year working in Lake Forest IL, and we corresponded regularly for a while, even becoming engaged, with announcements in the Newcastle Journal and the Kentish Gazette! But at some point she became involved with a religious minister called Bill Gros in Lake Forest and although I saw her on her return, and we proceeded with arrangements for the wedding, she eventually dropped the bombshell and the whole thing was OFF.

While Judy was in Lake Forest, I met and dated several nurses from the Kent and Canterbury Hospital, one of whom, Carole Shepherd, became a very good friend, and with whom I am still in contact. We continued to see each other after my rift with Judy. She eventually moved to France, married Pierre Chassagnard, and had five children! They live in a Chateau near Morraineville in France. My daughter Carole was named after her.

Reviewing my diary for this period, I find that I was dating both Julie and Judy simultaneously for much of the time. But neither relationship proved lasting. Julie graduated at Swansea and emigrated to the USA, ending up as a marine biologist at the University of Hawaii, married to Richard Brock, with two children. We kept in touch and in fact we visited them in 2015 following a holiday with our son and his family in Kauai. Of Judy, I have no knowledge at all after she spent her year in Lake Forest.

At the Poultry Department, I continued to operate the selection programs with the R.I.R. and L.S. flocks, and also established a colony of Japanese

Quail. This species had become the darling of applied geneticists. The females started to lay at about 35 days of age, so the generation interval was very short, around 50 days, compared with a minimum of six months for chickens, and much longer if you had to measure egg production. And they were obviously of more practical application than the fruit fly (*Drosophila spp*) favoured by academic geneticists of the time. But we had problems with the quail! The newly hatched chicks were about the size of a bumblebee and very difficult to contain, and the adults were more aggressive than we had expected. We never really got going with the quail program.

I continued work with various local organizations and also national programs like the National Diploma in Poultry Husbandry (NDP) for which I was an examiner and also sat on the organizing committee. The same organization later developed the Diploma in Poultry Technology, a more advanced qualification, in collaboration with the University of Nottingham.

The routine of teaching, mentoring students and running the selection programs continued as usual through 1965, but I began to get itchy feet. The prospect of remaining in Wye *ad infinitum* lost its appeal, especially when watching one staff member retire after god knows how long as a lecturer, living with his aged mother!

The house provided a challenge; I built a coal bunker, painted the interior, and bought enough furniture to make it comfortable. Peter Bomford and I created something of a garden. After he married and left Simonside, I acquired another tenant, Alan Hunt, who worked in the Economics Department at Wye.

Just prior to starting the 1965-66 academic year, I took a trip with Len and Brenda (from The Bowl) in their Jaguar, to the Rhine and Mosel valleys in Germany. Talk about a "busman's holiday"! We spent a lot of time at wine festivals and in various bars. But we definitely enjoyed the unique scenery as well as copious wine and beer.

The new Poultry Postgraduate intake provided a truly international group; one each from Nigeria, Rhodesia (now Zimbabwe), Ireland and Sudan. We continued as in previous years to introduce them to the local industry. Now, twenty years after the end of World War II, the egg sector had rapidly developed into a viable and competitive business. A large farm was still in the region of 10,000 to 20,000 hens, and some were starting to pack and market their own product. Simultaneously, the large packers were consolidating, creating a source of supply to the rapidly expanding retail supermarkets. One of the egg producers we visited with the students was

Mike Weller. He had about 10,000 layers in a house with a raised wire floor, which for some reason was called the "Pennsylvania system". I later called it the 10,000 bird cage, and it was the least bird-friendly environment I ever saw! Mike eventually became the President of the International Egg Commission.

The meat chicken industry was rapidly expanding. Geoffrey Sykes' prediction of one million birds/year was long surpassed. Turkey meat was still a bit of a luxury and extremely seasonal; nobody thought of having a turkey except at Christmas. Thanksgiving was not on the European calendar!

I continued to have itchy feet. I applied for and was offered a secondment position as Lecturer at the University of Ghana in Legon, near Accra. Although an offer was made, I did not accept it. Whether this was cold feet or discouragement by Alan Sykes, I am not sure. I may have been approaching the realization that the academic life was not a permanent necessity, and other avenues existed.

After a visit home to my mother for Easter in 1966, I traveled back to Wye by way of Bawdeswell in Norfolk, where I had lunch with Jim Ingram, the Managing Director of Shaver Poultry Breeding Farms (GB) Ltd. This was by way of investigating the possibility of a job with the company. As I was later to discover, Shaver was a very centralized company, with all decisions made by the President, Donald McQueen Shaver, in Galt, Ontario, Canada. However, it was a useful first contact. Rob Gowe, a geneticist working in research at the Canada Department of Agriculture (now Agriculture and Agri-Food Canada) visited Wye later in 1966 and gave me more background to the company, for which he was an unofficial consultant. Early in September, I received a letter and a phone call from the company inviting me to an interview with Vice President Bob Gray at a hotel near Heathrow airport, and so my academic career began its final chapter.

The timing of my departure was probably propitious; only three new poultry students enrolled in 1966, and the College may have had a hard time justifying the undoubted resources needed to keep the program going.

The next four months were, of course extremely busy ones. I had to sell Simonside, resign the position at Wye and wind up the teaching and research programs as far as possible, and also make peace with my mother. She thought Kent was a long way from home so Ontario, Canada might as well have been on another planet.

Sale of Simonside did not go quickly and in fact was not completed until March, 1967, at a satisfactory price.

I continued a very intensive social life with Brian Freeman, a zoology lecturer, and his then companion, Sherry, who in turn introduced me to a plethora of her nursing colleagues, but none of these lasted. I also kept in touch with, and dated Carole Shepherd, and almost as a matter of pride, dated the new secretary to the Principal, Susan Hawes.

I am amazed to read in my diaries the number of pubs I visited on a daily basis. Often 2 or 3 at lunch time and more in the evenings. Probably just as well, as I had no idea at the time of the bleak situation I would encounter in Galt, Ontario, where my next job was located.

Emigration to Canada at that time was an easy formality for Britons. I spent no more than an hour at the immigration office in London, where I had an interview and a very peremptory medical exam. They even subsidized the plane ticket; one way London to Toronto for £10.

December 1966 was a frantic time. Farewell parties at the Senior Common Room, and at Alan Sykes home, and of course at all the numerous pubs that had been part of my life for the past few years. I unwisely traded my car for a Ford Cortina to be delivered to Canada a.s.a.p. All I took to Canada was contained on one large trunk, a suitcase and two wooden boxes sent separately by Canadian Pacific.

I took the train home for Christmas with my mother, saw a bunch of friends around Newcastle, and eventually flew to Toronto on December 29th, 1966.

Chapter 4

Commercial Breeding: My Early Years with Shaver

The interview with Bob Gray at London airport did not tell me much about the company. He offered me a job in research and a salary of CAN$8,250/*annum*, which sounded OK. (I was earning about £1,300 at Wye, which when converted at the then exchange rate of 3:1 was $3,900). I confirmed by mail with D.McQ Shaver, my intention to accept the offer. Later in September I met him in London for a couple of hours and learned a bit more about the company, but not much more about Shaver himself.

In October, I met Jim Ingram again and we visited the Houghton Poultry Research Station. Also visiting was Dr. R.K. (Randy) Cole, from Cornell University, with whom I would later have a great deal of contact, as he turned out to be the major consulting geneticist for Shaver. The same day, I was introduced at a Shaver G.B Distributor meeting in St. Ives. I think the meeting covered the problem of Marek's disease, for which there was then no vaccine. Dr. Cole was at the forefront of research demonstrating a quite strong genetic resistance to the disease. As I was to learn on arrival in Canada, Shaver was deeply involved in applying this to their White Leghorn breeding program.

Before leaving for Canada, I met more of the Shaver GB crowd at the London Poultry Show, and also visited the farms near Bawdeswell in Norfolk. Here I met with Geoff Matthews for the first time. Geoff was a "poultry man" through and through. Although major breeding decisions came from Galt, Geoff was in charge of daily operations and dealt with most of the detailed work of selection and breeding, specifically the brown egg lines, which were located at Shaver GB.

I arrived in Canada on December 29th, 1966, and was met by Henry Bayley, who shepherded me around between Guelph, where he lived, and Galt, 20 km away where the Shaver office and farms were located. The first day, we had a dinner party at the apartment of the late Brian Evans, who was a geographer at the University of Guelph, where Henry worked in the Department of Nutrition. Also there was Ed Moran, another poultry nutritionist who later moved to Auburn University and made a big name for himself in the field of broiler and broiler breeder nutrition. For dinner, we had some of Ed's experimental chickens.

January 1st was a Sunday, so I officially began work on January 2nd. I met some of the Shaver people, including Bert Munro, Cliff Luce, Bruce Murray and most of the office staff the previous Friday. I also had a short session with DMcQ and got my orders for the next five weeks.

This was basically an "ordeal by fire" to make sure I wasn't going to leave at the first sign of difficulty. It involved the reproduction, using AI, of a number of "gene pool" lines not immediately involved in the commercial programs. This took place at the Hobhill Farm, a newly constructed facility about 10 km out of town, and the first one with "shower-in" requirements. I worked with George Trenamen, a long term Shaver employee who was a true poultryman. He was also one of the few with a post secondary agricultural qualification, in his case a degree from the University of Guelph.

All the birds, including the males, were housed in individual cages. Although the biosecurity program was not nearly as stringent as it would be in 2021, it was deemed preferable that those of us working at this farm did not spend time at any other company facility the same day. So we kept going with our inseminations and egg collection until all the lines were reproduced. I think we hatched about 250 females from each line, expecting to have 200 to house for the next generation.

When I eventually completed this "indoctrination" I started to work more in the office. The official hours were 8.15 am until 5.30 pm Monday to Friday and to 12.00 noon Saturdays. But after a few weeks it became clear that many people in the office worked evenings, and basically most days including weekends, we worked until the job was done. The Advertising Manager at the time, Bruce Murray, often worked well into the evening, but after arriving a few minutes late one morning, was called on to the carpet. I think he won the day; after DMcQ berated him for being late, Bruce essentially apologized and then said he wished DMcQ was there to watch him leaving at 11.00 pm. Nothing more was said.

The hatcheries worked different hours, often governed by the need to have chicks to Toronto Airport at a specific time for long distance flights. For pedigree hatches, where each egg was identified and each chick had to be wingbanded, we would often start at 5.00 am and continue until the job was completed. I was involved with this process because geneticists needed to have confidence that the job was done precisely, and also have the ability to do the work themselves. When I later moved to Ross, I found this was not the practice, and immediately instituted it.

For the first month, I had full board and lodgings with a Mrs. Molnar, on Lowell Street S. in Galt. This was a long walk to the office but it could be done if no other way was available. However, I soon found a little flat not far away, more or less built into the attic of #10, Pine Street, belonging to a nice family, George and Jean Holtzhauer. My address was 10½, Pine St. I moved there February 1st, and furnished it with a package deal from a local furniture store, Grant Blackwell. This was an amazing deal; for $399, $499 or $599, they would supply a double bed, dresser, sofa, armchair, two end tables, kitchen table with 4 chairs, 4 cups, plates of two sizes, cereal bowls, knives, forks and spoons. So the flat was almost instantly furnished. I think I chose the middle level of quality, and took out a bank loan to finance it. I also commissioned the construction, at a local furniture maker, of a nice corner cupboard, which completed the living room. There was a shopping plaza across the street where I bought sheets and stuff, and groceries. My first lot of groceries cost $23! The flat also included a balcony, actually the roof of the carport, which made a wonderful place for drinks and relaxation, and even occasionally, breakfast. The place was not air-conditioned and the balcony offered a cool place in the evenings as it faced north.

Social life was a different story. I saw a lot of Henry Bayley and his then fiancée Christa (they married in May 1967) and Hansi, an Austrian friend of Christa's. But this was on weekends and because I still had no car, they had to come from Guelph for me. Nothing resembling a British Pub existed. I spent a few evenings with other Shaver people in a cocktail lounge called The Ebony Room (it was part of the Royal Hotel) but this was a far cry from the Rose and Crown! Once I moved to Pine Street, I had drinks at home. The beer parlours in Galt were appalling and I didn't go there much at all after the first few weeks. At that time, to buy beer in Ontario, one had to go to the Brewers Retail store, fill out a form with name, address and the beer required, and pay cash. (Since that time, the store has been renamed The Beer Store, and you don't have to identify yourself, but they still don't accept credit cards.) For wine and spirits, you had to go to the Liquor Control Board of Ontario (LCBO) store and follow the same rigmarole of i.d. and form filling. Much later the LCBO stores became a bit more consumer friendly but still a near-monopoly and very expensive compared with most other countries.

One interesting character from these early days was a Swede, Harry Krajenhagen, who was working for the Shaver distributor in The Netherlands, but was being groomed for work at Shaver France. He was in Galt for a few months of indoctrination and training. Harry had a car, and we spent quite a bit of time together sharing meals, trips to the movies, etc. On one memorable Sunday in March, we went to Niagara Falls, an absolute necessity for all newcomers. It was a raw, sunless day, and we gazed at the falls and the ice-encrusted surroundings, walked around a bit and had lunch. At that time, Ontario was "dry" on Sundays, so we decided to cross the Rainbow Bridge to the US side, where we knew we could get a beer. But we had to first pass through US Customs and Immigration. The agent leaned out of his booth and asked where we were born. My answer that I was born in England seemed OK, but Harry didn't quite understand the question and in any case when they found he lived in The Netherlands, and was visiting Canada on a Swedish passport, they declined to admit him. They gave him a form stating that on this date, "H. Krajenhagen was refused admission to the United States of America", and told us to turn around and go home. We thought the form would make a nice souvenir, but then we had to pass through Canada Customs and Immigration, and they confiscated it!

After a lot of back and forth with cables and letters, my Ford Cortina finally arrived in Montreal in mid March. I flew there and spent about 24 hours getting it out of the dock, to a garage for inspection, securing a temporary license plate and sundry other paperwork. Eventually I drove to Ottawa to visit the Animal Genetics people at the Department of Agriculture. I spent the evening with Rob Gowe, stayed the night in a motel and drove home the following day. This, my first experience of driving on the right, was quite traumatic, and driving through Toronto quite terrifying. However, this fear quickly evaporated, and soon I was visiting Toronto quite often, sometimes going for an evening show and returning the same night. There was a distant relative of my mother's, a Miss Hume, that I had promised to visit, and I went there in March for lunch with her. She introduced me to "the young people", mostly a family called Vanstone, whose relationship to her or to me I never understood. I dated Alice Vanstone once (took her to see *Spring Thaw* at the Royal Alex. This was a tradition in Toronto for many years.) Anyway, having a car again was a huge step forward, even though the Cortina was not really suited to the conditions. I kept it for only 11 months, after which I traded it for a Chevrolet Camaro, which at the time was an appropriate car for a youngish single man in my position!

In April 1967, I drove to New York City for a long weekend. Patricia Mulvihill, whom I had known during her visit to Wye, was now married to Michael Forhane and living in Queens. So I arranged to meet them, along with Michael Bertram (formerly from Ponteland) and his wife Patti, who were passing through on their way to the Far East. Pat showed us the tourist sights; Times Square, the Empire State Building, the UN, and a trip on the Staten Island Ferry, and we ate in some of her favourite pubs and restaurants.

Then at the end of the month, I went on the first of many business trips for Shaver. This involved firstly a trip to Cullman, AL, where a new branch operation was established. It should be mentioned at this point that earlier in the 1960's, when the company was rapidly expanding, DMcQ was faced with the need for external capital. He either had to take the company public, or find a private partner. He chose the latter, in the shape of Cargill Inc., the huge grain merchant based in Minneapolis MN. They purchased

49% of the company, but DMcQ retained all management responsibility. Cargill provided capital for the newly planned US farms in Cullman, and also for Shaver France which at this time was in the planning phase. Cargill was at this time expanding rapidly into the livestock production field, with integrated layer, chicken and turkey operations mainly in the US but also in central and south America. While at first sight, these may have appeared as captive markets for Shaver, this was by no means the case, and we sometimes felt at a disadvantage, as the Cargill managers strove to demonstrate their independence.

Cullman was a small town in central Alabama between Huntsville and Birmingham. It was in what was then "chicken country" with a large processing plant and associated farms and hatchery nearby. Shaver found a location not far out of town relatively remote from other poultry and built a grandparent farm and hatchery called Hickory Ridge. A second farm was added later. Local people were hired to manage both farm and hatchery, and in the early days, Ellis Cross was the general manager and Phil Dietz, his assistant. They were both experienced in the industry and well able to manage the operation, though neither had experience of the primary breeding business. I found them easy to get along with and they were kind and sociable to this relatively naive import from the UK. For a newcomer, the Alabama accent has to be heard for several hours before it becomes remotely understandable. They probably felt the same way about me. I often felt that if some of the farm workers (few of whom could write) were to be dropped in the centre of Glasgow, Scotland, they might as well be in the middle of China in terms of mutual understanding. At this time, and it may still prevail, Cullman County was "dry" and if you wanted to buy booze, you had to drive to the county boundary where there was a convenient Package Store. Each Sunday morning in the local newspaper, there was a list of people charged the previous night with breaking the Prohibition Law. But the Cross and Dietz families were not dry and so our Saturday evenings were quite convivial.

From Cullman, I traveled to Kansas City MO, for the Poultry Breeders of America meeting and the Poultry Breeders Roundtable. This was the meeting from which the British Roundtable took its name and format. I think DMcQ had doubts about allowing me to go to this meeting, because before I left, he admonished me to "Keep your ears and eyes open and your mouth shut". He was quite paranoid about company secrets and stock security, but subsequent events proved him more right than wrong. However, I quite enjoyed the opportunity to meet many of my peers in academe and the industry, and several of them became good friends over time. These included Ken Goodwin (Penn State Univ.), Arne Nordskog (Iowa Sate Univ.), Ben Bohren (Purdue Univ.), and many others among the academics, and George Godfrey (Honegger Farms), Gerry Havenstein

(H&N Inc.), and Jack Hill (Babcock Poultry Farms Inc.) from industry. We would meet and enjoy good conversations on an annual basis.

These travels also allowed me to become familiar with several parts of the U.S. Meat chickens, then still known as broilers, were concentrated in the South, so I visited the Carolinas, the Delmarva peninsula, Georgia, Arkansas, Louisiana, Mississippi, among other states. The egg industry had a somewhat different distribution, with concentrations in New York, Pennsylvania, Ohio, California, and elsewhere. At some points in its history, egg production was concentrated near populations centres, but later moved to the grain belt, closer to feed sources.

Flying at this time was very much a pleasant experience. Everybody wanted to feed you and the meals in Economy were probably better than you get in Business Class today. Drinks were cheap and plentiful, and cabin staff went out of their way to be friendly and helpful.

Henry Bayley and Christa were married while I was in Kansas City so I was unable to attend the wedding. Interestingly, because Christa was German, Henry's parents refused to come to the wedding, but one of his aunts came instead. Shortly after my return, I helped them move to a new apartment on Edinburgh Road in Guelph, and after their daughter Anya was borne in 1968, to their house on Bellevue Ave., where they still (2021) live.

I saw quite a bit of DMcQ in this period and learned how the company worked. He was very formal and quiet most of the time, but it became clear that delegation was not something that came easily to him. His intellect was huge; even without formal training he could embrace the rather simple genetics that was being practiced at the time, and on which continued improvement of our commercial product depended. Although Watson and Crick's description of DNA was published during the 1950's, even in the late 1960's there was no apparent way in which it could be applied to our work. Another 30 years would elapse before the chicken genome was mapped, and associations sought between commercial traits and identifiable pieces of DNA.

The layer program in the 1960's was based largely on the population genetics principles I had been teaching at Wye, but angled according to the Cornell duo of Hutt and Cole, who were suspicious of statistics but great promoters of the progeny test. DMcQ was very much hands-on with the breeding program, as with everything else. Using summarized egg production data on the new generation of laying pullets, Randy Cole produced lists of females to be placed in breeding pens (everything was floor managed at this point, although we moved to cages later) and the families from which the cockerels were to be taken. DMcQ then handled the cockerels and decided which of several brothers would be used in the breeding pen. Anecdotally, he seemed to pick the most aggressive ones, and after many generations, the Shaver male lines gained a reputation for this trait when used in natural mating in the field.

Another feature of the breeding work in the late 1960's was the method of recording and data processing. All the birds were trapnested 5 days/week and the hand-written records transferred to the office. Here they were manually summarized using an old fashioned adding machine, by an aged Scotsman, Archie Crawford, for shipment by mail to Randy Cole at Cornell. DMcQ was most reluctant to start using computers, and only after Gowe and his associates in Ottawa developed a program to compute these family summaries did we enter the modern era. And this meant using IBM equipment, that is, 80-column punch cards, shipped to Ottawa by truck overnight using Bankers Dispatch.

One of the features of life at Shaver was that regardless of qualification, everybody did everything! So as well as trying my best to be a geneticist, I also helped write advertising copy and began what turned out to be a major occupation, the composition of technical service literature. The first of these dealt with lighting. Pioneering research at Auburn Univ. in Alabama, followed up at Reading in the UK, showed that laying hens responded dramatically to changes in day length. This was the stimulus that caused wild birds to lay eggs in spring time. Chickens can lay eggs all year round, but they reached sexual maturity much earlier during periods of increasing day length. But if/when they matured early, they tended to lay smaller eggs, so precise control of day length was an important part of layer management. Technical knowledge became an important attribute of successful breeders, and Shaver soon realized this and appointed long term staffer Chris Fowler as Tech. Services Manager. Chris had managed the Shaver subsidiary near Dusseldorf in Germany, and a joint venture in India, prior to this appointment.

Shaver also introduced one of the first technical service magazines in the industry, *SHAVER FOCUS*, which started in 1968 and continued, with some changes of name, until about 2016. I was its Editor for the entire time, except for the period 1974-1977, when I worked for Ross Poultry. *FOCUS* was strictly a technical publication; the only promotional aspect was the masthead. Another publication, *SHAVER NEWS* was strictly promotional, with news of distributors, Shaver travels, Random Sample Test successes, etc. However, some time in the 1970's, the two were combined and it was a continuous challenge to maintain a balance between technical and promotional content. Many well-known international specialists contributed to *FOCUS*. I remember Don Bell, the renowned poultry specialist from UC Riverside, writing several articles, along with

John Summers (Univ. Guelph), Arnold Elson from the UK, and many others.

Shaver was involved in two major poultry health initiatives at this time. First was the application of Randy Cole's discovery that there was an important genetic component in resistance to Marek's Disease (MD). For this, we hatched sample families from the key White Leghorn lines (grandparents of the Commercial Shaver Starcross 288), injected them with MD virus, and grew them at a remote location. At 8 weeks of age, these birds were killed and examined for evidence of MD, and relatives of those families **not** showing symptoms were adjudged more resistant.

The other program was the elimination of *Mycoplasma gallisepticum* (MG, which at the time, we still called PPLO, for pleuro-pneumonia-like organism). To accomplish this, fertile eggs were injected with the antibiotic Tylosin, and resulting chicks placed on a farm with strict biosecurity (shower-in, etc.) thought to be MG free. Within a few years, all of the Shaver farms except the original one, Whitecraigs, were MG free. Whitecraigs, where DMcQ had his residence until the early 1970's, was eventually closed and sold for real estate development.

Shaver made its reputation as a breeder of white egg layers. The Shaver Starcross 288 would lay more eggs than its competitors and enabled the company to expand internationally, as well as supplying a significant part of the Canadian egg industry. However, it seemed intuitively correct that a company in this position should expand its activity to other types of chickens, brown egg layers and meat chickens being the obvious choices. Although several breeders of meat chickens were already established (and dominated their market much as Shaver did the egg sector) there seemed to be economies of scale if a company could market both types. So Shaver established Maple Lane Farm as its centre of meat chicken breeding during the late 1960s. A number of key lines were already available. Where these originated, I am not sure. At this time, the sole criterion in the meat chicken business was weight for age. Broilers were being killed at 10 weeks to yield a ready-to-cook bird weighing 2.5-3.0 lb. So really all the breeder had to do was to place as many chickens as possible at day old, grow them to 10 weeks, weigh them and select the heaviest. Some attention was paid to conformation; particularly of the breast. It turned out that George Trenamen was an expert at this subjective evaluation, so we spent many hours weighing and evaluating birds at Maple Lane. DMcQ appointed me as leader of the Meat Program. This did not sit well with George, who had been with the company longer, and in fact knew a good deal more about meat chickens than I did. But in any event, all of the major decisions came from the fountainhead, so we pursued an armed truce and everything worked out reasonably well.

DMcQ spent between one third and half of his time traveling. He was almost solely responsible for securing all the overseas customers. He not only signed them up as distributors, but also encouraged them to visit the company headquarters in Galt, where they were further indoctrinated. We also tried to help with technical education, as in some cases, the customers had very little practical experience. So those of us resident in Galt were expected to host and help a wide variety of visitors. In my first years, I spent time with personnel from The Philippines, Portugal, Japan, Pakistan, Spain, France, Mexico and many other countries. All of these contacts confirmed the need for continuing technical service at an advanced level. And of course in some areas like nutrition and lighting, we were learning ourselves as we followed research reports from around the world, and took advice from several excellent consultants at the University of Guelph and elsewhere.

The huge US layer market was important to Shaver, largely in establishing a reputation for the performance of the bird. Profit was hard to come by because of intense competition with other breeders, and the cut-throat efforts of franchise hatcheries to secure more business. DMcQ did not spend much time in the US; he appointed his brother-in-law Doug Rundle as Sales Manager and left him to deal with it, one of his few acts of real delegation. I enjoyed traveling with Doug on several occasions; many of the franchise hatchery owners were wonderful people and very loyal most of the time. But they too found it hard to make a profit; for years the standard price of a day-old layer chick was US 50 cents and this may have been discounted, payment delayed, or otherwise "adjusted" to secure a sale. This made it hard for the breeders to get their regular price of about $5.00 per mated female out of this market. Among the memorable characters with Shaver franchises were Duke Perron in Georgia, Bill Smithey in Florida, Bob and Ben DeWitt in Texas and Jay Greider in Pennsylvania. Since that time, the franchise system has almost completely disappeared, with chick production now concentrated in huge hatcheries owned and operated by the few remaining breeding companies.

DMcQ's departures for overseas always raised tensions in the office. His last-minute instructions, sudden changes of plans, and insistence on covering every eventuality that might take place in his absence, made life difficult for all of us. The sigh of relief when he walked out of the office bound for the airport was quite audible! The next day, of course, the telex machine ran continuously as he flew from one place to another, sending back instructions on an hourly basis. Some of us felt that he tried to do too much, too quickly. On one occasion, Peter Quail, another expatriate Brit who was Marketing Manager, included in his trip report after two weeks in

South America, the suggestion that " - - - there is plenty of business here for us if we spend time beating the bushes rather than flying over them".

Although most Shaver chicks left Canada by way of the airport at Toronto (now Lester Pearson), some large shipments left by charter flight from Waterloo Wellington Airport (now Kitchener Waterloo International). This required many hands on deck to load the boxes into a non-air conditioned DC3, which quickly took off with a Shaver employee inside to adjust the natural ventilation in the fuselage. Most of these shipments were to Mexico and Colombia and involved at least one stop *en route*. Sometimes the plane would back-haul cut flowers or other cargo.

Life at 10½ Pine Street continued to be quite acceptable. I enjoyed doing my own cooking, entertained modestly, and found all the services I needed like the coin laundry, dry cleaner, grocery and hardware stores close at hand. In the summer of 1967 I bought a do-it-yourself Stereo system from Heathkit, and learned how to solder! Amazingly, it worked the first time I tried it after spending many hours on the assembly process. This was before the era of transistors and cheap ready made sound systems, and it ran well for many years.

Social activity included reconnecting with two other ex-Ponteland families. John and Brenda Purvis lived in Kitchener with their three children, Nigel, Miles and Ingrid, while Mike and Margaret Crossling lived in Toronto. John worked for a large Artificial Insemination (for cattle) service near Guelph. He had a small sailboat and later built a cottage near Point Clark on Lake Huron. During the late 1970's he was convicted of theft of semen from the company and did some jail time. He and Brenda separated and divorced.

The Crosslings subsequently moved to Montreal but we kept in touch and still see each other from time to time. They suffered in the Quebec separatist situation in the late 1970's. Mike, who worked in the financial industry, was let go as many such businesses were forced to downsize. Then they could not sell their house. He and Margaret eventually purchased a small farm in south western Quebec, and she trained and worked as a Canada Customs agent in Cornwall ON. They finally retired to Port Elgin ON, and we visit them occasionally.

In August 1967, I took my first week of holiday. I decided to see a bit more of Ontario. I drove to Parry Sound and stayed a couple of nights in a motel, and toured the surroundings. Then on to French River and another motel, this one with quite a congenial bar, where I spent a couple of evenings. I rented a small power boat and explored the French River and really enjoyed this very different (for me) and gorgeous scenery. From here I continued north through Sudbury, which at this time was a ghastly town surrounded by mountains of mine waste, and looked a bit like the moon. Sudbury has since massively improved, the mountains of waste are green and the town is quite prosperous even though much of the mining has ceased.

After Sudbury, I continued west and then south on to Manitoulin Island, with much nicer and quite unique scenery, passing through Little Current and ending up at South Baymouth, where the ferry left for Tobermory. The Chi Cheemaun was then quite new, I enjoyed the crossing and had an excellent dinner on board. I also enjoyed one of Lake Huron's beautiful sunsets.

Later, in September, after a poultry conference in Quebec City, I took more holiday at EXPO 67, a World's Fair mounted on an artificial island in the St. Laurence River in Montreal. This coincided with Canada's 100th birthday and was a fabulous affair, with pavilions from all over the world. Of course I was drawn irrevocably to the British Pavilion, which contained an authentic pub, The British Bulldog, where I drank British beer and chatted with mainly British visitors, most evenings. Shaver had donated 500 eggs to the "Man The Provider" exhibit, so I was able to attend a VIP reception and have a grand tour of the whole site by minirail. EXPO was a huge success for Montreal and for Canada, and is still well remembered.

When I left Wye College in December, 1966, I still did not have a Ph.D. However, most of the work was completed in rough form, so during the first year at Shaver, I worked on it in what can only be referred to jokingly as my spare time. In September I took this (literally, "hand written") manuscript to Sybil Parkinson, a former Secretary at Shaver, for typing. We worked on it together over perhaps a couple of months until it was complete. I paid her $78.68! She did an excellent job, with two onion skin copies. The original and two copies were bound in the appropriate format, in Guelph. I mailed the original to Prof. Holmes, my supervisor at Wye. Then in November during my first overseas trip with Shaver, I took the oral examination with Douglas Falconer as external examiner, at the University Senate House, and passed, to my great joy and relief. I telephoned home to my mother, and sent a cable to Shaver in Galt. On my return, I received a very nice hand-written letter from D. McQ, along with two bottles of Champagne. I still have the letter! Henry Bayley arranged for a celebration of the event in the party room of his apartment, and we had a splendid night there in mid December.

In the absence of much scientific expertise (other than my own) Shaver relied heavily on consultants, and about twice a year, we held Consultant Meetings in Galt. Besides Randy Cole, we had, on a regular basis, John

Summers and Stan Slinger, both nutritionists from Guelph, Art Ferguson and Bruce Truscott from the Ontario Veterinary College, Fred Jerome, geneticist from Guelph, and Rob Gowe from the Canada Department of Agriculture in Ottawa. Rob was not officially allowed to be a consultant so he came as a personal friend of DMcQ. These meetings were carefully structured with formal agendas and very thorough reports for which I was responsible. The meetings covered the gamut of our own research, updates on relevant research at Guelph and elsewhere, and most importantly, technology and research to help commercial customers in the field.

One of the challenges I faced was that when someone like Doug Rundle, who traveled almost full-time in the US, returned from one of his trips, his first priority was usually the complaint from the last customer he visited! And he also would be concerned about alleged shortcomings of Shaver when compared with competitors. However, out of this, over time, it became obvious that one of our "problems" (we weren't supposed to have problems, only challenges) was in the area of egg shell quality. This was something that we had only begun to study and monitor.

It is intuitive that as the number of eggs laid rises, other traits like egg weight and shell quality might be expected to change, usually in the opposite direction to that needed commercially. The Shaver Starcross 288, our flagship product, actually laid quite large eggs, and this trait was already included as a selection criterion. Shell quality had not received the same amount of attention, and we hoped to remedy this in future generations.

In short order, we established a small laboratory to obtain detailed data on all the pedigree birds during their early production phase, prior to initial selection for reproducing the lines. In this, we were fortunate to have as a model, the procedures being followed by Gowe and his associates for their experimental layer lines in Ottawa. Our program was slightly different, as from my own experience I wanted to include measurements of egg shell colour, and strength. Most shell quality work prior to this had used egg specific gravity as an index of shell quality. Whole egg specific gravity is a good indicator of shell thickness, but I and others were skeptical as to the validity of this as the only measure of shell quality. Research in The Netherlands had developed a piece of equipment that measured the amount of deformation that an eggshell demonstrated when exposed to a standard load. We acquired this equipment and incorporated it into our egg quality assessment. We also purchased equipment for measuring egg shell colour, using percentage reflectance that I had seen in England at Sterling Poultry Products. We used this for both white- and brown-egg lines: producers of white eggs wanted them perfectly white, while those producing brown eggs liked a uniform brown colour.

So our little laboratory, in which we could assess 500-700 eggs daily, would measure on each egg, the following:

- egg weight (to the nearest g)
- egg shell colour
- egg shell deformation
- egg shape index
- visual shell imperfections (subjective)
- albumen quality (measured as Haugh units; albumen height corrected for egg weight)
- presence of blood spots
- presence of meat spots

These data would be incorporated with those for egg number and body weight obtained at the farm, and used for Randy Cole's selection program.

In 1968, Shaver began to hold Training Schools for employees from overseas customers. We gave lectures, introduced visiting speakers such as John Summers, Art Ferguson and others, did farm tours, seminars, and of course some social time including trips to Toronto. These lasted a couple of weeks and were valuable ways to get to know our customers, and to indoctrinate them into our methods. One of those attending was Chris Bennett from Trinidad, with whom I holidayed one Carnival time.

On the Dominion Day (now Canada Day) weekend I went on what would be the first of many trips to Algonquin Provincial Park. This one was with Henry, Christa, Bruce Knight (ex Wye) and two of Christa's friends. We drove to Canoe Lake and camped overnight, then rented canoes and paddled across the Lake, portaged to Joe Lake and thence to Burnt Island Lake, where we set up camp for the weekend. Although we had huge thunderstorms, the weather was hot and we enjoyed swimming in the lake. Henry and Christa stayed for a week, but the rest of us came out and back home on the holiday Monday. My first experience of canoeing!

This year I also learned to water-ski. After a futile attempt, helped unsuccessfully by Dave Roberts, Shaver publicity man, in Puslinch Lake near Galt, I finally made it on to the water surface in Smith Lake, AL with Ellis Cross, the manager at Cullman. Once up, I skied all over the lake several times. The following day, I was rigid from the neck down, having used and strained muscles as never before. But this led to the purchase of a small boat at home, soon replaced by another, with a 40 hp Chrysler outboard, which I used until 1974.

In late July, 1968, I shared the drive from Guelph to Winnipeg with Brian Evans, who was moving there. A chance to see more of the Great Lakes, and the beginning of the Prairies. We did not hurry, staying at motels in Spanish, Nippigon and Sioux Narrows, on the way. Brian later bought a small house and I visited a couple of times. It later transpired that he was gay and eventually his partner moved in. Unfortunately, this led to his suffering from AIDS and Brian died in 1993. This was tragic, such a clever and sociable person, but of course the treatments for his condition had not been discovered at the time.

Flying home from Winnipeg in a window seat, I was able to see in about two hours what had taken four days to drive. The flat prairie, the endless lakes and bush of northern Ontario and parts of Lakes Superior, Michigan, Huron and Ontario were laid out like a giant map below.

In November 1968, Peter Quail and I spent two weeks at Shaver GB promoting the Starbro meat breeder. It had been decided that instead of visiting customers, we would invite them to Norfolk, wine and dine them royally, and give them our pitch on our own turf. Over ten days, we must have spoken to a large majority of the UK meat chicken industry. We also ate our way through a very upscale menu at the Phoenix Hotel, where we stayed and gave the presentations. On the weekend, I made a quick trip to revisit Wye, meet some old friends and stop by some of the old haunts, mainly pubs of course.

Before continuing on to Spain, I had time in London to meet up with Carole Shepherd, take her to dinner and to see *Man of La Mancha*.

The trip to Spain included Valencia, Tarragona, Larrida and Barcelona, and some very spectacular scenery, in between the broiler breeder farms and hatcheries I was attempting to persuade to buy our Starbro stock.

On European trips, I always had the opportunity to make a side trip to Newcastle to see my Mother, and some of my old friends from around Ponteland. This time I spent the weekend there prior to returning to Canada.

In January 1969, I made another trip to the Southern States to travel with the folks from Shaver in Cullman. We did a good week of sales visits and then headed to Atlanta for my first experience of what was then known as "The Atlanta Show". I'm not sure when it started but by the later 1960s it was already an established part of the poultry industry. While predominantly aimed at the US market, a lot of Canadians attended, and a smattering of South Americans and Europeans. It has since become truly international in scope.

In the early days there was a lot of hard drinking and "partying" of various kinds. This was centred on the American Hotel, known to all as the Americana. Some of the salesmen would share adjacent rooms, with one for drinking and girls doing informal stripteases, and the other for more advanced activity. I think that the story of the salesman who phoned the Bell Captain and said "Send up the pussy", to which the Bellman replied "Yessa, black or white", is probably close to the truth. As time progressed, these activities have become less common.

There were also innumerable "hospitality suites" offered by some of the big companies, including breeders, equipment suppliers, etc, and a huge party, (now no longer) the night before the show opened run by Watt Publishing. Watt was a pioneer in publishing for the poultry industry, and the family owned business still exists, although many of the publications are now digital.

Shaver ran a hospitality suite for a few years but the expense escalated to impossible levels. The hotels insisted on supplying the drinks at bar prices. However, for a year or two at least, some of the salesmen would "smuggle" cheap booze into the hotel for use in the hospitality suite.

I went to Atlanta at the end of January almost every year from 1969 until 2011. In later years this was on behalf of the Egg Board or World's Poultry Congresses.

In 1969, Shaver hired its first Veterinary Officer, Otto Weninger. Otto was originally from Hungary, and graduated from the Ontario Veterinary College in Guelph. He was a big asset to Shaver; in house veterinary advice was becoming increasingly vital as the business expanded. It was also important for assisting commercial customers, and ensuring that they had good professional information from a reliable source.

An important visitor came to Galt in February 1969. This was Stan Tirlea from Romania. Stan had been one of the M.Sc. students at Wye and I had become quite friendly with him. On returning to Romania, Stan had quickly risen to the top of the government-run poultry industry, and DMcQ had persuaded him that he could establish a breeding operation in Romania using Shaver stock. We ended up supplying pure lines of white egg, brown egg and meat lines (although not those used for the Starcross 288). Stan established a research program using fully pedigreed lines with the potential to supply their industry with parent stock. In some ways, if the program had been run optimally, it could have created a competitor. However, during the life of the communist regime in Romania, efficiency was abysmal and although competitive birds may have been produced, they never went outside Romania. However, Shaver had a long-term contract to supply not only breeding stock, but also technical back up. This involved one visit annually by a geneticist (usually me) and others including nutritional and veterinary specialists, often from Guelph.

That same month, I moved from 10½ Pine Street to a newly built apartment on Hespeler Road called Somerset Place. This was a 5 floor block with perhaps 10 units on each level, built in very conventional style. A rectangular living area, made L-shaped by putting a kitchen in one corner, plus a bedroom and bathroom. Mine was on the fourth floor and had a nice north-facing balcony. I also had underground parking. The rent was $150/month all inclusive.

Although I had no problem with the Ontario winters, I was beginning to find it was nice to have a break, and that South was the direction to go. The first of these excursions was to Trinidad, where I was hosted by one of the trainees I had become friendly with in Galt, Chris Bennett. Chris lived in Mayaro on the North-east coast, and I spent several happy days around their lovely plantation house, just 100 yards from the beach. We also visited Port-of-Spain and other parts of the island. This was Carnival time and we got thoroughly involved in many activities, with some of Chris's friends in the feed industry, along with their wives/girl friends etc. including the previous year's Carnival Queen. I loved the Trinidad girls, black, brown and white!

Before returning to the frigid Canadian winter, I spent a few days in Tobago, with more gorgeous beaches and interesting places. I came quite close to buying a piece of real estate there but in the end, did not.

In March I was invited to speak at the Texas Commercial Egg Clinic at College Station. Bill Krueger, one of the great old fashioned poultry scientists met me and shepherded me around. This meeting confirmed my continuing fascination with accents, and elicited the following quote by Tip Smith in the Texas Poultry Times: "We particularly enjoyed Peter Hunton. His subject was the genetic inputs of layer performance. All we understood about that was when he referred to ladies and gentlemen. But oh boy, we loved his clipped British accent. He speaks the Queen's English for sure". At this time, almost every state with a significant poultry population had an extension service, government funded and usually associated with the state university. Most ran one or several meetings for producers each year. These were always fun, and gave commercial scientists a great opportunity for some free publicity for their companies.

Social life at this point was quite varied. A new arrival was another ex-Wye friend, Peter Gooch. Peter worked in the feed industry and he and his wife Pam eventually moved to a beautiful house in Hanover, Ontario, walking distance to Peter's office at New Life Mills. They also had a cottage on Rosalind Lake, just a few miles out of Hanover and I left my boat there part of the time.

In August 1969, I spent a week with Brian Evans, who was still living in Winnipeg. We did a nice circular tour of southern Manitoba including the Riding Mountain Park.

As to dating, I was all over the map! But nothing remotely permanent. I joined a "singles club" in Toronto which turned out to be a dancing academy. I attended hourly sessions for a few months, to little avail. They signally failed to teach me to dance; neither did I meet anyone particularly interesting. I was now 33, the age at which my father married my mother. I dated Adele, who worked in the office; Susan Miller, a friend of the Purvises and aspiring actress; Dot Elmes, who lived downstairs and had two teenage kids. Her husband, a veterinarian, had died of a heart attack in his forties. Joe and Lindy were really nice kids and we all became friendly, but I couldn't get beyond platonic with Dot, though she may have wished otherwise. Joe eventually qualified as a veterinarian too, but had a heart attack and died at 32. Lindy moved to Alberta, working as a laboratory manager, and married, but resisted having children. I met with her a couple of times in Alberta, and communicated when Dot died in 2014 at the age of 89.

But none of these "relationships" could be considered long term.

Work at Shaver continued to be all-consuming. I was much involved with early and very basic data processing. This still involved producing 80-column punch cards to be processed elsewhere. Selection work on the meat lines was becoming more complex; we had some lines fully pedigreed. The relationship with Cargill was becoming a little more fruitful; we had experimental layer crosses on their farm at Elk River MN, with nutritional treatments superimposed, under the direction of the company nutritionist, Norm Magruder. Cargill had a huge research building fully staffed, library, labs, etc and I spent quite bit of time there. They had tremendous resources but somehow they didn't lend themselves to Shaver's way of doing business and research, and so we missed out, I think, on some real possibilities.

In November 1969, I made another trip to Europe. This was typical of European trips at that time: Overnight flight, this time to Brussels; met by our franchise people, and in the hatchery by breakfast time. We visited several farms during the day, had dinner at a Mussel Restaurant in Zeeland (The Netherlands) and finally to bed. The next day was spent partly with people from Hens Feeds (a Cargill company) and then to a trade show in Ghent for three days. Then on to Dusseldorf and Shaver GmbH, which at this time was managed by George Sandkuhl, whom I knew well from his time in Galt. We visited several of the Shaver franchises and generally had a good time. The German industry was at that time dominated by Lohmann; in addition to a successful breeding company, they also supplied commercial chicks and were involved in the egg industry. Our distributors had to use every trick in the book to compete, but they succeeded for many years.

From Germany, I flew to London and managed a quick private trip to Sussex to see Dan and Margaret Durrant and their children, and also met up for a meal with Carole Shepherd, before traveling to Norwich for a visit to Shaver GB. Arriving on a Sunday permitted a nice noon pub session with Managing Director Jim Ingram (and a ride in his E-type Jaguar) and Geoff Matthews, before visiting one of the breeding farms. After this, I attended the British Poultry Breeders Roundtable in Harrogate, and then on to Newcastle and Ponteland to see my mother. I spent three days there and spent some time in my old haunt, the Blackbird, meeting old friends. Returning to London, I rented a car and had a splendid two days in and around Wye and Stelling Minnis, again revisiting pubs and friends.

My final destination in Europe was Edinburgh, for a useful session at the Poultry Research Centre with its Director, Toby Carter. They were involved in research into egg shell quality and as this was one of the "challenges" with our Starcross 288, it proved a useful stop. I flew home from Prestwick, which at the time was a major portal, serving both Edinburgh and Glasgow. For a three-week trip, I accomplished quite a lot, both for Shaver and for myself. In those days overseas trips were usually three weeks or longer, in order to reduce the cost of the airplane ticket.

In early December, my diary notes that I started receiving a new salary, at $14,500/year! I was still converting this to £ for comparison and it seems to have been about £5,500, or about four times what I was being paid at Wye in 1966. I wrote "Not bad for a Geordie lad". But I worked hard for it, and later found that it was startlingly low for that kind of professional position.

Socially, I was still seeing the Purvises in Kitchener, Henry and Christa Bayley in Guelph, and several Shaver staff, especially Pam and Malcolm Gee. We shared meals, drinks and general sociability on a regular basis. I saw Dot Elmes regularly for drinks, coffee, mostly in our apartments but also with her relatives in Guelph. I was also dating Alison, and Karen (Miller) whom I now, to my shame, cannot remember at all! Karen lived in Fergus when I first met her, but later moved to Richmond Hill. So we would meet up in Toronto, and regularly visit the old Riverboat coffee house in Yorkville. This was quite famous as a venue for folk singers, and among those we saw there were, Catherine McKinnon, Murray McLaughlin, Bruce Cockburn, Gordon Lightfoot, and Sonny Terry and Brownie Magee. Amazingly, many of these trips took place on week nights, with me driving to Toronto after work, dining, drinking and seeing a show, and then driving home by 3.00 or 4.00 in the morning. At the ripe old age of 34, those were definitely the days.

As well as the Riverboat, I began to patronize the Colonial Tavern on Yonge Street. This was the home of jazz; the first visit, with Karen, we saw the legendary trumpeter, Wild Bill Davidson. Later the same month, I saw pianist Earl Hines, and in June 1971, by this time with Nita, Oscar Peterson. On several occasions later, we went to see The World's Greatest Jazz Band with Yank Lawson and Bob Haggart. They played what was then my favourite kind of music; traditional Dixieland jazz. I still have some of their music, transposed from vinyl on to CD.

One of the things I had determined to do when I emigrated to Canada was learn to ski. In 1970, I took lessons at the Chicopee slopes in Kitchener. I can't say it was easy going, even on those simple hills, but I practiced and practiced. Dispelling the fear of falling on even the easy slopes was a priority, and partly because of this, I think, I never really achieved competence as a downhill skier. I even took a trip to Colorado in March, managed to break my new skis and enjoyed the scenery, but didn't raise my skill level a great deal. This trip was in good company. While completing my Bachelor's degree in Newcastle, I became friendly with one of the secretaries in the department, Margaret Johnston. Margaret was obviously not your typical clerical worker; in 1968 she emigrated to the U.S, settled in Denver, and eventually enrolled in the medical school there, later graduating as a M.D. We communicated by phone and I ended up going on a ski trip to Aspen with her and several of her local friends. We all lived in a motel room, ate out and brought doggie bags home for lunches, and generally enjoyed ourselves. I took an all day lesson and felt a little more confident. Of course, the rest of the crowd were all high up on the slopes while I struggled about on the short runs near the chalet. By this time, I had bought new skis, which helped quite a bit. They got lost in Chicago on the flights home, but eventually turned up, like most lost luggage.

Meanwhile, work at Shaver continued as usual. While the work tended to be repetitive and sometimes tedious, I think we were all inspired by the success of the company and its continued expansion. Everyone felt a part of the enterprise, and it was undoubtedly competing well in most markets. From a genetic standpoint, we knew we were doing most of the right things and ought to be making progress, although there was no way of knowing the extent of this for sure. Nobody thought of unselected genetic controls in a commercial environment, although Gowe and his group in Ottawa created a number of such lines both for egg and meat strains in their research program. Several years later, while I was working at Ross Poultry, we did create an unselected control line for one of the commercial meat strains, and it proved of great value for many years, enabling the company to demonstrate the actual extent of progress, rather than indulge in speculation like its competitors.

One of the new Shaver staff based in Cullman was John Nay, and I got to know John very well. He had worked in the broiler industry for many years, most recently for Pilch Breeders, who sold a competitive female broiler parent. It was another company founded and led by an aggressive and highly motivated individual, Chester Pilch, and of course DMcQ knew him well. John had been involved in international sales and had some hair-raising tales to tell, especially from time spent in Eastern Europe, then part of the Communist Bloc. John knew everyone we needed to know in the US broiler industry and was a great asset. He hired several excellent sales people, including Hugh Thornburg and Charles Overstreet, before he was shipped off to Germany to take over Shaver GmbH when George Sandkuhl came back to Canada.

Once I joined the Poultry Science Association, I began getting to know many of the poultry scientists working around the US. In May 1970, after the Poultry Breeders Roundtable in Kansas City, I visited Bob Reid and Chuck Weber at the University of Arizona at Tucson. DMcQ would permit, and even encourage, these visits as long as I also gave some sort of talk while visiting, and where possible, helped with local distributors' sales efforts. In this case, I gave a talk at the university, but we had no local franchise, and I flew on to California, where we had recently sold Starbro (meat lines) grandparents to Foster Farms, located near Fresno. Here I worked on selecting birds for use in that breeding program and visited a broiler parent farm with 77,000 breeders and its associated hatchery.

At this time, we had also recently completed an agreement with Ed Demler, President of Demler Farms, for him to have the Shaver franchise for California. Demler was a long established presence in the California egg industry, having run an independent breeding program for many years. The farm was in Anaheim, not far from Disneyland, and to get there from Los Angeles airport, one used a helicopter service.

All the birds there, including breeders, were kept in large colony cages (20-50 birds) raised about four feet off the ground, and beneath lean-to roofs. Manure dried where it fell! Demler had grandparents and one of the largest customers, Goldman's Egg City, also had their own parent breeders, purchased from Demler. At the time, Egg City was one of the US's largest egg farms, with 2 million layers housed in cages, in open sided houses on a mountainside. With its own hatchery, feed mill and egg processing, this was an operation to be reckoned with. However, from a poultry health viewpoint, it was a nightmare, with all 2 million hens effectively one flock! By this time Shaver was delivering PPLO-free stock, but chances of maintaining that status here were a fat zero.

In one day driving with Dick Baker, one of the Demler salesmen, we covered 366 miles and "talked to" 4.6 million hens. Shaver Starcross 288 was to do very well in California for several years.

Selling grandparent stock carried an outstanding risk of line theft by competitors. This was especially so for Shaver because at the time our commercial Starcross 288 was a two-way cross. Males from one pure line crossed with females from another, so even parent stock sales were vulnerable to theft to some extent. Although our sexers were extremely accurate, there would always be a few sexing errors. To minimize the risk of these being used to reproduce the pure lines, we would deliberately add to them with "salts" from an unrelated line, in all parent and grandparent stock sold.

On the social scene, I was still dating here and there, but failing to enjoy any potential long-term involvement. One such "partner" was a very glamorous red-head from apt#504 in the apartment building (mine was #404 and in fact Liz [from 504] complained of the noise one night when I was having a party, and then joined us!) She had a little girl, Patty, from a failed marriage, and we dated on and off for a few months. At one point, I thought it might become serious. In some respects, she partly replaced Dot Elmes as a location for late night coffee. With the benefit of hindsight, this was a mistake! I was also seeing Mary Dahms, as well as Karen Miller, referred to earlier. With all of them, I variously wined, dined, water-skied, and went to theatres and movies. Although there were plenty of places where one could go for a drink now, my notes from the time show that many had quite serious dress codes. Friends and I were refused admission to the Holiday Inn bar in Cambridge, and the roof-top bar at the Skyline in Ottawa, for not wearing ties. It was said that girls wearing pant-suits were similarly unwelcome; they solved the problem by taking off the pants! Short skirts/jackets were deemed OK.

I continued to entertain numerous visitors to Shaver's with dinners, drinks, farm tours, lab tours, visits to Guelph to see our consultants there etc. etc. One such was Stan Tirlea from Romania, who came several times, and of course I was one of the contracted visitors to Romania as part of the Shaver agreement with their government. These visits mostly took place in January/February until I left Shaver in 1974.

In August-September 1970, I had another trip to Europe. I was able to visit my mother in Ponteland for several days, as well as trips to Sussex to see Dan Durrant, and Wye to meet old friends. I then spent a week in Romania with Stan Tirlea, visiting the farms where they had the Shaver program, and also Mamaia on the Black Sea, where Stan had assembled a collection of Romanian breeds as a gene pool. Most of this visit was by road; the roads were not good but the scenery was wonderful; the Romanian Alps, the Black Sea etc. I ended up the trip at the Worlds Poultry Congress in Madrid. I spent a lot of time on the Shaver stand at the Poultry Fair and some time at the Congress, but the timetable there was a catastrophe with papers given haphazardly if at all. This was my first Worlds Poultry Congress, but I was to attend all but one (1974) every four years, until Brazil in 2012.

After the Congress, we spent considerable time with Shaver's new Spanish distributor, Granja Vila, in Reus, near Barcelona. We met the family owners, and staff, and I gave a presentation there on the breeding plans we were pursuing.

I flew home by way of Montreal, visiting the Crosslings, who showed me around the city, which I hadn't really got to know on my visit to Expo in 1967. They also gave me contact information for Gail Preston, a friend who lived in Toronto, and I followed this up later in the year. Gail was most attractive and we began dating in September. Many Tuesdays, I drove to Toronto after work, had drinks, dinner and various shows, and finally coffee at Gail's place on Avenue Road before staggering home at 3.00 the next morning. But this relationship also came to naught after a few months. One of the highlights was seeing Peggy Lee performing at the Royal York Hotel.

In November 1970 I went to Jamaica for some warmth and sunshine. I stayed first of all with Brian Freeman, whom I had known from the days at Wye College. He had moved to the University of the West Indies in Kingston, and married a Jamaican, primarily so that he could purchase a house in Irish Town, in the hills above Kingston. We spent time around his place and the UWI Senior Common Room. To justify Shaver's purchase of the 'plane ticket, I spent a couple of days working with people from the local poultry industry, who were interested in buying breeding stock. I ended up with three days in a delightful hotel, the Tower Isle at Ocho Rios. I swam to Tower Isle, lazed on the beach, and also took a boat trip to Dunn's River Falls. Nice "business trip"!

Some time in this period, I and the Research Department established a tradition of Christmas parties. These followed a fairly tame office party a day or two before Christmas, and took place in my apartment. They were anything but tame, and generally lasted well past midnight! We continued the tradition after moving to the house in St. George. Anyone was welcome and many came, leaving in various stages of intoxication. This was well before the crackdown on drinking and driving, and we were fortunate that nobody ever had an accident.

At the end of 1970, DMcQ announced the appointment of Bob Gray as President of Shaver Poultry Breeding Farms Ltd., while he became Chairman of the Board. I didn't know there was a Board to be Chair of, although in retrospect, Cargill would probably have insisted on it. My feeling, quite justified by subsequent events, was that little would change. Bob Gray was an extraordinarily nice person, but he was best at carrying out orders, not giving them.

Interesting factoids from my 1971 Diary: The population of Canada was 21,061,000. It cost 6 cents to send a letter weighing <30 g anywhere in Canada, 10 cents to the US, 15 cents for <15g to the UK and Carribbean and 25 cents anywhere else. In 2017, the population was 36,600,000, a letter for Canada cost 82 cents, the US, $1.20 and overseas, $2.50. Of course, by 2017, no information of importance was sent by post, and Canada Post existed mainly to distribute junk mail, except at Christmas, but even that market was disappearing as the younger generations abandoned Christmas greetings in what we oldies considered the traditional manner.

February 1971 saw me in the US again for two weeks. I spent time at a convention in Kansas City and with our distributor in Arkansas, Bob Legan, who owned Blue Ribbon Hatchery in Russellville. Another of the old time franchises; hard working, hard playing and thoroughly committed, he was easy to work with and we visited some of his customers together and with Sonny Clements, one of his salesmen.

I also traveled with the Shaver people on sales calls for Starbro (our meat breeder) and some existing Starcross customers. The trip ended up in Texas with a new distributor Charlie Dodd, who owned a hatchery in Joachim. I stayed with him over the weekend and spent Saturday fishing, for the only time in my life! I caught one fish (the others caught dozens) which we ate for dinner Sunday night.

In March I again visited Europe and had a few days with my mother. I finally persuaded her to visit me in Canada. She agreed and would be accompanied by Elizabeth Henderson (neé Dobson, an old flame of mine) later in 1971. I spent two days at Shaver GB and one night in London, when I took Carole Shepherd out for dinner. I spent a day in Paris at a trade show and then on to Romania for my annual visit. Arriving on a Saturday evening, my Sunday was "free". This was the closest I ever came to international intrigue! A "student" befriended me in the hotel, and showed me around Bucharest. It turned out that what he wanted was to buy US dollars! Fortunately I did not have any but I did see a bit more of the city.

The following day, Stan Tirlea collected me and we flew to Bacau, where one of the farms housing Shaver stock was located. Security was strange; at Bacau we landed and stopped in the middle of the runway, before being picked up by a military truck. Actually it was at this time that hijacking was becoming a factor in international travel. At many international airports, including Zurich later on this trip, landing planes would be surrounded by armed soldiers.

At the farms in Romania, I was struck by the cultural challenge of the Communist era. Stan, his colleagues and the managers are all "us" and the workers, "them". When Stan needs something, it was like a pantomime as people rushed around to ensure he got it, and quick. The towns were drab and impoverished, except for the nice hotel where we stayed, but even this sometimes frayed at the edges. The journey from the hotel to the Brad Farm passed through Bogdan Voda and Dumbrava, the names and the scenery brought scenes from the movie Dr. Zhivago to mind.

The stocks Shaver supplied to the Romanian project could, in the right hands, have enabled them to develop into a competitor. However, whether by luck or judgment, it was clear to me that this was most unlikely to happen. Things just moved too slowly. However, they were always most hospitable and gave me (and of course themselves) a good time. The other bigwigs here were Dmitri Bosoanca and Peter Placinta, a very military type. Bosoanca I think was scientifically trained but spoke very little English. This was another obstacle in terms of our communication.

My next stop was in Spain to again support our distributor Granja Vila in Reus. By now I was becoming accustomed to the Spanish meal routine; minimal breakfast, huge lunch from about 1.00 to 3.00 p.m, no siesta, and huge dinner from 9.00 p.m. to who-knows-when. Vila were actively selling both Starcross and Starbro brands. They had grandparents for the Starbro, and I spent some time at the isolated farm in the mountains where these were housed. My host for most of my Spanish visits was Juan Louis Blanch. He was a real gourmet, and after the first trip, I told him that in future, he should order for me and I promised to eat whatever came. The only thing I ever criticized was octopus cooked in its own ink, which was like eating a dark blue rubber glove! Blanch didn't particularly like it either.

My final stop in Europe was in The Netherlands to work with our very enthusiastic Dutch distributor, Rotzhuisen NV. Ernst Rotzhuisen had met DMcQ at the end of the second World War, and loyally represented Shaver for about 20 years, until he eventually switched to Lohmann. As I was leaving for the airport in Amsterdam, the Rotzhuisen sales manager Henk gave me a bottle of gin as a parting gift, and wouldn't you know, I already had my allowance of booze and the Canada Customs charged me $4 to bring it in! This also made me miss the limousine back to Galt, so I was late getting home. But all told, a great trip.

Another part of the Romanian contract was the attendance in Cambridge of pairs of personnel from their breeding farms, and two such visitors arrived the next week. We gave them farm tours, lots of lectures, visits to Guelph, and did our best to entertain them for the week or so they were with us. From my visits to the country, it became obvious that this would be a most sought-after perk, and those chosen were extremely lucky.

Our research department was thriving now. We had data processing using shared computer time at a local business (Canadian General Tower) and continued to use the government system run by Gowe and his staff at Agriculture Canada. We had state-of-the-art equipment for measuring egg quality, and the Engineering Service at Ag Canada helped in developing improved versions for us. We had three full time staff operating in a nice building attached to the main office, and it all worked very well. We finally were able to use the pedigree records system developed in Ottawa to maintain records on the layer pure lines, and receive data summaries that Randy Cole used to make his selections. We did not, however, go as far as Eric Maddison had done 10 years previously, in terms of allowing the computer to make the selections. That would probably not happen for another 20 years if DMcQ had anything to do with it.

Socially, 1971 was a year of change. I still spent a lot of time with John and Brenda Purvis, having meals, sharing boating activity. Henry and Christa Bayley were also regularly visited and provided much hospitality. But in April I subscribed to the "Cupid Computer" service that promised lots of congenial dates. This was a very basic kind of service run on a computer share system somewhere in Toronto. One filled out a fairly detailed form at home, mailed it to Cupid, who ran it through their system and mailed back a print out of supposedly compatible women. One was encouraged to phone and set up initial dates to confirm whether any compatibility actually existed, then take it form there. (This was certainly primitive compared with today, when my internet browser sends me, without asking, all kinds of dating services, and some not just dating.)

My first date was with Carol Duke, who lived in Toronto. We met only twice before calling it quits. But it was a worthwhile experience for both of us, and certainly justified the cost of Cupid! My second date, Edna Teiman was English, teaching school in Toronto, and we had only two dates. She was extremely thin and I learned later, suffering from *anorexia nervosa*. Third time lucky, they say! Before agreeing to a date at all, my third candidate, Nita Scoffield, asked how tall I was. At that time I could claim 5ft 10in, maybe in shoes. So that's what I said. It turned out Nita was the same height and didn't want to date anyone shorter than herself. So we met for drinks at Malloney's on Jarvis Street in Toronto and the rest, as they say, is history. I described her after the date as "most attractive, dark hair, blue eyes and a gorgeous sun-tan". She originated from Nottingham, England and was teaching at an inner city school in Toronto. She had a nice place, the upstairs of a house on Marjory Avenue in the Greek neighbourhood in east Toronto. Nita had been briefly married before leaving England about a year after I did, but had no children. I don't think either of us aspired to "love at first sight", but we obviously shared some quite important needs: A stable relationship and pleasant company. Avoiding singles bars and events. An appreciation of the outdoors. And sex. And so on.

I traded cars again this spring; after shopping all over the place, I got a nice gold coloured Pontiac Firebird from Highview Motors in Galt for $2,400 plus my two-year-old Camaro. List price of the Firebird was $4,455, so it seemed a good deal to me. I borrowed $600 from the bank to pay cash.

Shaver hired a young man called Peter Evans in 1970, and he and I became friends. He and his wife Ann were both from Trinidad, where his family had a farm. They made great rum punches in large quantities, and also had a lot of Trinidadian friends mostly in Toronto. One such was a lovely girl called Lyris Tracey, whom I got to know quite well. She was tall and slim, and coffee coloured, and along with her long time boy friend Binky, made a pleasant couple. Lyris was a physiotherapist trained in London, England. She lived in downtown Toronto and over the next many years I visited often, even staying overnight when circumstances demanded. Lyris died in 2019, but until then, lived in the same apartment on Sherbourne St. that she had in 1971. Peter Evans did not stay long, eventually joining Cobb Breeding Co., a competitor, and moving several times, eventually to Mexico, and he divorced Ann along the way.

I made two trips to the US in the summer of 1971, promoting Shaver products, both egg and meat. There were still plenty of franchise hatcheries for our egg production stock, and broiler companies willing to try something new. And it was fairly common for a salesman and geneticist to travel together; the geneticist provided some credibility to go along with the sales pitch. I enjoyed the experience although it meant time out of the office and away from the research program.

I was also deeply involved with company PR at home. I spent a half day in August at the Master Feeds Research Farm near Georgetown, just west of Toronto. The Director at the time was Doug Morrison, later to become Chair of the Animal and Poultry Science Department at Guelph. The Farm Manager was Dan Price Jones, a poultryman *par excellence*, with whom I kept in touch for many years. Dan had been to Harper Adams College in England at the same time as Chris Fowler. He later worked for Craig Hunter Hatchery, a Dekalb franchise, but he was also interested in preserving fancy breeds. I came to work with him much later on gene conservation generally.

By the end of May, Nita was becoming a regular part of my life. She had acquired her own car, a bright yellow Chevelle, and drove herself to Galt most times. She came down for a very wet Victoria Day, which we spent with the Bayleys. We dined luxuriously at La Chaumiere on Church St. in Toronto. And she learned to water ski! Just about 150 ft. the first time but that is all one needs for the confidence to do it again. We had a nice picnic and ski session at Bellwood Lake with the Bayleys at the end of May. Nita enjoyed the company, and the sunshine. She was then very keen on tanning, and hated tan lines!

We began spending some weekends in Hanover, with Peter and Pam Gooch and their growing family. We would take the boat and everyone skied. One such weekend we took the whole family including Peter's mother, to eat at the Hartley House in nearby Walkerton, where I had the biggest T-bone steak of my life – I think it must have been close to 2 lb.

For my 35th birthday on June 12th, Nita brought a 3½ lb cheese and a bottle of Moselle, and we took these, plus the boat, a barbecue and a lot of other food, to Bellwood Lake for a great party. We were joined by Peter and Ann Evans and their kids, Trevor and Beryl Sykes (Trevor had been at Wye), Pam and Malcolm Gee and David, and Pat Attridge, Pam's sister, who was a long-time personal assistant to DMcQ.

By this time, I learned that my second Cupid date, Edna, was actually a friend of Nita's; they had joined at the same time! So it was fortunate that Edna and I did not "click". In July, Nita had a visit from her mother and her nephew, and they all, plus Edna, went on a 3 week car trip to the Grand Canyon. They covered 6,000 miles in total. While they were away, I dated the last Cupid candidate but this was not a success and I don't even have a name to go with the experience.

In late August my mother and Elizabeth arrived on a charter flight from Gatwick for an eighteen day visit. In those days the charter airlines somehow managed to undercut the majors as long as they could fill a plane with members of some largely fictitious "club". I vaguely remember joining such an organization to facilitate this trip. They stayed in the apartment; mother and Elizabeth in my room, and I on a borrowed bed in the living room. I took two weeks vacation (I think that was all we got at the time) and we had a splendid car trip into the US, starting, of course at Niagara Falls, Canada. After the mandatory look at the Falls, we drove through New York state, part of Pennsylvania and ended up very late at a Holiday Inn in Winchester, Virginia. The next part of the trip was to see the Skyline Drive on the top of the Appalachian Mountains through Virginia. It was hot and hazy but altogether enjoyable. After a second night in Winchester we headed north through the corners of West Vitginia, and Maryland, across part of Pennsylvania and into New Jersey. I drove through New York City to show the tourists the sights before emerging northbound to New Haven, Connecticut and another Holiday Inn. We toured New Haven including Yale Univ. and then kept going north, around Boston, through part of New Hampshire and into Maine, where we stayed in a charming little two-bedroom cabin in Wiscasset.

From here we visited Reid State Park, right on the Atlantic, but although the weather was hot and humid, the water temperature was 54°F, much too cold for swimming. I knew this ahead of time from visiting a beach in New Hampshire with Henry Bayley during the Poultry Science meeting in 1968. Anywhere north of Cape Cod was the same.

We continued heading north and stayed the next night at a nice motel in Conway, New Hampshire, in preparation for the drive to the summit of Mont Washington the following day. The weather was hazy but we got some good views, and some memorable photographs. At this time I was using a single lens reflex film camera, mostly for coloured slides, as the fidelity of colour prints still left much to be desired. I have recently (2013 – 2017) digitized many of these old slides for posterity.

We headed back through the White Mountains and into Vermont. More gorgeous mountain scenery, which my mother really enjoyed. All much grander than her favourite Lake District hills in England.

We got back to Galt on September 9th after a total distance traveled of 2,545 miles in the Firebird. This really was a nice holiday for all three of us.

Before they left we spent a day in Toronto. Ontario Place had just opened with the first IMAX theatre, and we saw the great movie "North of Superior". I still remember having to clutch the arms of the seat during the "flight" across the forest and out over the lake. We went shopping at the Colonnade, had drinks in Stop 33, and a splendid dinner *chêz* Nita. Mother and Elizabeth flew home September 12th.

In October, Nita and I spent a long weekend at Arowhon Pines in Algonquin Park. This was an upscale lodge and these were still the days when obviously unmarried couples were looked upon with a hint of suspicion. However, they were happy to take our money and we enjoyed the weekend. The food was exceptional. On one short canoe trip, we followed a swimming beaver for a few minutes. We also caught some of the best of the fall colour. Although we had both been in Canada for 3 or 4 years, the colours were still magic. We revisited Arowhon Pines in 2021; we remembered very little but had two wonderful days canoeing the lakes. The food was still exceptional.

I went on another European trip in early November, this time to Portugal, where Shaver had a good national distributor, and then Spain for more work with Granja Vila (and more excellent food with Blanch). From Barcelona I flew by a highly circuitous (and originally unplanned) route to Sweden and eventually met up with Geoff Fairhurst, who was guide and interpreter for my trip. Geoff had moved from his job with Thornbers in the UK to manage an egg layer complex in Sweden, but by now was an independent consultant. We ended the trip at Geoff's home for a splendid dinner and overnight. Geoff had married Chris in Suffolk; she brought 3 children from her first marriage, and they now had one of their own.

Finally I flew to England and spent a couple of days with Shaver GB, prior to the annual Breeders Roundtable, this year hosted by Shaver. DMcQ attended and spoke at the opening reception.

I spent a couple of days in and around Wye before coming home. Even after nearly five years, the pubs were still quite a draw!

Christmas day, 1971 we spent at the home of Flora and Arthur Attridge, parents of Pat and Pam (Gee). They had run a London pub before retirement and emigration to Canada. Arthur was a handyman and Flora, an excellent cook. We started the day with real champagne cocktails and continued with the traditional turkey with all the trimmings. Games and chatter, and more drinks, kept us going the whole day, and more guests would show up for the evening.

Towards the end of 1971 and in to 1972, I was negotiating the purchase of a 2½ acre building lot on the Concession V road near St. George (it's now called McLean School Road), and a house designed to go on it. I eventually bought the lot for $6,000. It was quite close to one of the Shaver farms (Maple Lane) although this had nothing to do with the decision to buy it. The design and building of the house played an increasing part in life away from work which, as could be expected, continued to occupy most of my time. One of my colleagues at Shaver, Doug Ridsdale, had a brother Cameron in Toronto who was an architect, so he came down and inspected the lot, and produced a very nice house design for me. We found a contractor who lived on the same concession road, Fritz Schweitzer, who agreed to build it, once the winter was over. We had to haggle about the price and ended up getting another estimate, but Fritz eventually agreed to do it for $31,000, which was close to what we wanted. Cameron advised me throughout this time. I arranged a mortgage for $30,000 with Fidelity Trust in Brantford. But before ground was broken, I had all kinds of run-ins with the local Township about the entry from the road, and the fact that they like 150 ft. of frontage and my lot was only 123 ft. The disputes continued into June, with multiple lawyers, councilors, me, Fritz all working in different directions. My own lawyer, David Charlton, was particularly inept and I made a great mistake in selecting him. I found with some items it was easier and quicker to do the work myself. The plans were eventually approved and construction began in August, after I and friends had cut down enough trees to allow for a driveway to be made. Elgin Smith, whose wife Mary worked at the Shaver office, had a contracting business and bulldozed the driveway. I also had a well drilled before construction began; it went down 128 ft before striking water, but the quality was good, unlike the one at the Shaver farm just down the road which was rusty and sulfurous.

I had yet another trip to Europe in February, 1972, the first part retracing the route I took the previous November; Portugal, then Spain. I did a number of calls with Granja Barca Nova, Shaver's national distributor, up the east coast of Portugal, based in Porto. On one of these, we got there mid-morning and were invited for lunch. This farm was virtually on the Atlantic coast and the owner was out fishing when we arrived. He returned bearing copious *lampreia* which we ate much later, cooked in tomato and garlic sauce with brandy. This, I think, was the same species that had recently been (accidentally) introduced to the Great Lakes and was playing havoc with the lake trout. I was not sure how it survived in both salt and fresh water.

After the Portuguese part of the trip, I was driven to Viseu in central Portugal, where we were met by Blanch from the Spanish distributor, Granja Vila. Blanch drove me to Santiago de Compostela, famous as the end point of the famous *Camino Real* which began in France. It surely was spectacular. From here we drove to Pontevedra, Vigo, Valladolid, and Orense with appointments all along the way, before finally arriving in Reus after four hectic days. Both the Portuguese and the Spanish drove with typical European verve; after 4,000 km I felt as though I lived in the passenger seat of a vehicle on a permanent S-bend. So it was a relief that the next part of the trip, to Romania, was by air! There wasn't much new in Romania and I spent a week working with Stan Tirlea and many of his colleagues that I had met there previously as well as on their visits to Canada.

From Bucharest I flew to Germany for time with John Nay, now General Manager of Shaver GmbH in Dusseldorf. I noted in my diary how nice it was to be in a hotel where one got ice in one's drink, reliable plumbing, a radio in the room and a telephone operator who spoke English. We visited a number of hatcheries and their customers. The Germans by this stage (27 years post-world war II) had regained a lot of prosperity and we enjoyed great hospitality in some really wonderful old homes; great courtyards, foursquare brick or stone houses and excellent food. The customers were generally boisterous but friendly. In my early visits to Germany I tended to feel slightly intimidated, when the customers pounded the table and shouted their complaints. By now, however, I had discovered that what I needed to do was pound the table while shouting my rebuttals, and all would be well! This was greatly helped by Hans Grauke, who was then the traveling representative for Shaver, who drove me around, and translated for me.

The German trip was followed by one day with Rotzhuisen NV in The Netherlands before flying to Great Britain.

I spent the night near Heathrow, managing a nice dinner with Carole Shepherd. This was followed by a day in Edinburgh to visit the Poultry Research Centre, a very productive time arranged for me by Director Toby Carter. Finally I took the train from Edinburgh to Newcastle, a lovely trip down the Northumberland coast, and spent a couple of days with my mother. I then rented a car and drove to Prestwick airport near Glasgow, for my flight home.

Nita and I had planned a holiday in the Caribbean but soon after I returned from the European trip, she canceled it. I never knew why. We had an "estrangement" for a few months although we communicated frequently. It was on-again off-again, though more off than on, for both of us. I re-joined Cupid, and dated several women on the new list.! I also joined a Graduates Club in Toronto, which held regular dances and booze-ups, and made friends with a nice nurse called Sybil. This went on until the end of May, when I got a somewhat tearful phone call from Nita, basically wanting to turn back the clock, and frankly, it wasn't a hard choice for me.

Peter and Janice Bomford, whom I originally met in Wye, had now moved to the Agricultural College at Ridgetown, far down in south-western Ontario, and I visited from time to time. Compared with south-east England, Ridgetown was a bit of a backwater and they weren't exactly happy there. But Peter had a decent job teaching agricultural engineering and so they stayed for 6 years. By this time they had established a nice life and several good friends, but the lure of England got them back to a job for Peter at the Seal Hayne Agricultural College in Devon. We kept in touch with them for the next forty years. Peter died suddenly of lung cancer (he never smoked in his life) in 2015. Janice visited us in 2017 and spent several days in Ridgetown, so there must have been something about it!

It was about this time that I became friendly with Doug and Ivy Brown, and their family, in St. George. I had met Doug while waiting for the ski-lift at Chicopee. Originally from Scotland, Doug was an entrepreneur. He had a furniture factory in Kitchener, making cabinets for stereos etc. but when that business showed signs of collapse, he opened up another business in St. George where they made leather and plastic stuff. Among other things, they made turkey saddles! They also made footballs for one of the big American name brands. Doug and his wife Ivy had two sons and two daughters, and lived in a large and lovely old house in St. George. One of the big events in their lives was the Burns Supper, held each January. They did the whole thing properly; the haggis was piped in, and then addressed by one of the family, who was not identified until the very day. An invite to this was a must (in spite of my well concealed dislike of the bagpipes) and Nita and I attended on a number of occasions. We often exchanged hospitality with Doug and Ivy, and Doug was helpful in many ways when we moved. Doug's sons both joined the Company (although the younger one, Richard, did not stay long) and after he died, Douglas Jr. ran it for a number of years until he himself retired.

I had another trip to the US in June 1972, centred around Cullman AL, where Shaver had recently opened its second farm for the selection and multiplication of Starbro grandparents. I did sales calls in several of the southeastern states with Charles Overstreet and Hugh Thornburg. This was one of my longer US trips, and ended up on the Delmarva peninsular, one of the most dense chicken production areas in the country, and of course, a prime target for Shaver. While in Virginia, I spent a couple of days with the Rocco company, who were our Starcross distributors as well as being a major broiler prospect. The management of this company, mainly the Strickler family, was greatly respected throughout the industry, and we were very fortunate to have an excellent relationship with them.

The work part of the trip completed, I then spent time with Michael Forhane and two-year-old daughter Alexandra. Mike was married to Patricia (née Mulvihill) but they were now separated, so this was an interesting visit. They were living in Chestertown MD and I stayed there a couple of days before going to Washington DC to stay with the Donaldsons, Graham and Robin and family, whom I had known from the days in Wye. By now, Graham was working for the World Bank and Robin, the Brookings Institute. They lived in downtown Washington and I enjoyed the usual relaxed time with copious wine and excellent food. I flew home from there and was met by Nita, with whom I was now reconciled.

Later, towards the end of August, we went on a camping trip to New England. We borrowed a tent and some equipment, just enough to fill the (minuscule) trunk of the Firebird. We drove east through Ontario and through Montreal before heading south into Vermont, and stayed the first 2 nights at Smugglers Notch. We really enjoyed the scenery in the Vermont Green Mountains. A combination of a short rain shower, bumpy, hard ground and inadequate planning convinced us that we were not cut out for camping, and so the next stop was 3 nights in a cabin at Perry's Rest in North Conway NH which we rented for $7.00 a night! We enjoyed the White Mountains and for the second time that year, I drove up to the summit of Mount Washington. This time the weather was clear and we had magnificent views all round. We spent a day near Cape Elizabeth and in Crescent Beach State Park, and on the way home, visited The Flume, to which I had also taken my mother and Elizabeth earlier in the year. We stayed the night in Ottawa with Jim and Liz Parlour on the way home.

On my return from this trip, I had expected all kinds of progress with the building of the house, but it was not to be! I wrote in my diary that "the builders are worse than the lawyers". However, by September 6th, the hole for the foundation had been excavated. After another hiatus, the foundations were completed the first week in October and it proceeded quite well from then on. The framing was essentially done the third week in October. There was a falling out between Fritz and Cameron; Fritz did not take well to supervision, and that was what architects expected to do. However, in the end I had to pay off Cameron as there was no choice; getting another contractor at that stage would have been a nightmare. And I was expecting to move in before Christmas.

Work at Shaver continued as usual; lots of overseas guests, some unexpected turnover in lab staff as we continued to need IBM cards punched and verified. We continued to hold Consultant Meetings about twice annually, and these were valuable events. We still were under-staffed at the technical level but the Consultants often filled in for us. The breeding programs all proceeded according to plan and the company continued to be highly successful, especially in the white egg sector.

I continued to have a lot of fun after work with George Sandkuhl, Ed Hubbard and others in various bars. The Rascal Lounge had become a favourite but I don't remember where it was.

After several months of ups and downs, Nita and I finally decided to marry. I think her words on Sunday October 22nd were "Lets do it!". In retrospect I can partly understand her hesitation. She had been married before, and it had not been successful, primarily due to her first husband's infidelity. I was pretty certain I wouldn't be guilty of that! We eventually got the marriage license and an appointment for the ceremony at Toronto's Old City Hall for December 29th. This turned out to be a highly propitious date; on my 1972 income tax return I had to answer the question: "How much did your spouse earn in 1972, while married?" Answer: $0. So I got the full spousal allowance for the whole year!

Thus, in addition to moving house, we were also joining forces for the final construction and decoration phases in the house on Conc.V. We purchased appliances secondhand, and all were good deals except for the fridge, sold to us by a tricky lawyer in Toronto. We eventually bought a new fridge but when it was delivered, our driveway was ice-bound and the guys had to lug it up the hill by hand. I got home just as Nita was plying them with coffee and beer as compensation. We bought carpets, light fixtures, draperies, furniture, and chose the flooring in the entrance way and the kitchen cabinets. We chose the paint and I and Nita painted the whole interior. I don't think I did a very good job, because in the ensuing 45 years, I have not painted a single square foot.

The house had a sunken living area called a conversation pit which would hold about 8 people sitting on carpeted benches, and we got an Acorn fireplace to go in it. This room also had a walk out on to a huge deck where we entertained in summer. There were three bedrooms on different levels; the master bedroom had a walk-in closet and its own bathroom. In addition, there was a full bathroom half way up the stairs and a powder room adjacent to the front door. There was a fairly large, unfinished basement where we had the laundry, and some crawl space for storage. The basement also had access to the carport, which held two cars.

I had to personally arrange for a lot of the services; heating, hydro, telephone etc and this all took time, so it was a fairly frantic three months. With the interior construction taking place in cold weather, I had to rent and install temporary heating until the oil furnace was operational. I rented sundry trucks to transport appliances, furniture etc from Toronto and from Nita's and my own apartment. Part way through December, Pam Gee hosted a surprise shower for Nita, and the same night, Ron Jones (Shaver Production and Hatcheries Manager) hosted a stag for me. I don't remember what happened to Nita, but I got home at 3.00 am.

I had given notice to the owners of my Somerset Place apartment for the end of December and I cleared out the place and moved everything to the house by December 15th. I actually slept in the house on the 16th, but couldn't cook anything until a few days later. We installed a lot of our own stuff, carpets etc and this all took time so December was a lost cause for everything but the house. But many friends helped, and were generous with their time; some brought food, some champagne, so all in all we did not suffer.

Our wedding at Old City Hall in Toronto took place during a snowstorm but in spite of this everything went more or less according to plan. Our witnesses, Henry and Christa Bayley, Malcolm and Pam Gee made it on time and we actually had a half hour wait for the judge. He turned out to be a toothless old guy about five feet tall but he knew how to go through the motions and we were duly married. Then on to the Holiday Inn adjacent to new City Hall where we had some champagne in the room, before lunch in their revolving restaurant. The Bayleys and Gees left about 3.30 and Nita and I relaxed until the evenings activities; *Twelfth Night* at the St. Lawrence Centre and a good steak dinner with wine at Barberians. The following day, back in St. George, we entertained 24 guests in our new home with Deutche Sekt, sundry other drinks and a large volume of coffee. All the beds were full with overnight guests including Peter and Pam Gooch and Edna Teiman.

And so to 1973. Nita had secured a temporary job teaching English as a second language to immigrant children at St. Peters Catholic School in Galt, and I continued my job with Shaver. Nita really enjoyed the teaching, although not so much the Catholic environment. The children soaked up the language voraciously and progressed rapidly; Nita would sometimes see them interpreting for parents in the grocery stores. She found a permanent job starting in September, at St. Andrews School, which was part of the Public School system encompassing Grades 6-9.

Although we were living quite comfortably in the new house, it was by no means finished in terms of decoration, and we spent most of our non-working hours varnishing, polishing, installing yet more light fixtures, and all and sundry things to make life easier and more comfortable. We also acquired a jet black cat (he must have been part Siamese, to see and listen to him) and a Jack Russell puppy.

At work, I continued with my responsibilities in research and data processing and traveled as usual. In January, I was in California to work with Demler Farms, followed by more calls in Mississippi, Georgia and the Carolinas with the Cullman salesmen before going to the Poultry Show in Atlanta. While in California, one of the Demler salesmen, Frank Mendonca, drove me into the mountains east of Sacramento to visit a remote chicken farm, supposedly owning some "giant chickens" that had been widely publicized. The chickens turned out to be unexceptional and the farmer, pretty much the same! How the publicity evolved, I will never understand. But it was a nice day out nevertheless.

I went to Europe again in February, first to Spain and then to Romania for what were now quite predictable, but enjoyable in a way, stays. From Romania I went to Poland for the first time. Shaver had both business and friends in Poland, which at this time was still very much under the communist boot. I had a guided tour of Torun, birthplace of Copernicus (500 years ago in 1973) and sometime home of Chopin. A most graceful and attractive city. After a visit to a large poultry farm, I was taken by my interpreter, Andrezy Koslowski to his home in Bydgoscz for a celebration dinner. Andrezj had visited Shaver in Canada and he clearly wanted to return our hospitality. His family went all out and I am sure they used a weeks worth of rationed food in one meal. And of course none of them except Andrezy knew much, if any English. I thanked them profusely and wished I had some tangible gift, but of course I didn't carry anything with me for such an event.

After this very social event, I had a most pleasant visit with Dr. Prof. Ewa Potemkowska, whom I had previously met, and who was also a long time friend of DMcQ. We talked academic genetics, quite a change for me. She was a woman of great charm and enthusiasm, and I very much enjoyed the visit. A few years later, Prof. Potemkowska led a bid by Poland to host the World's Poultry Congress. It was awarded to the country but politics intervened and later it had to be canceled. After a few days in Germany and The Netherlands, I was again able to spend one day with my mother in Ponteland, before returning to Canada.

In March, 1973 we had some of the worst winter weather. Both our cars got stuck in the driveway and on the Concession road in both directions. Proximity to the Shaver Maple Lane Farm came in handy, as the manager at the time, Ron Markel, helped clear the driveway and pull cars out of the ditch. Yet, by the end of the month, we had our morning coffee on the deck outside the living room.

I again attended the National Breeders Roundtable in Kansas City, and followed this with trips to Arkansas, Texas, the Carolinas and Delmarva. In Arkansas, my visit coincided with the state Poultry Festival, where one of our hatchery sales people, Sonny Clements and his wife Bobby were in charge. My diary reminds me that "I ogled the Princesses and drank some illicit booze" during this event.

In Texas, I was hosted by Monroe Fuchs (pronounced "fox"), who at that time was still operating a private breeding company, Ideal Poultry Farms, in Cameron TX. We ate a wonderful dinner at the Stagecoach Inn, built in 1848, in Salado, and also looked round his farm. I had a day at Texas A&M University, hosted by the legendary John Quisenberry, which I very much enjoyed.

The Belated Honeymoon

Because of the timing of our wedding, Nita and I did not have a honeymoon. So we counted our summer trip to Poultry Science in South Dakota, and on to the west coast, as a belated one. We drove the whole way. For some reason I failed to keep a mileage record for the whole trip, but it was 1260 miles to Brookings SD, so the total must have been close to 6000 miles. We still had the Firebird, which was very nice to drive, although with limited trunk space. We established the habit of each driving about 2 hours, then a pee and meal or coffee break followed by another 2 hours drive by the other person. So 500 miles each day was quite comfortable, and more at a stretch.

Our route took us north on the Michigan interstates and then west through Wisconsin and Minnesota to Brookings SD for the four day Poultry Science meetings. I was involved with the meetings, chaired one of the genetics sessions, and attended most of the lectures and seminars. Nita joined the spouses tours (at that time, exclusively wives) and made several new friends that became regulars at subsequent meetings over the years.

After Poultry Science, we continued west through the Badlands, Rapid City and the Black Hills, and stopped to see Mount Rushmore. We stayed the night in Deadwood, and visited the graves of Calamity Jane and Wild Bill Hickok. These were all new to both of us and we had a great time. The spectacular scenery only improved when we entered Wyoming, and drove through the Bighorn Mountains, then over near-desert to Cody, and on towards Yellowstone Park, where we rented a small cabin at Canyon Village.

To "do" Yellowstone park in one day was impossible, but we did our best! We stopped at Artist Point and did the 500 ft descent to see the Lower Falls (and back up of course). We saw the Mammoth Hot Springs, Yellowstone

Lake, and Old Faithful, and then spent the following night in what I referred to as a shanty town, West Yellowstone. The next day we continued our westward journey, but with a diversion through the Bitterroot Mountains in Montana to Salmon, and then south following the Salmon River. The scenery here reminded us of Scotland, but without the heather. We ended up for the night in Boise, Idaho.

To make up some time, we used I80 the next day, through the northeast corner of Oregon and over the Columbia River into Washington State, and stayed the night in Rainier, with great views of its eponymous Mountain. We actually started walking the trail towards the ice caves, but encountered snow, and since Nita and I were both in shorts, turned back. But not before taking many photographs.

Since Nita had never seen the Pacific Ocean, we headed in that direction, through Olympia, Aberdeen, and finally to Ocean City, right on the water. It was here that we found how cold the Pacific can be! One thinks of southern California's balmy beaches but up here immersion any higher than the ankles was not pleasant. But the weather turned sunny and we spent an afternoon mooching on the beach among the rocks and driftwood.

We drove north from here to Port Angeles and stayed overnight in order to catch a morning ferry to Vancouver Island. This was an American ferry, and it wasn't until we were well on our way to Nanaimo on the east coast of Vancouver Island that we discovered the BC ferries were all on strike, and the only way off the Island was by another American ferry. I think there were only two; the one we came on, and another which ran from Sydney to Anacortes WA. Since we had a commitment in Saskatoon in four days time, we had no choice but to join a many-mile long line-up for the Sydney ferry. We joined the line about lunchtime Friday, hoping to get on a ferry at 5.00 pm Saturday. We were able to get some food in a corner store before it ran out, and people along the road were generous with their washrooms. But a Firebird was about the last car you would want to spend the night in, and we got up cold and stiff after very little sleep. We got to the ticket booth at 1.00 pm Saturday, loaded on to the ferry at 6.00 pm, and arrived in Anacortes at 10.00 pm It took us an hour to clear town and drive to Bellingham where we got the last motel room available, and went to bed about 12.30.

We were up at the crack of dawn and drove north to Vancouver, crossing the Canadian border without incident. We did a very quick tour of Stanley Park before heading east on the Trans Canada highway, via the Fraser Canyon, Kamloops and the Thompson River, spending the night in Revelstoke. By this time we were more or less on schedule, so the following day had time to linger a while on the summit of Rogers Pass, and at Lake Louise with a beer in the Dick Turpin pub. We visited Moraine Lake before heading out of the Rockies and stopping in Red Deer AB to visit friends of Nita's, Lee and Kate McQuillan. Kate was a College friend of Nita's from Exeter.

The commitment in Saskatoon was a meeting of the Canadian Hatcheries Federation, which I attended as a Shaver representative, along with Marketing Manager Peter Quail. Nita again joined the Ladies Program. The meeting was only one day, and ended with a nice banquet and some lighthearted speeches at the Western Development Museum.

After this, all we had to do was get home, except for a commitment for a night in Winnipeg staying with Brian Evans. Brian was very hospitable, gave us dinner, a tour of the city and a comfortable bed for the night. We took just 2½ days for the drive from Winnipeg to St. George, with overnight stops in Thunder Bay (where we had a drink with Binky, Lyris's boy friend) and Thessalon, on the north shore of Lake Superior. A truly memorable trip and a great honeymoon.

Back to Work

While reading through the trade magazines on my return to work, I noticed an advertisement for a job with Ross Poultry in Edinburgh, Scotland. If I had tried to write my ideal job description at the time, this would have been it. Although I was not crazy about leaving Canada for Scotland, professionally it was the right thing to do. The job was Senior Research Geneticist. It had been occupied by Bob Osborne, whom I had met at Breeders Roundtables. Bob had died suddenly and Ross wanted to find a replacement. The only person I told about this whole thing was Nita, because it would have been quite unacceptable for anyone at Shaver, or elsewhere, to have wind of it. So I wrote an application and put it in the mail.

We had a lot of visitors at Shaver in September. Dr. Potemkowska from Poland was one of them and she insisted on visiting Maple Lane Farm, which was a shower-in facility. Dr. P. was a big lady and I had to ask Nita to buy underwear for her to wear on the farm visit! It worked out OK. We also hosted Dr. John Lancaster, a disease specialist originally from England but long employed at the Canada Department of Agriculture, in charge of poultry matters. A big group of Japanese visitors, a few from The Netherlands and Sweden also occupied some time.

Towards the end of October, Doug Rundle (DMcQ's brother-in-law and North American Sales Manager) and I, along with John Summers, Nutritionist and Shaver Consultant from Guelph, drove down to Lancaster PA for a joint Greider Hatchery/Shaver producer meeting. I always enjoyed these affairs. It was a chance to meet, first hand, the end users of our products. The hatchery owners and sales people were always a joy to work with especially when things were going well. Pennsylvania was at the time a huge egg-producing state with a large number of independently owned farms. This was an excellent meeting and we all felt very good about it.

We had a lot of snow, even before Christmas, this year, which tested our abilities getting in and out of the house and up and down the driveway. The day of the planned Research Department party, the roads were totally blocked and we had to cancel it.

At year end, I was informed of a raise in salary to $20,000.

Early in January I had a telephone call from John Archibald at Ross Poultry in Scotland, telling me they wanted to interview me for the Senior Research Geneticist position. At the beginning of my European trip in February, I had most of a day free in London and met with John, and his boss Struan Wiley, at the Imperial Group offices. Ross at this time was owned by Imperial, as part of their policy of diversification away from being strictly a tobacco company. This interview went well and we agreed to meet again in Scotland in a few weeks.

After this, I worked with the Shaver GB people for several days in Suffolk and Norfolk, talking to many customers and potential customers, before flying to Lisbon to again work with our distributor Granja Barca Nova. This time we visited customers in Faro, in southern Portugal, locally known as "little England" for the huge number of British tourists and indeed, residents. And from here to Spain, and another trip with Juan Louis Blanch. In true Spanish style, on the second day there, we visited a hatchery and farm near Pontevrdra around noon and then drove 1½ hours to a special restaurant near the coast for a seafood lunch, which lasted until 5.30 p.m. The next day we flew back to Madrid for a half day meeting with Paco Vila and several of the Granja Vila staff. In those days business was booming and the atmosphere was very positive.

From here I flew to Dusseldorf and found a strike of ground staff and everyone had to carry luggage from the plane to the terminal. My suitcase was totally destroyed as it looked as though it was thrown from the hold on to the tarmac. I eventually received DM329 from the airline so was able to buy quite a nice new one. Germany was as always enjoyable, though I got a bit of a grilling from some journalists and one of the hatchery customers.

Then it was onward to the annual visit to Romania. The trip was on an old Ilyushin prop-jet which sounded like nothing on earth, but it got me to

Bucharest, be it all 1½ hours late. I arrived on a Saturday and they put me up at one of the best hotels, the Athenee Palace for the weekend. I relaxed a bit and caught up on some paperwork, reports etc. which were always easier to write immediately after the event.

This year's Romanian visit was a full working week on the Shaver pure lines at two locations and then a "genetics lecture" followed by questions, on Saturday morning. Stan Tirlea had not been present during the week but we had a nice dinner together the night before I left. It was never clear to me what exactly Stan's position was but it was clearly very senior. In North American terms he was definitely "Mr. Poultry" for the whole of Romania.

I flew home via Zurich, and then to Montreal on a Swissair DC10; this was Douglas's answer to Boeing's 747 and I found it a lot more comfortable and the Swiss service, excellent. Of course in those days there was no chance to fly any class other than economy; there was no Business Class and first class was totally *verboten*.

On my return to work, my diary notes some "niggling notes" from DMcQ and my resolve to proceed with the Ross negotiations, which I did by means of a cable from home. This resulted in a request to visit Scotland for a weekend in March, where final negotiations with John Archibald would take place and I would get a chance to see some of the facilities. This had to be a clandestine affair and in case anything went wrong, I booked the flight to Prestwick, near Glasgow, using a different travel agent from the one the company used exclusively.

So on the appointed Friday in March, I left work early, packed an overnight bag and headed for the airport. The flight to Prestwick, with a stop in Montreal, was 4 hours late, making the in-flight dinner a 1.00 am affair, and we landed about 6.00 am. John met me and we had a lightning tour of some of the Ross facilities including a hatchery and farm near Dumfries, and another farm near Ecclefechan before ending up at his home in Newbridge for tea. After this, we visited the main office and hatchery, also in Newbridge, before a very good dinner at a pub in South Queensferry. Even on this short acquaintance, it became evident that Ross's ideas of entertainment and hospitality were a world apart from Shaver's! Sunday morning saw us again on the road, this time to one of the broiler growing facilities used in the meat chicken program, before heading back to Prestwick for my flight home. In the course of the weekend, I was asked how much salary I would require and I told John £7,000 *per annum*. This was, I thought, the minimum to make the move worthwhile. A week later I had a phone call from Struan Wiley offering this salary; John later told me it was the maximum they would consider.

The flight home, also *via* Montreal, was delayed, but then encountered fog near Montreal and so flew straight to Toronto, my one lucky break in a lifetime flying! But pity the Montreal passengers!

By the end of March, the negotiations with Ross were complete, and I gave DMcQ notice, effective at the end of April. My diary notes that he was "not overjoyed" and that is hardly surprising, as I had been a loyal employee for more than six years and clearly enjoyed his confidence. But he still didn't delegate much, if any responsibility. This was not just to me; there were quite a few others equally dissatisfied.

So began the process of untying knots, dismantling the rather pleasant life we had established in Canada, and planning a new one in a strange land. For while Scotland was a part of the United Kingdom, it was not necessarily welcoming to English people, as we were to find.

Chapter 5

Three Years With Ross Poultry

Moving From Cambridge to Edinburgh
The last month at Shaver was not a barrel of laughs. Of course the routine work continued but I was naturally excluded from any and all PR, sales, planning and the entertainment of visitors. Colleagues were friendly, some probably envious, others accepted it as part of company life. I don't think DMcQ spoke to me at all.

Because Nita had a formal contract at St. Andrews School, we decided that she would work out the school year, while I would go to Scotland at the beginning of May. This would mean Nita would be responsible for selling the house and moving the contents. We expected she would arrive in Scotland in the summer.

We advertised the house in the Toronto papers, to no immediate effect. Then we put it in the Galt and Brantford papers, with more interest but mostly just curiosity. (I should explain here that in 1973, Galt became a part of Cambridge, following its amalgamation with two smaller towns, Preston and Hespeler. Cambridge was a compromise for the name of the amalgamation) Being one of a kind, and in an out-of-the-way place made the house difficult to sell. We eventually listed it with a realtor for $95,000, but it was several months after I left that Nita was able to finalize a sale. She made the very smart, as it turned out, move by having our lawyer invest the cash proceeds in a second mortgage on a corner store in Cambridge.

Of course we also had to sell the boat, and both cars. For the latter, we had a friend in the business who made it easy for us, although it was probably very good for him too. But we had the cars right up to the day we no longer needed them. The dog and cat found a good home with Mary and Elgin Smith near Rockton, and the Jack Russell quickly learned to round up both chickens and sheep!

Ross agreed to pay our moving expenses so we got a couple of estimates, and it cost more than $4000. One of them quoted by the pound; I think it was 49 cents/lb, which was one way of quickly deciding if something was worth taking.

My last day at Shaver was April 30. The following week I again attended the National Breeders Roundtable in Kansas City, this time on a Ross ticket. There I met, among others, Dick Udale, who had worked for Ross in The Netherlands, after training in Scotland on the breeding program there. He then headed up the first Ross operation in North America, at Thorntown, IN. Both of us visited Thorntown after the Roundtable meetings.

I got home from this trip on Saturday May 4, had a last look at our house, changed my clothes and left for Scotland the next day. I again flew to Prestwick and was met by James Laughton, one of the Ross employees. I stayed in the Norton Hotel in Newbridge for a couple of days, before moving to a flat in Edinburgh that the company had arranged for me. Two bedrooms, quite large and a bit gloomy but on Grosvenor Gardens, right in downtown Edinburgh, not far from Princes St. and the Caledonia Station. The rent was £95/month.

The Learning Curve at Ross

Work at Ross Poultry could not have been more different from Shaver. At the Ross Office in Newbridge, there was an organization chart and a deliberate hierarchy existed with John Archibald at the top. In Grimsby, where the headquarters of Ross Foods was located, there was another hierarchy, and presumably yet another at Imperial Group Headquarters in London. At Newbridge, everyone had a specific position and defined responsibility. Where, at Shaver, I remember saying "Everybody did everything", here it was the opposite. I think it made for a generally more efficient operation, although there were some areas where cross fertilization between departments may have been missed.

Of course, the main reason for the difference was in the history and structure of the Company. Shaver was a family organization, even though only one generation was involved. But people were hired because of family connections as well as on merit. Ross Poultry was a relatively recent invention; the Breeding Department embraced all the operations of a number of previously independent companies that had been accumulated over a relatively short period of time. The reason for the location in Newbridge was that the office of Chunky Chicks (Nichols) was located there and this was one of the larger components of the breeding side of Ross. Chunky had imported pure lines from (among others) the Nichols Breeding Company in New Hampshire. Another reason for locating in Scotland was that, although there was no formal border between England and Scotland, Scotland had developed and maintained a *cordon sanitaire* which enabled stocks to be sold to countries that would not, for reasons of disease control (primarily Newcastle disease), accept them from England. Another major component of Ross was Sterling Poultry Products, a breeder of laying stock that had existed independently for many years. Latterly it had itself taken over several other breeders, including F. & G. Sykes in Wiltshire and Fairbairns in Carlisle (where I had worked as a student!). F.& G. Sykes main claim to fame was the Sykes Hybrid 3, a cross between a White Leghorn (thought to be imported, perhaps from Babcock) and a local Rhode Island Red. This hybrid had tremendous egg production but the eggs were tinted, neither brown nor white. Somewhere along the way, Sterling or Ross acquired the pure lines for the American brown egg layer Hubbard Comet, which we called Sterling (or later, Ross) Ranger. There were also swine breeding operations in Wiltshire and Yorkshire, and a turkey breeding company in Yorkshire, the same one at which I had been consultant geneticist in the 1960's. Finally, and incredibly, there was a pheasant breeding operation somewhere in East Anglia. Pheasants were hatched and sold, presumably to be shot by the local aristocracy.

Ross Poultry was in fact much more than a primary breeder. All of the former Sterling hatcheries were still in business, selling commercial layer chicks under the Sterling and Ross brand names. The Company owned the largest broiler integrators in the country producing a multitude of chicken products, as well as the turkey production facility in Yorkshire of which the breeding company was a part. It also owned a large egg production complex at Ross-on-Wye in Herefordshire. Not long after I left the company, Ross Breeders became a separate division of Imperial Foods. Subsequent amalgamations including one with Arbor Acres Farms resulted in the formation of Aviagen, which over the years had a variety of ownerships before becoming part of a German multi-national breeding company, EW Group.

So this made for a very different working environment, but one to which I found it very easy to adapt. The other huge difference was the absence of a DMcQ! I can't remember the specific issue, but within a few days of joining, I encountered something that I knew would have to be decided "above", and so I went to see John Archibald. His response was quite brief: "Peter, this is what we are paying you for. So go ahead as you see fit". Wow! Another big difference from Shaver was that all of the management staff had company cars, sized according to job status. I got quite a nice Ford Cortina, a big step up from the one I had imported to Canada 7 years previously. This was somewhere near, but not at, the top of the automobile scale.

First priorities were getting to know colleagues, and also the workings of the breeding program for the egg production stocks. My job was to oversee all aspects of genetics, but specifically to head the egg program, as that had been Bob Osborne's responsibility. In addition, the company was in the process of upgrading its Data Processing system, and I was expected to participate in these activities.

At the time, Data Processing would be undertaken at the headquarters of the company in Grimsby. Computers of the capacity needed were too expensive for us to have one in Newbridge. The people in Grimsby were very helpful but had a lot of prejudices in terms of methods for data collection, which I personally didn't think were really suited to our needs. I doubt the systems we adopted survived long. The agreed system used Optical Mark Recognition (OMR) for all our records. This technology used a printed form on which boxes had to be marked for reading by a specialized machine. Certainly better than the IBM punch card, but a long way from what would become available within a few short years. Data were input in Newbridge and transmitted by phone line to Grimsby. The technicians from Grimsby, led by Dennis Crawford, spent a great deal of time with us, at Wreay (see below), the hatcheries in Dumfries and Newbridge, and at the research farms.

As to the egg production program, this was centred in Wreay, (pronounced "ree-ah") near Carlisle, where Bob Osborne had resided. One of the pedigree farms was located there as well as the office. There was a small staff under the direction of Vernon Pollard. Vernon was a most charming individual, in his 60's, a former professional tennis player, and a very good organizer for the job. I don't think Vernon had any poultry background but was good at the job he was given. The Data Processing at Wreay used a large Burroughs calculating machine. As I remember, information was entered manually and the machine summarized the data by pedigree families in a manner similar to that used at Shaver before the use of Gowe's computer system in Ottawa.

My first visit to Wreay was on my second day at work, and was just for the day. But it coincided with a visit from three of the company veterinarians, including Tony Harris, and I stayed and had dinner with them. Tony was the head of the veterinary services and another man of great character and charm. He also knew how to spend the company's money. One great thing about Wreay was it's proximity to the Crosby Lodge. This was a former country house converted to a Hotel and Restaurant. We always stayed at the Hotel and ate at the Restaurant. It was owned and operated by a youngish couple, Patricia and Michael Sedgwick. Michael had trained as a chef in Europe and the cuisine was extraordinarily good. Patricia made desserts and looked after the Hotel. A typical evening consisted of drinks (several), in the bar, usually a three course meal with cheese to follow, followed by more drinks after. Residents were not restricted to pub opening hours. The other nice thing about the Crosby Lodge was its proximity to the Lake District. It was quite feasible after a day in the Wreay office, to drive to somewhere like Ullswater or Keswick, have a drink in a pub and still be back to Crosby Lodge in time for dinner.

During my second week at work, I stayed there for three nights and completed my indoctrination as far as the egg program was concerned.

There were a number of farms, including grandparents and research in the general area of Carlisle, Gretna and Dumfries, all within about 50 km. The hatchery used for pedigree reproductions was located in Dumfries. I also met the farms' managers and the supervisor, Bob Goldie. Another hostelry we frequented, usually for lunch, was the Queens Arms at Warwick Bridge. This was run by two brothers, David and Laurie Keene and their respective wives, and did a great trade in beer and lunchtime meals.

After returning to Newbridge, I also got to know David Butler, who was Technical Adviser to the Breeding Department. David lived in East Anglia, where his wife ran a pub, and he spent most of his time away from home. His capacity for beer was unequaled. When he realized he was getting over weight, he stopped eating and lived for days on beer alone. I am not sure what David's qualifications were, but he seemed to know chickens and was a pleasant fellow.

The genetics staff, who reported to me, consisted of Alan Gristwood and Nigel Barton. Alan had been with Chunky Chicks prior to the merger into Ross, and was a master at evaluating meat chickens for conformation. He personally handled all of the selected males to be used in the breeding program. At this time, the selection program for meat chickens was still quite simple, and very similar to the one used at Shaver. Large numbers of chicks were placed, grown to market age (at this time ~ 8 weeks) and then weighed. The heaviest were then examined for conformation and stature before final selection to reproduce the line. Alan Gristwood supervised all selection activities in this program.

Nigel Barton had worked for F. & G. Sykes prior to its merger into Ross, and had moved to Edinburgh. He had an agricultural degree and good genetics skills, and at the time I joined the company, was responsible for the turkey and swine breeding programs, located in Yorkshire and Wiltshire. He had also kept the egg programs running following the death of Bob Osborne. I felt that at this point, Nigel felt himself lucky to have a job, as many geneticists were let go when breeders merged. However, he was competent at this work, made good contributions to our discussions and developed more confidence during my three years at Ross. Much later, he became much more assertive and for a while was the head of Ross Breeders, after it relocated its headquarters to Alabama.

In the egg breeding program, we were moving from floor management to cages, and this necessitated a move to artificial insemination. Having the experience from both Wye and Shaver helped me to train key workers at Ross's Eaglesfield Farm in these techniques. I also consulted with Peter Lake at Edinburgh's Poultry Research Centre, who was a world authority and researcher in the AI field.

Domestically, I enjoyed living in the flat, but was frustrated by the slow pace of the banking system (more of this later). It took forever to get a credit card (in Canada, they had started to come in the mail, unsolicited) and the banks closed for lunch! I cooked at home a lot but also ate out (on expenses of course) but social life was pretty limited. I visited my mother in Ponteland which was only a 2 hour drive, and she was, of course delighted by my return to the UK. I also visited Dan and Margaret Durrant and their two little girls. Dan by this time was living in Carlton Minniott in Yorkshire. He was nutritionist for Nitrovit, a feed company that was part of the chicken and turkey integration and another arm of Ross Poultry. I would sometimes go there for the weekend and then work with Nigel at the turkey breeding farms the following week.

I also explored the surroundings looking for a house to buy. I had decided that I would prefer to live outside of the city, and so looked at villages in a wide arc with a radius of about 30 miles. Cottages were for sale but mostly very small. We would be bringing our king-size bed, which served to eliminate many places. In Scotland, the majority of real estate sales were directly through lawyers. Real estate brokers existed in Scotland but not on the scale we knew in Canada. And their commissions were less than 1%, so it was obvious that they did not do the same amount of work that we were used to. (Canadian realtors took commissions of 3-5% at that time).

The Ross Working Routine

Our Breeding Department held regular breeding and genetics meetings to discuss the selection and breeding programs. For each commercial product, we had a Blueprint which described in great detail the methods for selection and reproduction of each pure line. All of us were involved in fine tuning these important documents; not only geneticists but also production and veterinary departments. The Blueprints were living documents and we reviewed them often, but once established, they provided foolproof instructions that everyone could understand. This again was a huge contrast with Shaver, where only DMcQ knew exactly what was going on.

In June I spent 2½ weeks "on tour" to see the rest of the Ross breeding program. Most of the first week was spent at Wreay, and then I took the weekend off with my mother and Bill Clarke, who were on holiday in Garlieston, near Wigtown on an offshoot of the Solway Firth. We did some nice car trips in this very pleasant part of Scotland.

After another couple of days in Wreay, I headed south. Until this point, I had been driving a temporary car, and I picked up my new Cortina in Manchester on my way to Chepstow in Wales for a meeting of the Sterling

Management Committee (SMC). This was another example of the lavish environment to which the senior people felt entitled. I actually didn't spend much time at the meeting, but ate and drank quite liberally with them. I got to see some of the nearby egg production units at Ross-on-Wye, and met the general Manager, Robin Lucas.

Following this, I had an appointment with a Dr. Stuart of the Home Office to discuss some of the company research, and also visited Harper Adams College to see Dick Wells, who was in the year after me in the Wye M.Sc program, and now worked at Harper Adams. He later became the Head of the Poultry Department following the retirement of Harold Temperton. I spent the weekend with Elizabeth and Alastair Henderson in Bramhall.

I then went to Grimsby for meetings with some of the senior people in Ross, and with the EDP group who were working on the new information system for our breeding work. I had drinks with John Foster and his wife Joyce. John was one of the original Sterling hatchery managers and now quite senior in the commercial chick business. We visited the newest commercial hatchery at Woodhall Spa and I was shown the workings of Sterling's northern division. I stayed the night at the Dower House, the pub run by David Butler's wife, where we drank late into the night.

From here, I drove back *via* Scotch Corner and Penrith to Wreay for the rest of the week. That weekend I was delegated to entertain a group of Bulgarian visitors, and took them to Dalhousie Castle for its Medieval Banquet. This was an event that quickly palled, but the first experience was OK!

Most weekends were now spent with my mother in Ponteland, but I was also preparing for Nita's arrival in September. I bought a decent sized refrigerator (all the local ones seemed to me about the size of a bar fridge) and shuffled the furniture in the flat around to make it more habitable. This included moving the two single beds together to more or less make a king-size.

Mid July I visited the National Laying Test near Godalming in Surrey and also met Chris Hann, who had replaced Rupert Coles as Chief Poultry adviser at the Min. of Ag. Naturally, being so close, I went to Wye for the weekend and spent time with Alan Sykes and Eric Maddison, who had returned there after his adventures in the commercial world. Also, of course, I renewed my acquaintance with several of the old pubs I used to patronize.

I took the train to Yorkshire and stayed one night with Dan and Margaret Durrant before a two-day review of the turkey program, which John

Archibald (henceforth JDHA) attended. We also reviewed some of the swine program located near Thirsk, overseen by another real character, Ted Dickinson. He reported to Nigel Barton, but I was to meet him frequently in the course of the next three years. He was a great "pig man" in the way some of my other colleagues were "chicken men" and earned great respect for this.

I often phoned Nita and on July 24, she told me she had accepted an offer of $80,000 for the St. George house, which was a great relief. Still a lot of details to be worked out but the deal seemed to be done. At Ponteland the following weekend, Brenda Purvis visited my mother's and we had long talks relating to her problems at home. John had been charged with stealing semen from the AI company he worked for, and of course Brenda did not work outside the home. Her parents, who lived in Ponteland, would probably have to help.

At the beginning of August, I finally found the house I had been looking for, and as this coincided with confirmation of the sale of the house in Canada, I decided to go ahead. The house was modern, 3 bedrooms and a nice garden, located in Pattiesmiur, a tiny hamlet near Rosyth and Dunfermline. So it meant driving over the Forth Road Bridge every day, but that was not a huge challenge. The price was £25,000 which I determined was not quite out of sight. I eventually financed it through an arrangement with a life insurance company. We paid only the interest on the principal, plus premiums on a life insurance policy which would mature after 25 years.

Meanwhile I was working most of the time at Wreay and staying at the Crosby Lodge. I had to fit in the negotiations for the house purchase whenever I was back in Edinburgh. Everything was handled by lawyers, and I acquired one Ross Drurie, a port-faced man who achieved what was needed for, of course, a generous fee. We eventually agreed a price of £27,750 with closing on October 31. At that time, the Scottish real estate system was based on what they called the "upset price", which was the lowest the vendor would accept. This was a big contrast with the Canadian system, where the price quoted was a faint hope and was usually negotiated downwards.

Also during this period, I became re-acquainted with Ann Murray, who taught at Wye for a few years. She had left the poultry industry when the breeding company she worked for, W.D. Evans, failed and she subsequently taught high school. She lived not far from the Crosby Lodge and we occasionally had drinks there together.

The Scottish business of Ross for commercial chicks was based on a hatchery near Inverurie, in the north of Scotland. It was presided over by Norrie Semple, known in the company as the King of Scotland. I visited Norrie and got to know him quite well, in addition to learning more about the egg business in the country. This was a part of Ross that I found unusual; I felt it important for the geneticist to have first hand experience of what went on in the field. This was not generally shared by others in the company. Apart from the business side of things, Norrie was an enormously generous and gracious host. Whenever I visited that part of Scotland, I stayed at his home and of course got to know his wife Ada. Later, when we had our first baby, PJ, Norrie would invite us for the weekend and detail one of his kids to babysit. The Semples lived in a large old farm house with a huge kitchen and similarly large living room, complete with a very high end sound system. Norrie was a jazz fan which was another thing we had in common.

In the summer of 1974 I had a surprise visit from Brian Evans, whom I hadn't seen, except for an overnight stay at his home in Winnipeg, since he moved from Guelph in 1967. He was on a sabbatical year and spent the weekend with me. We explored some of the neighbourhood pubs and I took him on a long drive around the border country. We went as far south as Otterburn, then east to Alnwick and up the coast past Craster, Seahouses and Berwick and back to Edinburgh. The following day, we explored a lot of Edinburgh, as well as visiting Pattiesmuir, and dining royally at Nivingstone Country House near Clieth in Fife.

I hadn't realized it at the time, and in the 1960's it was still well hidden, but Brian was gay. By this time he had a companion living with him in Winnipeg.

I was still spending a lot of time at Wreay, and staying at the Crosby Lodge. One night in August, Tony Harris, the veterinarian, was there too, regaling us with stories from his recent trip to the Worlds Poultry Congress in New Orleans. Besides his veterinary skills, Tony was also a very good jazz pianist, and while at the Congress, played in some of the clubs on Bourbon Street. I very much regret that I missed this Congress, but plans wee already complete when I arrived in May. It was the only Congress I missed between 1968 and 2012.

August also saw a change in the sale of the St. George house, which we thought was settled. Evidently not, as Nita had to accept a $20,000 drop in price, and a delay in the cash payment for a year. So we needed to borrow more to buy Roseburn, the house in Pattiesmiur. I first of all went to the bank to talk about financing the house and they suggested "you might like to try your Canadian banking contacts." For someone working and banking in Scotland, and buying a Scottish house, they wanted me to finance it in Canada? I eventually secured the additional funds through a contact at Imperial Foods, so that was settled. On September 11, Nita gave over the St. George house to the movers, having already evacuated the dog and cat. They all stayed with Mary and Elgin Smith until Nita left for Scotland. The deals on the St. George house and Roseburn were both finalized on the 13th, which was a Friday!

In early September I went to London for the day with John Archibald to meet some of the top brass from Imperial Foods and to secure approval for our future developments in the egg program. This involved a meeting with Imperial Chairman Sir Alex Alexander. Sir Alex had a remarkable ability to remember everyone's name and position. He had been involved with the Ross Group (fisheries, frozen food etc.) before it acquired the poultry interests, and engineered its takeover by Imperial Foods. While remaining Chairman of Ross Group after the takeover, he also joined the Imperial Foods board, eventually becoming Chairman. We seemed to have sold him on our future plans and returned to Edinburgh well satisfied. Following his retirement from Imperial in 1979, Sir Alex went on to revive the Lyons restaurant chain as Allied Lyons, a subsidiary of Allied Breweries.

Nita arrived at Prestwick at 6.15 a.m. on Tuesday September 17th and of course I met her off the plane. I find it hard to believe that we then drove to the flat in Edinburgh, unpacked and re-packed, visited Roseburn just to look, and then drove to the Crosby Lodge for the night and a company dinner with guest Jeremy Holmes. I can't remember what Jeremy's connection was with Ross, but the following day, he and I went to Harper Adams College for a WPSA Symposium, leaving Nita at Stoke-on-Trent where she took the train to Nottingham to see her mother.

I had arranged a weeks holiday time after the Symposium, so I collected Nita at her mother's and we drove through London to Wye, where we stayed at the Kings Head. By this time, I had been gone from Wye for eight years, but there were still plenty of my old friends about. Ken and Ann Pearce were there and we saw them often. The George was still open and I played darts there, though I must have been spectacularly out of practice. We visited Stelling Minnis to look at my old house, and visited Marjorie Bailey, Julie's mother, in her house in Bossingham. Canterbury was another destination, along with Dover, Folkestone and Hythe. We visited a friend of Nita's in Farmingham, and also Michael Bertram, my old school friend, who was staying with his in-laws at Broadstairs. Michael and I were borne one day apart and our birth announcements appeared together in the Newcastle Journal. By the time we saw him in 1974, he was established in the Merchant Navy and lived in Australia with his wife Patti. Many years later, both Nita and I would spend time with them in Sydney.

From Kent we headed west, with a dinner in London with Nita's friend Tricia on the way. We stopped overnight in Winchester and stayed long enough to see the cathedral and the old city, before continuing west through Stockbury and Salisbury to Stonehenge. We looked around this extraordinary monument and stayed the night in a B&B at the old Almshouses in Moretonhampstead. Our eventual destination was Porthleven in Cornwall, where Nita's friend Jill Simpson lived, in a tiny cottage overlooking the harbour. We stayed with Jill's parents in nearby Helston.

Although the weather was mixed, I was able to enjoy my first trip to this part of England. Nita knew it well, having visited Jill in Porthleven many times. So she navigated us around the coast including the Minack Theatre, Lands End, St. Ives and the ancient village of Chysauster.

We headed back north at the end of the week, and stayed overnight with Elizabeth and Alastair Henderson in Bramhall. By this time the weather had improved and we had a wonderful day driving through the Yorkshire Dales with a stop in Dent, where I had camped with the Royal Grammar School, and holidayed with my parents. I don't think Dent had changed in 100 years. Then through Sedbergh to Kendal in the Lake District on the way to a night at the Crosby Lodge. We visited my mother in Ponteland before arriving back at the Edinburgh flat on a Sunday night. Prior to Nita's arrival, I had found a very good Indian Restaurant, the Star of Bengal, within easy walking distance and we ate there on our first night together in the city. We ate there again a few weeks later following a great concert at the Usher Hall by the Worlds Greatest Jazz Band. This brought back fond memories of the Colonial Tavern in Toronto.

Back at work, I met the newly appointed veterinarian, Mark Pattison, who would report to Tony Harris but be based in Edinburgh. He and his wife Sue (also a veterinarian) soon became good friends with both me and Nita. They already had two small children and a golden retriever. I spent a few days with Mark, showing him the farms around Wreay and introducing him to the relevant people. I see from my diary that at this time, my position as Senior Research Geneticist was confirmed; I don't remember there being a probationary period but there was a general reorganization of the Breeding Department at the end of September, and I seemed to be a part of it. Working non-stop for almost five months, I certainly felt that I had earned it.

My predecessor, Bob Osborne had been well respected and a Memorial Lecture at the Institute of Animal Genetics had been established. The first lecture was given by Gordon Dickerson, whom I had met at the US

Breeders Roundtables. I think he worked for USDA at the time, but later worked with Rob Gowe in Ottawa before ending up at the University of Nebraska. He gave a good lecture, followed, in true British tradition, by copious sherry.

In early October I went to Madrid for the first Congress of Genetics Applied to Animal Production. The papers were OK and the social aspects good. All of the commercial breeders were represented and at this time there were still a lot of us. I met Jack Hill (Babcock), Frans Pirchner and Dietmar Flock (Lohmann) among others. I met lots of American, Canadian and European geneticists from a variety of Institutions, including Gowe and Dickerson, Crad Roberts and John Turton from Edinburgh and Hans Abplanalp from California. The Congress lasted a week, which by any standards was excessive; I think future versions were reduced to 3 or 4 days.

We took possession of Roseburn, our house in Pattiesmuir, at the end of October. Transport strikes delayed delivery of the container from Canada which contained our belongings. We bought carpets, appliances and various other necessities ahead of the takeover. When we finally got there after getting the keys from lawyer Ross Drurie one evening, we found all the light bulbs had been removed by the previous owner. How cheap can you get? In the meantime, we had bought a car for Nita, so she would be able to work in the house to make it habitable, and supervise the arrival of the container when it finally arrived on November 11th. We had used a well recommended firm, Tippet Richardson, in Canada, and they really lived up to their reputation. Their counterparts in Scotland could not have been more different. They wouldn't move a thing until Nita provided tea, and had to be talked into putting runners down to prevent soiling our new carpets. We had already done a lot of decorating, removing wallpaper, caulking, painting etc. so when the container had been emptied and things unpacked, we were ready to move in, which we did on November 12th. We brought our electric stove from Canada; it worked on UK voltage, but we had to have the counters moved to accommodate it. Fortunately a neighbour in Pattiesmuir, George Springthorpe was a builder and made the adjustments for us. We also brought our washing machine and several other appliances, for which we had to buy a transformer. This was eventually accomplished but not before Nita almost committed murder of sales people who refused to deal with a woman. In retrospect, bringing the appliances was not a good idea. As well as using 120 volt power, Canadian a/c operates at 60 cycles/sec, while the British used 240 volts at 50 cycles/sec. So even when the voltage was converted, motors ran only at 80% of their rated speed.

Over the next several months, we pretty much redecorated the whole house, replacing wallpaper with paint, filling cracks etc. and it looked very nice when we were done. Nita has a good eye for colour and decor, which helped a lot.

Before we got the stove installed, we had to have meals in local pubs. In Limekilns, we preferred The Ship to The Bruce Arms, but the best place of all for dinner was the Sealscraig at South Queensferry. This became our go-to place for dinners out; their Chateaubriand for two was out of this world; I don't think we have enjoyed anything more in the subsequent 48 years. Of course in 2018 the platter would serve four people with our much reduced appetites.

We had previously visited the Linlithgow and Stirlingshire Hunt kennels and bought a Jack Russell puppy, and through one of the secretaries at Ross, a seal point Siamese kitten. We brought these to Roseburn a few days after we moved in. The house had electric under-floor heating, and the animals loved it. The puppy, about 3 months old, had lived alone in a straw pile for several weeks before we got her and had to be house trained. The lack of company in this period seemed to have eliminated the capacity to play; she was a very taciturn dog all her life. She was called Maggie (after Maggie Tulliver of the *Mill on the Floss*), and the cat was Simon. They got along perfectly from their first meeting, and the cat even managed to persuade the dog to play a little.

Work at Ross continued apace. We conferred with the people at the Houghton Poultry Research Institute concerning our proposed research on leucosis; met with Ross International Division to talk about overseas sales, and in November I attended the British Poultry Breeders Roundtable in Birmingham. This was held at an hotel close to the airport and the first evening, we had to evacuate the hotel because of a bomb threat. This was at the time of "the troubles" in Northern Ireland. For us, it was a half hour inconvenience, but of course later, it became much more serious when the hotel in which Margaret Thatcher, by then Prime Minister, was staying was actually bombed, and she was injured.

The Roundtable was, as always, interesting and challenging, and an invitation from Ross was accepted to host the meeting in 1976.

In December, we visited Dan and Margaret Durrant in Yorkshire, combined with work on the turkey program at the Dalton office. On the weekend we took a walk along the escarpment at Sutton Bank, and on the way back, stopped in Kilburn to visit the showroom of Robert Thompson, the "mouse man". He had begun making ecclesiastical furniture but by then made a large range of tables, benches, chests, etc, each one with a small carved mouse in a prominent position. Throughout the small village of Kilburn, every vacant space was used to store oak boards while they aged. When we left the UK in 1977, Nita brought several pieces back to Canada, which were generally admired and made a nice talking point.

In the end-of-year review, my salary was increased to £8260, which I considered pretty good! But I think that was the last raise I had, as the newly elected Labour government subsequently froze all of our salaries.

When we originally decided to move to Scotland, it had been Nita's intention to continue teaching for a while. However, on investigating the possibilities, she found that the Scottish education system would not accept her English Teachers Certificate and would require a further year of study. So we decided that instead of being a provider of education, we would be consumers, and in December 1974 Nita became pregnant.

For Christmas 1974, my mother and her companion Bill Clarke came to stay. Proximity to parents was certainly a benefit of moving to Scotland. And both were far enough away that significant effort was needed for visits! My mother enjoyed the Pattiesmuir environment, and walked happily with Nita and the dog on her usual hour-long trips.

At Wreay, January saw me doing selections and mating plans for all of the layer pure lines, based still on the data summaries produced using the old system. In many ways this was similar to what Randy Cole had done at Shaver, and I personally handled the candidate males and assisted with the AI for the first few matings. I also attended the Dumfries hatchery for all the line replacement pedigree hatches. The system of wingbanding and family identification I also "imported", as I knew how well it worked in Canada. This required a degree of re-education of key staff but it all worked out in the end. With the reorganization of the data processing now well advanced, we decided to close the Wreay office and concentrate all the work in Newbridge. JDHA had the sad task of informing the Wreay staff, as we really didn't see any way of offering them work in Newbridge. There was a nucleus of three or four good people whom we had to let go. But it saved a fortune in hotels and meals for me and others. Vernon Pollard, who lived near the Eaglesfield farm, would continue to supervise these facilities. The Wreay office closed finally at the end of July, 1975.

Ross Poultry re-organized itself early in 1975, with Struan Wiley, JDHA's boss, becoming Managing Director of the Company, and John himself promoted to the main Company Board. I think this may have been largely symbolic, to enable them to receive new, higher salaries, thus thwarting the government's wage freeze. The rest of us were unaffected by these changes, as far as I could see.

At home in Pattiesmuir, we gradually redecorated the ground floor rooms and tended the garden. We got to know our neighbours, including some other English migrants but also some of the "natives". It was a tiny community and generally friendly although the dour Scottishness came through with some people. One old lady couldn't figure out whether we were English or American; when she found we were from Canada she became quite friendly! Nita developed a nice social life as well as daily walks in the countryside with the Jack Russell. Interestingly, the Siamese cat also liked to walk, although he didn't go as far as the dog; he would wait in the hedgerow until Nita and the dog came back.

In February, 1975, Nigel Barton and I spent the best part of a week on pig business. So Nita and both animals came south, with the cat left with my mother in Ponteland and Nita and the dog with her mother near Nottingham. Nigel and I attended the Meat and Livestock Commission conference in Cambridge. For one who spent 90% of his time with poultry, this was a welcome eye-opener to the pig business. After this, Nigel and I spent two days at the Ross pig breeding operation near Sutton Veny in Wiltshire. As usual, we stayed in nice hotels, and ate and drank in lovely old pubs as often as we could.

We had another visit from Brian Evans in March. He knew more about the local history than we did, especially the Andrew Carnegie connection. (Carnegie was born in Dunfermline in 1835) Brian was a great house guest and we enjoyed his visit enormously. Edna and Gill Teiman also came to see us; Edna had been one of my "Cupid" dates, and a friend of Nita's, and her sister Gill had moved to Toronto to help her manage her anorexia. They both wanted to return to the UK and were interested in how we were adapting. At this stage, we were OK, Nita perhaps more enthusiastic than me about life in Scotland. In the event, Gill stayed in Toronto, Edna returned to the UK and Nita and I ultimately moved back to Canada.

In early April, Nita and I took a holiday in south and southwest England. We first visited Kent to see old friends and pubs, and then headed into Hampshire where we stayed with Peter and Val Halliwell. Peter was in the second clutch of Poultry M.Sc. graduates from Wye and was employed in the poultry feed business. They lived in the lovely little village of Upper Clatford, not far from Andover. Most of the houses had thatched roofs, including the gorgeous old pub just a few steps from Peter's front door. We spent a day touring the New Forest, and then headed further west, skirting Bournemouth and stopping at the old Thomas Hardy cottage near Dorchester. We stayed two nights in the Moonfleet Manor Hotel near Weymouth. The coast here was beautiful, but in spite of it being April, we had snow flurries and actually saw primroses poking out of small snow banks! We did quite a bit of driving and some walking along the coast. The weather remained cold and we stayed in one really frigid B&B where there was frost on the inside of the windows when we got up.

We spent time on and around Exmoor staying in B&B's and eating in pubs. We were puzzled by the size of the Cornish Pasties we often ate for lunch. The first occasion, they were so small we could have eaten two; the next time we could have shared one between us! But they were universally tasty, along with the inevitable beers. We again visited Nita's friend Jill Simpson in Porthleven and stayed in the best B&B of the trip. We toured a lot of the villages along the Cornwall and Devon coastlines, including, of course, Lands End. In Tintagel, we visited a quaint old lady, Mrs. Wiffen, who was the Aunt of our neighbour in Canada, Kay Bean. Small world!

At the end of the second week, I left Nita at her friend Tricia Ellis' place west of London, while I attended the Pig Breeders Roundtable in Wye. I think the meeting was good, but the high point of the weekend for me was scoring 3 double 20's at darts in the George! Our last port of call was the Agricultural College at Writtle in Essex, where Eric Maddison had taken the position of Principal. We spend a nice night with him and Gwyneth before traveling home, collecting the dog and cat *en route*.

On my return to work in Newbridge, I had my first meeting with Lord Edward Fitzroy, who was at the time in charge of sales for Ross's Sterling division. As the second or third son of an aristocratic family Edward apparently had no chance of an inheritance and had to work! He was a pleasant enough character, but somehow one always felt a slight inferiority. I think he did an excellent job and after our first meeting, I mostly enjoyed his company.

In early May I made a trip to the US and Canada. I spent some time at the Ross facility in Thorntown IN and attended the Breeders Roundtable in Kansas City MO. I also visited Purdue University and had a very good lunch with Ben Bohren, one of the great geneticists of the day. At this time, they were still doing excellent work on practical selection experiments.

I flew in to Toronto and stayed a night with Lyris Tracey, and then headed to Cambridge to see old friends there. I stayed two nights with Doug and Ivy Brown in St. George while visiting the Attridges, the Gees, Alix Malcolm and Flo MacLeay, our neighbours on the concession road in St. George, and sundry others. I spent some time in Guelph with people at the University and then flew to Ottawa to see Rob Gowe and the genetics team at Agriculture Canada.

My final stop before returning to the UK was Northport, Long Island. Here I met with Margaret Johnstone Troiano and her husband and five week old son. Margaret had been a secretary at the Agriculture Department at Kings College in Newcastle, emigrated to the US (I went skiing with her in Colorado) became a Doctor and married another. Quite the life for a Geordie lass.

When I got back to Pattiesmiur, we almost immediately hosted Henry and Christa Bayley, plus their first two children, Anya and Christopher, for a couple of days. This was a very welcome visit that we all enjoyed.

Meanwhile, Nita was now five months pregnant and because of her age (and mine, although this may not have been relevant) we had, with some difficulty, obtained amniocentesis and ultrasound tests to determine the normality (and incidentally gender) of the baby-to-be. At the end of May, we learned that as far as could be seen from these tests, the fetus was normal and male. So we began to discuss names, a process now reduced by 50%.

The vacation allowance at Ross was quite generous; I think it was three weeks for me, increasing as my tenure was prolonged. So I took another ten days in early June. My mother and Bill Clarke came for a few days, and stayed to look after the cat and dog while we were gone. Nita and I traveled to the Yorkshire Dales and the Lake District. We stayed first at the Bluebell Hotel in Kettlewell, and from here took wonderful walks in Wharfedale, Buckden Pike, and Arncliffe. After leaving the Bluebell, we stopped at the Ingleton Falls and did the whole walk from beginning to end. Then we drove *via* Kendal and Ambleside to the Old Dungeon Ghyll Hotel in Great Langdale in the Lake District. I had camped nearby with the school back in the 1950's and remember being essentially washed out one stormy June. But our weather in 1975 was much better and we did some lovely walks including to Striding Edge and Hellvelyn. On my birthday, we took a picnic lunch and walked up Oxendale, Three Tarns, Bow Fell, Angle Tarn and Rosset Crags. We visited the Beatrix Potter cottage and bought a Peter Rabbit book for PJ. We had a nice lunch at the Crosby Lodge on the way home.

During this time, we had acquired a reasonably good colour TV and for the only time in my life, I watched it regularly. One of the main attractions was a series called "The Ascent of Man" featuring one Jacob Bronowski, which I found extremely interesting. I even sought it out in hotels if I was away from home. British TV was far superior to both American and Canadian TV, largely because of the density and timing of advertising. We also watched "The National Dream" a TV version of Pierre Berton's book about the construction of the Canadian Pacific Railway.

Work with Ross involved a huge amount of traveling within the UK. Apart from the selection and reproduction of the egg lines housed at the farms in southwest Scotland, I also visited broiler research facilities near Buxted in Sussex, worked with the turkey and pig programs in Yorkshire and Wiltshire, kept in touch with commercial sales and service for Sterling, headquartered in Grimsby but in reality, all over the country, and maintained contact with academics at several universities – Reading, Nottingham, Wye, the Poultry Research Centre and the University in Edinburgh. There was also the West of Scotland Agricultural College, its Poultry Department presided over by the redoubtable Tom Whittle, which I visited regularly. I also attended all of the pedigree pure line hatches at the Dumfries Hatchery. I probably spent about half of all week nights away from home. Of course some of this was by choice: I wanted to make sure that the pedigree lines and experimental work were managed according to our very precise expectations, and so regular visits were essential. We also established an egg quality laboratory in a converted garage at the Dumfries hatchery which I designed and equipped, very similar to the one in Canada.

International travel was however, much less than with Shaver. Ross had its own export division and they worked independently and saw no need for geneticists to be a part of their team. With so much domestic travel, I did not argue.

The summer of 1975 was among the hottest on record but our garden thrived. We had a great crop of strawberries early on, and onions, cabbages, broccoli, beans, beets, green peppers and tomatoes later.

Nita enjoyed the sun and spent sufficient time in it that when she went to the hospital for pregnancy checks, everyone came to admire the tan!

In early September we enjoyed a visit to the office of a group from J&M Poultry in Arkansas. This was a result of Imperial's merger or takeover with Pillsbury, which also owned Howard Johnson Hotels. I had always enjoyed the contacts with the US industry. Albin Johnson and Coy Skaggs were our guests, and with all our wives, we had a great dinner at the Hawes Inn, one of our favourites. At this time, the Ross presence in the US was still comparatively small, so we had to convince our new colleagues that this was only temporary. Of course it wasn't long before Ross became a major player in the US and eventually moved its HQ there.

A New Family Member

Our son Peter Jon (mostly PJ and later, Peege) was born at 4.45 pm on Wednesday September 24, 1975, in Dunfermline Maternity Hospital, weighing 4,080g. Nita went into the hospital just after lunch; the birth was assisted by midwives but mostly she and PJ did it together! I visited about an hour after the birth and found them both full of life. Nita's mother Flo was with us and we both went back later to visit. The village neighbours all came over in the evening and we toasted the birth with Henckel Trochen. These were the good old days and Nita and PJ remained in the Maternity Hospital for a full week before returning home. Of course we visited every day and I managed to avoid any company travel. Nita maintained she could have come home after a couple of days and would have preferred to do so; the hospital was noisy with newborn infants and nursing staff at most times of the day.

PJ was a bit of a celebrity in the village, as the first boy born there in many years. There was a little girl, Kate Foster a year older, but boys were more important! One of the older Scottish ladies came to visit and gave him ten shillings! The Fosters, Andrew (Scottish) and Linda (American) became good friends, and when we left Pattiesmuir, we kept in touch. Andrew was an engineer specializing in helicopter design. They left Scotland soon after we did, and spent time in Montreal and Texas before he took a job in Mississauga, near Toronto. They eventually moved to a house close to ours in Cambridge, and for the second time, we shared the same postal address.

Once home, Nita, who was breast feeding, soon established a regular routine and PJ was a model baby. He was fed every four hours for the first few weeks, he slept a lot and within a relatively short time, could go through the night without waking. He always slept soundly and when we visited neighbours, we could take him with us in a carry-cot and put him on a strange bed without waking. Same procedure when going home!

We began giving him solid food after about five weeks, to which he adapted quite quickly. We shared diaper duty. In those days, disposable diapers were available but not widely used. We were glad we had brought our large Canadian washing machine, and it ran practically every day.

Company travel soon resumed and in October, with Tony Harris, I spent a day at the Houghton Poultry Research Station near Huntington. They were doing a lot of research on lymphoid leucosis and Marek's disease, which was of interest to us. I also visited Cyril Thornber, retired but still breeding chickens as a hobby. It was always fun to talk to Cyril, and swap stories of former times and people. He still had a fairly old Rolls Royce with the license plate CT 404, this being the brand name of Thornber's most successful layer, and he drove us to lunch in it.

I attended a week long course run by Imperial Group at their Temple Street Training Centre in Bristol. The course was called "Developing Skills in Communications" and was run by a psychologist, Neil Rackham. There were all kinds of people there but no one else from the food sector. I found it interesting, but a whole week? On the way home, I stayed the night with John and Brenda Butlin, whom I had known at Wye, and stopped to say "Hello" to Elizabeth and Alastair Henderson, who now lived in Bramhall, near Manchester.

At the end of November we hosted Lyris Tracey from Toronto for a week. She was on holiday and we showed her the local sights and enjoyed long and interesting conversations. Lyris worked as a physiotherapist in Toronto. By now, her long time companion Binky had returned to Trinidad, but she had three brothers and other relatives in and around southern Ontario. During the visit, she persuaded us to visit Trinidad with her the following year and to stay at her mother's house. Company policy was that no more than two seeks vacation could be taken at once without prior approval, but JDHA agreed I could go for 3 weeks.

Having crossed the Forth Road Bridge almost every day for over a year, I had conceived a plan to photograph it at sunrise. This would provide a colourful backdrop to a very photogenic structure. I knew very approximately where I needed to be to get just the right picture. Saturday December 6, 1975 dawned clear and bright, so this was the day! I drove Nita's car towards the Naval Dockyard at Rosyth and wandered about with my camera. This wasn't quite the right spot but I eventually found it a few hundred yards nearer the Bridge, and took my pictures. I was in the shower at home when the Military Police phoned to ask what I had been doing with my camera outside the Dockyard. No choice but honesty; "I was photographing the Forth Bridge at sunrise". There was a long pause, then a polite "Thank you sir", and nothing more was heard. A neighbour, Bill Elford, who worked at the Dockyard, told me that the incident would be on file forever. They could have confiscated the film. The photograph turned out very well and I still have a poster size print, framed, hung prominently in our home.

Christmas 1975 saw us in party mood. My mother and Bill Clarke came to stay and on Christmas Eve (her birthday) we hosted about 30 people. Most of the village, and the rest from work, enjoyed *buffet froid*, punch and exotic desserts. We had two outside guests; Ray Salmon and his wife Judy from Swift Current, Saskatchewan. Ray, a turkey specialist with Agriculture Canada, was on sabbatical, so it was very nice to welcome him. While in the UK, he gave a useful seminar to our turkey people in Dalton, Yorkshire.

By this time, I think it had become a tradition that I dressed and cooked the turkey for Christmas dinner. I had a recipe for very tasty stuffing (called Grandma's stuffing) from the Chatelaine cook-book that I acquired when purchasing a long term subscription to Macleans magazine. For this year, we had an 18 lb turkey which must have taken forever to finish. Mum and Bill maybe took some home with them and we had a lot of cold turkey lunches and dinners.

I noted in my diary that after dinner, we watched TV, seeing the movie "Butch Cassidy and the Sundance Kid" and Michael Parkinson interviewing Bob Hope.

Ross had agreed to host the 1976 Poultry Breeders Roundtable in November. So in January, I began to look at possible hotel venues. We finally settled on the Marine Hotel in North Berwick. This was on the coast a few miles east of Edinburgh. Since most people would arrive by road, this avoided the need to drive in or through the city, which was a challenge even for locals. I liaised with a small committee of geneticists (John Bowman, Toby Carter and John McCarthy) to develop the program and social events.

In January, Sterling held its annual sales conference in Leicester, and I was heavily involved with the Breeding Department presentation. This went off very well. On the second day, Sir Alex Alexander participated in a Q and A session about the corporate giant, Imperial. He was an imposing and memorable character. I had about five minutes conversation with him during the reception prior to the final dinner. As always, the Ross/Sterling people did themselves proud in terms of food and drink.

Ross had a large grandparent operation in The Netherlands, which I visited in March. We saw quite a few customers and also the renowned research institute at Spelderholt.

Later the same month I spent a day at a Sterling producer meeting in Huntingdon to get some more grass-roots feedback, and a day at the Houghton Research Station again discussing the work on leucosis and Marek's disease. I also attended the WPSA seminar on egg shells; I would become much more interested and involved with these as time progressed. At this meeting, I was elected to the Council and Joint Standing Committee of the WPSA, beginning a long and fruitful relationship with the Association.

In early April, we spent one of our most enjoyable weekends with Norrie and Ada Semple. We left home on Thursday and drove to Inverurie. Nita took PJ to Norrie's, while I worked with the Sterling people including Robin Johnston, who was Norrie's second in command. One of Norrie's kids was appointed babysitter while we explored the local countryside; the River Dee, Glen Muick, and Crathie. After more of Norrie's fabled hospitality we drove home *via* Dufftown, Granton-on-Spey, Aviemore and Perth.

At this time, there was an annual event called the European Poultry Fair. It was held at the BOCM (for British Oil and Cake Mills) Research Farm at Aston Clinton in Buckinghamshire. I attended and worked the Ross stand, but also took a tour of the show. I met with the Shaver people and felt ever so slightly sad! We stayed at the Bell Hotel, which was very comfortable except for a lot of hooliganism the first night. This turned out to be mostly the Ross Poultry and Imperial Foods Board members! I was not amused.

Following this, I spent a day visiting Marks and Spencer's in London. They were getting into the food business in a big way and had hired Peel Holroyd to oversee the poultry aspects. He had a big staff and a lot of power; all the breeders were spending time with him to secure "preferred status" as suppliers.

The pile of paperwork awaiting me after most of a month's absence was a cruel homecoming, but a bonus was the visit of Prof. F. B. Hutt from Cornell University. John Archibald made a bit of a mistake flying the US flag; Hutt was born in Canada! Even I did not know this. Anyway it was an interesting and useful visit. John, Nigel, Alan, Mark Pattison and Ray Thorpe joined Hutt for a good lunch at the Bridge Inn, and he had tea with Nita and me at our home.

Shortly after our return from our holiday in Trinidad (described in detail in chapter 16), I celebrated my fortieth birthday, which fortunately fell on a Saturday. We had 34 people, a mix of neighbours, work colleagues, and family, plus Brian Evans, still at the Univ. of Winnipeg but visiting the UK again. We served a good punch, beer and wine, home barbecued chicken and sundry salads. My mother and Bill Clarke and Brian stayed in our spare rooms; Norrie and Ada Semple parked their house trailer in the driveway. It was a very good party.

About this time (June 1976) we were beginning to feel the pinch of price inflation, and salary stagnation. I began to make wine and beer at home; the beer kits came from Boots, the chemist! The baby food PJ consumed started at 25p and kept increasing, briefly reaching 75p, as did many other staples. So when I got a letter from Rob Gowe in Ottawa saying that "Shaver wants you back" I didn't rule it out!

In September, Nita accompanied me to the European Poultry Conference, held in Malta. There was only a small poultry industry in Malta, but Rupert Coles, former Chief Poultry Adviser to the Minister of Agriculture, had retired there and started a WPSA Branch, which then sponsored the

Conference. We arrived a couple of days before the Conference, stayed at the Corinthia Palace Hotel and did some sightseeing in Valetta and surroundings. We also spent some time at the beach, but it didn't measure up to Trinidad! The Mediterranean was clear but quite cold compared with the Caribbean.

The Conference provided an opportunity to meet many friends, old and new. One such was Philip Lee, whom I hadn't seen since leaving the UK in 1966. He had originally worked for a feed additive company (Vitamealo) but was now working for a holding company that was part-owner of Arbor Acre Farms in the US. The Ross contingent included Struan Wiley, Lord Edward Fitzroy, Nick Chandler, John Powell and some others. One of the challenges, especially for Nita, was that dinners tended to be late, and only after a lot of "hospitality" at various company suites (including Ross) and bars. We survived but moved quickly to our room and bed after dinner. Some, including Struan and Edward, continued to party far into the night, and we heard that they went out to the Gut, the local red light district.

The Conference and associated exhibition took up some of my time but there was a lot of tourist oriented activity and it was hard to call this "work". Much more professional was the UK Branch WPSA Symposium that took place in Sutton Bonington, near Nottingham, a week later.

At home, we had our Jack Russell mated with one of the Ross farm manager's dogs, and at the end of September she produced a litter of five fine puppies. This was the only time we regretted the under floor heating, as before the puppies were trained, the area where they lived was essentially dried dog poop and pee! We eventually sold all the puppies for £15 each and then had the dog spayed.

We continued to entertain lots of visitors from overseas. Geoff and Christine Fairhurst came for a couple of days; Jim Smith, head geneticist at Hubbard Farms, and his wife Joanne also stayed with us. Jim was a golfer so went to St. Andrews as part of his stay. Ed and Nancy Moran, from Guelph, came with their daughter Thea.

By the end of September, we had decided to return to Canada if at all possible. There was a job at Shaver if I wanted it. We all too briefly looked at buying a farm with an egg production unit already established including, of course, quota. But the price looked out of sight. Hindsight being 20/20, within ten years we realized our mistake. The value of egg quota, about $5.00/hen at the time, kept rising. By the time I retired from the Egg Board in 2001 it was well over $100. And of course the farm itself would have increased in value.

I flew to Toronto in mid October. I stayed with Lyris on arrival and then went to Cambridge. I met with DMcQ and he offered me the job of Director of Research. No job description or salary were discussed at our first meeting. I visited all of our friends in Cambridge and St. George and generally had a great time.

Of course this was not known to anyone at Ross, and on the same trip, I visited Dick Udale at the Ross farm in Thorntown, Indiana, as well as the Arbor Acre farm near Hartford, Connecticut. At this time Ross was selling male broiler parents with Arbor Acre females. I also went to see Jim Smith at Hubbard Farms in Walpole, NH.

Back in Ontario, I stayed a couple of nights with Henry and Christa Bayley, and met again with the Morans, John and Marian Summers and realized how many good friends we had here, and how nice it would be to be back among them. I met with DMcQ again just before leaving and we agreed a salary plus moving expenses. No job description, but what did I really expect?

I arrived home to find neighbours looking after PJ and Nita in hospital, after a second miscarriage. We really wanted our children close together, but it was not to be.

I did not immediately inform Ross of the possibility of my return to Canada, because we had a Sterling sales meeting in London and the Breeders Roundtable at North Berwick which we were sponsoring.

While in London, I went to the Canadian High Commission to inquire about re-emigration. This would not be easy, because we did not take out Canadian citizenship, and the moment we left, we might as well never have been there! In fact, it was worse: Why didn't we become citizens? Did we have criminal records? Had we paid all our taxes? Even having a job to go to was not enough; Shaver would have to prove that there was nobody in Canada who could do it! A huge difference from 1966 and 1967, when the "welcome mat" was well and truly laid out for both of us.

I was due for a new company car, and chose a Ford Capri 2000, a very sporty number which was delivered to the Ford dealership in Edinburgh.

The Breeders Roundtable went off without a hitch and much to Ross's credit. The papers were excellent, the hospitality just right and I think everyone enjoyed the whole event.

By the end of November, some news of my impending move had leaked out and I had to formally make my resignation official. JDHA and Struan

Wiley were, I think genuinely sorry to see me leave, and I spent an hour in London with the latter, who tried all kinds of inducements to persuade me to stay. But we had made our decision and so that was that. We put the house up for sale but the market was very slow and we had few inquiries. One offer was made, but for little more than we had paid. Then another that looked "certain" fell through. We again had problems with our Scottish bank; of course we would need some bridging financing while the house was sold but they were not interested. Eventually Nita found a branch of the Bank of Nova Scotia (now Scotiabank) in Edinburgh who were happy to set up a loan account with the house as security.

So began another period of turmoil for us. Now we had PJ to think about, as well as the dog and cat. This time the animals would come with us, but they had to be vaccinated against rabies which, curiously, was absent from the UK but present in Canada. We all had to have a thorough medical examination, at our own expense, and a formal interview at the Canadian Consulate in Glasgow. The contrast with our original emigration was stark. I had been welcome with almost open arms and a subsidized flight; Nita got her teaching job after a very superficial interview and paid no income tax her first year.

1976-77 turned out to be quite a severe winter for the UK. Our village had rutted snow in the street for several months and the road in was partially blocked with the pile of snow plowed from the main road. On the whole most of Great Britain was unprepared for snow. There were days when no snow plow appeared and the use of salt and/or sand was sporadic. Nobody had snow tires, and few had any idea of how to drive in snow; the general tendency when the wheels wouldn't grip was to hit the gas! At one point I was driving from Carlisle to Grimsby on a snowy day and doing OK until I came to a snow covered hill, just littered with cars half in or right in the ditch, or abandoned. I eventually gave up and found a hotel in Leeds where I stayed overnight. The next day everything thawed, all the abandoned cars were recovered and I made my way home, having given up on Grimsby.

Of course I continued to do my job with Ross, and to deal with the breeding program in a professional way. We had a pleasant visit from Norman Overfield, the egg quality expert with ADAS (Agricultural Development and Advisory Service) and also Dr. Ricardo Aleson from Gallina Blanca in Spain. I had met Ricardo at various times while in Spain and it was good to see him again.

Ross was actively seeking my successor, and I spent two hours with a "head hunter" to describe the work that I was doing.

My mother and Bill Clarke came for Christmas and we did the traditional things. We had a party for the village people on Christmas Eve (mother's birthday).

Christmas morning was time to open presents. PJ, at 15 months, soon got the hang of things and learned to open parcels! We had several visitors during the holidays, including Eric Wainwright (my Godfather and mother's best friend) and his daughter Pam, Don and Joan Legg, now living in London but long time friends from the days in Ponteland.

Early in 1977, I was told by Struan Wiley to expect a delivery of hatching eggs in plain boxes from an unknown source. These, I was told, would be the three pure lines used for the Shaver Starcross 288. This caused raised eyebrows on my part, as to the best of my knowledge, Shaver was still using a two way cross. After they were hatched we sent some samples to Elwood Briles for blood typing and, sure enough, two of the "lines" were the same. I eventually discovered that this purchase had been brokered by Lord Edward, that the eggs came from the Shaver farm in Ireland, and that Ross had paid Jim Ingram (Managing Director of Shaver GB) and Gordon Edmondson (Shaver GB Marketing) £100,000 for them. Needless to say, I conveyed this information to DMcQ when I returned to Shaver, and both Jim and Gordon were summarily fired.

In a curious case of *deja vue*, in 1986, Alan Gristwood took early retirement (I really wonder about this) from Ross and arrived in Cambridge for consultations with Shaver! Interesting to speculate what they talked about. DMcQ had long claimed to have some lines originating from Ross, and Alan would surely recognize them if he got to handle them. We enjoyed Alan's visit: We gave him some meals, took him canoeing, a trip to the McMichael Gallery of Canadian Art in Kleinburg and a drive through downtown Toronto.

I formally left Ross on Friday February 25, 1977. The farewells were long and sincere; I made good friends there and did a good job but the British economy drove us out.

Chapter 6

Return to Canada; Shaver Round 2 and the move to the Ontario Egg Producers Marketing Board
(Soon after I retired in 2001, the organization changed its name to **Egg Farmers of Ontario**)

Before I returned to Canada, I visited Shaver GB with DMcQ, Len Zoller and Donald Jr and his wife Cathy. Donald Jr. would ultimately work for Shaver Beef Breeding Farms, a separate company involved in creating new lines of beef cattle. We also went to Shaver France and to Paris for the *Salon d'Agriculture*. From there I flew home by way of Amsterdam.

Because Nita would remain in Scotland until the house was sold we had to arrange Power of Attorney for her through our lawyer, and confirm the arrangements with the Bank of Nova Scotia, which actually worked out very well. We also did a money deal with Peter and Janice Bomford, who were leaving Ridgetown to return to England. As we were not allowed to take more than £5000 out of the UK, we swapped our pounds for their Canadian dollars. We also bequeathed to them our 240 volt – 120 volt transformer. And Nita bought a lot of furniture from Robert Thompson, "the mouse man" in Kilburn, Yorkshire. This included a blanket chest, coffee table and a nest of tables and was another good way to get assets out of the UK without breaking the law.

I flew to Toronto from Gatwick on March 18th. I bought a return ticket on Laker Airways that was cheaper than one way on any of the major airlines. Shaver's driver met me at the Toronto airport and drove me to the office, where I was able to borrow a company VW Rabbit for a few days. I stayed with Doug and Ivy Brown and family in St. George until I found a temporary residence.

Doug and Ivy were great friends, and hugely hospitable. They had a heated pool in their small backyard and when our kids were old enough, we were invited there on hot afternoons, which sometimes extended into drinks and dinner. Sadly, Douglas died quite young of a rare iron excess, while on a Caribbean cruise in late 1989.

I settled on an unfurnished basement apartment on Dudhope Avenue, quite close to the office. It was part of a three floor walk-up, a format that was quite common in the neighbourhood. It of course had a stove and fridge, and I bought used basic furniture. I did not expect to be there long. In fact, by early April I was spending many hours with realtors driving around Cambridge and the surrounding countryside looking at houses and building lots. As I wanted to buy quickly, we decided on a standard home that could be re-sold if/when the dream home materialized. So we bought such a place at 15, Dakin Crescent in the St. Andrews subdivision in west Galt for $58,000, $3,500 below the asking price. It was quite new, had 3 bedrooms, kitchen/dining area, living room, a family room, 2 car garage and an unfinished basement. Because we would have the Jack Russell with us soon, I decided to have the backyard properly fenced; got a quote for $460 and decided to do it myself, for around $260. The Jack Russell was out under the fence within 30 seconds the first time she saw it! I moved into the house a few weeks before Nita, PJ and the animals arrived on June 30th.

I quickly re-united with friends; Pam Gee (husband Malcolm had left), Henry and Christa Bayley, Alix Malcolm, Chris Fowler (from whom I bought a used Chevrolet Chevelle) and others from work. George Sandkuhl and Ed Hubbard were still around and we had beers after work. I had lunch with Mary and Elgin Smith, where Nita had stayed before moving to Scotland, and who took both our dog and cat. Neither had survived; the cat died and the dog ran under the wheel of a moving tractor. Of course I quickly renewed contact with Lyris Tracey, and spent several weekends in Toronto with her and friends.

On April 1st, Nita phoned to say our Scottish house was sold for £29,000 (our upset price only) with closing May 23rd. Not an April fool joke; I felt a huge weight removed from my shoulders. We heard from our friends in Pattiesmuir that five years later, the new owners sold the house again for £60,000. Our timing on house sales has always been like this.

Work at Shaver was slow to start; of course my activities would be controlled by DMcQ and he wasn't around until I had been there a week. There were now two geneticists full time with the company; Howard French who worked with the meat program, and Al Kulenkamp who did the egg side. They were both well qualified and competent, but my work relationship with them was not clear. What was clear was that little had changed. I resumed my travels for the company. In this area I was probably more suited to the job than either Howard or Al. I had a nice trip to the southeast US in late April, stopping in Washington DC to visit the Donaldsons *en route*. I traveled with Hugh Thornburg through Virginia, North Carolina and Georgia. I met one of the new salesmen, Doyt Dauler, and we had drinks at his lakeside home. Doyt had previously worked for one of the other breeding companies and knew the industry well. We ended up in Cullman, Alabama and dined with John and Fran Nay; John was now the General Manager for Cullman. Old colleagues Riley Smith, Charles Overstreet were still around, along with another new salesman, Bill Hicks, who had previously worked for Vantress Farms, by then taken over by Tyson Foods. The trip ended with the National Breeders Roundtable, still being held in Kansas City MO, where I met up with Howard and Al and of course, lots of friends working for other breeders. Jim Smith from Hubbard was among those. I flew home *via* Winnipeg, where I spent the weekend with Brian Evans. We explored the city and Assiniboine Park Zoo on foot, and on Sunday drove to the Museum of Man and Nature. It was good to see Brian again.

One new feature of the Shaver scene was the new Technical Manager, Dr. Manuel Soares Costa. He replaced Chris Fowler, who was now managing Shaver operations in New Zealand. Manuel, a former University Professor, had migrated from Portugal during a political upheaval. He was an excellent addition to the Shaver staff and we quickly became friends. Not long after my return, he and his wife (who unfortunately spoke not a word of English and never learned one) and Ricardo Aleson from Spain had a splendid dinner at the Knotty Pine in Preston. For many years, this was the only place in Cambridge where one could get a decent steak dinner and a glass of wine to go with it. Manuel eventually returned to Portugal, and resumed his University career. He also established a highly successful micronutrient supplement business as a profitable sideline.

Surprisingly, DMcQ called a Breeding Meeting in May. But it was a travesty; we (Howard, Al and I) really were no closer to having any real responsibility. Disappointing, but I had a job! A good part of it involved liaison with the consultants at Guelph and elsewhere. John Summers, Art Ferguson and others at Guelph, Rob Gowe in Ottawa, along with fellow geneticists Jan Gavora and Jim Chambers were all good friends and valuable assets. I resumed the editorship of *Shaver Focus*; this I thoroughly enjoyed as it involved writing material myself and soliciting articles from outside specialists. As the magazine was not an advertising medium, except for the masthead, most people were prepared to write for it. I think we paid a modest honorarium. Among the external writers was Don Bell, long-time Poultry Adviser at U. Cal. Riverside, and a world authority on all things to do with egg production. Several contacts from my time in the UK also contributed; Arnold Elson on housing and environment, Norman Overfield on egg quality. This use of outside authors gave *Shaver Focus* a status that it could not have achieved if all of the writing had been done internally, or if it contained much company advertising and promotion. I took on myself the composition of the Editorial and this was always on the front page! We were still hosting visitors from Romania and I was involved in teaching and entertaining them.

For a "dream home", I looked at a few building lots. One on a St. George sideroad, near our old house, was on the market for $40,000! I passed.

Shaver provided staff gardens in a corner of a field at one of the farms. I took a plot and grew lettuce, radishes, tomatoes, beans, peas, sweet corn and a few other vegetables. But the weeds were terrible; within a week they could smother any but the most aggressive crops and with my absences traveling, I had a hard time keeping on top of them. And of course all the crops were ready at the exact time the same stuff could be had at the market or in stores at very reasonable prices!

Reuniting with Nita

Nita, PJ, the dog and cat and a lot of luggage arrived by plane on June 30th. The flight was quite an ordeal for all of them; it was 4½ hours late and of course we had to wait while the animals were unloaded and cleared through customs and immigration. PJ did not recognize me in spite of Nita's constant reminders that I still existed. We drove home to Dakin Crescent through light rain arriving around midnight. I took the following day off work and helped with the orientation of everyone. It was a cold day and we had hoped to use the community pool, but no such luck. We looked at the Shaver garden and Churchill Park.

The container with our furniture and effects arrived the following week. It was still "in bond" and I had to clear it through customs in town, which I did with help from Dave Roberts, who handled customs affairs at Shaver. We had used the same company, Tippet Richardson, that had moved us out of the St. George house, and our faith here was amply justified. Two highly competent and efficient men worked almost non-stop until the container was empty at about 8.00 pm. For one horrible moment, we thought the cat had gone with the container, but then he showed up quite unconcerned.

The animals adapted quickly to their new home. The cat of course was happy to be fed and watered and allowed to explore the neighbourhood. The dog learned the surroundings too, and within a couple of days encountered a groundhog almost her own size. They fought to the death (of the groundhog) and the dog Maggie came home covered in blood, almost none of it her own.

I had a short trip to the US, starting with a drive with Doug Rundle to Ithaca, NY for the annual New York Poultrymens Get-Together. Cornell at this time had a full scale Poultry Extension service and the meeting was attended by a large number of egg producers, plus suppliers like ourselves. I gave a paper at the meeting. Doug and I also visited Randy Cole at his home in Ithaca. We talked with our local hatcheryman, Norm Hecht, another great asset for Shaver. Norm was later to spearhead the campaign to reinstate eggs as a safe food after the cholesterol scare. He sent a dozen eggs to every doctor in town, accompanied by a letter saying he was proud to produce food but wouldn't do it if he thought it would be bad for his children or grandchildren.

From Ithaca, I was driven to Syracuse and flew by way of New York to Raleigh NC and spent three days traveling with Hugh Thornburg. I was only home for a week before spending another week with Hugh traveling North and South Carolina, and Georgia before ending up at the Poultry Science Meeting in Auburn AL. Here it was extremely hot; my motel room had no air conditioning and was still intolerable even after I bought a 21 inch fan, so I moved in to a room on campus. These meetings tended to be "dry" but anyone wanting a beer had only to find John Summers and all would be well. I found him most evenings and contributed to the beer supply as part of my expenses. DMcQ gave the keynote speech at the Annual PSA meeting, which was well received. He was very good at this kind of thing. The Shaver group left Auburn and drove to Cullman for the evening, after which I flew home.

While life in Dakin Crescent was OK, we were still looking for a country lot and eventually bought one, almost opposite to our old place on Conc.V road. We had to pay $30,000 for it, and of course there were no services. We had a local architect, Joe Somfay, design a solar house for us, but it was never built. Before we even started, Nita found the "dream house" on West River Road in Cambridge. But we cleared a spot for the solar house, which resulted in a supply of rather green logs which we used in our family room fireplace at Dakin Crescent.

When I returned to work after the trip to Poultry Science, I found that our egg lab and the warehouse of which it was a part, had burned to the ground. It was reconstructed and included my office.

Work now included liaison with both the Animal Research Institute (Rob Gowe and colleagues Jan Gavora, Allan Grunder, Bob Hamilton and others) and the Animal Diseases Research Institute, where the poultry section was under the control of Lloyd Spencer. These were important sources of information and informal assistance for the Shaver breeding program. I was also involved with the many visitors we received; customers, colleagues from other Cargill poultry operations around the world, occasional visiting scientists, etc. etc. DMcQ was still 100% in charge and although we had occasional "breeding meetings", they tended to be formalities with little of the long term planning that we, as geneticists, needed, and which were a basic feature during my years with Ross. The day-to-day selection work continued with DMcQ signing off on every Directive. We still lacked in-house computing power, with everything farmed out to Ottawa or local time sharing. I did attend a Computer Show in Toronto with Bob Jones, now the comptroller after George Sandkuhl's retirement, but nothing came of it.

I represented Shaver at the Ontario Poultry Council, and attended the Ontario Poultry Health Conference, along with a new veterinary assistant, Patricio Liberona. Patricio was a refugee from Chile. He had a valid DVM from Santiago but took a long time before he was able officially practice in Ontario. He was another good friend and we maintained contact for many years. The Council also ran a one-day Poultry School in Guelph which I attended with Doug Ridsdale.

I represented Shaver on the Poultry Council's Research Committee. This group had little money or power, but worked on issues that we subsequently lobbied government for support.

By September 1977, Nita was pregnant again, and underwent amniocentesis and ultrasound tests in Toronto. On determining this one would be a girl, we again faced the naming challenge and settled on "Carole Elizabeth". Both names of my good friends in England. Carole was born on March 25, 1978.

The winter of 1977-78 was a typical, traditional one. We had a huge snowstorm on December 5th, with cars stuck in drifts etc., white Christmas, more snow on and off, and still piled in the driveway when Nita came home with Carole from the hospital at the end of March. One of the highlights of the Christmas season was (the new) Mrs. Shaver's St. Lucia feast at their newly renovated home, the Shellards Farm. The low point was finding out, on December 23rd, that I had shingles. At that time there was no treatment, no cure and no vaccine; one just sucked it up. I was in pain for about a month, but continued to work and do things at home.

We had a traditional Christmas, with Nita's mother Flo and her husband Mick visiting for the holiday. They were both good grandparents and PJ had a great time with them. Their presence allowed us some time out for visits, and we re-united with Roy and Kay Bean, our former neighbours when we had the St. George house.

In January 1978, I made a trip to Central America. First stop was Nicaragua, where Peter Quail had identified a prospective customer. This was San Francisco Estates, owned by an English immigrant family, the Vaughans. They owned half the hens, and sold 80% of the eggs consumed, in the whole country. The farms and hatchery were good and up to date. I had a good session with the owners, lunch, and then tea, before leaving to stay at the Intercontinental Hotel. Managua at this time was still recovering from an earthquake in 1972 and was called the donut city. The next day I took the short flight to San Salvador, where Cargill had established a broiler production complex. I spent the day with the local managers and talked up Shaver Starbro.

The next stop was Mexico City, but only after another chaotic central American airport experience. They were all pretty bad but San Salvador was the worst. I later discovered that on the day I left, there was a government coup, and I was lucky to be on my way, as the airport was closed later in the day.

Shaver was well established in Mexico with a distributor based in Monterey. Our meetings in Mexico City involved one of my standard company genetics lectures to a group of hatchery employees and salesmen, and the following day after a short flight to Monterey, I repeated the performance, but with more of a sales pitch included. From here I flew to Guadalajara for a short meeting with another prospect, the Anderson Clayton Company, and then on to San Antonio, Texas, where I was met by our Shaver salesman, Bill Hicks. We drove to Lockhart, where our distributor, Bufkin Farms was located, and visited some of the breeding flocks. This was followed by another visit to College Station, where Texas A&M had recently opened a new Animal and Poultry Science building.

We saw a lot of Texas on this trip, including a visit to the Poultry Times office in Nacogdoches, still presided over by Tip Smith; by this time I think he understood me better than when we first met in 1968! I ended up in Dallas, from which airport I flew to Orange County, California to spend four days in "Demler country". We met with many current and potential customers and also with Don Bell, the famous poultry adviser in Riverside. I did a fifteen minute radio interview with Bob Daniell of the Farm Bureau. I was by this time traveling with Cliff Stuart, who was the Shaver representative for the west coast. We ended up Friday afternoon with the weekend to kill before going to San Jose in northern California. Although we had plane tickets, we decided to rent a car and drive, and this was an excellent decision.

I had never seen this part of the Pacific coast before. We drove north and about the time we thought of stopping, arrived quite by accident in Solvang. This was settled much earlier by Danish immigrants and they had built the town along Danish lines with traditional buildings and businesses. The thing that gave it away was the mountain backdrop! We stayed here overnight and dined at the Danish Inn.

The following day (Sunday) we drove back to the coast at San Luis Obispo and admired the ocean from Morrow Bay. We then turned inland and drove through the Salinas Valley, which was Steinbeck country. I had read a lot of Steinbeck and many place names were familiar. And the Valley was really beautiful. We stopped to sample wines at the San Martin winery, and arrived at our Holiday Inn in San Jose late afternoon. A splendid weekend all round.

We were met at the hotel by Lloyd Merrill, long time Shaver distributor based in Idaho, and Dr. Walter Hughes and his wife. Walter had worked for Kimber Farms in California, the first breeder to hire a full time geneticist (Dr. Will Lamoreux, in 1943) and one of the first to exit the industry (some time in the 1960's). He now worked for the University of California at Davis. We had an interesting dinner with them all.

We spent a couple of intensive days calling on existing and prospective customers. Shaver had lots of competition on the west coast, but very good representation with Demler in California, Lamont's Featherland Farms in Oregon, and Merrill's hatchery in Idaho. On the broiler side, we were still in start-up mode here, but we visited Foster Farms on this trip, and they eventually, for a short period, took Starbro Grandparents. This was a gorgeous trip from a scenic point of view, with drives around the San Francisco Bay, and into the Napa Valley wine country. One customer there was air-drying manure from layers and using it as fertilizer for grape vines.

We flew on to Eugene OR and drove to Corvallis for a visit to the Oregon State University. Its Poultry Department at the time was headed by a Canadian, Prof. Paul Bernier. Cliff Stuart and I gave a seminar entitled "Shaver – Its life and Work" to the poultry students. In those days, Profs had some privileges and we lunched very well in the Triad Club, part of the Union Building. The trip ended with visits to our distributors in Washington State, and Mickey Sanders hatchery in Abbotsford, BC.

The trip finished, as did most Shaver trips, on a Friday night, with a Saturday flight back to Toronto. I was up at 4.00 am for the 7.00 am flight, and got home at 6.30 pm, just in time to change clothes and head out to Douglas and Ivy Brown's Burns Supper. It is amazing to me now (at the age of 85) how we burned the candle at both ends! The following Saturday, we hired Dave Roberts's daughter Terry to babysit, while we drove to Toronto, met our friends Ted and Janet Jones for drinks, followed by dinner/theatre show: *Tonight at 8.30 - 9.00 in Newfoundland.* Then coffee at Ted and Janet's apartment. We got home at 2.00 am. Janet had taught with Nita before either of them was married. They did not have children and Janet continued teaching until retirement. Ted sold company insurance and benefit packages. He and I would occasionally lunch together, and when, later, they bought a cottage on Crego Lake in the Kawartha district, we visited with both children.

110

My usual winter trip to Europe began less than two weeks following my return from the west coast. I had a couple of days in Ponteland with my mother before flying to Norwich and two days at Shaver GB, now in the capable hands of Len Zoller. I had talked to Len after hearing from Geoff Fairhurst that he was looking for an opportunity to leave Sweden. Len was open to the idea of hiring Geoff and by the time of this visit, had done so, although Geoff had not yet arrived in Norfolk. This was to be a good move for Geoff, and a good hire for Len, who needed more technical help than was currently available. Len had married Louise in France, and they now had a very pretty rented rectory to live in.

Next stop; The Netherlands, where our distributor Rotzhuisen was helping us to introduce Starbro, and then my annual week in Romania. They were still working on the breeding program we set up, but it was hard to estimate whether they were making progress, or whether it was making "commercial" sense for Romania's poultry industry. This seemed to be a very hard winter in Europe; I had some snow in Scotland, England, The Netherlands, and then lots of it in Romania. We were staying in Braşov near a ski area and a group of us took the chair lift to the top one afternoon. Beautiful views all round; one of the party skied down while the rest of us walked. As always, the Romanians went out of their way to offer the best hospitality; maybe they used it as an opportunity to indulge themselves, but I certainly enjoyed it. From Bucharest, I flew home *via* Frankfurt, to be met by Nita with PJ. Now 2½, he was talking a blue streak and I was thrilled to sit in the back seat with him on the drive home. Ontario had a hard winter too, and I was soon shoveling snow out of our (thankfully very short) driveway.

Our daughter Carole was born on March 25th, 1978. I continued work at the office but took some time off to visit the hospital.

Following her birth, I proceeded with my plans for a vasectomy; Nita and I had agreed that two children would be enough and now we had them, why delay? The operation was performed a few weeks later. A twenty minute procedure for a lifetime of security seemed a very good deal, in spite of the temporary discomfort.

Work at Shaver was not satisfying. Throughout 1978 and into 1979, my diary notes "boredom" and numerous meetings with DMcQ at which I told him I thought most of my work to be trivial. The travel was obviously useful, and also my work with visitors to the office, but as to being Director of Research? At a meeting in August 1978, DMcQ specifically said that I could keep the title but my main job in R&D was to work on the brown egg program. This was mostly in the UK and a relatively small part of Shaver's business. It too was largely under DMcQ's control. With all my complaints, it is amazing in retrospect that I wasn't fired. The main reason, I think, was that DMcQ genuinely liked me and respected my qualifications, but was not prepared to delegate at any price.

An additional "insult" was the company vacation policy, explained in a very blunt memo from Bob Gray; two weeks was all we would get for the foreseeable future.

I was involved with writing technical literature and this was rewarding in the sense that Shaver's material equaled or excelled that of our competitors. And of course I always enjoyed writing.

Meanwhile we put our house on the market for $64,900 in anticipation of building on the lot at RR4 St. George. We did not expect much, if any profit; this was to be expected with owning the house for such a short time, sky-high realtor fees, plus the housing market was not great. We didn't even have a nibble the first month it was on the market. We got a conditional offer at the end of July for $62,500. But since they could not dispense with the condition, the offer lapsed. By this time, the listing had expired and we re-listed with a different realtor. After this failed, we tried to sell privately. Our neighbour sold his this way but had to drop his price considerably in order to clinch the deal. His place was similar to ours but the basement was finished. He got $64,000 having started at $75,000.

Nita's mother came for her now annual visit in early June, 1978. She brought Mick's sister Doris with her. This enabled Nita and me to do a little gallivanting; one memorable night we drove to Toronto, and met Ted and Janet Jones for a concert by Oscar Peterson and Joe Pass at Ontario Place. As if this was not enough, we then went in to the city to the Bobbins Wine Cellar for a liter of hock while listening to Louise Lambert, a wonderful singer/songwriter/character we had seen featured in the Globe and Mail. Home at 2.00 a.m! Another night Nita and I went to the Royal Alex to see the late, great Robert Morley perform in *Picture of Innocence*. It was worth the trip just to see Morley's classic British style and humour.

I continued my Shaver travels, with trips in May to the Breeders Roundtable and visits to customers and our franchise hatcheries in the mid-west, and another in June to Winnipeg for an industry Convention, and more mid-west visits with Cliff Stuart. On one of these, I had my first exposure to the Hutterite colonies, which were large and loyal customers. On these colonies, there was no private ownership of anything: The colony owned the land, buildings and the poultry farm. All work including preparing and consumption of meals and rearing of children, was communal. The "chicken man" looked after the poultry system and was responsible for purchases. When the colony reached a certain size and

112

further expansion was considered impossible, a new colony would be created. The colonies I visited were mostly in the Dakotas, but later, I visited several in Alberta, where the system was also well established. While this communal system seemed to work well, it was not without challenges. Cliff Stuart told me the hatcheries sometimes over billed for the chicks or pullets and then rewarded the chicken man through a kickback!

During 1978, I learned from Doug Rundle of a small business in Smithville, Ontario breeding Quail. The owner, Jack Pannachetti, had an integrated business (a sideline, I think) with a few hundred quail, involving breeding, growing for meat, processing and sales. He was having hatchability problems and I tried to help. I was paid in kind, and also tried to sell a few frozen quail to the local restaurants and ethnic food stores. This never became a formal consultancy but was interesting, and a welcome break from the monotony at Shaver.

Another diversion this summer was sitting and passing the IQ test to join MENSA. One had to be in the top 2% and I just made it. I joined the local Kitchener chapter and attended a few meetings. But in the end, I did not keep up the membership, because there was a lot of infighting at the national level that I couldn't be bothered with, and there was nothing particularly special about the locals. Nita took the test later and found herself at the 97th percentile and was therefore denied membership. Not a significant difference, I always told her, but it still rankles.

The four of us, plus Flo and Doris, spent a week at the Cedar Haven cottage near Wiarton the first week in July. Quite a crowd in the cottage but we had a good time. Nita and I took the opportunity to take a day off and drive to Tobermory, and thence on the good ship Captain Ahab to Flowerpot Island. This was our first visit and we have been back many times since. On that first occasion, Nita described it as the quintessence of Canada; it was peaceful, serene and unspoiled. In 2017, we found it besieged; boats full of noisy people arriving and departing every few minutes and a gift shop near the lighthouse!

Both Nita and I were eating and drinking too well and agreed to go on diets – the Scarsdale Diet to be precise. Nita joined a group of teachers in a contest to lose weight , which she eventually won after losing 9 lb in a month. So we took ourselves to Cambridge's finest eating place, which, at the time, was the "Bouquet Garni" housed in an old button factory in Preston. We spent the whole winnings and had a great meal.

My mother came to visit in August, and we took a week at Birch Glen Cottage near Baysville on Lake Of Bays in the Muskoka region. By this time we had two cars (no company car here!) and with three adults and two small children we really needed them. This was still the era of huge American cars and even the "second car", a 10 year old Ford Fairlane had plenty of room and a huge trunk. This cottage was right on Lake of Bays and came with a row boat. The cottage was perched on a cliff above the lake with steps down to the dock. The dog enjoyed sitting at the top of the steps to watch for prey, and we got a nice photograph, later transformed into a large painting by one of our neighbours Laurie Koehler. We also took what became one of our favourite pictures of my mother, holding Carole, who was fascinated by a twirling maple leaf.

For the rest of 1978 and 1979, work continued to be a challenge in terms of finding meaningful tasks. I made useful forays into the US and elsewhere, and enjoyed traveling with the many loyal, hard working Shaver franchises, customers and marketers. The company was doing well in an era of great competition. At one point DMcQ told me I was to be Marketing Director for Central America, but nothing came of this, and I continued my travels as usual. During a three week sortie to the west coast in the fall, I made my first visit to Hawaii, with Dick Baker from Demler farms. At this time Hawaii had its own egg farms, being so remote from the US mainland, and Demler was supplying them with chicks. I managed to swim twice on Waikiki beach at 7.00 before work! I also visited Julie Brock (née Bailey), who worked at the University of Hawaii in marine biology. I enjoyed the visit with her, husband Dick and baby Vernon.

Shaver attended the Worlds Poultry Congress in Rio de Janeiro, Brazil in September 1978. DMcQ was there and he was a different person when "on tour". Much more relaxed but also looking out for any business that happened to appear. South America at that time was opening up and offered great opportunities to the international breeders. Shaver had good contacts but may not have made the best of them for lack of presence on the ground. Peter Quail had nailed this one with his note about "beating the bushes, not flying over them" a few years ago. He and I ran and walked on the famous Ipanema beach before breakfast most days during the Congress.

After the Congress, Manuel Soares Costa and I visited some of the egg industry people. At this time the egg business in Brazil was almost entirely controlled by Japanese migrants and we met a number of them, making sure they were aware of Shaver and its local distribution network.

One of the memorable aspects of this time with Shaver was some of the employees who came to join the company, several from other breeders. Cliff Stuart came from Hy-Line. He had worked for them for many years and of course had a huge network of industry contacts. I'm not sure why he left Hy-Line but he was a big asset for Shaver. I traveled with him several times in the midwest and the west coast.

Another old timer who came to Shaver was John Nay. John had worked for Pilch Breeders, another one-man operation based in New England, that bred broiler breeder females. John had worked there a long time and done a lot of overseas travel including behind the iron curtain. He had some hair raising tales! John was a great person to have around and we saw quite a bit of each other over the time he worked at Shaver. One night I had dinner with him at the newly opened Holiday Inn in Cambridge. He refused a drink on the ground that he had to lose weight, and then consumed the entire contents of the bread basket! John was eventually made General Manager of Shaver's German operation, Shaver GmbH in Dusseldorf. He complained bitterly about being paid in $US when he had to spend Deutchmarks, which continued to rise in value against his salary. When he returned from Germany, John brought us 6 very nice hand cut crystal wine glasses as a gift. We used these for years and as tends to happen, they were occasionally broken. There is only one left today (2020) but I still think of John Nay every time I use it. John eventually became the General Manager of the Cullman office.

A great recruit to Shaver was Jack Hessler. Jack came from Cargill's head office but had international experience, and was himself originally German. He had huge management capabilities, but these were never fully exploited while he stayed at Shaver. I don't remember how long he actually stayed, but even after he left, he still enjoyed D.McQ's friendship. Long after they both retired, they ended up in the same retirement home in Cambridge, and spent quite a lot of time together.

In Mexico, Shaver was doing well with the Reproductoras Shaver in Monterrey and Anderson Clayton in Guadalajara. We ran a three day technical school for their key staff in January 1979.

At home, the children were growing nicely. I constructed a two-level bunk bed for them in one of the bedrooms (so that we could still retain a spare room for visitors) and this worked out very well for a number of years.

We did a lot of entertaining and, of course going out for reciprocal hospitality. It is a sign of those times that for one party of six, Nita prepared crab crêpes, beef with green peppers, followed by cheesecake for dessert. All washed down with a lot of homemade wine most of the time. And a full bar before and after.

While at the Breeders Roundtable in Kansas City in May 1979, I learned that Margaret Thatcher's Conservatives had been elected as the new government in the UK. Should I have stayed? Several years of great prosperity for the UK ensued. I also heard of an opportunity to work with Jim Smith at Hubbard Farms in New Hampshire, but didn't pursue it.

We had good holidays in 1979. By this time, our renting at Cedar Haven Cottages had become an accepted part of the summer and both children loved it. It was great relaxation for Nita and me. The facilities were very basic but that was a part of the attraction; making do, and devising our own amusements was a good way to spend our special time together. And even with the limitations imposed by our young children, we began to realize what a wonderful place the Bruce Peninsula was. In later years we would return many times and explore it in detail. We also got to know our hosts, Betty and Charles Seigrist, very well and kept in touch with Betty until she died in 2017. One of their secrets, to which we were carefully introduced, was the Lady's Slipper in the swampy bush across the road, which they also owned. The yellow one was fairly common but there were a couple of patches of a gorgeous pale pink variety which was quite rare. Of course we took pictures.

We had almost the same holiday in 1980, by which time the children were a year older, but they still enjoyed the simple life.

My mother visited again in August 1979, now able to fly directly from Newcastle airport to Toronto. PJ and I met her off the 'plane. Flo (Nita's mother) and Mick also visited, in order to babysit while Nita, my mother and I took a holiday in the west. We flew to Calgary and rented a motor home for a week. It was specified to sleep 5 or 6 but it worked out very well for just the three of us. The learning curve was steep: the first night we ran the battery down by keeping the heat on while not "plugged in". We also learned how anything not screwed down would end up on the floor! But we had a great time once we learned how everything worked. My mother shared my fascination with mountains and was completely awed by the Rockies. Nita never did share this passion but enjoyed the trip anyway. I had recently read a book called *Men For The Mountains* written by Sid Marty, a former Canada Parks warden and we went to Yoho National Park in eastern BC based on his writing. The scenery everywhere we went was totally different from either eastern Canada or Europe, and we thoroughly enjoyed it. We visited Kananaskis Provincial Park in Alberta, and, of course the tourist spots like Lake Louise, Banff and Jasper. We took the cable car in Jasper to the mountain top; my mother couldn't believe the alpine flowers and spent most of the time on her knees! We went on the boat rip on Maligne Lake and saw the most photographed island in Canada (I think) and of course more and more mountains. *En route* to Jasper we stopped at the Columbia Icefields to see the glacier. On the way back to Calgary we stopped in Red Deer to see Nita's friend Kate McQuillen and her husband Lee.

Never had we had so many visitors! In early October, Norrie and Ada Semple came to stay for a few days, before going on to Detroit to visit relatives. Norrie was one of my favourite people from the time at Ross Poultry and we were both delighted to see him and Ada. We showed them the sights, including a trip to Niagara Falls. We had been to the Falls so often that we now made it mandatory to stop for the buffet lunch at the Beacon Inn at Jordan Harbour. The Stone Crock in St. Jacobs was another place we discovered with the Semples. It featured a buffet; the kids loved it and it was excellent value.

In August 1979 I heard on the local grapevine that the Ontario Egg Producers' Marketing Board (henceforth the Egg Board or OEPMB) was looking to hire a technical liaison/extension person to advise producers. This seemed like a possible alternative to staying at Shaver, which I was still not enjoying. I went for an interview in St. Marys at the home of Tom Graham, along with Gerry Long and Ross McEwan. Tom, Gerry and Ross were all Directors of the Egg Board and constituted a committee struck to look for a Poultry Specialist. Tom was, at the time, vice chairman of the Egg Board. He had a few thousand layers at another farm outside of town and grew pullets at the home farm. Gerry Long was President of Woodlyn Farms, a corporate structure near London with layers, pigs and crop land. He had recently sold a substantial egg grading business, but kept the production facility. Ross McEwan had a relatively small egg farm on the Niagara Peninsula and also worked for a local feed mill. All three were men of considerable charm in different ways, and I felt there would be no difficulty working for such a group. The interview was very informal and went quite well, but at the time they wanted me to move to Toronto, where their office was located.

The Egg Board was one of ten in Canada, one for each Province. The Provincial Boards worked under the umbrella of a Federal agency, then called the Canadian Egg Marketing Agency (CEMA). Together they administered the system of Supply Management for which Canada was noted, not always politely, but with great loyalty from its members, the producers. The background dated back to the 1960's and 70's when the egg industry in the US and Canada endured a series of boom and bust cycles. During the bust phases, surplus American eggs were shipped into Canada, depressing already low prices. In 1973, the CEMA was established, and each producer was allocated a production quota based on existing flock size. Since this allocation was advertised well in advance, many producers expanded their flocks. So, the first thing that confronted CEMA was a serious surplus of eggs. Some of them were allegedly dumped in the ocean, which did not make for a good start to the system. However, by the late 70's, supply and demand were fairly well balanced and the system flourished. Not only was production controlled but also the price the farmer received. The price was set based on a calculation of production cost, plus a "reasonable profit". Imports of shell eggs were prevented by very high tariffs. Each Provincial Board deducted a levy from the producers' egg cheques to finance its administration and to fund CEMA. This is not the place to debate the rights and wrongs of the system; however, it achieved stability, which was its primary goal, and most producers welcomed it.

I had another interview with the Board at its office, located at 5799 Yonge Street, Toronto, in what used to be called Willowdale, about 3 km north of Hwy 401. They offered me the job of Poultry Specialist at a competitive salary and gave me ten days to think about it. After a lot of heart-searching, I decided to stay with Shaver. Then at the end of October, after another pretty boring month at work, I met Brian Ellsworth, the Egg Board's General Manager and he said the post was still open and would I reconsider? He telephoned about three weeks later to see what I was doing. I went for another interview at the office on Yonge Street in mid-November and they sweetened the offer; I didn't have to move to Toronto. By this time rumours of my possible move began to circulate in the industry and I knew I would soon have to make the decision. I finally resigned from Shaver on January 18th, 1980, ending a 13 year career in the Poultry Breeding business. I had some misgivings but also excitement at the new challenges. In retrospect, it was a good move, for two reasons. First, the breeding industry was undergoing great change, with rapid consolidation into a smaller number of larger units. One-man operations like Shaver would not survive. Secondly, within ten years, the field of molecular genetics would mature to the point that it might be useful in commercial breeding. I had no skill or knowledge in this area, and might be superseded by more recently trained professionals.

Within a few days, DMcQ asked me if I would be a consultant for Shaver. This was an interesting development and a welcome one. It was mainly aimed at my continuation as Editor of Shaver Focus, composition of Management Guides, and included some work selecting breeders in a few pure lines. There would be potential conflicts of interest, but I cleared this with the Egg Board Chairman, Jimmy Johnstone, and accepted. Obviously, if questions of breed selection arose with producers, I would declare an interest and they could make their own decisions. I never had any issues with this as long as I worked for the Egg Board. I worked cooperatively with people from all the hatcheries. Breed competition was fierce and I doubt I could have had any influence in favour of Shaver even if I had tried.

Chapter 7

Work at the Ontario Egg Producers Marketing Board

I started work for the Egg Board on March 3rd, 1980. Prior to this, I had attended, with Brian Ellsworth, its General Manager, a Zone meeting in Petrolia in south western Ontario, which gave me a taste of things to come. I had to learn about the local industry politics. The egg producers were prospering under the protection afforded by control of production level and prices. Many who previously purchased 20 week old pullets from independent growers were beginning to grow their own, thus putting pullet growers out of business. So these growers were beginning to ask; "Why can't we have quotas too'?" Eventually they would get their own quota system, but only after a long and arduous struggle and much belligerent opposition from the prosperous egg farmers.

The commute from Cambridge to 5799 Yonge Street was a bit of a chore but I got used to it. In any case, much of my job was expected to be in the field, and the 400 egg farmers were spread (unevenly) across the Province, literally from Windsor in the west to near Hawkesbury in the east, and a handful in the north, as far up as Kapuskasing and Hearst.

The staff at the office were varied. There was an accountant and a book keeper. A quota control manager was based in the office for whom ten fieldmen worked in their defined areas, literally counting chickens in producers' barns, to ensure that everyone followed the rules. These fieldmen also checked out any non-compliant producers; the maximum number of hens that could be kept without a quota was 100. Another employee was responsible for liaison with grading stations, which received eggs from producers and paid for them, after deducting the levy forwarded to the Board. We also had an advertising department; both CEMA and the Egg Board promoted eggs in a variety of media including television, radio, print and attendance at food fairs and related events. A home economist was on staff, who developed and promoted egg recipés. There was a continuous development of promotional literature distributed from the office. Later, a Public Relations person was hired.

One big benefit with the Egg Board was a company car. I looked at many cars and eventually got a Ford LTD, at the time an oversize car with seating for 6 and a V8 engine. Only Brian and I, and occasionally another staff member had this privilege. It made commuting more acceptable. We kept the cars for about 2 years or 200,000 km before trading them. The LTD did not turn out well. In late 1982 a rattle began and it needed a new crankshaft! Almost all highway driven and all the prescribed maintenance done on time. It was traded in December 1982 and I have never had another Ford! The next car was a Pontiac, then an Oldsmobile and then a Buick. In 1994 I got the first of two Chrysler Intrepids. In many ways these were my favourite cars, and I bought the second one from the Board when I retired. Brian was careful with the Board's money and always had a better car than I did, but mine was a significant advance on our family cars! We still kept a car of our own, as Nita needed mobility for her and the kids' activities. One thing about the Board cars; we always had air-conditioning, and our family car soon followed suit.

I spent most of my time at the office for the first several weeks. The Directors met monthly for two days and I attended most of the first meeting after I joined. Subsequently, I gave a monthly report and was expected to be available throughout the meeting if needed. The meetings dealt mostly with "political" matters: quota infractions, production reviews, budgets and advertising and a host of matters in which I had little interest and no responsibility. But in my later reports, I detailed my farm visits and often provided information of interest. Later, as our research commitments increased, this also featured in my monthly reports

I started a monthly technical newsletter, eventually entitled "The Ovum". It was printed and mailed to all producers along with "The Cackler", which consisted of Board news. I wrote up reviews of current research of interest, and reprinted items from the numerous other Extension newsletters published, mostly from US University Extension services. Of these, California, Georgia, North Carolina, Ohio and Pennsylvania were perhaps the most useful.

One of the reasons for my appointment was the lack of any government poultry specialist. The Ontario government provided extension services in some areas but not poultry. The University of Guelph had a significant Department of Poultry Science (later merged into Animal and Poultry Science) with some extension capability but by no means full time, and the faculty did not expend much effort out in the field. In the 1990's the Provincial Government appointed a Poultry Specialist, Don Luckham, based at the Ridgetown College. When he retired he was replaced by Dianne Spratt based in Guelph and this position is still (2021) active. However, my position with the Egg Board was maintained until I retired and there was little or no overlap with the Provincial Poultry Specialist. No successor was appointed after I retired, so the Provincial Poultry Specialist then achieved a broader remit. However, the circumstances had changed from 1980; producer numbers were smaller and producers themselves were much better informed.

I was "on call" from my first day, although I soon found that I might have made one call a month if I had waited in the office. Some calls came as a result of complaints from grading stations regarding egg quality. Small producers (there were still many with less than 1000 hens) only had eggs picked up once every week, or sometimes two weeks, and unless they had refrigerated storage, then internal quality would suffer, especially in summer.

Over the first few months, I made a point of visiting each Director at his home farm, and was mostly made welcome. It was as much a learning experience for me as for them, but on the whole was mutually beneficial. Some of the facilities were recently updated, while others were old and needed new equipment. I made myself familiar with what was available and was soon able to offer intelligent suggestions and comment on renovations and updating.

Just a week after I started, the Egg Board held its Annual General Meeting, which was a really big deal. In those days it was held at the Inn On The Park in eastern Toronto. I think it lasted three days in quite plush surroundings. All of the staff and producers' expenses were paid and most of the farmers brought their wives, so this was a great opportunity to meet people and set up farm calls for later. The level of expense was nowhere near that experienced with the Ross and Imperial affairs in England, but it was a nice change from the day to day activity.

The first afternoon I spent meeting the fieldmen (impolitely known as chicken counters, but that is what they did). Each of them had a specific area to cover, roughly comparable to the Zones represented by a Director. They were in some ways policemen and in fact some of them were retired military police. One of them covered the handful of producers in northern Ontario and also did "enforcement". His name was Wally Chaulk, and he hailed from Newfoundland. He was one of the retired military police, was about 6ft.6in. tall, maybe 300 lb and had an intimidating skill with profanity. But, I think, a heart of gold. Wally dealt with unregistered producers with flocks larger than the exemption of 100 hens, preparing court cases if necessary and following up the inevitable convictions. We followed our discussions at the Annual Meeting with drinks and dinner, and then attended the Chairman's reception for more drinks.

Jim Johnstone, the Chairman, was quite a character. He had been Chair for several years and would remain in that position for many more. He owned quota for about 10,000 hens but at the time, this was inactive, or rather rented out. His farm was on the edge of Alliston, about 2 hour's drive north of Toronto; the town was rapidly expanding, and his property had been sold. Alliston exploded later when the Honda Motor Company built a factory there. Jim's hen barn was eventually demolished and replaced by a Church, and they built a new house and barn a few km outside town. Jim was a charmer! He knew everyone, including all the important politicians, both federal and provincial, who needed to be kept on side to protect the supply management system. He knew most of the producers personally and of course all of the Board staff. He worked closely and seamlessly with Brian Ellsworth and in many ways, the two of them "were the Board".

The Annual General Meeting included reports from all the Board Departments, from Brian, the Chairman and myself. At this stage all I was able to say was what I expected to do, and to invite contacts. The meeting was covered by the agricultural press; the Editor of the Canada Poultryman always attended, as did Jim Romahn of the Kitchener Waterloo Record. Jim was one of the Boards severest critics but I found him largely fair in reporting and a useful contact. Most producers brought their families and Nita came with our kids. Our friends Ted and Janet Jones came and babysat while we attended the Board Banquet, and the following day, Nita and the kids used the hotel pool.

Over the following weeks I continued to work from the office but also started visiting the Directors' farms, and a few producers who contacted me. At the time, some new cage systems were reaching the market to replace the old "stair-step" systems. These consisted of two or three levels of wire cages in a "A" configuration over a shallow manure pit cleaned by a mechanical scraper. An alternative was to mount them over a deep pit in which manure would build up over the whole life of the flock. One of the new systems, called Cagemaster, consisted of plastic cages stacked three or four high with manure collected by means of an endless belt under each row of cages. Other stacked cages made of wire also came on the market. I made a point of visiting many of the newer installations and became familiar with their characteristics.

Having previously worked almost exclusively with geneticists, I now found myself requiring contact with all of the other disciplines involved in the egg industry. I found a wealth of knowledge within easy reach, even within Ontario. Guelph was home to some of the best nutritional knowledge and research in Canada, if not the world. The duo of Stan Slinger and John Summers was world renowned and they had recently recruited Steve Leeson from England, who later became extremely well known. The federal Animal Research Institute (Gowe's shop) had a fine nutrition team including Ian Sibbald, Bob Hamilton and Nick Cave. Veterinary Science was also well covered; the Provincial Government operated the Post-Mortem clinics at Guelph and three or four Provincial Agriculture Colleges, and of course I already knew Art Ferguson who ran the clinic in Guelph.

Although the animal welfare movement was not an issue in the early 80's it was to emerge soon, and Frank Hurnik was one of the early specialists working at the University of Guelph. Later on, Ian Duncan, whom I had known when he worked at the PRC in Edinburgh, moved to Guelph and by the early 21st century, welfare probably had more faculty and researchers at Guelph working on poultry than any other discipline.

I decided to start a program of Producer Seminars with technical speakers drawn from this rich pool of talent, and it proved successful for several years. We would invite two or three speakers for an afternoon session in one of the Producer Zones and invite those in adjoining Zones to attend. If the speakers came from a distance, we often hosted them overnight and repeated the program the following day at a different location. Each meeting might attract 30 or 40 producers and most enjoyed the experience. We continued with these producer meetings until demand for them (manifested in audience numbers) declined in the 1990s.

I attended any and all industry meetings held by hatcheries, feed suppliers etc. and gave talks when asked. Egg quality was a favourite topic, but welfare was beginning to emerge as a future challenge. The hatchery meetings were fun. At one held by the Craig Hunter Poultry Farms, I wrote in my diary; "Listened to all the Dekalb bullshit - much like Shaver's"!

Farm visits soon took up a significant amount of my time. I began to learn a lot of the country roads and started to put considerable kilometres on my LTD. Distances in Ontario could be deceptive. From home in Cambridge to producers in Lambton County would be close to 200 km, a two hour drive before seeing anyone. Going east was even further; we had a number of producers (mostly French speaking) in St. Isidore de Prescott, more than 500 km away. For the eastern visits, I would try to combine several for one trip, visit producers *en route* and stay one or two nights. For the French speakers I had to call on the local fieldman, who was fluently bilingual, to help, although it has to be said that the majority of these producers understood English very well.

In the "near north", we also had a few producers. Craig Hunter Poultry Farms operated the Dekalb franchise in Stroud (150 km) and there was one producer in Orillia (200 km). Further north, there were originally about ten farms scattered over a huge area, with its own Zone and Director. I attended the Zone meeting at which the Director was elected in May, and visited several of the farms. After a couple of years I began to take a one week trip and visit them all. My first trip included Cobalt, Moonbeam, Hearst, Timmins, Chapleau, Iron Bridge and Massey, taking six days all told. This was a 2000 km round trip with five nights away from home.

These were memorable people; far from any' suppliers, they were independent and resourceful. Most of them graded their own eggs and sold them "locally" but this might mean within a 200 km radius from home. Ferne Trottier, who had a farm at Warren, between North Bay and Sudbury, even got a slaughter license and killed his own spent hens. He got them New York dressed (plucked and bled but not eviscerated) and sold them door-to-door in Sudbury, rather than pay a southern processor to take them away. Eventually, the southern graders began to truck eggs into the north, putting great pressure on the northern producers, and I believe none has survived.

I also visited the two producers in Thunder Bay (by air); Amin Dewji owned Thunder Bay Fresh Eggs and the Vanderwees brothers owned Vanderwees Poultry Farm. These were both good professional farms, although Amin eventually sold out, left the industry and moved to BC. By the mid-eighties Vanderwees brothers were the only producer in town, with their own feed mill, egg grading station, and several other farming interests as well.

For several years in the late 1980s, my tours of Northern Ontario included Ellen Badeski, one of our promotion team. We did North Bay, Sudbury, Elliot Lake, Sault St. Marie and Kapuskasing radio and TV stations, and visited all of the producers in the area. With the media, I talked about technical matters, Ellen did cooking demo's and talked about eggs in our food. Don Luckham, newly appointed Provincial Poultry Specialist, accompanied me in 1985, and in 1987, Eleanor Marshall, who did my secretarial work for several years, came along for the ride.

On this occasion, one of the producers, whom I hadn't visited before, had 7,000 layers in cages, and had designed and built an anaerobic digester to produce biogas (mostly methane) from the manure. He used this for home heating and to generate electricity. This was quite new technology at the time, and highly inventive on the part of the farmer. I heard later that the digester eventually exploded, causing significant damage.

I always enjoyed my visits to the North. Not just the producers, who were, as I've said, a breed apart, but the scenery on the drive there and back. In August, 1998, after a quick trip to Iron Bridge and Massey to visit producers, I was looking for a place to stay overnight on the way home, and found "Yesterday's Resort" on the French River. It was not cheap like the motels, but it was gorgeous! I had my own balcony for pre-dinner gin and tonics, and a splendid pickerel dinner overlooking the placid French River. It was calm and peaceful; I wished I could have stayed a week.

I made sure I became familiar with many of the ancillary industry suppliers. Feed companies, drug and vaccine suppliers as well as equipment manufacturers mostly welcomed my existence and I learned a great deal from them, some of which I passed on to producers. I got to know the Poultry Veterinarians too; Lloyd Weber, Conrad Van Dijk and later, Elizabeth Black and Mike Joyce. They served the entire poultry industry and it was important to keep in touch with them. Towards the end of my time with the Board, McKinley Hatchery hired their own veterinarian, Mike Petric, who was another useful contact and a great resource for the industry.

Meanwhile, I continued to expand my contacts with egg farmers. The farm visits were instructive on both sides. I became familiar with the field problems; dirty eggs, cracked eggs, flies, manure utilization, etc. etc. The farmers realized that I was not all "white coated scientist" and actually had something to offer them.

I also became familiar with the Board's and CEMA's advertising programs, produced at the time by Ogilvy and Mather. Both organizations used TV and were at pains to avoid conflicting or overlapping messages. I think the Ontario advertising budget in 1980 was in excess of $1 million and at the time, this bought quite a lot of TV space. CEMA's budget was a lot more, all of it from the levy deducted from the producers' egg cheques. Long term, I believe that these expenditures paid off, especially after the "cholesterol scare" that emerged in the mid 1980s.

In 1989, the Craig Hunter Poultry Farms Dekalb franchise went bankrupt. This had many ramifications: suppliers were left with unpaid bills, employees without wages and expense reimbursements, and customers scrambling to find new sources of day-olds or started pullets. There was quite a bit of personal animosity towards Craig, as he had been the owner and the boss in every way. He actually left the Province for several years, but eventually returned and became a manager at Burnbrae Farms. I always got along well with Craig and was glad to see him succeed in a very challenging position. Joe Hudson, the owner of Burnbrae, would have been a very difficult person to work for, probably on a par with Don Shaver.

Some of the border states in the US had excellent poultry facilities and staff, and several had Workshops or Seminars to which we were invited. I usually took a car full of our farmers and it was always worthwhile. April 1980 saw Harold Linn and Scott Graham (son of Tom, who interviewed me for the job. Scott later became a Director and, ultimately Chairman of the Board) accompany me to the Penn State Poultry Conference. Pennsylvania was and is still a big player in the egg business and this two day meeting was excellent. The social aspects were fun too; extension specialist Floyd Hicks hosted an "Industry Smorgasbord" the night before the meeting started. A bonus for me was contacting scientists whom I had previously met at the Poultry Science meetings, and the chance for private sessions before or after the conference. At Penn State I always tried to meet with Ed Buss, a geneticist who also specialized in egg shell structure and quality.

Another favourite US event was the New York State Poultrymen's Get Together, held in July. I had attended one of these meetings while working for Shaver. Cornell University (home, of course to geneticists Hutt and Cole) had a great Extension service, headed by Charles Ostrander. It was also home to Prof. Milton Scott, world renowned poultry nutritionist, and a full department of Poultry Science. For several years, I drove with some of the Ontario producers for this two-day event. The meetings were good and one year they held a banquet to honour F.B. Hutt, which I thoroughly enjoyed. One of the great Cornell characters, Bob Baker was the MC. Bob was a food scientist and developed many egg and poultry products, but if he hadn't been a scientist he could easily have been a comedian. A wonderful man all round.

They later changed the name to Cornell Poultry Conference and it continued well into the 1990's although with a diminishing program. When Ostrander and the "old guard" retired,, he was replaced by Kavous Keshavarz, who continued the extension programs until he himself retired.

I gave talks at some of the meetings and we all went to the barbecue in the State Park at Taughannoch Falls. This was dry of course but there was a bar in the hotel!

The London Poultry Show was another occasion for meeting producers and suppliers and naturally, the Board had its own exhibit. I spent most of my time at the Egg Board booth, along with other staff members. I managed to see most of the show on the second day, which was always slow.

Stemming from our interest in promoting egg quality, the Egg Board sponsored an Egg Quality Contest at the London Poultry Show, each year starting in 1981, in collaboration with Agriculture Canada, whose inspectors did the judging. We would receive entries of 2½ dozen eggs from over 100 producers – of course they could select the eggs from a whole days production - but the main thing was to show visitors what good quality eggs looked like. A small sample was broken out to determine interior quality and shell thickness. The winning entries were auctioned off and the proceeds went to charity. It was not unusual for a winning entry to fetch $1,000!

Hotel service and food could be less than fun. We were staying one year at the Holiday Inn tower in London and I had dinner with Jan Gavora; my diary states that it was "unforgettable for the ineptitude of the service, the ordinariness of the food and the grandeur of the bill". Oh well, the Egg Board payed. One great thing about traveling for the Egg Board was that I could pretty much stay and eat where I wanted, or at least I knew the limits! Crummy motels out in the country were unavoidable but in places like Ottawa I always stayed in decent hotels with either their own restaurants or good ones close by. In April 1982, I noted often eating at Sammy's Macey's Steakhouse, where I got, soup, salad bar, lamb chops and ½ l of Italian red wine for $17.65, tax and tip included! Aunt Lucy's in Kingston was another favourite. (I visited Kingston in 2018 and found it had closed after 60 plus years in business)

I'm not sure how I convinced Brian that I should travel to the Poultry Breeders Roundtable, now in St. Louis, MO, but I attended anyway for a year or two. I suppose knowing what the breeders were planning would be useful, and it gave me the chance to just keep my foot in the door of genetics.

One of the many benefits of working for the Egg Board was the opportunity to work with my counterparts in other provinces. In July, 1980, after our annual holiday on the Bruce Peninsula, I had a visit from Keith Macmillan, my opposite number in Saskatchewan. Keith was a qualified veterinarian, but had seen many less live hens than dead ones, so I took him out to see a selection of our producers. This was a useful activity for both of us. In September I spent a week in Saskatchewan, part of the time with Keith. Energy efficiency was a particular concern there because of the cold winters, and Dick Van Ee at the University was deeply involved with the development of heat exchangers. We saw one installed in a broiler house and talked at length with Dick. He ultimately set up his own company to produce them and quite coincidentally, we purchased one of his units for our home in Galt. While in Saskatchewan, I also attended the Canadian Hatchery Federation's annual Convention in Regina. This was a bit of a junket but nevertheless enjoyable. Particularly welcome was a dinner/theatre evening which featured Robert Morley's play *A Ghost On Tiptoe*.

Another regular event for the Egg Board was the International Plowing Match, held near London in September, 1980. I stayed in London and worked the show for three days. This year was great weather (some times they were knee-deep in mud) and a very well attended show. The opportunity to meet our consumers was important and a show near a large city accentuated this aspect. The Board's accountant Leo, a very brash

Irishman, was also there and he got quite drunk most nights, embarrassing the rest of the group. At the end of the show, he and one of the office staff, Mary, stopped in to our home for a look round and the inevitable drinks. Leo overindulged and left, alone, about 8.30. At 10.45 he phoned from the Police Station in Preston asking if he could stay the night, after being charged with speeding and impaired driving. He slept in the sun room. The next morning we had to get his car from the pound before we all drove to the office. After the Plowing Match closed on Saturday, we had a much nicer visit from Michelle, Linda and Veronica, all from the Advertising Department, who came for a cold supper on their way home.

The following week I participated in a staff school for the employees of Embury Brothers Farms near Napanee in Eastern Ontario. This was a really good idea. The Embury Brothers had a large operation with one brother, Doug, entirely devoted to pullet rearing and the other, Elwyn, running the egg layer side. Elwyn had a son and daughter in the business as well as a range of employees. Doug was unmarried. They also made their own feed using home grown corn and purchased protein and micronutrients. I think their quota at this time was around 300,000 layers. For some inexplicable reason, when Doug married a few years later, the business was split and the two brothers hardly spoke to each other. Elwyn's son joined his uncle! Eventually Elwyn came to own all of the egg and pullet quota and greatly expanded, and gradually passed the business to his daughter Pauline.

Winters in the 1980s were cold and lots of snow. Our house, known then as The Folly, had a circular driveway which we almost always cleared by hand, sometimes taking several shots at it before it was clear. Night time lows of -25C were not uncommon.

On one winter farm trip to Fred Bader's near Elmvale, it was blue sky and fine all the way to Stayner, then white-out to the farm which was between Wasaga Beach and Elmvale. I checked the farm, stayed for lunch, hoping it would clear. I set out again about 1.00, still snowing wildly, but ran out into blue sky south of Barrie for a clear run home. Many journeys were delayed or altered because of snow, although I became used to driving in less than perfect conditions. One of our Egg Board Seminars in Petrolia coincided with a big storm and only 4 producers made it.

Helping the farmers keep good records was a priority in the early days. The first formal method used the Texas Instruments TI59 programmable calculator, and a system developed by the extension staff at Cornell Univ. I did a deal with the local TI dealer and quite a lot of the more progressive producers adopted this system. I would demonstrate the system and deliver the machine at the same price we paid for it. Later, when reasonably priced

PCs became available, Cornell produced software using the same logic, and I helped many of the producers to set this up.

We also introduced a formal system of monitoring flocks, keeping records of body weights of a marked sample of hens, egg production, egg weight and feed consumption. This began in 1986 and we hired a co-op student from Guelph to introduce and promote the program. Once started, this practice spread and of course all of the larger, professional egg producers quickly adopted either our system or developed one of their own.

We hired another co-op student in 1987 to conduct a survey of egg shell quality, using the Gravity (SG) method. This was introduced to producers as a possible add-on to the monitoring program already in place. While the relationship between SG and level of cracks observed at the grading station was not strong, producers could use SG declines as an early warning system, and make nutritional adjustments if possible. Many producers used supplementary vit. D3 as a way of maintaining shell quality in older hens.

My main focus in the 1980's was egg quality. This was a big educational effort for the producers and for the small graders. Most of the large, professional producers had coolers and gathered eggs several times daily. The smaller, part-time units were more of a challenge. Many did not have coolers, gathered eggs once daily, and often only had them picked up by the grading station once weekly. Some of them had below average management and produced a lot of dirty eggs, especially those with floor operations and some of the older types of cage. If the eggs were washed, it was frequently not done according to our recommendations. The favoured method was to immerse the eggs in warm soapy water in a bucket that would then be mechanically agitated for a few minutes. While this may have removed some external soiling, it also allowed much of the dirt to enter the egg contents through the pores in the shell when they cooled.

The Egg Board office on Yonge Street was leased for ten years. As the termination date (January 1985) approached, the owner proposed a huge rent increase. When it was built, it was basically in the boondocks; now it was the middle of North York and so a much more desirable location. The Directors, led, I think, by Gerry Long, decided it might be desirable to own our own building, and so they began searching for a location. It boiled down to two places: Markham or Mississauga. I was grateful beyond words when they chose Mississauga, effectively cutting all the grief out of my commute, and reducing it to a predictable 50 minutes from anywhere between 1½ and 2 hours. When we first looked at the almost completed building, I was allocated an inside office with no window, and I protested! They eventually did some shuffling and I got a very nice office on an outside wall, which I occupied until my retirement in 2001. For the official opening of the new building at the end of October, we hosted local MP Jack Riddell, federal Minister of Agriculture, Eugene Whelan and the Mayor of Mississauga, Hazel McAllion.

When I first joined the Egg Board in 1980, it was in the days when everyone had a secretary, either his own or shared. I shared. I had a variety of different girls at first but in 1981, we hired Joy Fujino. Joy stayed with us for a number of years including the move to Mississauga. She married and eventually left to start a family. She was followed after a few false starts, by Eleanor Marshall, who carried on until we all learned to keyboard, and no longer had secretaries. While my work involved typing from dictaphone tapes and other clerical jobs, we also developed an information retrieval system once the office had a computer. This would today be a very simple process, but in the early days of office computers we had to have special software. I had seen a system when visiting the Cargill head office while I was still at Shaver. So I attempted to replicate this at the Egg Board. Basically, whenever I read anything I might later need to refer to, I highlighted the title and any key words (sometimes adding my own), and kept a hard copy. Eleanor then numbered each item sequentially and entered the title, key words etc. into what was essentially a searchable database. Google was not invented until about 10 years after this! Eleanor was also most helpful with some of my writing work – not the sideline work that I did at home, but speeches and other work involved with the Egg Board, especially the monthly newsletter *The Ovum*. When editing my Elsevier book, *Poultry Production*, most of the initial work was done by her. She also did the work on my Chapter in Mark Pattison's book, *The Health of Poultry*, a lot of it at home while recovering from a car accident. Interestingly, after Eleanor left the Board, she purchased a small egg farm and quota. I think she was advised to do this by Bruce MacMillan, a hatchery salesman, with whom she had a long term relationship. She didn't keep the farm long, but probably made a handsome profit when she sold it, also on Bruce's advice.

By late 1987, a few of our producers began to buy their own computers, and in general the market for home computers was starting. I got my first desktop, plus a dot-matrix printer, for about $2000 around this time after seeing one at one of our egg farmers. One of the lecturers at Ridgetown College, Randy Ross, was helpful in advising on both hardware and software

In August 1983 I again explored the possibility of getting back into genetics. Hybrid Turkeys, at that time owned and run by the Shantz family, were looking for a geneticist. I had several interviews, with brothers Ross and Milo Shantz and eventually decided to stay where I was. I sensed that

130

while I would be working for Ross, Milo, much the brighter of the two, would be calling the shots. Interestingly, the company was soon sold to Euribrid, which evolved into Hendrix Genetics, the ultimate owner of Shaver.

During the mid to late 1980's, the poultry industry was under constant threat from Avian Influenza (AI). I attended a very good 3 day Symposium on the subject in Athens, GA in September, 1986. At this time it was a notifiable disease which meant that outbreaks were reported and all birds in an infected flock were destroyed, and a large surrounding area placed in quarantine. Repeated outbreaks elsewhere made industry very conscious of the risks, and so the term "biosecurity" was coined and became of great importance. It involved great care on the part of the Egg Board field staff, who of course, drove from farm to farm counting hens, presenting a ready method of spreading not just AI but any other infectious disease. So in cooperation with Dr. Lloyd Weber, we developed an improved system for the field staff, including clean coveralls at every visit, carrying disinfectant for boots and/or paper overboots, gloves and bonnets. Many of the larger producers developed their own protocols for visitors, which Egg Board field staff also followed. Of course, I too had to observe all of these precautions. Generally as time progressed, I would try to avoid more than two farm calls each day.

Part of my job was to make sure producers understood these risks and challenges, and also how to minimize them on their own farms. I did this by speaking at meetings and writing often in our newsletters.

In 1999, a fairly large producer in Prince Edward County actually had a confirmed case of AI, and his flock was accordingly slaughtered. I helped him with the aftermath and he eventually received almost full compensation for his costs and loss of income.

In 1985, we looked briefly at the possibility of using high moisture corn in farm-mixed feed for layers. Many of our producers who grew corn ensiled it in the sealed Harvestore containers, mostly for feeding to ruminants, and the possibility of using this in layer feed was suggested. After a lot of talk, we provided some funding to one producer, but got nowhere and the project was abandoned. A few farmers actually did use high moisture corn to feed their layers, but it did not become widespread. Feed once mixed, could not be stored, so it involved mixing fresh feed every day, and few were able to do this.

The egg industry faced two separate crises during the 1980's. First was the Cholesterol affair, started in public by the infamous Time magazine cover showing two eggs and a strip of bacon making a very sad face. The accompanying text purported to show how consuming eggs would raise peoples' serum cholesterol and thus the risk of cardiovascular diseases. The eventual outcome is by now clear – eating an egg a day did more good than harm and had little to no effect on cholesterol levels in the vast majority of people. But achieving this took about ten years, and egg consumption was depressed in a major way for several years. At the Egg Board, we talked this down as much as we could but straightforward denial was not useful. Mainly as a result of sterling work by the American Egg Board and its Egg Nutrition Center initiative, sufficient research was sponsored to confirm that eggs were not only supremely nutritious, but also had no measurable effect on serum cholesterol levels. I think it was during or shortly after this crisis that I got my personalized car license plate IM4 EGGS, and I still have it.

The second crisis was the Salmonella scare. It had long been accepted that contamination of eggs with Salmonella serotypes harmful to human health was restricted to the shell surface. Efficient egg washing at grading stations was responsible for avoiding this threat. However, in the mid 1980's it was shown that one serotype, *Salmonella enteritidis*, could contaminate the egg contents. It was further shown that this contamination did not come only from the environment, but was sometimes transmitted from parent to offspring. This presented no human health problems as long as the egg was fully cooked, but of course some uses of eggs do not involve cooking, for example mayonnaise. This was made with raw eggs and frequently stored for significant periods, sometimes un-refridgerated. Other dishes such as custards and some puddings also used uncooked or under-cooked eggs and were similarly risky. How the *Salmonella enteritidis* reached the commercial egg industry was not clear; it may have been through breeding stock. Once identified, however, it quickly became a serious challenge for industry. While the contamination was by no means widespread, the publicity was everywhere. It was at one time estimated that the incidence of eggs with *Salmonella enteritidis* contamination was of the order of 1/1,000,000. However, if this one egg happened to be used without cooking, then improperly stored, human health was compromised. Industry quickly began to test commercial flocks for *Salmonella enteritidis*. The Egg Board developed a program in which any flock found to be contaminated was destroyed, and the owner compensated. All of the sampling was done by Egg Board field staff. I did some myself. The testing was done by Silliker Laboratories in Mississauga.

This program evolved into a full scale Hazard Analysis, Critical Control Points (HACCP) program that was operated by the Board for a number of years. We got a grant of $173,000 from Agriculture and Agrifood Canada to get going, and hired two Guelph co-op students, Barb Keith and Sigrid Boersma, in the summer of 1999 to start it off. They worked hard to recruit volunteers and soon had a good nucleus of cooperating farms. The program was at first, voluntary, but soon became compulsory.

Sigrid stands out as one of the best co-op students we ever hired. Bill Stevens spotted her and when she graduated, persuaded her to take a job with Cuddy Foods, for whom he acted as consultant. I kept in touch with Sigrid as she progressed with Cuddy, and I attended her wedding. She eventually moved to Nicholas Turkey Breeders in West Virginia, until family life beckoned and she left to raise children.

Before both Barb and Sigrid returned to University, we interviewed two recent Guelph graduates for a permanent position, and chose Pam Kuipers. Pam began work in August 1999, a few days before the two co-op students returned to University, so they were able to help her get started. She was quick to learn and a very hard worker, and we soon realized we had hired the right person. She began to arrange Producer meetings solely concerned with the HACCP program and they were well attended and appreciated. As the commitment expanded, Pam eventually needed assistance and we hired another Guelph graduate, Lorraine Stevenson. Lorraine only stayed a few years, but as of 2020, Pam was still working for the Egg Board (now called Egg Farmers of Ontario), but with somewhat different responsibilities, as the HACCP program was subsumed into a national program that also embraced bird welfare and was administered at the Federal level.

There were all kinds of provincial and federal meetings; a Salmonella Task Force was established to discuss how to deal with the problem. A lot of talk but the Egg Board was already taking concrete action. We shared our experience widely; at an International Egg Commission meeting in Toronto in late 1997, Bill Stevens and I informally met with 3 people from BC, one from Saskatchewan plus Walter Debicki from CEMA, to explain what we were doing. I also had a visit from Narine Singh, who worked for Alberta Agriculture, to discuss our program.

We involved the University of Guelph Food Safety Institute as auditors for the HACCP program. While expensive, this provided good evidence to consumers that Ontario eggs were as safe as they could be.

Another co-op student from Guelph, Brian Keunen, worked mainly on the Northern Fowl Mite (NFM), which was a constant challenge in these days. Many infestations were missed until they were quite serious and hard to control. Fortunately they do not live on the human body; otherwise many of us would have been permanently itching! The hiring of co-op students was ideal for us, a win-win situation. We paid the going rate, we got an enthusiastic individual who worked on a given project for three months, and he/she got to see the egg industry. Dana Waterfall joined us in January

1991, helping producers with records and flock monitoring. And in the fall semester, Ken Carson was with us and worked on advising producers about composting mortalities. In 1993, Steve Kells spent four months working on northern fowl mite research, using our producers' flocks and working with Gord Surgeoner at the University of Guelph.

One good thing to emerge from our battles with the NFM was that I was able to create a poster presentation on the subject for the Western Poultry Disease Conference, when it was held in Acapulco, Mexico.

In the late 1990's animal agriculture was beginning to hear about antibiotic resistance. This came from the medical profession, the challenge being the use in agriculture of antibiotics that were also used in human medicine. The egg industry was not really impacted in practice, as antibiotics were seldom used to treat laying hens. But they were almost universally used in meat chicken diets for their growth promotion effects. However, public concern would not make this distinction, so I attended a two day conference in Toronto to learn what was going on. The controversy continued for many years and eventually the meat chicken industry began to reduce antibiotic use. How much animal agriculture contributed to antibiotic resistance affecting humans is still, to me, an open question.

We also began to hear about differentiation in the egg market. Bruce Winkler, a sales representative, talked to me about free range eggs and Ralston Purina, then a feed supplier, was looking at nutritionally enhanced eggs. This was definitely a taste of things to come, as at the time, most stores just sold white eggs, large and extra large. In September 1997, I visited a Fortino's store in Burlington for a look at the retail business. They had by this time a significant "Natural Foods" section, and large brown eggs were selling for $3.29/doz. White eggs at the time time often sold for $0.99/doz and the origin of the brown eggs was unknown. Certainly the omega-3 enhanced eggs were genuinely "different" and could be shown so by laboratory analysis, but the other varieties like free range, barn, and other names, while attracting premium prices, would be indistinguishable on a nutritional basis. But while consumers bought them, and paid the extra, who could argue against it?

It was nice to visit producers in other provinces, and in October 1994 I was invited to the Alberta Poultry Servicemans Workshop (they renamed it later!) to give two talks. The meeting was held at Chateau Lake Louise, Nita came with me and we got a VIP room on the third floor overlooking the Lake! All the Western provinces were represented and it was an excellent event. We stayed for a couple of days after the meeting and did some walks and touring in the locality, including Morraine Lake. After leaving Lake Louise *en route* to Calgary, we stopped in Banff for most of the day. At this time Banff still had a "village" feel about it and was not crowded. We walked the streets and did the gondola ride to the top of Sulphur Mountain. When we re-visited in 2018, everything had changed: parking was almost impossible, the line ups for everything were endless and the place overrun by tourists.

In the early 1990's manure management was becoming an issue. While most of our producers were small compared with some of their US counterparts, there was room for improvement in manure utilization. In the US there were several Poultry Waste Management Symposia and I attended a couple of them. Later, producers were encouraged to create formal Nutrient Management Plans. This became essential in the early 2000's, after a serious outbreak of *E. Coli* in the water supply in Walkerton ON was traced to contamination with cattle manure. The fact that the outbreak was due to failure of the water treatment system did not diminish the political furor or the impact on animal agriculture. The silver lining was, of course, much improved utilization of a valuable resource, especially by many egg producers. I became involved with the technical side of the discussions with a variety of government departments.

We began to seriously encourage producers to work on nutrient management plans, both for their own benefit and to bolster efforts to limit government interference with their regular farming business. We had two very good Producer Seminars with Paul Patterson from Penn. State Univ. as guest speaker. Paul was a good friend and an expert in this field. We hired a co-op student the summer of 2001 who drew manure samples from a variety of layer systems with the object of providing baselines for producers' nutrient management plans. Because of my impending retirement, I would not be there for his whole period of employment, we liaised with Hugh Fraser, the nutrient management specialist for OMAFRA, who also had a summer student in the field, to coordinate their efforts.

Research Quota

An important issue I had to deal with was quota used for research, in contrast to regular commercial egg production. Clearly, a breeding and genetics operation like Shaver had a legitimate claim to be able to carry out breeding stock development, line multiplication etc. They had a large quota allotment that was usually expanded if requested, with few questions asked. But we had several other less obvious requests, from a variety of sources, for "field testing" of experimental crosses. Some of these were legitimate and permitted; others were not. My main criterion for advising the Board whether to accept or deny these applications was an acceptable experimental design, a clear system of records and a perceivable paper trail to a breeder's research department. An example of a denial was a house of about 10,000 hens, already in production when I was called to see it. There were four rows of cages with a different variety in each one. No replication and in fact no systematic records. This was shut down after one laying cycle, but of course the hatchery involved made a fine profit from that one flock.

A much better and successful request came from Bob McKay, formerly with Shaver but then working for Dekalb, in the late 1990s. The farm belonged to Scott Helps and was located in Wyoming in Western Ontario. This was testing a number of experimental crosses and involved a highly complex experimental design with full replication. Hard work for Scott, but excellent field data for the breeder. It was at one of my meetings with Bob to discuss this that he asked me if I had ever heard of Google. I hadn't!

There were in addition, several research farms owned by feed companies. These were legitimate and important for the commercial industry, in terms of keeping up to date with new feed formulations and ingredients. Shur Gain, later Maple Leaf Foods, was an excellent example of this with their farm in Burford.

Some of the Directors were at best, lukewarm about research quota, so in early 2000, they requested a meeting of all the holders. This elicited high level response; Jim Arthur came from Des Moines IA to represent Hy-Line, Bob McKay from Illinois for Dekalb, George Ansah from Ithaca NY for Babcock, plus representatives from Shaver and Shur Gain. They all told the Directors how important research was, and I didn't have to say a word! Some of the Directors were still skeptical, and this must have been coming from the producers, because they passed a rather stupid resolution at the subsequent AGM to limit research quota. Fortunately these resolutions were not binding.

When the major consolidations took place in the breeding sector, the new owners of Shaver, Hendrix Genetics, wanted to concentrate their white-egg layer research at the Cambridge farms, and this involved a significant increase in their quota. The Board's Quota Manager and I spent some time touring the facilities and the additional quota was granted. This was good, not only for Hendrix, but also the community of Cambridge, as it led to sustained employment of staff at the farms and the hatchery, which by then was supplying breeding stock to most of the Americas. The impact on the commercial egg supply was minimal, since as many eggs as possible would be used for incubation.

General Egg Board Business

Both Brian and I would regularly attend the annual "Southeastern" poultry show in Atlanta. (this show. had several different names over the years but everyone in N. America knows it as "Southeastern" or "Atlanta"). I sometimes went to Southern Poultry Science, a scientific meeting that took place a couple of days before the show. These were useful trips to keep up with new trends in equipment and supplies to the industry, but also for meeting old friends. I would regularly spend time with David Martin, then Editor of Poultry International, for which I was a regular freelance writer. In 1992, I met Philip Lee, one of my cohort at Wye in 1958-60. The show attracted visitors from all over the world and was a great social occasion. In the 1990's, the hospitality was lavish and most evenings one could eat and drink adequately without going to a restaurant! I think this diminished over the years – probably a good thing!

In June 1995, I attended a meeting in Guelph on Electronic Communication; for the first time in my life, I surfed the internet. In my diary, I wrote: "Not a great experience, but I can see the potential"!

In early January 1996, the Egg Board received a recommendation from a management consultant that my position as Poultry Specialist be terminated. Fortunately for me, the Directors did not agree, and I continued my work as before. Some of the Directors were also gunning for Brian, so we quite often talked privately together. I never knew who was after his blood, bur I think I knew who wanted mine.

With our various international connections, Brian and I received more than our share of foreign visitors. Many were interested in Supply Management, and by the mid '90s, Canada was probably the only country in which it was still in place. In June, 1996, we had a visit from Joe and Carmen Vella, who produced and marketed eggs in New South Wales, Australia. Supply Management had recently been dismantled there, so it was interesting to meet them and hear what had happened. They stayed at the Holiday Inn in Cambridge and I showed them around and spent quite bit of time with them, and we had them home for dinner. Although I did not know it then, our hospitality was repaid many times over when Nita and I visited Australia in 1997.

The Egg Board was ever mindful of the vulnerability of supply management. Many media people, and quite a few academics condemned the system as favouring farmers over consumers. They pointed to higher prices and lack of competition.   While there was some truth to these statements, they ignored the fact that if the system was abandoned, Canadian producers could again be faced (as they had been in the 1960's) with predatory US imports from sometimes subsidized farms (in the case of dairy) and dumping of other products in times of surplus production, which were frequent. Both the Provincial and Federal agencies made certain that the elected politicians were kept informed and on side. The Egg Board ran an annual Egg Producers' Breakfast at Queens Park (seat of the Ontario Legislature), where we prepared and served a good egg breakfast to our politicians. I attended this once and found it excellent pubic relations. The Federal agency ran a similar event in Ottawa. The fact that the system was still in place in 2021 is evidence that these strategies paid off handsomely.

Most of the producers were, naturally, in favour of the system, but one, whom Brian and I visited in 1998 to sample his barns for Salmonella (there had been a previous positive test) regaled us with his plans for 5 million hens, "when the system is gone"!

By the late 1990's the poultry interest at the University of Guelph was in serious decline. Most of the "old guard" had retired. Steve Leeson and a small number of others at the Department of Animal and Poultry Science were still active, but several spaces existed where retirees were not replaced. The Egg Board and the Poultry Industry Centre were particularly concerned. Brian still had good contacts at the University and at The Ontario Ministry of Agriculture and Rural Affairs (OMAFRA) and eventually, a Memorandum of Understanding regarding financing by industry was signed. The signature was celebrated with lunch at Guelph's Cutten Club, with Brian, myself, Bill Stevens, Deborah Whale, Ann Gibbins (then Chair of the Department of Animal and Poultry Science), and David Hume (CEO for the contract between Guelph and OMAFRA). Several positions were secured, but at great cost. When Steve Leeson retired, his position as non-ruminant nutritionist had to be bridged and eventually, following an endowment of $1 million from Jim and Brenda MacIntosh (both Guelph graduates and long-time egg producers), the post was secured. The scale of poultry teaching and research at the University never approached what it was when I first arrived in Canada, but it did not completely vanish. The study of Animal Welfare and related sciences dominated the field. Meanwhile poultry research and teaching expanded in other provinces, especially Alberta and Saskatchewan, so there was, on a national basis, no shortage of resources.

I kept detailed records of all farm calls, especially how to get there. These were the days before everyone had a GPS and some of the farms were quite hard to find. Subsequently, in the 2000s, all farm locations have been entered into a database to facilitate rapid response to any disease outbreak requiring quarantine. Sometimes I helped by taking mortality samples to either private veterinarians or the several government labs around the province. The same with feed and water samples. Although some of the other service people carried out on-farm *post-mortem* examinations, I never did, believing that since I was not a veterinarian, I had no business doing so and would prejudice my relations with the professionals. In general, I think this was a wise decision; I enjoyed good relations with all the private vets and also those in the government labs.

For my work with the Egg Board, it was important for me to liaise with OMAF vet labs. These were originally located at Guelph, Centralia, Kemptville. Ridgetown and Brighton. (Since the time I worked with these laboratories, most of them have closed). Drs Josephson, Sanford, Doug Galt and Fred Harden were very useful and friendly contacts. Dick Julian and Art Ferguson at the Ontario Veterinary College were valuable resources, and both were extremely skilled at post-mortem examination and interpretation. The Poultry Science Department (later Animal and Poultry Science) had an extension department, but its importance was much diminished. Nevertheless, Earl Hunt, Bert Reinhart and Hank Orr were still around and available if needed. OMAFRA also had two agricultural engineers on staff, Harry Huffman and Ron MacDonald. They were both helpful in designing and evaluating new and existing buildings and equipment. Ron later left to start his own private engineering practice and worked with the Egg Board in various capacities until and after I left. He was a great asset as well as a fun person to work with.

By late 1999, Brian was asking me about retirement and also talking about his own. He was two years older than me so could retire any time, but basically couldn't make up his mind. I said I would retire at 65. Brian told the Directors he would go some time in the next few years. Meanwhile, they would hire an "assistant" who would ultimately replace him. The man they hired was Harry Pelissero. Harry's father was one of the original quota holders from 1973, and the family farm was now run by Harry's brother, Roger. Harry had a varied career including a term as a member of the Provincial Legislature, so he had lots of political smarts. He eventually manoeuvred the Board into pushing Brian out well before he wanted. But he had a good run all the same – more than 30 years!

At the Board's Annual Meeting in March 2001, they recognized my 20 years of service (it was actually 21), and Brian Ellsworth's 30. They presented me with a cheque for $2,000, which was a pleasant surprise.

I presented a modified version of "100 Years of Poultry Genetics" at this meeting.

As my retirement approached, and it was obvious that I would not be replaced, we began to support Poultry Update meetings sponsored by OMAFRA. These would replace the Producer Seminars I had previously arranged.

I worked full time for the Egg Board until my official retirement at the end of June, 2001. We had a formal farewell dinner at one of the better restaurants, and a staff lunch at the office. The Board presented me with a new hand-held computer, which I much appreciated – better by far than the traditional gold watch! I never had a formal job description, but of course my prime responsibility was to the producers. I was always "on call" and endeavoured to respond whenever called upon. I always said I was supposed to know everything there was to know about hens and eggs, or where to find it if I didn't know.

The Ontario Poultry Council, Poultry Industry Council
The Ontario Poultry Council (OPC) was a long-established trade organization representing the entire industry, but mainly funded by feed companies, hatcheries, and other suppliers to the egg, broiler and turkey producers. It had an elected Board and when I joined the Egg Board in 1980, was run by Dr. David Mitchell from his home office in Mississauga.

The OPC ran two major activities: one was the London Poultry Show (Poultry Industry Conference and Exhibition or PICE). This was Canada's Poultry Show and administered by the Western Fair Association in London, Ontario. The OPC shared the revenue from exhibitor fees and patron entry charges. However, most of the leg work was done by employees of the Western Fair. OPC worked on the speaking program, which was never particularly popular; most people just wanted to see the show and meet their friends.

By the year 2000, the PICE was very firmly established as Canada's showcase for all things poultry. The poultry health company Intervet ran a full day conference the day prior to the show opening. The Egg Board held its monthly Directors' meeting there too. The morning the show opened, Cuddy Foods held a breakfast. This year they celebrated 50 years in business and Bill Stevens, their major scientific consultant, gave the keynote speech. Shaver ran a lunch the first day for its customers and anyone else who cared to go, and the Turkey Board subsidized a lunch as well. On the second day, The magazine Canada Poultryman gave an Exhibitor's Breakfast and the Egg Board provided a subsidized lunch. Both of these, of course, featured as many of our products as we could reasonably use. Like most shows of this kind, the first day was always crowded and busy; the second day less so, but this gave a chance for people like me to cruise the exhibits and meet friends.

OPC's second initiative was the Ontario Poultry Health Conference. Modeled after the eponymous New Hampshire event, this was held annually. I worked on the planning committee for many years and gave presentations most times; unfortunately I kept no record of my subjects. When I first began attending, the meeting was held at the old Skyline Hotel in Toronto, with a satellite meeting in Trenton the following day. More than 300 people regularly showed up for the Toronto event. Later, it was moved to Bingemans in Kitchener. The subject of Health was interpreted very broadly and almost any aspect of management could be covered. For the 1986 meetings, we invited Gerry Havenstein, a geneticist and formerly head of research for breeder H&N, but now Chair of the Department of Poultry Science at NC State University at Raleigh. Gerald was the keynote Speaker. Subsequent to my involvement, the Health Conference became known as the Poultry Innovation Conference and the location moved again. By this time, the Ontario Poultry Council had been subsumed into the Poultry Industry Council, which still organized this and other events.

In September, 1990, the Kay House, and old stone dwelling near Arkell, south of Guelph belonging to the Ontario Ministry of Agriculture and Rural Affairs, was opened. It was the office of the newly appointed Poultry Specialist, Dianne Spratt. It had a large Board room and a selection of offices and was intended for the use of the whole poultry sector. The OPC moved there but David Mitchell declined to do so.

The Ontario Poultry Council also created an Award of Merit, and in 1992 it was awarded to Tom Graham.. Tom had always been a big supporter of my position and also a good friend, so I was delighted to be asked to make the presentation. I met the whole family prior to the event, and along with a resumé that Tom already had, was able to prepare a really effective citation. Tom died suddenly in late 1997. I wrote at the time that he "died with his boots on"; he was still active but succession was not a problem, as Scott and several other family members were well able to take on the business. The celebration of Tom's life was a big affair with lots of his Egg Board colleagues, friends and family taking part.

I received the Award of Merit in 2000, a few weeks prior to the Worlds Poultry Congress. Bill Stevens made the presentation. Both Nita and PJ were there for this event.

The Poultry Industry Centre (PIC) was established in 1990 and was also based at the Kay House. It worked in parallel with the Ontario Poultry Council but its mandate was much wider, embracing research, education and industry promotion. It planned for a paid Executive Director and a Board representing all of industry plus government, university, etc. It had commitments from a variety of sources for funding adequate to meet its new responsibilities. Although located in Ontario, it was expected to have a national outlook. The Egg Board was a primary funder of the PIC and had two representatives on its Board. I was there to address technical matters and an Egg Board Director dealt with politics. I became Chair of the PIC Research Committee in 1991.

There was a long and tangled series of negotiations in 1991 regarding the position of Executive Director of the OPC after it moved to the Kay House. I was touted for the position but there was insufficient funding. They had to at least equal my Egg Board salary plus benefits, and this proved challenging. In early 1992, the committee decided to appoint Ellen Olechowski from Ridgetown College to the position. Ellen worked hard and began the process of fundraising, something I would not have been good at. This worked well until September, 1993, when several of the supporting companies withdrew their support, and we had to reduce the Executive Director position to part time. This was not acceptable to Ellen, so in the end, the Egg Board agreed to my spending one day a week at the OPC as its interim CEO until a permanent position could be adequately funded. I usually worked a full day and sometimes called in to the Kay House on the way home from the Egg Board office.

It was obvious to anyone who looked carefully that OPC and PIC had so much in common that they should merge. But there were some strong personalities in play that made this difficult. John Hoover became the Chair of PIC, while Tom Fleming was Chair of OPC. John Hoover's family had owned Curtis Chicks for many years but it was now owned by a broiler integrator, Maple Lodge Farms. So John had lots of time to spend with the PIC. Tom Fleming was the son of Art Fleming, founder of Fleming Hatchery, located in the Niagara region but selling broiler chicks province-wide. I worked with both of them, but was very wary of John, whom I did not completely trust. Tom, on the other hand, was good to work with, so my loyalties definitely lay with him. The two organizations continued talking merger, and eventually accomplished it in July1997. The new organization was called the Poultry Industry Council. They were able to hire a full-time Executive Director, so my days working at the Kay House came to an end. But I did have a say in the hiring of the new person. It was widely advertised and attracted a deluge of applications. The selection committee was Deborah Whale, one of PIC's Directors, Roger Bennett, General Manager of the Ontario Broiler Hatching Egg and Chick Commission, and me. We reduced the field to five, whom we interviewed, and eventually offered the position to Alan Bentley. Alan worked for AAFC in Ottawa, and was also Secretary of WPC2000 Inc. I think his seniority at AAFC and the few benefits we could provide, led to him turning down the offer. Also, his wife, Betty did not want to leave Ottawa. I never could understand anyone wanting to live there who didn't have to: dreadful long, cold winters. There is no doubt Alan would have done a good job.

After more committee discussion, the job was offered to another candidate, but due to the delay he had already taken a job elsewhere. Finally, we hired David Nodwell, who started work in June 1998.

David did a good job as administrator but needed direction. When he was hired, Maurice Smith, a veterinarian who variously worked independently and for a large drug company, was the Chair of PIC. Maurice was a procrastinator; decisions came only with difficulty. At the first Directors meeting after David's appointment, Deborah Whale was elected Chair; she was the exact opposite. Highly opinionated, "my way or the highway" was her motto, but this was good for the times and circumstances. I occasionally locked horns with her, and always lost, but she did a fine job for the PIC, spending a great deal of time at the office in addition to working from home, which was a family run broiler farm.

Early in 1999, PIC received a visit from Prof. Roger Buckland (Macdonald College of McGill University) to discuss its potential as a national coordinator/focus for poultry research, education and technology transfer. Of course, this was PIC's ambition, but how far and at what speed it could be achieved was the question. I have mentioned previously my feeling that with these activities spread so thinly across the country, there would inevitably be overlap, missed opportunities, and a lack of cohesion.

Some of the other commodity Boards eventually established research funding and in several cases, delegated PIC to administer their programs, and after I left the Egg Board, I think it did the same. So in the fullness of time, the PIC became a significant source of industry funding for poultry research across the country. Their grants never covered the entire cost of most projects, but relied on the researchers to secure matching funds from other sources.

In July 1999, PIC's Research Committee, now led by egg producer Ed McKinlay, reviewed 6 research projects with total budgets of $1.7 million, while the PIC's budget was $470,000. But this was the kind of leverage that we expected; if the projects were to proceed, they would need a lot of matching funds. The budget in 2000 was approximately the same. Some of the awards were in the form of graduate student awards, and these were anonymous. We discovered in 2000 that one of them went to the son of PIC's Chair, Deborah Whale! I subsequently resigned from the committee.

Although the PIC had the ambition to become national in scope, a variety of people across the country (including the Canada Branch of the World's Poultry Science Association) felt that a truly national organization was needed, and so the Canadian Poultry Research Council (CPRC) was created. It formally began operations in 2001 and I was its first Chair.

Since most of the activities of CPRC took place after I retired, they are described in Chapter 8.

Egg Board Research Funding

The Board in the early 1980s began to provide funding for research. A Research Committee was established that met monthly prior to the Board meetings. Finding suitable projects and working with the scientists occupied an increasing amount of my time. Initially, we funded research primarily at the University of Guelph. John Summers and Steve Leeson (in the Department of Poultry Science, later, Animal and Poultry Science) were active in the field of layer nutrition and this had immediate application among feed suppliers. We also funded work at the Ontario Veterinary College and occasionally in other departments. Later, when the word got around, we extended our reach to most parts of Canada. I regularly visited the Agriculture Canada Research Station in Ottawa, overseen by Rob Gowe, but in addition to genetics, embracing a very active poultry nutrition department with Ian Sibbald as the leader. Lloyd Spencer at the Animal Diseases Research Institute was another valuable contact. These Government departments were not allowed to receive external funding but it was important for me to maintain contact. This worked in two directions; I was able to get first hand information that might be of use to our producers, and I may have had some minor influence on the direction that new research might follow.

In the late 1980s I was approached by Dr. Jeong Sim, at the University of Alberta, to partly fund a study on enhancing hen's eggs with omega-3 fatty acids, by feeding flax seed. None of us at the Egg Board knew Sim, so I made the trip to Edmonton to meet with him. This was in the days when most eggs were sold as an undifferentiated commodity. You could get different sizes, and maybe a premium pack, but choice was very limited. Sim had a good study planned, having done some preliminary trials, and was optimistic as to the potential, so I reported positively to the Board and they agreed to fund the study as requested. A few weeks later, Steve Leeson phoned me from Guelph, asking if we would fund an almost identical study there. Having already agreed to the Alberta work, we declined, but he got the funding elsewhere and proceeded with the study. Both experiments were successful; results were published in Poultry Science a few months apart, and both obtained similar results. This work was quickly applied and most of the local grading stations began marketing omega-3 enhanced eggs. Sim established his own brand in Alberta, called Dr. Sim's Designer Eggs, and they did well for a few years. He tried and failed to get the same thing going in Ontario. So did Paul Born, who's brother Frank marketed "Born 3" eggs in BC, and for a short time in Ontario.

Sim also established an International Egg Symposium that took place in Alberta every four years until soon after his retirement. The first, in April, 1992, was held at the Banff Springs Hotel. I traveled there with Geoff and Marcela Fairhurst, in Canada on a visit. I chaired the session at which Geoff spoke, on the subject "The Egg Industry in 2000". This series of meetings led to a number of initiatives in terms of enhancing the nutritional profile of eggs, and, of equal importance, the extraction and utilization of various components that were valuable in the pharmaceutical industry. It soon became apparent that they could not afford the Banff Springs and so the meeting retreated to the Banff Centre. To me, it made little difference: just being in the mountains was a bonus.

One of the important observations I made on farm calls was the variation in the incidence of cracked eggs. The cracked egg was bad news at every phase of the production, processing and marketing system. In the early days, when many eggs were gathered by hand, big differences could be observed between different people in their ability to handle the eggs without breaking them. Mechanical systems also varied in the number of cracks resulting from their use. We were able to track sources of breakage using an electromechanical egg, invented and sold in the UK. This egg was placed on the egg collection belt and if it was subjected to the type of impact likely to crack an egg, it would light up to identify the potential problem.

There was also variation among the lots of eggs themselves, caused by genetics, nutrition, age of flock, etc. The egg shell is composed of about 95% Calcium Carbonate ($CaCO_3$), so providing this in the diet would be the first priority. But nutritionists already knew that $CaCO_3$,when digested in the hen's gut, was broken down into its individual components, and then re-synthesized to form the egg shell. Some quite classic work conducted in the 1980s by Dr. Milton Scott and his associates at Cornell University showed that not only the amount, but also the physical form of $CaCO_3$ would strongly influence the quality of the egg shell. The secret was particle size; Scott compared ground limestone (the standard product used to provide $CaCO_3$ in layer diets) with oyster shells, chemically identical but with much larger particle size. The oyster shell diets produced much superior egg shells. The explanation was that the larger particles were held for much longer in the hen's digestive system, and were still being digested during the night when, incidentally, most of egg shell formation took place. It was also noted that hens would seek out large Calcium particles late in the day, to be available at the time of shell formation. So it was important for feed suppliers to find a way to include large particles of $CaCO_3$ for at least half of the total amount.

My experience at Shaver had shown me the potential of genetics to enhance shell quality, and probably by the time I started observing the performance of different breeds in the field, all of the breeders would have been paying some attention to it. There may have been small differences between the commercial hybrids used in Ontario at the time, but I believed they were minor.

But remarkably little was known about the fine structure of the shell, and how it affected shell strength. My interest in this grew as I worked at the Egg Board, and I was able to persuade the Board to begin funding some of the basic research in a small way. One summer, we had a request from Dr. Max Hincke at the University of Ottawa to fund a part time technician to study some aspect of egg shell structure. Hincke worked in the Medical School and his primary interest, prior to this, had been in bones. I am not quite sure how he came to be working with egg shells but research on egg shell structure has greatly benefited from his decision to do so, and as of 2021, he is still deeply involved.

At the University of Glasgow in Scotland, Dr. Sally Solomon was studying the fine structure of egg shells using an electron microscope. She was not the first to do this; Piet Simons (of whom much more later) had undertaken such a study for his Ph.D. and published an excellent monograph, about ten years prior, but with less sophisticated equipment. I talked to Dr. Solomon at a meeting and she asked if we would fund some of her work, and eventually, we provided some money, matched with much more from other sources. Subsequently, she, and her graduate student and eventual successor, Maureen Bain, visited us in Canada and spoke at one of the Board's Semi-Annual Meetings.

A year or two later, I attended the WPSA European Federation Egg Quality Symposium in Tours, France. Both Max Hincke and Sally Solomon were there, along with Yves Nys, a French scientist also working in the field of egg shell physiology. All three spoke to me privately about the Egg Board funding more of their research. After thinking about this, it occurred to me that we might get more bang for our buck if the three of them presented a joint request, with each contributing his/her own expertise to a single project. I was thrilled to receive such a proposal a few months later. In the end, the three labs levered the funding to the point that the total project was worth $180,000, of which the Egg Board paid $15,000. This led to continuing collaboration between the three laboratories, and several years of modest funding from the Egg Board. Many subsequent publications included the names of at least two and sometimes all three of these highly competent scientists. After about 10 years of his work on egg shells, Max Hincke gave a very good talk on his activities to the Annual Meeting of the Egg Board in 2002.

In 2005, at the European Federation Symposium on Quality of Eggs and Egg Products, I gave a presentation entitled "Forty Years of Egg Shell Research" which included a review of some of these joint efforts, along with other work in the field.

The research work and the nutritional studies had direct application to producers' activities and was easy to justify. As time went on, our research support became less and less related to producer profitability and thus, harder to sell to a skeptical Board of Directors.

In the late 1980s and the 1990s, molecular genetics was evolving rapidly. Traditional population genetics was still the basis of commercial breeders' stock improvement, and they were only marginally interested in molecular genetics. In any event, producers were not too keen on supporting research that primarily benefited their suppliers. Nevertheless, the Egg Board was persuaded that there were long term benefits, and so became significant supporters of studies in molecular genetics at Guelph. Professors Ann Gibbins and Rob Etches were the chief recipients of this support. Their studies and those of their graduate students undoubtedly advanced the science, but with little or no direct impact on producers. Etches eventually left Guelph to enter the private sector with a genetics company in California, where he stayed for a number of years before leaving to start his own company. When he eventually sold it for several million dollars, he admitted to me that the Egg Board funding, while gratefully accepted, never yielded anything of direct benefit to the egg industry.

In early 1988, we were made aware of a proposal by Dr. Joe Tedesco who was testing ways of removing cholesterol from egg yolk products. I think we put up $100,000 to start with; the project continued for several years but was not ultimately successful.

While poultry nutrition, physiology and other disciplines continued to be actively taught and researched, they were joined in the 1980s by poultry behaviour and welfare. Frank Hurnik came to Guelph in the 1970s and later, Ian Duncan, whom I had known in passing at the Poultry Research Centre in Edinburgh. In the late 1970s, I helped Frank Hurnik by acting as an advisor to one of his graduate students, Patricia Ross, who studied the potential for using water restriction instead of feed restriction to limit the growth of broiler breeders.

In December, 1985, the Egg Board provided $1 million endowment for a Research Chair at the University of Guelph, which ended up in the Department of Food Science. After many false starts and interviews, the first scientist to hold the Chair, Les Ferrier, was appointed in June, 1987.

But for some reason, this did not work out, and the Chair was not filled again until the mid 1990s, when Yoshinore Mine, an egg scientist from Japan, was appointed.

Once a vibrant and exciting centre of poultry knowledge and expertise, this part of the University of Guelph declined during the 1990's and early 2000's. As faculty retired, they were not replaced. Industry funds were used to "bridge" faculty positions so that if someone retired, a replacement was possible.

When we funded Dr. Sim's work on omega-3 fatty acid enhancement of shell eggs, the University of Alberta was just beginning its progress in the poultry research field. This was immeasurably accelerated by the presence of Dr. Frank Robinson. Frank's enthusiasm in both teaching and research soon had Alberta rivaling Guelph as a centre for poultry science. He encouraged very good research and introduced an experiential teaching program that at the time was quite revolutionary. Students would be assigned a research project, and then have to find out for themselves how to feed, manage and generally conduct the necessary experiment. A report was required in the format of a paper to be submitted to the journal *Poultry Science*. Many of the graduates from this program went on to become respected players in both research and industry.

The University of Saskatchewan was also involved in poultry research and teaching in a significant way, led by nutritionist Prof. Hank Classen. Geneticist Roy Crawford spent most of his career there, and more recently, Karen Schwean-Lardner has developed a major teaching and research presence in the area of poultry management and welfare.

Industry and Government committees
It was clear that I would be the "science and technology" representative for the Egg Board on any committees that needed one. The political committees would be attended by Board members or other Board staff as appropriate. Sometimes there would be two of us, as on the Ontario Poultry Council, but I would deal with technical and scientific issues. The Poultry Council (OPC), and later its successor the Poultry Industry Centre (PIC) took up a considerable amount of my time.

The Ontario government had an Animal Research and Services Committee, which I attended starting in 1986. It's amazing how many of these "useful" committees existed, that are now long gone and not missed at all. This one also included a very nice dinner in the Whippletree restaurant (also, lamentably, long gone) in the University of Guelph administration building.

In 1986 I joined the Agriculture and AgriFood Canada Expert Committee on Animal Breeding and Reproduction. This Committee met annually, usually at a University Campus. The first meeting I attended was in Saskatoon. The day prior, some committee members had a tour of the Veterinary and Infectious Diseases Organization (subsequently renamed Vaccine and Infectious Diseases Organization). This was an ambitious and, as it turned out, hugely successful initiative, being an independent adjunct to the Western College of Veterinary Medicine. It had no teaching function, but did excellent research and had, from the start, a lively poultry interest.

The Expert Committee meetings were interesting, being mainly involved with guiding the work at the Ottawa Animal Research Institute. There was also a long discussion led by Roy Crawford, from the University of Saskatchewan, on his proposal to edit a new book on poultry breeding and genetics. At the time, there had been no book on this subject published since F. B. Hutt's classic *Genetics of the Fowl,* published in 1949. (See Chapter 9 for my contribution to Crawford's book)

The 1987 meeting of the Expert Committee was held in London ON. By this time it was becoming clear to me and most of the Committee that while our deliberations and discussions always resulted in fine recommendations, these were almost universally ignored, or occasionally contradicted, by Government! Of course, this was almost entirely due to the fact that our recommendations involved spending money, while government was looking for ways to save it. I continued to attend this committee until it was disbanded some time in the 1990s.

I also attended, on the Egg Board's behalf, a Poultry Research Program Review, organized by the Federal Government in 1986. The review tended to be a bit self-serving but the government liked this kind of thing, so it was done. This meeting coincided with Rob Gowe's retirement as head of the Animal Research Institute. There was an official presentation at the Central Experimental Farm, and then a private dinner at the Gowes' with several of the VIPs including Gordon Dickerson and Bob Shoffner, both Americans, and Pierre Mongin from France. I attended this along with Jan and Eva Gavora. Following his retirement, Rob worked at Shaver for a while, but this ended with the ISA takeover.

All kinds of committees were struck during and after the Salmonella scare, including the Canadian Food Safety Council for Poultry. This was primarily a federal government initiative, and was only started long after the Ontario Egg Board, CEMA and most of the other provinces had established protocols for *Salmonella enteritidis* testing and responses to positive results. However, the Council had a wider remit and would become useful in the event that other pathogens emerged. I don't know how long the Council survived, but I was Chair for its first Annual Meeting in May 1998, and its second in 1999, after which Arnold Read from CEMA took over.

I also attended, along with several other Canadians, mostly from Quebec, a very good Salmonella Conference in Baltimore, MD in July, 1998. This meeting helped us to stay abreast of current thinking and technical developments.

One very important function I became involved with was the preparation of welfare codes of practice. Public concern for animal welfare, especially intensively managed poultry, began in the late 1980s and progressively intensified. Initially, only a small, vocal minority of the public was involved, but the public at large became increasingly aware, largely due to the activity of the original minority. At first we consulted with animal behaviour people at the Universities, Frank Hurnik, Ian Duncan and others. They were more or less sympathetic to industry but made sure we knew that we could not continue indefinitely without some respect being paid to the opinions of the humane societies and other purveyors of public opinion. Frank was good enough to have me give a lecture as part of his course on animal welfare.

In September 1987, we began working with the Canadian Federation of Humane Societies to develop a Code of Practice for the Management of Laying Hens. The first version of this document, basically enshrined existing practices, but with some limitations on space allowances and a few other details. Many of the recommendations were in the realm of common sense. At this time, I was the Egg Board's authority on animal welfare, and even did a phone-in radio show on the CBC Winnipeg radio station.

Future versions of the Welfare Codes, most of which I was involved with until my retirement in 2001, became ever more restrictive. Space allowances were greatly increased for both layers and meat chickens. In general, industry people could work with those in the community and Universities who were genuinely concerned with animal welfare. After all, farmers who kept poultry for their livelihood had their birds' welfare at heart. When we came to members of the public proclaiming animal rights, industry had a much harder time finding common ground. Subsequently, in the 21st century, many countries have banned cages outright, or required so-called "furnished cages". Canada expects to phase out cages some time in the 2020's. This of course led to all kinds of (for both farmers and the public) unintended consequences. Diseases that did not occur in caged flocks reappeared; behavioural activities like feather pecking emerged, and ironically, the practice of beak trimming, which could mitigate the effects of feather pecking, was also discouraged or prohibited on welfare grounds.

All the committees on which I represented the Egg Board had their place and the potential for benefits to the producers. But I found that a lot of time was spent on internal discussions – who does what? The actual impact on industry was, in many cases, slight. At the time the Canadian Food Safety Council for Poultry was established, the Egg Board was just about ready to launch its HACCP program, which we had developed independently of CEMA and all the committees! This was a good case of action, not words.

I represented the Egg Board and/or the Poultry Industry at many scientific or technical meetings across Canada and occasionally elsewhere. These included the Canadian Society of Animal Science (where poultry was definitely a tiny minority and myself, a curiosity), the Midwest Poultry Convention in Minneapolis, both the Canadian and Ontario Hatchery organizations, and many others. Outside Canada, I mostly tried to explain how our supply management system worked. Some were curious; most Americans were justifiably dismissive, except when producer prices were low during their frequent boom/bust cycles. I reduced my talk of genetics as the science rapidly overtook me, but was able to talk intelligently about other areas, especially egg shell structure and quality. I scanned several Journals to which the Egg Board subscribed, and used information from them for composing lectures and newsletter articles, as well as passing it directly to producers on farm calls.

I attended most meetings of the Canada Branch of the Worlds Poultry Science Association (see Chapter 10) and also World's Poultry Congresses that took place every four years. Although these were quite costly, all being held overseas, they were useful in terms of new information and networking with international scientists. It was an unwritten agreement that I would work with WPSA while Brian, the CEO, worked with the International Egg Commission. Brian was a very enthusiastic member of IEC and served a term as its President. This was a good arrangement for both of us in terms of international travel. The IEC was very marketing- and economics-oriented, while WPSA was, of course, concerned with science and technology.

In 1984, the Poultry Science Association Annual Meeting was hosted by the University of Guelph, and I helped with the administration as well as attending the scientific sessions. Both Nita and I led tours on the Wednesday, visiting wineries on the Niagara Peninsula and culminating at the traditional barbecue, held in the park at the Brock Monument in Queenston, near Niagara Falls.

This was followed immediately by the World's Poultry Congress in Helsinki, Finland. This was a good meeting and some nice tourist outings too. Lots of Canadians attended including Rob Gowe, Jan Gavora, and a contingent from Guelph. One of the tours on the water was quite reminiscent of Canadian scenery. Even though it was salt water, the islands and landscape might have been Georgian Bay. We also had a splendid reception at the Canadian Ambassador's residence, the only time I can remember this at a World's Congress.

I was invited to attend meetings of the Ontario Academy of Avian Medicine. Contrary to their reputation in some other species, poultry vets were pretty broad minded and sought out involvement of people in associated fields. So going to these meetings was, I think, mutually beneficial.

Poultry meetings were held across Canada. I've mentioned the Alberta Service Workshop where I spoke in 1994. In February, 1995 I gave a talk at the Atlantic Poultry Conference in New Brunswick (it moved around the Atlantic Provinces) on the subject, "The Information Highway". Reading this today shocks me; it sounds like the blind leading the blind. But I suppose we were at the beginning of the internet age and with my information system and the newly available online capabilities, I was perhaps a few months ahead of at least some of the audience.

One of my earlier gripes about Canada's poultry science community was that I always felt it was too strung out across the country. By the time I retired, I had come to realize that this was not going to change, and we were just a strung out country. The fact remained that our national poultry science effort may have been less than that of, for example North Carolina State University at Raleigh, or the University of Georgia at Athens.

Chapter 8

My Consulting Career

Shaver Poultry Breeding Farms

I had a consulting arrangement with Shaver from the first day I worked for the Egg Board. They paid me a small quarterly stipend, for which they received tremendous value! I don't recall the level of the stipend, but it remained the same for many years. When Geoff Fairhurst came to manage the place after it was purchased by ISA, he raised the payment significantly. I did some selection work on a few of the egg lines, and continued to edit *Shaver Focus*, which was published four times annually. In addition, I attended all of their consultant meetings, which took place two or three times each year, always on weekends. I assisted with the composition of the various layer management guides. I still had a mailbox in the office and probably visited at least twice a week. An additional bonus was I was entitled to staff eggs: 2½ doz/week and this continued until I ceased to be a consultant at the end of 2014.

DMcQ retired in 1985: Cargill had at the time a strict policy that everyone, regardless of their position in the Company, retired at age 65. The Company sponsored a Symposium in recognition of his leadership at the Royal York Hotel in Toronto and I gave a talk about Supply Management. Many Shaver customers and staff were there for this "farewell" occasion. DMcQ gave an outstanding address following lunch and the meeting concluded with a fabulous Canadian Sea to Sea Dinner.

Prior to his retirement, DMcQ had passed the Presidency of the Company to Bob Gray, while he became Chairman of the Board. This was largely cosmetic; he still called the shots. Bob Gray was a hugely loyal and hard-working man, but he never seemed to me to be a decision maker. After DMcQ retired, Bob was very much in charge, but it was not long before Cargill, who now owned the entire company, parachuted in a young man called Tom Schmidt to become their man in charge. Tom was a management man; as far as I know he knew nothing much about poultry (and had little interest in learning) but a lot about business. It soon turned out that his primary mission was to find a buyer for Shaver, and within a year, ISA (Institut pour Selection Animales) purchased the company. ISA had evolved from a privately owned company (Studler S.A.) into a subsidiary of Rhone Poulenc (or Rhone Merrieux – I' m not sure which), a huge French conglomerate primarily in the pharmaceutical business. This was interesting because several of the previously independent, family owned breeders had followed a similar pattern; Hubbard Breeders, Babcock Farms, H&N, all at one time or another were owned by pharma companies. None of these relationships lasted. By the time of the Shaver takeover, ISA had also purchased Babcock Farms in Ithaca NY, one of Shaver's big US competitors.

Geoff Fairhurst became Vice President of Shaver (really the "Hatchet Man") in September 1989, when the ISA takeover was completed. Geoff had been one of the M.Sc. students at Wye while I was teaching there. His arrival resulted in the firing, one day, of Tom Schmidt, Peter Chapman (Marketing Director), Drew Orocz (Marketing assistant), and 3 clerical staff. While Geoff was living in Cambridge, we entertained him frequently, usually Sunday dinners. His original plan was to have his wife, Chris join him in Cambridge as he expected to remain for quite a while. However, on one occasion she had visited, and they returned to France together, Chris suffered a fatal brain hemorrhage and Geoff was left a widower in his early 50s. He continued to live in Cambridge, in a small Shaver-owned house adjacent to the old hatchery on Branchton Road, for several years. We entertained him frequently and I often stopped in the Shaver office on the way home from work to chat. During this time, he began dating (very inconspicuously) Marcela, who worked in the office. She had an unhappy marriage that was falling apart, and when they eventually "came out" we were delighted and Marcela became a great friend. Originally from Mexico, she had two boys born in Canada, and they went to live with their father in Mexico City. But when Geoff and Marcela returned to France, the boys often spent their summers there. The boys were both fluently bilingual (English/Spanish) and both ended up working on Toronto several years later.

Following the 1990 WPSA meetings in Barcelona, I visited Geoff in France. He collected me from the Paris airport and took me to his house, Les Jobards (translates, he told me, to "the idiots") near Courtenay, where the Shaver operation was located . The house was a beautifully converted stable, with a nice garden and an overgrown pond complete with waterfowl. Geoff was busy at work but lonely at home so we had a grand time drinking the local wine, which he bought in bulk, and reviewing the poultry world, and our parts in it over the years.

Several years later, ISA itself was taken over by Hendrix Genetics, which after this, owned a string of brand names. Originally called Euribrid and using the Hisex brand name, they had subsequently acquired Bovans and Dekalb, and now added Shaver, Babcock and ISA to the range. Hendrix also by then owned Hybrid Turkeys, based in Kitchener, Ontario, and a swine breeding operation based in Saskatchewan. They later expanded into breeding several species of fish.

Although it was a huge organization, Hendrix' CEO Thijs Hendrix, had many of the characteristics of an old-fashioned poultry breeder. He loved chickens, and last time I visited, had photos of Don Shaver, Monroe Babcock and many of the other former independent primary breeders, on his office walls. When Don Shaver died in 2018 (aged 97) Thijs made a special trip from The Netherlands to his memorial service.

While Geoff was still in Cambridge, he arranged for me to deliver a lecture to Shaver's Japanese customers. The lecture dealt with the history of incubation and I spent a lot of time researching and writing it. I was royally hosted by the Japan Shaver company and their distributors and thoroughly enjoyed the trip, which lasted 5 days including the flights there and back. I visited a couple of the Shaver franchise hatcheries and helped as best I could, but the language barrier in Japan made things difficult.

Geoff suggested to his superiors in France that I might re-join Shaver (third appearance!) in a technical capacity. So in early December 1990, I made a very confidential 3 day trip to France – by air to Paris, TGV to Lyon for 2 hours of interview with Michel Perrot, who was the CEO at the time. All for naught – they made no offer so I carried on with the Egg Board. Geoff persisted for a few months, trying to get me appointed Technical Director, but his efforts were in vain.

I also went on a 9-day trip to Argentina and Brazil with Geoff in July 1990, and Patricio Liberona was there to translate for us. In Argentina, we had a good meeting with Albayda, the local Shaver distributor, visiting their hatchery and an egg breaking plant. In the evening they hosted a meeting of 80 producers, representing around 5 million hens. The meeting ran until 11.00 pm, after which, Spanish style, we had dinner! We had time for a little sightseeing and shopping in Buenos Aires before leaving. As we realized then, it was a very pleasant city with quite a European flavour.

We flew from Buenos Aires to Sao Paulo, and were met by Eduardo Bernardi, ISA's man in Brazil. Eddie (as he became known) subsequently had a varied and successful career outside of Brazil. He joined Shaver in Canada for a while, then worked for a feed company there, moved briefly to Germany, and ended up in New Zealand working for a veterinary products company. I caught up with him in New Zealand when we went there on holiday in 2009. But in Brazil in 1990 he was our host and drove us many hundreds of km.

We spent a day in Sao Paulo, meeting with Shaver's distributor, and one of their customers who at the time owned 3 million hens, all HyLine. I never did find out whether they tried Shaver!

The main object of the Brazilian trip was to attend the *Festo do Ovo* in Bastos. Bastos was a small town, with a population of about 20,000, 550 km from Sao Paulo. It was Brazil's Egg City. A huge industry was based there, almost entirely owned by Japanese families. Even the sidewalks had alternating black and white egg-shaped paving stones.

We both gave our speeches at the opening of the *Festo*, then Geoff spent time at the exhibition, manning the Shaver booth. I gave a short talk to an industry organization about the Egg Board's promotion and advertising programs. I helped with the booth later, an activity enlivened by the presence of Angelica, our receptionist, and our giving out of small shots of Canadian Club whiskey to all and sundry, including ourselves.

During the show, we visited several potential customers, all of Japanese descent, so language was a bit of a challenge. I was asked to make a pitch on the subject of egg quality. At the time, eggs in Brazil were marketed very much on a commodity basis with no differentiation. I was able to show them how high quality eggs could command higher prices once consumers realized the difference. The journey back to Sao Paulo took us through huge tracts of prosperous agriculture; we saw oranges, bananas, sugar cane, as well as big open ranges where cattle were growing. The cattle were mostly grey coloured, zebu type.

I left Geoff and Patricio in Sao Paulo; they were continuing to Venzuela while I flew back to Canada.

In late 1991, Geoff's replacement arrived from France. Olivier Behagel was a long time ISA employee and he led Shaver quite successfully until the Hendrix takeover.

Spring 1998 saw me again Sao Paulo, on behalf of Shaver/ISA, where I gave a paper at the VIII Symposium on Egg Production. Geoff Fairhurst had accumulated a big volume of data on egg production costs around the world and I used these for my presentation. It went very well and I enjoyed the rest of the meeting most of which was presented in English. One of the papers was by Tony Churchill from the UK, the inventor of the original Marek's disease vaccine. After the Symposium, the ISA people took me to visit Saito Farms, one of their major customers. We spent four hours talking about egg quality and marketing. We then drove to Mogi Las Cruces, to visit Granja Nagao, another customer. They were innovators, and were just launching a "Quality Egg" claiming low cholesterol, high Vit. E and high omega-3 fatty acids. They also owned a paper recycling plant where they manufactured their own egg flats.

The final call was with Granja Shinoda, near Campinas. They managed about a million layers, mostly HyLine but a few Babcock. They graded and sold their own eggs, and were about to embark on further processing.

Because labour was cheap in Brazil, most farms were not highly mechanized, but this complex included one house with mechanized feeding and egg gathering.

Meanwhile, Geoff continued his work with ISA based in France. When he officially retired in 1999, they had a big party in Cambridge for him. Although he had originally come as a hatchet man (and a lot of people suffered) he also developed a very loyal and efficient staff to keep the place going and improve the way it worked. So those attending the retirement party were all good friends, and it was a most enjoyable event. I told the crowd how we met and our early history. I remember Geoff's speech very well. The message was how much he had enjoyed his career, but how glad he was to retire now that the industry was in the throes of such rapid change. He was of course referring to the huge emphasis currently applied to food safety and bird welfare. It wasn't that he disagreed with it; just that he didn't have decent answers to give to farmers under pressure. The reason I remember it so clearly is that I felt exactly the same!

Geoff retired early, but he planned to remain in France until he became 65 and eligible for a full pension. Meanwhile, he and Marcela bought a house in Nuevo Vallarta, on Mexico's Pacific coast, to which they planned to move permanently. It was a lovely place located in a quiet neighbourhood, on a canal. Water was important because Geoff liked fishing and Marcela was a SCUBA diving instructor. The house had a boat launch and they even bought a boat. Before they moved, Geoff told us we could use the place for winter holidays and we did so several times. We actually lived there more than he did, because in 2005, Geoff developed lung cancer and died before they could move to Mexico. A very sad end to an illustrious career.

I continued my consulting arrangement with Hendrix Genetics until the end of 2014.

Newfoundland Chicken
In late 1981, I was involved in a consultation led by Woods Gordon, an accounting firm, to study and make recommendations regarding the broiler industry in Newfoundland. The whole industry was, of course hugely subsidized as there was no economic sense in growing and processing chickens on the island when all the inputs had to be brought in from the mainland. Nevertheless the provincial government had decreed that there would be an industry and so it was. The industry was comprised of a handful of small (10,000 birds) producers near St. Johns and a processing plant plus a similar set up around Corner Brook on the west coast. Each of the plants processed 1,200 chickens/hour.

It was my first visit to "the rock" and we (my contact, Glenn Manderson and I) arrived on a Saturday and did some sightseeing, including Cape Spear, which at that time was not nearly as formalized as now.

We met with the Agriculture Department Poultry Specialist, Lloyd Barnes, and the Veterinarian, Alt Smith, and with people from the St. Johns processing plant. We visited several of the producers in the St. Johns region (one of whom was Joseph Smallwood Jr., son of the politician who had engineered Newfoundland's entry as Canada's tenth Province) before flying to Deer Lake to visit the Corner Brook area. We attended a meeting of the ten producers in the region and spent a few minutes at the processing plant.

I think one of the recommendations was to close the Corner Brook plant and concentrate processing in St Johns. As we learned, the situation was highly political and economics was not the only priority. On the way back to Toronto, I had a stopover in Fredericton and a nice dinner with the local Shaver distributor, Donny Clark.

I note from an internet search that in 1997, the Newfoundland producers banded together in an effort to purchase the money losing company. I presume this initiative resulted in the creation of the current (2018) company, Country Ribbon Inc. that processes and markets locally grown chickens.

Euribrid
Another very interesting call came from Ad van Hedel of what was then Euribrid. I made a very quick visit to their headquarters in Boxmeer, The Netherlands, in August 1981. I was "grilled" on the Shaver and Ross breeding programs by Ad and Cees Hajer. Obviously since I was still getting a cheque from Shaver I did not reveal much. They gave me **cash** for my plane ticket and honorarium. I hid the money in three different places on my way home. Not a bad trip! Euribrid was then owned by Thijs Hendrix and has since morphed into Hendrix Genetics.

Farmax Environmental Control System
In the spring of 1994, I was asked by the Nova Scotia Agriculture College (NSAC) to evaluate a newly developed computer system to control the environment in poultry houses. The software was developed by Jim Shand, and called Farmax. This was far ahead of its time in 1994. Sensors throughout the poultry house scanned for temperature, and the computer created a "heat map" of the building. In turn, the computer then activated air intakes and fans to obtain a pre-programmed uniform temperature throughout the building. I spent 2 days at the College learning about the system, and then visited two farms where it had been installed. One of

these belonged to Dave Coburn, near Fredericton, NB. Dave was always an innovator and a big booster for Farmax. It worked well for him. and he was an excellent example for them to show off the system. I was well pleased with what I saw and wrote a very positive report. The system was marketed and promoted, but never really achieved the widespread use I thought it deserved. This was partly due to the personality of its inventor, Jim Shand. He seemed obsessed with retaining total control, and refused to delegate. A large egg production company in Pennsylvania wanted to use it and market it to others, but Jim made it virtually impossible for them to do so. Of course, within the next ten years, all kinds of competitors developed systems that were equal or better, and ultimately cheaper, but this always seemed to me an opportunity squandered. The Nova Scotia government paid me a fee and expenses, and I wrote them a 37 page report, which I delivered in person as part of a holiday trip to NS.

Indian River

In 1994 I had a message from the Shaver distributor in Columbia, Sen. Camargo after he bought out the Indian River broiler breeding program, which by this time was located in Nacogdoches, Texas. He of course needed genetic advice. I wrote in my diary that it "seemed exciting". I discussed it with Chris Fowler, whom they had also approached, and eventually decided against it. Chris and Olive actually moved to Texas for a short while to manage the farm. They hired Wayne Fairfull (formerly with Agriculture Canada) as geneticist and Rob Gowe did some consulting, but the whole enterprise imploded quite quickly and the stocks reverted to Lohmann, and subsequently the EW Group which now includes about half the world's meat chicken breeders.

Watt Publishing

Watt Publishing asked me to moderate and report for their first "Poultry Summit", held on the University of Georgia campus in Athens in April 1996. This was an interesting initiative for them. It was the kind of event that would, today, be held successfully online, but in 1996, everybody still flew about the continent very cheaply. And it lasted 3 days!

First Visit to China

In January, 1999, I received an invitation from the (American) National Renderers Association's Hong Kong office to visit mainland China and do a lecture tour on their behalf. The letter came from Dr.Yu Yu, who had previously worked for United Co-ops of Ontario, a local feed company. Although I wasn't really looking for more travel opportunities, I thought it would be interesting, so I accepted. One thing I insisted on was Business Class flights to and from China, to which they reluctantly agreed. I managed to combine the trip with attending the Western Poultry Disease Conference, held that year in Vancouver. This was always an interesting meeting, though held only rarely in Canada. Vancouver in April was wonderful: cherry blossom in full bloom and very spring-like weather. The meeting was excellent, and the hospitality also splendid. It included a complimentary Chinese lunch courtesy of Eng Hong Lee. Dr. Lee was a veterinary graduate from Guelph but he subsequently invented and developed the first vaccine against coccidiosis. The product and the company were called Immucox. Friends there included Bill Stevens and Ed and Dorothy Moran, and we spent some time together.

From Vancouver I flew direct to Hong Kong, landing in what was then its brand new airport. Dr. Yu Yu met me there and we flew straight to Guangzhou, site of my first lecture. The subject was the modern Canadian egg industry and I had nice slides of some of our better farms and a good talk. Yu Yu did consecutive translation. As I knew absolutely no Chinese, I was never sure exactly how good his translation was, or whether he was editorializing. I know sometimes his translation seemed much longer than my English! We were given a little sightseeing tour in Guangzhou, including the Sun Yat Sen Memorial. Sun was billed as the Father of modern China, living about 30 years prior to the Communist Revolution.

The next stop was Shanghai. I remember all of the hotels we stayed in were quite palatial, and fairly English-friendly. This one was a Westin; I was left to myself for dinner and ate an excellent Italian meal. All of the meetings were the same; my lecture followed by Q&A, then lunch, always the same with large round tables and a Lazy Susan with the food. Chinese beer if I wanted it. Attendance was good, varying from 50 to 100. We also did some sightseeing in Shanghai – the old city and the new. At the time, the population was 18 million and growing fast. In 2016, when I visited while on vacation, the population was 24.3 million. The waterfront buildings were just beginning in 1999. When I was there in 2016, it was unrecognizable.

The next lecture was in Qingdao. Here again we had some sightseeing, this time Qingdao's answer to Disney World, the Tsingdao "Goddess of Beer" sculpture. The building boom was everywhere we travelled; apartment towers and mansions, beach houses, etc. And transportation in Mercedes, BMW, and once in a very beautiful vintage Lincoln Town Car.

We visited one of the National Renderers' customers in Lanshan; they sold 300,000 tonnes of layer feed annually and I learned a lot about the nascent Chinese egg industry. This was a rural area and certainly lacked the apparent prosperity of Shanghai and Qingdao. Even the hotel we stayed in, though it looked palatial from outside, was seriously fraying inside.

This trip was hard work, especially the fact that unless YuYu translated, I was totally unaware of what was gong on. But they paid me a daily rate as well as all expenses and I did not complain!

I gave my final lecture at the Beijing Agricultural University, where I met Dr. Ning Yang, who was Secretary of the China Branch of WPSA. Fortunately, he spoke excellent English, having done graduate work at Virginia Tech. with Paul Siegel. So we had a good talk and I said I hoped he would come to WPC2000. Dr. Ning Yang eventually bid for the 2016 World's Poultry Congress, and it was held in Beijing, following which he became President of WPSA.

On my final day in China, two University students took me to see and walk along the Great Wall for 1½ hours, a very good way to end the trip, as I went straight from there to the airport for my flight home. The wall was built in 700 BC for the same reason Hadrian built his wall in Northumberland; to keep out marauding invaders! The Chinese version, however, had been massively restored and rebuilt and was now a huge tourist attraction. My visit was early in the day and it was quite civilized but by the time I left, it was besieged. I visited the same area again in 2016 and the wall was the same, but the surroundings transformed by the massive tourist presence.

I flew home with a change of plane in Vancouver. On arrival in Toronto, I stayed at a hotel near the office, as it was too late to go home and then back the next morning. It was the Directors' meeting at the Egg Board, and when they invited me to lunch with them at the local Chinese restaurant, I politely, but firmly declined!

Consulting for the Egg Board

Following my official retirement at the end of June, 2001, I continued some of the work I had been doing on a consulting basis. This included my monthly technical newsletter, *The Ovum*, which I now wrote at home, and my work on the Board's research activities. The Board paid me on a *per diem* basis, a bit less than I expected, but they kept up some of my benefits in compensation. I received telephone calls and emails at home and responded as needed. When I first retired, a Guelph co-op student was still working on manure sampling, and I continued his supervision, and the associated work on nutrient management programs for producers. His data provided a good baseline for nutrient composition of manure stored in different ways, and I presented a summary of them at the Ontario Poultry Health conference later in the year. We held producer meetings throughout the province to encourage and help with the development of nutrient management plans.

In the summer of 2002, another co-op student was hired to further develop the procedure for Nutrient Management Plans, and we created a policy Manual for this purpose.

I was still deeply involved with the HACCP program, along with Bill Stevens and, of course the Egg Board staff, Pam and Lorraine. We held frequent meetings, mostly in Guelph to review progress and make adjustments to the program. We also began, with the help of engineer Ron MacDonald, placing dataloggers in producers' egg rooms to monitor conditions and assure good compliance with storage protocols.

Once Harry Pelissero was installed as General Manager, and my former boss Brian, "put out to pasture", I wondered what my future role might be. I met with Harry in 2004 and although he had replaced several of Brian's hires, he assured me he considered me a valuable resource, which I took as license to continue as before. As time progressed, the work load diminished and I finally decided to quit some time in 2005. It had been a good run.

Canadian Egg Marketing Agency

In anticipation of my retirement, I made good contacts at the federal agency, then called the Canadian Egg Marketing Agency (CEMA). (It is now Egg Farmers of Canada, or EFC). The office of their CEO seemed to have a revolving door most of the time I worked for the Egg Board, and at the time of my retirement, it was occupied by David Clement. David had had a long career in the dairy industry and was familiar with the sort of work CEMA did, and I got along very well with him. It had always seemed strange to me that CEMA had never employed anyone with a scientific or technical background and clearly, David saw the same deficiency. They created a Research Committee and invited me to join it. They also nominated me as their representative on the newly created Canadian Poultry Research Council (CPRC). And at my first meeting with them, a few weeks before my retirement from the Egg Board, I was asked to review a draft of CEMA's Production Management and Welfare Code. All of this was right up my street and I welcomed the opportunity. They also paid me a *per diem* and of course my expenses. Expenses were significant because their office was in Ottawa, This was a good 5 h drive or one hour flight from Toronto airport. Of course, some of the work could be done at home but most meetings, both with CEMA and CPRC took place in Ottawa. We also did quite a few conference calls.

Peter Clarke, the CEMA Director from Nova Scotia chaired the Research Committee and I very much enjoyed working with him. Many of the Research Committee meetings were half-day affairs tied to CEMA Board

162

meetings, and I was able to fly there and back the same day. Expensive for them, but it kept my time commitment down.

In 2002, CEMA was starting to develop its HACCP program, which would ultimately take over from the Ontario Egg Board's system. I was often involved in the planning process and of course this was mutually beneficial, as sooner or later both programs would merge.

The Poultry Welfare Codes were revised again beginning in 2000, and CEMA represented the egg industry in negotiating with the Federation of Humane Societies and other contributors. This was a long drawn out process that was not complete until late in 2002. Frank Hurnik, from the University of Guelph, was a major contributor to composing the draft codes and insisted on many changes to the industry proposals.

CEMA held a Producer Conference in Saskatoon in July, 2002 and as part of their Research Committee, I was invited. Nita accompanied me and we had a weekend holiday before the meeting, including two live theatre outings. We had a short meeting of the Research Committee ahead of the main proceedings, to hear a request from Jeong Sim, for a very large grant, which we had to decline. The Producer meeting was very good, with a keynote speech by Patrick Moore. Moore had been a founding member of Greenpeace, but later saw the light and by this time was working as a forestry consultant, calling himself a "science based environmentalist". Closer to CEMA's real mandate was a presentation by Dr. Don Macnamara, the technical Director of the Egg Nutrition Center, based in Washington DC. Don was a good friend and we always enjoyed our meetings. He was in large measure responsible for the gradual turnaround in the public perception of how consumption of eggs affected (or more correctly did not affect) blood serum cholesterol and the risk of heart disease.

After the CEMA meeting, I spent a day at the University, hosted by Hank Classen, to talk about the Canadian Poultry Research Council (CPRC), and to see first hand the staff and facilities they had involved in poultry research. As well as the Agriculture building and the Poultry Farm, I again visited the Veterinary and Infectious Diseases Organization (VIDO – it later changed its name to Vaccine and Infectious Disease Organization, and extended its remit to human diseases).

On CEMA's behalf, I attended the annual meetings of the Canadian Agricultural Research Council (CARC) for several years. Apparently there had been no poultry representative for several years and now I was "it". The meeting was interesting but I thought again of all the government committees I had participated in, and how ineffective they generally seemed. Busy work for the civil servants? The second meeting I attended was in Lethbridge AB and of course with all expenses paid, it was a good way to see the country! The meeting was scheduled for a full day but many people didn't show up so we were done by lunchtime. For me, the best part of the trip was a day in the field following the formal meeting.

In some circles at this time, "agriculture" was becoming a forbidden word. Not here! We spent the whole day "celebrating agriculture". Lethbridge's Ag. Tech. Centre was focused on engineering, with a great combination of commercial and government applied research. Lehtbridge Research Centre was mostly funded by the Federal Government, but here too there was local emphasis and partnership. Some crop plots were 100 years old; it reminded me of Cockle Park at my old college in Newcastle.

From here we went to the farm of Albert Kolk, now run by his son John, and including a broiler farm with a capacity of 180,000 birds. Their house overlooked the Oldman River, and we enjoyed the views while our lunch steaks were cooking on the barbecue. We learned that John's daughter, Ashley had just completed Frank Robinson's unique poultry course at U. Alberta. Following lunch, we toured "Feedlot Alley" including John's place with a capacity of 5,000 beef cattle. This was currently losing millions of dollars due to the boycott of Canadian beef exports resulting from a single case of BSE several months earlier.

Another farmer, Bill van Roocaellar, who farmed dairy and beef, guided us the rest of the day. We learned how increased irrigation from the Oldman River dam had permitted growth of previously exotic crops such as potatoes and corn, as well as the more traditional wheat and barley. We saw the dam, completed 10 years previously, which we were told had positive outcomes for farmers, wildlife and human recreation – altogether a win/win/win situation. Finally we got to Head Smashed In Buffalo Jump but by this time it was dark!

The 2004 meeting of (CARC) was in Fredericton NB. As usual, the pre-meeting tours were very interesting, more so than the meeting itself! We visited the Federal Government Potato Research Lab. and the Acadian Seaplant Company, which harvested seaweed and converted it to animal feed and fertilizer. We also saw, from a distance, several Atlantic Salmon farms and visited the Atlantic Salmon Interpretive Centre.

In June 2003, I went to Halifax for the Expert Committee on Eggs and Egg Products, yet another government committee whose value I wondered about. I was a member as CEMA 's representative and as the Chair of the CPRC. The silver lining of a visit to Halifax was being able to meet my daughter, Carole, who was living there at the time, and giving her a very good dinner at the Economy Shoe Store, and yes, it was a restaurant! The next day was my birthday, so I took her out again, this time to the Five Fishermen. This was quite up-market but we got "free" mussels and salads! We also took a trip in my rental car to Lunenberg and Peggy's Cove.

I continued consulting for CEMA for several years, mainly working on their Research Committee. Most of the meetings were held by Conference call, and I was able to do this from home. By this time the CEO had again changed; Tim Lambert took over some time in 2003 and interestingly, he looks like a permanent fixture; as I write in 2020 he is till there!

Canadian Poultry Research Council
As described elsewhere the CPRC resulted from the desire to have a truly national poultry research effort. Although the Poultry Industry Council had that ambition, it was prevented from doing so by a few provinces, notably Alberta. The concept for the CPRC was developed in the late 1990s and it came into being in 2001. Its members, and funders, were the four marketing agencies for chicken, eggs, turkeys and broiler hatching eggs and chicks, plus the Canadian Poultry and Egg Processors Council. Each was represented by one Director.

I represented CEMA on the Council and became Vice-Chair at its inaugural meeting in January 2002. Political factors (mainly my being a resident of Ontario) prevented me from being the Chair, for which position I was, in all modesty, best qualified. At this point, it was decided to have the Poultry Industry Council as Manager, since they had a staff person in Dave Nodwell who could carry out administrative tasks. A few months after its formation, the elected Chair resigned and I took his place. At this point, my province of residence seemed not to matter.

In June I visited the University of Alberta on behalf of CPRC. Poultry Head Frank Robinson invited me on condition that I spend a day working with their research team and I was happy to comply. They held a Showcase Event to launch their newly built Hatchery and Poultry Processing Plant. We also visited the environmentally controlled chambers and the teaching and computer facilities. The entire setup was highly functional for both research and teaching and I was hugely impressed.

My day of "work" was equally impressive. I was picked up at 6.00 am and the job was the slaughter and analysis of a group of 146 turkey parent breeders at the end of an experiment. The birds were slaughtered and my task was to remove and weigh the livers and fat pads. Faculty, support staff and students were indistinguishable and worked together until the job was done. My conclusion was that at this point, Alberta clearly had the most Producer-friendly and practical research and teaching programs for poultry in Canada.

While in Edmonton, I also met with Dr. Jeong Sim, whose work on omega-3 enrichment of table eggs had been partly funded by the Ontario Egg Board. He was now looking for funding from CEMA for more research, and in addition, planning for the next Post Harvest Egg Symposium. I had helped with editing the Proceedings of the previous Symposium, and agreed to do this again.

Meanwhile, to give the Council some exposure and assure members we were active, it was decided to hold a national conference in Ottawa to identify research priorities. We asked Dr. Jim Pettit, who had recently retired, to work on this. Jim was a veterinarian with a long career working for the Ontario government. He continued to help with CPRC affairs for several years. David Nodwell, from the PIC, made most of the arrangements and we hired a facilitator to run the meeting. We had very good representation from all parts of Canada. The format was to have a few introductory speeches and then break-out tables to discuss and identify national priorities. Prof. Roger Buckland, from McGill, and I gave two of the main speeches: the third was Roel Mulder from The Netherlands, who gave a European perspective. The break-out tables were very enthusiastic and I think we achieved what we intended. The Alberta group, led by Frank Robinson, were very active and gave me quite a hard time over financial affairs: Did CPRC have a big pot of money to spend? The answer was "No", but if we could build on the outcome of this meeting, maybe we could create one.

At its January 2003 Board meeting, CPRC began the process to establish a funding capability, but it would be very slow. First, however, we established a Scientific Advisory Committee, with representatives from institutions across the country. This group met in November 2003 for the first time. Members included Frank Robinson, Andrew Olkowski, Rick Holley, Fred Silversides and Roger Buckland. One of our challenges was to persuade more of the Directors of the member agencies that our mission was necessary. Many of these Directors were hard working farmers more concerned with current production issues than with scientific and technological developments that might enhance future profitability. The four agencies held a joint Annual General Meeting in Ottawa every year, and I spent an evening there in March 2004 trying to drum up support. Within a few years, CPRC had developed secure commitments from its members and was able to begin funding significant research across Canada.

CPRC also organized and ran a one-day workshop on Avian Gut Microbiology at the Ontario Ministry of Agriculture and Rural Affairs building in Guelph ON. This was at the time when use of antibiotics, and also some of the anti-coccidial drugs, was being questioned, so it was timely and well attended.

As the PIC was still doing the administrative work, meetings of CPRC were often held in Guelph, with some members on the telephone. The Annual General Meeting in 2004 was held by Conference call, while I was at another meeting in Banff, but there were no major issues and I was elected to a further term as Chair. This year we hired Gord Speksnijder as part time administrator. Gord ran his family broiler farms and worked part time for CPRC, replacing David Nodwell, who continued working for the PIC.

Several of us, including Gord Speksnijder, Roger Buckland and myself, spent considerable time in Ottawa, where we canvassed the marketing agencies and we were eventually able to secure sufficient funding, guaranteed for several years, to be able to start looking for suitable projects to support.

The Scientific Advisory Committee, under Roger Buckland's Chairmanship, began establishing guidelines for funding. We also met with AAFC's Assistant Deputy Minister, Bruce Archibald to discuss possible matching funds for CPRC projects. It was never the intention for the Council to fund projects in their entirety.

When I decided to retire from my activities with CEMA and CPRC in 2006, I suggested that CEMA approach Dr. Helen Anne Hudson to replace me. Helen Anne was Joe Hudson's daughter and worked for the family company, Burnbrae Farms. She was a graduate of the University of Guelph with M.S. and Ph.D. degrees from the University of Georgia, and thus very well qualified.

Of course, I talked to Helen Anne first and she was quite agreeable. She not only became CEMA's consultant and Research Committee member, but also later became Chair of the Poultry Industry Council in Guelph. She was CEMA's Director on the CPRC and became its Chair in 2017.

Fast forward to the latest available (2021) Annual Report from CPRC. Since inception, the Council has spent $5.1 million on 112 projects. This has been more than matched by the Federal Government ($11.6 million), Provincial Governments ($8.2 million) and other industry sources ($4.7 million) for a total of $30 million. The Council now has a full time Executive Director and two support staff.

Farm Livestock Genetics Conservation

I began to take an interest in this at the behest of Don Shaver immediately after I retired. It is included as "Consulting", but was entirely voluntary and unpaid.

I first attended a meeting in Guelph to "get my bearings" It appeared that while conservation of crop plant genetics was already well advanced in Canada, with an Agriculture and Agri-Food Canada laboratory associated with the University of Saskatchewan in Saskatoon, there was absolutely nothing done about farm animals. Of course, this was not surprising, as the costs of conserving seeds, while significant, were manageable. Those associated with animals were on a different scale, and in the case of poultry, even the technology did not exist. Bovine semen, ova and embryos could be frozen and were mostly viable when defrosted. No such technology existed for poultry. Even semen storage was unreliable, and with the embryo being associated with the entire egg, no method was available for its long term preservation.

A Foundation was established (the Canadian Farm Animal Genetic Resources Foundation) in an effort to collect funds and stimulate interest, but regretfully, neither of these objectives was achieved at anything like the scale necessary to actually accomplish much. I was President and Jim Dalrymple, a retired animal scientist who had worked for the Ontario Government, was Secretary. Don Shaver recruited people from across the country to form a Board of Directors.

In November, 2002, the Board of the Foundation met in Ottawa, and then went to the Parliament Buildings to meet with the Research and Education Caucus, a very lively group of MPs and Senators, to make them aware of the challenge we were dealing with. I think as a result of this meeting, along with support from Ed Lister, who succeeded Rob Gowe at the Animal Research Centre, we were instrumental in persuading the federal government to consider adding an animal laboratory to the existing plant conservation activity in Saskatoon. After another full-day meeting with Agriculture and Agri-Food Canada in July 2003, a decision was made to proceed with this initiative. And at the meeting where the Business Plan for the Livestock and Poultry Germplasm Centre was announced, Minister Lyle Vanclief made a presentation to Donald Shaver recognizing his contribution. I thought his speech on this occasion was excellent, much better than the one he made at our World's Poultry Congress. This time he really sounded as though he knew what he was talking about!

Several members of the Foundation later visited the Saskatoon laboratories and met with the newly appointed staff. We were suitably impressed and believed that our efforts had been successful. The laboratory was adequately, if minimally, staffed with a competent group of scientists and support staff. However, a recent (2021) search of the Agriculture and AgriFood Canada web site indicated that the page on Animal Germplasm had "disappeared". The Foundation was later wound up, mainly for lack of financial and personal support.

The concept of germplasm conservation was not hard to understand. The breeding industry practiced selection for commercial traits and inevitably, some potentially valuable genetic material was being lost in the process. Sometimes entire populations (lines thought of lesser value) were discarded because of cost. The competitive nature of the industry was such that conservation might not be feasible. When I first joined Shaver in 1967 there were at least 20 lines being held as gene pools that were not part of the commercial program. Over time, some of them were discarded, others combined, and one or two may have risen to become part of the commercial system. But I doubt if such programs exist among today's breeding companies simply on economic grounds.

When Donald Shaver retired, he took with him a few layer lines and maintained them, with selection, for several generations, until he moved off the farm and was no longer able to look after them. He attempted to sell them but got no offers, and eventually, small populations were given to the Universities of Guelph and Alberta. They survive today (2021) but costs are high and there is no guarantee that they will be held forever. No doubt a few other populations around the world exist in similar circumstances. There are still a few small independent breeders remaining who have useful stocks, probably unrelated, or distantly related, to those used by the major breeders. They offer some degree of conservation but this too is fragile. To me, the dilemma is insoluble.

Chapter 9

My Writing Career

I have always enjoyed writing, but it wasn't until early in my career at Wye College as a teacher that I realized that it could, indeed should, be a source of income!

University faculty are recognized sources of both information and opinion. I soon learned how to write acceptable scientific papers. Both my M.Sc. and Ph.D. theses were in this format, although neither was ever published. Subsequent scholarly publications were prepared for peer reviewed journals, and my first was published in *British Poultry Science* in 1969. Several more, reporting on the results of the selection programs at Wye, followed, mostly in *British Poultry Science*. Much later, I began to publish scientific reviews in the *World's Poultry Science Journal*. But these, of course, while essential to upward mobility in academe, attracted no direct financial reward.

Even prior to publication in peer reviewed journals, I began writing for trade papers like *Poultry World* and *Poultry Farmer and Packer* (which later merged into one, *Poultry World*), and *Chicken* (the journal of the British Chicken Association) But it wasn't until several of these were in print that I realized I should be charging for this service! I continued writing for these British trade magazines while I remained in the UK, and for their Canadian counterparts after I moved to Canada.

When I first arrived, there were two competing magazines in Canada; *Canadian Poultry Review*, and *Canada Poultryman*. This was in the late 1960's, before supply management was introduced. But in the run-up to its introduction, *Poultryman's* editorial policy was much in favour, while *Poultry Review's* was opposed. Once the system was in place, some of the Agencies and Provincial Boards started purchasing *Canada Poultryman* in bulk for their producers, and *Poultry Review* was not long in folding. I knew most of the editors of *Canada Poultryman* personally and wrote regularly for them. One in particular, Tony Greaves, became a friend and as well as publishing (and paying for) my articles, he also bought several photographs from me which he used on the magazine's front cover.

In the United States, Watt Publishing had a range of magazines for the poultry industry: *Egg Industry, Broiler Industry* and *Poultry International* published in English, and *Industria Avicola* in Spanish. I began submitting articles to them and continued for many years. When my old friend, colleague, drinking and darts partner David Martin became editor of *Poultry International* I published there quite regularly. Watt's main competition was Misset, based in The Netherlands, who published *World Poultry*. I knew little about them until 1996 when I was approached by the publisher to become a regular contributor and provide their monthly Research page.

Of more lasting interest, however, might be my contributions to scientific text books, and I will deal with these first.

Poultry Breeding and Genetics
In 1987, Roy Crawford, at the University of Saskatchewan, began assembling authors for his book, *Poultry Breeding and Genetics*. This would be the first formal publication of its size and complexity since F.B Hutt's *Genetics of the Fowl*, which was published in 1949. I was assigned the chapter on commercial breeding. While my experience with Shaver and Ross gave a good start to this, I had been away from direct involvement with the breeding industry for more than seven years, and I felt unable to write the chapter without re-visiting some of the companies currently leading the industry. So I arranged personal visits with the geneticists working for these companies to get a better insight into current practice.

I spent a day at the Ross Breeders headquarters in Scotland in November 1987 to discuss their programs with Nigel Barton. On the same trip, I visited Cliff Nixey at British United Turkeys and Janie Barnard at Cobb UK. I hadn't been close to turkey breeding since my time consulting with the Yorkshire people in the mid 1960's and the B.U.T birds were truly impressive. This was also the first time I learned that turkeys are quite immune to flash photography!

After this, and a visit in Sussex with my old school friend David Bourn, I flew to Amsterdam, and spent a very interesting day with the Euribrid group (fore-runners to Hendrix Genetics). Then, after another short flight and a fast drive to Kiel, I met Dietmar Flock from Lohmann Tierzucht. He worked part time at the University and that is where I met him. Before returning to Canada, I spent a half day with John Powell, then head geneticist for Cherry Valley Farms. John had been a senior geneticist at Thornbers before its demise, but really fell on his feet at Cherry Valley, which for some time had almost a monopoly in the breeding of meat ducks.

During their stop in Toronto, I met with Gerald Hubert and Alan Emsley, at that time the ISA genetics team.

Later, I took a trip to New Hampshire to meet Jim Smith at Hubbard Farms. This was interesting timing, because he told me when I got there that he would be taking early retirement, and "would I be interested in applying for his job?" We had a good meeting, but I think a few of the people there thought I was after the job! I did, in fact, apply for it later, and had an interview, but the position eventually went to his erstwhile assistant, Ira Carte.

After Hubbard Farms, my next call was with Bill Rishell and Verne Logan at Arbor Acres Farms in Connecticut.

So after these multiple consultations, I had a very good background to prepare my contribution to Roy's book. I wrote the chapter beginning late 1987, and finished it mid 1988. The book, published by Elsevier as part of their series, *Developments in Animal and Veterinary Science*, was published in 1990. It was 1,100 pages (at least twice the length of Hutt's book) and at the time, quite comprehensive and current. But time has not been kind to some of the chapters, especially mine! The section on New Directions in Poultry Genetics dealt with the emerging science of genomics, which has now become mainstream in research and applied breeding. In contrast, those sections dealing with Qualitative Genetics are still very useful.

In terms of Commercial Breeding, if the chapter was to be composed today, in 2020, I would need much less travel commitment; Hendrix Genetics and Aviagen, based in The Netherlands and Germany respectively, control the majority of layer, turkey and meat chicken breeding for the world's commercial poultry industries. Cobb/Vantress, owned by Tyson Foods in Arkansas, is significant in meat chicken breeding. Cherry Valley still breeds ducks, as do Grimaud Frêres in France. But after these companies, there are very few significant contributors to the global parent stock supply.

Around the turn of the century, there was talk of a second edition of the book. It got as far as the recruitment of Jan Gavora and me as Associate Editors, but Elsevier wanted all the work done without payment. By then, Roy and I would be facing retirement, and certainly I would not be looking for unpaid work. So no second edition was ever produced.

The Health of Poultry

Mark Pattison, who had been one of the veterinarians at Ross, contacted me in 1990, while I was working for the Egg Board to ask if I would contribute a chapter to a book he was editing called *The Health of Poultry*. There were many text books about poultry diseases, but viewing the subject from a different perspective was a new approach. Mark wanted a review of how the breeding industry contributed to the overall health of commercial poultry. Although I no longer had intimate contact with the breeding industry, I was close enough to Shaver, and had good contacts elsewhere, to agree to write this chapter.

Breeders, of course had two primary approaches. Firstly, they eliminated and controlled those diseases that might be passed as active infections from their farms to customers of parent stock. Prime examples of these were *Salmonella pullorum* and *Mycoplasma gallisepticum*. Another was Lymphoid leukosis. These were detected by primary breeders in their foundation flocks, and either individuals or occasionally entire flocks were removed from the program if infected birds were found. In this way parent flocks sold to customers could be guaranteed "clean".

The second approach was to endeavour to select for genetic resistance to specific diseases. In the 1960s, this was the approach taken to control Marek's disease before vaccines became available. It was much slower and more expensive than elimination of specific infections. One must always be mindful of F.B. Hutt's statement that "Genetic variation in disease resistance can be found wherever it is looked for".

The book was published by Wiley in 1993 and was well received.

World Animal Science – Poultry Production
In 1990, I was approached by Elsevier to edit a volume in their *World Animal Science* series to be entitled *Poultry Production*. I visited the publisher in Amsterdam and a Mrs. De Jong told me what was involved. I saw the list of people who had already turned it down and it was a veritable "Who's Who?" of the poultry science world. I'm not sure what motivated me to accept: certainly not money, as there would be a huge amount of work and very little reward – just minimal royalties on an expensive book with very small sales potential. Fame and glory? I suppose this may have had something to do with it, but also the fact that many other available textbooks were significantly out of date. In retrospect, this would probably be close to the last hardcover textbook on poultry production before the emergence of huge volumes of online information, which could be cheaply and effectively kept up to date.

During the ensuing year, I assigned authors to the 23 Chapters. Many of the writers were from Canada and the US and all would be accepted as world authorities in their respective fields. There were also four from the UK, one each from Israel, France and Australia. Most of the authors were personally known to me, or strongly recommended by someone I trusted.

Assigning authors was relatively easy; acquiring copy was another story. However, only one chapter had to be re-assigned: Bruce Sheldon promised and promised but never delivered. He did however, find someone to write what would have been his chapter, and she delivered as promised. Bruce loved to travel and I think this prevented him from writing. The book was finally published in 1995. I personally wrote the chapter on Egg Production, Processing and Marketing.

This was before the days of standard word processing software, and most of the chapters were submitted as hard copy and had to be re-typed on our office word processing system. My ever helpful Eleanor Marshall did most of this work. I was happy with the outcome, but financially, as expected, it was a bust!

When I look at the book today (2021), much of it is as far out of date as the other books were when it was conceived. However, some of it stands as a useful historical record, and I am grateful for the opportunity to have put it together.

Technical Writing, Newsletters, Magazines

Throughout the time I worked at the Egg Board, I prepared the monthly newsletter, the *OVUM*. I also continued to sell articles on a variety of topics, mainly to *Poultry International* and *Canada Poultryman*, but also to anyone else who asked. These were mostly technical in nature. I scanned *Poultry Science, World's Poultry Science Journal* and the *Journal of Applied Poultry Research* regularly and used these as the basis for composing "popular" pieces that editor's welcomed. "Translating" scientific papers into a format that was comprehensible to non-scientists was something I enjoyed, and continued to do for many years.

At that time, there were also many regular newsletters published by extension services in various US states. The Editors of these publications, including me, had an unwritten agreement that we could reproduce each others' work in our own newsletters, with suitable acknowledgement as to source. The California publication, edited by Don Bell was always useful, but Georgia, Arkansas, North Carolina, Ohio and Pennsylvania were frequently used as well.

Material for *Poultry International* had to be mailed to England. Most of the time this did not matter, as David Martin, the Editor, allowed for it and made his own deadlines. Offices by now all had fax machines but international connections were expensive. I persuaded Brian Ellsworth to let me use the Egg Board fax but he insisted my international faxes had to go prior to 8.00 am, when the long distance charges doubled. This worked OK. With Misset, they gave me a Fedex account number so I could drop stuff off at their Cambridge location. Of course, all of this changed when email became universal and everything was transmitted around the world "free".

Misset, later Elsevier Business

At the Poultry Science meeting in Louisville, Kentucky, in 1996, I met and talked a lot with Soledad Urrutia, the Editor of Misset's Spanish Language magazine, *Avicultura Profesional*. A month or so later, and no doubt as a result of this interaction, I was visited in Mississauga by Vincent Konig, who was publisher of the Misset magazines. He was suggesting a consulting role and part time work with *World Poultry*. They also published a suite of magazines on the other species in animal agriculture. This would mean severing my contact with David Martin and the Watt magazines, but at this stage I was thinking mainly of the $$ side of things. Misset eventually made me an offer I could not refuse, equivalent to about 20% of my Egg Board salary, so I readily accepted. Apart from David Martin, with whom I remained friends indefinitely, I had no real connections to Watt, so the break was not difficult. The writing would include a monthly Research page in the magazine plus feature articles as determined by the Editor. It also included writing part of a *Poultry Production Guide*, a loose leaf binder with multiple authors. Looking at my diary now (2020) I see that after a few months, I would work about 10 hours/week on Misset projects.

The first consulting mission for Misset began a few months after my signing up. It was an exercise to evaluate their magazines compared to those of their competitors. It must be emphasized that most of these magazines were distributed free to "qualified readers". "Qualified" basically involved saying that one was employed by a *bona fide* company that might be a customer for the magazines' advertisers. Although Watt Publishing was the largest and most aggressive competitor, there were a few others. In the UK, Nigel Horrox published two magazines, one on poultry and another on hatcheries. There was another published in Italy called *Zootecnica*. Misset had a consultant, Karl Geil, working on the issue and of course they had a large staff involved. I went to their head office in Doetinchem, in November 1996 for three days. The most important issue was of course, *World Poultry* (WP) *vs Poultry International* (PI). Independent statistics showed WP had greater circulation, but there was a feeling it had less respect. We felt that the quality of writing was adequate, but I had found that more of the WP content was written by authors who were not independent. So we would try to improve on this score. All told, it was a very interesting trip. Misset had good staff, all English speaking. In addition to Soledad, who was based in Chile, they included Naheeda Khan and Sarah Mellor, both working in Doetinchem. The Editor of WP was Weibe van der Sluis. At the time of these meetings, he seemed a bit "distant". I thought he might feel threatened as to his position by Soledad, or even me. However, I think we straightened this out over a good lunch before I left, and I worked very cordially with him until he retired. The Publisher, Vincent Konig, was also an important feature of these

175

conversations. I think he had recruited several of the people I met and they all seemed to enjoy working for him.

I went to Doetinchem again in November 1997 for more consultations, and further work on the *Poultry Production Guide*, mostly with Naheeda, who was the chief coordinator for this project.

Vincent did not stay long with Misset, and moved to another position outside of publishing soon after this, and several of the staff left.

I kept in touch with Sarah Mellor. She subsequently left Misset and briefly returned to her native England to work for CABI as an Editor. She later moved to Germany in another Editorial position, and married Christian. Naheeda also left and moved to England and is married with children. I see them both on Facebook.

In September, 1997, I bought a new computer (running OS 486 I think) which included an internet connection, email, etc. so I could now send everything everywhere without charge. Of course it was a dial-up modem, not very reliable, but a big step forward. It took a while to get used to, but what a change! By now I was writing a regular Research page monthly for *World Poultry*, several feature articles for them and also *Shaver Focus*. I did occasional pieces for *Canada Poultryman*, and *Farm and Country*, a local ag paper, as well. I continued to replace computers as the technology developed, but modems were unreliable at least until the mid 2000's. I bought a tiny hand held computer that I could carry in my pocket (about twice the size of today's smart phones) and used it to take notes which could then be transferred to my desktop computer. Of course by about 2000, laptops were as reliable as desktops and easily portable, so that is what I have had the last many years. And of course reliable wi-fi at home.

The vast majority of my writing work in the late 1990s was for Misset/Elsevier. I went to Doetinchem again in September 1998, and found that Vincent wanted to be a Premiere Sponsor for WPC2000. That was a pleasant surprise. I spent most of the visit working with Naheeda Khan and Wiebe van der Sluis, and also "brainstorming" ideas for the Misset magazines. I learned that they had just launched a new magazine called *Flower Tech* and Wiebe was the Editor. I also had a short meeting with Piet Simons to discuss WPSA business.

One of my most interesting trips, solely to gather information for an article in *World Poultry*, took place after the PSA meeting in Arkansas in 1999. I flew to Jackson, MS, and spent the day at the head office of Cal-Maine Foods. They were, at the time, the US's largest egg producer, with somewhere in the region of 25 million hens. This would be about 8% of the entire US flock, and 80% of Canada's. Cal-Maine consisted of at least three formerly independent companies: Dairy Fresh in California, which included the old Demler Hatchery company, Maine Egg Farm, originally owned by Maurice Stein, and Fred Adams Farms in Mississippi. I met with the President, Fred Adams, along with Ken Looper and Dolph Baker. All three were most hospitable and forthcoming, but I will never forget sitting with Fred Adams, who used a spittoon next to his desk! I spent all morning in their office and in the afternoon, visited two of the egg production complexes. The one at Edwards held about 2 million layers, a complete egg packing and processing plant, as well as breeders and a hatchery. I took lots of pictures and I know my piece in *World Poultry* was one of my best. {According to their current (2020) website, Cal-Maine now has ~ 40 million hens and supply approximately 19% of US shell egg needs}.

Another interesting feature I worked on for *World Poultry* involved the cost of egg production in different countries. In the course of his international travels for ISA, Geoff Fairhurst established a set of contacts with large egg producers who agreed to send him regular data on their cost of production. Geoff assembled these and I helped to analyze them. He used these data in his marketing presentations, and I reviewed them on an annual basis in *World Poultry.* Of course, when Geoff retired, this process came to an abrupt halt, but it provided several years of interesting information about where eggs could be produced most efficiently.

New Life Feeds
In 2001, New Life, a major supplier of feed to the poultry industry in Ontario, decided to produce a series of producer guides and asked me to write one for Egg Producers. I had been working on similar guides for Shaver, and the Misset publications, so this was a natural task for me. I worked on it for about twelve months, with Bill Revington and Scott Houghton from the company, and it was eventually published. This was probably among the last of this type of guide to be produced as hard copy; all are now online, which means they can be updated and adjusted on a regular basis without recourse to costly printing and reprinting.

Winding Down
In 2005, Wiebe van der Sluis indicated that the arrangement with Misset might not last much longer. The consulting side was terminated but I continued to write the Research Page and any feature article requested. I also continued to write in *Canada Poultryman*, which, after a change of ownership, became the *Canadian Poultry Magazine.* Without my hands-on work at the Egg Board, I had no real reason to visit farms and so became a little out of touch with the very practical side of the industry. Some of my work strayed into advocacy, rather than strictly technical, and also straight opinion pieces. I finally gave up professional writing at the end of 2014,

when I edited my last issue of *Shaver Focus*, which had by this time been renamed for ISA and the thrust of the publication became much more of a marketing tool.

The urge to put words on a page did not diminish, and I ended up writing (it was called Editing) various publications including one for Cambridge Community Players, formerly Galt Little Theatre. When I joined the PROBUS Club of Cambridge in 2017, I soon acquired the reputation for swift response to a request for written material.

Chapter 10

The Professional Associations: Poultry Science Association and World's Poultry Science Association

The Poultry Science Association

Anyone working in a scientific discipline would expect to find specialist associations to foster collaborations and scientific development and Poultry Science is no exception. Two organizations dominate the field; they are the Poultry Science Association (PSA) and the Worlds Poultry Science Association (WPSA). Interestingly, they were formed only a few years apart, PSA in 1908 and WPSA in 1912.

PSA developed as a result of efforts of scientists in the US and Canada and although it welcomed international members, the great majority of its membership when I joined in 1967 was still from North America. Although in the early days it was largely administered and run by scientist volunteers from various universities, beginning in the 1970's it evolved into a professionally managed organization with well qualified and well paid staff. Its current membership is over 1000 members and its annual dues, US$120. PSA publishes the journals *Poultry Science* (now [2021] in its 99th year of publication) and the *Journal of Applied Poultry Research*, the latter acquired from independent publishers in the late 20th century. Both journals are available free online to all paid up members, and consist largely of original research, peer reviewed prior to publication.

PSA runs an annual meeting, most often in the US, occasionally in Canada, at which short papers are presented by members, and also includes invited speakers and a variety of workshops and symposia. These meetings, like the organization itself, have evolved over time. When I joined PSA after arriving in Canada, annual meetings were held on University campuses, delegates resided in student dormitories and were often accompanied by their families. There were programs for children, teens and spouses. Since 95% of the scientists were men, 95% of the spouses were women and the whole system worked very well. As more and more women became scientists, and more and more spouses worked independently, the meetings attracted fewer families and they are now held in Hotels/Conference Centres in major cities and the family programs largely discontinued.

I joined PSA primarily in order to attend the annual meetings and receive the journal, *Poultry Science*. The meetings provided a good opportunity to meet those with common interests, hear the latest scientific developments and network with like-minded friends. Starting in the 1980's we attended as a family: My wife Nita and the children made friends that they saw year after year. The programs were very well structured and supervised and our kids loved them. Nita made some lifelong friends.

The meeting format was the same most years. An opening session Monday afternoon, and a very American event, the "Ice Cream Social" Monday night. There would be a barbecue, often off-campus, Wednesday evening and a Banquet Thursday, at which the awards, Fellowships etc. were given out. The mornings and afternoons consisted mostly of short papers, often presented by graduate students. There were a few symposia with longer presentations, and on Thursday afternoon the WPSA Lecture, which generally was given by an internationally recognized speaker, jointly funded by the US and Canada branches of WPSA.

An exception to family attendance for us was the 1982 meeting in Sacramento, CA. I flew there specially for the meeting. It was notable for the full-day Winery Tour. I can't remember how many wineries we visited but at the first one, Beringer, we did the grand tour of vineyards, fermentation, cellars, bottling etc and then excellent tasting. I remember one of the red wines in particular – I could smell it long before the glass approached my lips. By the time of the last visit, we pretty much by-passed the tour and went straight to the tasting. The tour was followed by the traditional Wednesday night barbecue, accompanied by yet more wine.

The 1983 meeting was at the University of Maryland Baltimore campus. We drove there through New York and Pennsylvania and stayed on campus. The meetings were very good and afterwards, we drove over the Bay Bridge and had a memorable lunch at the Boon Dock Restaurant, which served crabs by the dozen along with beer and Chablis. We also visited Mike Forhane, now separated from my friend Patricia, in Chestertown, MD, before staying a couple of nights with the Donaldson family in Washington DC. They were originally from Australia. I got to know them when we were all at Wye College, met them again in Ottawa when they were on sabbatical and continued our contact well into the 21st century. Graham and Robin probably consumed more wine and beer than Nita and me! Graham had a wine merchant where he got special deals on case lots of Australian and other wines; beer was very cheap in the US grocery stores so they always had a full cellar.

After visiting DC in 1983 we continued driving south into the Shenandoah Valley and the Skyline Drive, staying in Harrisonburg, and then staying with Paul and Dianne Ruszler in Blacksburg VA. Paul had briefly managed the Shaver operation in Alabama after receiving his Ph.D at Texas A&M. But he left after a couple of years to take up a position in Poultry Extension at Virginia Tech.

The 1984 meeting was hosted by the University of Guelph, and we helped with administration and guided tours.

1985 provided us with a very nice drive west to Ames, IA. We traveled via Detroit and Chicago, where we spent time admiring the waterfront, which was a surprising contrast with the rest of this huge metropolis. Most of my visits to Chicago involved O'Hare Field; thus my somewhat negative feelings about the place. At this time the kids were 10 and 8 years old, and easily adapted to motel life, especially the pools! They were both good swimmers and we could let them loose without worrying too much. And we could trust them with an in-room, fast-food dinner while Nita and I ate a civilized meal in the restaurant. We took time to see the Mississippi before driving through the Iowa corn country to Ames.

Following the meeting, we drove north through Minnesota, and visited the Itasca State Park, which contained the headwaters of the Mississippi. Back in Canada, I did a couple of farm calls in Thunder Bay and we spent two days in Willy Vanderwees' camp (their word for "cottage") in Sibley Provincial Park. This was on the Sleeping Giant peninsular that jutted out into Lake Superior, and from which could be seen Silver Islet. The one downside here was the well known temperature of Lake Superior; we briefly put a canoe in the water, Nita and I sat on the seats but the kids were on the bottom and almost froze, and we had to put cushions for them! It was an idyllic spot and we much enjoyed the break from driving and motels. We left Sibley Provincial Park late Thursday afternoon and stayed the night in Terrace Bay just a couple of hours east. Friday we did a fairly hard drive to the Sault Ste Marie and stayed in a modest motel (the good ones being full) with no pool. We took a boat tour of the Soo locks. Next morning we agreed that we would not spend another night on the road but make the 750 km drive in one day, a long one for the kids but they were very good and we got home about 6.30, having left the Soo at 7.15 am.

Another nice cross country trip took us to the 1986 meetings at North Carolina State University at Raleigh. I always envied this place; they had as many poultry scientists on staff as in all the Canadian institutions combined. The meetings were the usual combination of short papers, and some symposia, and some good beer sessions in the evenings. After the meetings, we also met up with Hugh Thornburg, one of the former Shaver sales people I was very fond of, and his wife Tilley. We had a meal with them and went back to their place in Siler City NC. When we left there, we drove part of the Blue Ridge Parkway and in to Blacksburg VA where we stayed a couple of nights with Paul and Diane Ruszler. Paul took me to visit one of his client egg farms, with 1 million hens. That was quite a revelation and also an indication of what our industry might be like without our supply management system. We ended up the trip with a couple of nights with the Donaldsons in their new place, The River House in Centreville MD. This was a very old house beautifully maintained and modernized, with pool, river access, guest house, the works. As always, Graham and Robin were the most generous hosts, and we really enjoyed the time there. Graham continued to live there even after Robin died, and only sold the place in 2020.

For the 1987 meeting in Corvallis OR, we drove all the way! But we made a nice holiday of it too, spending time in Yellowstone National Park and visiting Mount Rushmore on the way. Carole and I visited the Buffalo Bill Museum. These drives really gave us an insight into how vast this continent really was, and the magnificent scenery there for the viewing. We covered 5,100 km from home to the Oregon State University campus.

At this time, the Canadian born Prof. Paul Bernier was still working at OSU, and the Poultry Department was vibrant and active.

After the meeting in Corvallis, we headed north, back into Canada at Blaine, WA. From there to Vancouver, where we stayed with Sandy and Eva Cairns in their gorgeous West Vancouver home, complete with pool! Nita had met Sandy previously and we had an open invitation. We did some sightseeing in Vancouver with the kids. Then I flew home and Nita drove family and car back on the Trans-Canada highway. My journey lasted five hours, hers, almost a week, but I think she enjoyed having the kids to herself and they behaved a lot better than they did when I was there!

The 1988 PSA meeting was in Baton Rouge, LA and Nita, Carole and I enjoyed a good drive there; a three-day trip through Michigan, Ohio, West Virginia, Kentucky, Arkansas and Mississippi. A good meeting and good tours for Nita and Carole (PJ was at camp). This year, I chaired the joint US and Canada Branch WPSA lecture by Roy Gyles, entitled "Poultry, People and Progress". I described this at the time as "very deep, challenging and philosophical stuff". First stop on our journey home was in Cullman AL, where I used to go when working for Shaver. It turned out to be still "dry" and the best place to eat, still the "All Steak" restaurant. We met up with one of my old Shaver pals, Charlie Overstreet, for breakfast before leaving.

The PSA meeting in 1989 was in Madison, Wisconsin; all four of us went by car *via* Chicago and stayed on campus. As usual, it was well attended and enjoyable. I frequently joined the Guelph crowd, with John Summers and his students. Also part of the group was Tony Costain, who ran his own nutrition consulting company from his home in Georgetown, ON. He formulated feeds for a number of independent feed companies throughout Canada. I found him a useful contact and also a splendid lunch companion.

This relationship lasted several years until suddenly he became "distant", not only with me but with most of his other contacts. We never regained the original friendship, and Tony later died of cancer well before his retirement.

For a change of company one night, I had beers with Don Bell and the Extension group from California. Don was a tremendous resource and worked tirelessly for the California, and indeed the international egg industry. At that time the State Extension services were important sources of information for industry; shortly after, however, a process of erosion began, when retirees were not replaced, and eventually publicly funded agricultural extension became obsolete in all but a few states.

We left Madison on the Friday morning and drove north into Canada, dropping PJ off at Camp Wanapitei on Sunday on the way home. He attended this camp for several years.

PSA in 1990 was in Blacksburg VA, and we drove there with Carole while PJ was again at Camp Wanapitei. We stopped at the Donaldson's *en route* and as usual stayed on campus. Of course, our friends Paul and Dianne Ruszler were hosting so we did not have the usual close contact. One non-academic highlight of this meeting was a lecture entitled *"The Confederate Women; The True Scarlet O'Hara"*.

As was becoming a habit, we had the Canada Breakfast at 6.00 am one morning. Also lots of beers with John Summers, Tony Costain, Nancy Fisher and several others. The annual lecture sponsored by the US and Canada Branches of WPSA was given this year by Frank Hurnik from Guelph. Entitled *"Ethics and Animal Welfare"* this was timely and surely a taste of things to come.

PSA in 1991 was at Texas A&M in College Station. Nita and Carole drove my car there, taking several days, and I flew down to meet them. We held the WPSA Canada Branch Annual Meeting during PSA and replaced Jim Atkinson, who had been secretary, with Roy Crawford at U. Sask. Jim had really let things slide and I as Branch President was glad to see the change, although apprehensive about dealing at such long distance. This would mean nothing in 2020 but in 1990, nobody had internet connections, and long distance phone calls were expensive.

Nita and I went to the 1995 PSA meeting, one of the few to be held in Canada, this one in Edmonton. We drove there after visiting PJ in Whistler, BC. The Alberta people did an excellent job, led by Frank Robinson, who at the time was the leader of the poultry group. They held a pre-conference symposium on Animal Welfare, which was well done, but the discussion dominated by an animal rights activist that left a sour taste in my mouth. They had a great opening reception, with a Canada/Alberta travelogue, and a performance by a very colourful and vibrant Ukrainian dance group.

The meetings were, as always, well organized and interesting. The Wednesday night barbecue, this year sponsored by Pfizer, was held in Fort Edmonton Park, and they had Klondike Days entertainment with a Dixieland Jazz band, dancers, and Barbershopettes! The WPSA lecture was on molecular genetics and given by Ann Gibbins from the University of Guelph. Canadians were elected as Second Vice President (Hank Classen) and Director (Frank Robinson) to the PSA Board.

While in Edmonton, I talked at length with PSA people about holding their 2000 meeting in Montreal, back to back with the World's Poultry Congress, and they were very receptive.

I attended the 2001 PSA meeting in Indianapolis shortly after my official retirement from the Egg Board. The meetings were becoming more expensive and the social and family programs gradually vanished! By this time the Journal was supplied online, and I scanned the contents while I was still writing newsletters, and my Research page in *World Poultry*. Retired members were entitled to *emeritus* membership, and so I could still look at the web site and the journals, which became open access anyway in 2019.

In July, 2003 I went to the PSA meeting in Madison WI. The sessions were useful in many ways, but primarily provided good material for my freelance writing, as well as the *Ovum*, which I was still producing for the Egg Board. It was also an opportunity to meet other Canadian scientists and extend the reach of the Canadian Poultry Research Council, of which I was by then the Chair.

The social activities were always fun, although the participants changed over the years. In my early days at PSA, the beer crowd was mostly from Guelph, John Summers and his students. Now it was mainly Alberta and Saskatchewan who led the way, but the scene was similar and enjoyable. And of course it kept me up to date on who was doing what and where.

One of the papers was presented by scientists from the University of Newcastle, my *alma mater*. I sought them out and found that the college of agriculture no longer existed, and they were from the Medical School!

After the meetings, I went with Francine Bradley (Treasurer of the WPSA) to visit the National Agriculture Library in Bethesda MD, where the WPSA archives were stored. Ray Scharr, long retired from USDA and a colleague, Cam Calvert, were in charge and gave us a very interesting review of what they were doing. Knowing about this facility was to be of great help to me when I later came to write my paper on 100 Years of WPSA.

In August 2005, Piet and Therese Simons can over from The Netherlands for the PSA meetings in Auburn AL. As this was mostly a holiday for all of us, it is dealt with more fully in Chapter 16. We did attend some of the PSA sessions, but the main reason we were there was for the WPSA Board meeting, presided over by Ruveyde Akbay from Turkey.

We also were able to see the newly built Poultry Science Department, a beautiful structure that I suspected might be the last such construction, at least in North America. We visited the poultry farm, which was soon to be replaced, primarily due to the huge value of the real estate that it occupied. One of the very pleasant social events was at the home of Ed and Dorothy Moran. Ed was to retire soon (he would not commit to a date) and we heard many anecdotes about his career. I told them the story of my first night in Canada in 1966, when a small party feasted on some of Ed's experimental chickens.

At the PSA Awards Banquet, I accepted the Egg Industry Award on behalf of Yoshinore Mine from the University of Guelph, who was unable to be there. This was my final personal appearance at a PSA event; by now retired and having no financial support, it made no sense to attend the meetings. I could still look at the journals and use the web site for any information I required.

The World's Poultry Science Association
The WPSA was formed in 2012 and was always international in membership and scope. Interestingly, one of the founding scientists, Prof. W.R. Graham from Guelph was also a founding member of PSA. Originally known as the International Association of Poultry Instructors and Investigators, WPSA was formed following a meeting in London, England in 1912. At this meeting, the following 14 countries were represented: Australia, Belgium, Canada, Cyprus, Denmark, France, Germany, Holland, India, Ireland, Norway, Russia, the United Kingdom, and the United States of America. Edward Brown (UK) was elected President and Raymond Pearl (USA), Secretary. Under its original name, it began to publish a journal which eventually morphed into the *Worlds Poultry Science Journal*. In the early days, the journal contained original research, practical advice, and anecdotal stories. It eventually became solely the publisher of peer-reviewed scientific review articles. In the early 2000's it became available to members online but hard copy was still

available on request. (For a detailed history of the WPSA, see Hunton, 2012; *World's Poultry Science Journal,* vol. 68, pp 758-767)

After World War II, the WPSA began to establish national branches, of which there are now more than 70, with a total membership in excess of 7,000. The Branches operate independently, levy their own dues and submit US$20.00/member ($10.00/member for low income countries) to the WPSA to cover the central administration and the production of the Journal. The administration is largely done by volunteers. The Secretary, Treasurer and Journal Editor's offices receive a modest honorarium, but there are no full-time paid staff. Thus the dues for the WPSA have remained low, by comparison with PSA, enabling almost anyone with an interest to become a member.

Another major source of revenue for WPSA has been sponsors; there are currently (2021) about 15 sponsors at various levels supporting the association.

Following the establishment of national branches, two Regional Federations were created, one in Europe and one for the Asia-Pacific region. The European Federation has been particularly successful and now holds a regional conference every four years, alternating with the World's Congresses. It also sponsors a number of discipline-based Working Groups, which hold their own symposia.

The WPSA sponsors, but does not manage, World's Poultry Congresses, normally held every four years. The first was held in The Hague in 1921, then Barcelona in 1924 and Ottawa in 1927.

I became a member of the UK Branch in 1962. They held a couple of meetings each year, which I attended. Once I moved to Canada in 1966, I joined the Canada Branch. Since most of the Canadian members also belonged to PSA, and attended its Annual Meetings, the *raison dêtre* for a Branch of WPSA in Canada, was unclear. One reason was to receive the Journal and as the dues were minimal, this was, for many, reason enough.

However, an important activity of the Canada Branch was fundraising in order to provide financial assistance to people, mainly graduate students, attending World's Poultry Congresses. While I was working for the Egg Board, I was ideally placed to persuade the federal agencies for eggs, chicken, turkeys and hatching eggs to contribute and most of them cooperated without too much fuss. I would sometimes meet with their Directors to make the pitch, and the WPSA was able to help many students who would otherwise not have attended.

At the time I joined the Canada Branch, the administration was concentrated in Ottawa at Agriculture Canada. Merv Mitchell was the President and Alan Grunder was the Secretary. Shortly after I joined, Alan circulated the information that the Life Membership dues were soon to be raised from US$100 to US$700, so several of us took advantage of this and saved ourselves quite a tidy sum. I later found this to be somewhat embarrassing, and made an annual donation to the Branch! I was elected President of the Canada Branch in 1984.

Finding a location, and even a reason, for a meeting of the Canada Branch was sometimes a challenge. Most often, we met during the PSA meetings, simply because that was where most members would be at the same place at the same time! We established the tradition of a Canada Breakfast at PSA, followed by our Annual General Meeting, and this worked fairly well.

The 1988 Worlds Poultry Congress, held in Nagoya, Japan, was the first that Nita and I attended together. By this time, former Canada Branch President, Merv Mitchell had retired from Agriculture Canada and set up his own travel agency, Ports of Call, and he organized a group for travel and tours around the Congress. Nita and I spent a couple of days in Vancouver with Sandy and Eva Cairns before joining the group for the flight to Tokyo, where we spent two days sightseeing. We found Japan very expensive, and were very happy to find a vending machine in the hotel where we could get a beer for US$4.00. We had our first experience of the famous Japanese Bullet Trains which took us to Kyoto. Assigned seats, numbered coaches, departure and arrival dead on time and the guide was standing exactly outside the exit door when the train stopped! The scenery viewed from the train was most spectacular, save for the fact that Mount Fuji was obscured by haze. But we saw rice and tea growing, lakes, mountains and occasional views of the ocean.

We had a day tour of Kyoto, and visited various religious (Buddhist and Shinto) shrines and monuments, the Imperial Palace and the Deer Park. We found very good hospitality at night with Al Kloosterman, who owned a prosperous poultry house building business near Peterborough ON. After another half-day in Kyoto, we took a short Bullet Train ride to Nagoya, where the Congress was held. We began learning what to avoid when running a Congress. First lesson: try to have the hotels and Congress centre within walking distance. In Nagoya, we had to take a subway and then a bus to get to the Congress site. In most Japanese train stations, you were lucky to see one small sign in English, so even this was a challenge. But once there, this Congress was well organized, and the Japanese WPSA President, Yukio Yamada, did a great job. Nita did the accompanying persons' tours and we met up at night. One memorable evening we were hosted for dinner by Chris Hann from the UK, and his wife Elaine. Nita described the meal as microscopic, and indeed it was; also expensive but quite delicious. We became good friends with the Hanns. Chris was Editor of the World's Poultry Science Journal for a number of years. They came to our house soon after the Congress, and we visited their home in Berkshire several times.

At the WPSA Membership meeting, although our bid for the 1996 Congress was unsuccessful, (we lost by 2 votes in a total of 116) I was elected as one of five Vice Presidents for a four-year term. This would oblige me to attend the annual meetings of the Association Board and they paid travel expenses. Nita and I enjoyed hospitality at both the Ross and Shaver suites, although we had to take taxis between them. At the final Banquet, Canadians Rob Gowe, Stan Slinger and Donald McQ. Shaver were inducted into the International Poultry Hall of Fame. (Stan wasn't there, so I brought his trophy home and delivered it later.)

Following the Congress, we flew from Tokyo to Hong Kong for three days as the final part of our tour. In Hong Kong we did all the tourist things, but the poultry people had a tour to the Research Farm in the New Territories, which was very interesting. One mistake we made was to buy a "Hong Kong Rolex", which so rusted up that when the battery expired, it could not be opened!

We got home at 10.00 pm, after the long, long journey including crossing the date-line for the first time. I had become accustomed to the jet lag experienced coming home from Europe, but the journey from the Far East always floored me.

In August 1989, I went to a WPSA European Federation meeting at Hohenheim University. Prof. Scholtysek was a long time WPSA member and an important part of the German Branch, one of Europe's largest. He and his wife held a dinner for several of us at the conclusion of the meetings and were most gracious hosts throughout. I presented a poster at the Symposium on Egg Quality, and acted as "reporter" at another session. The symposium was useful and informative, as they always were. We were also taken on several industry tours.

The 1990 Board meeting was in Barcelona, along with the European Federation Conference. I enjoyed the Spanish hospitality, led by Branch President Fernando Orozco, and met a lot of friends from Europe, including Norrie and Ada Semple from my days with Ross. They were part of the delegation from Glasgow, who were seeking and were awarded the privilege of hosting the next Conference.

In September 1992, I represented Brian Ellsworth at the International Egg Commission (IEC) meetings in St. Malo, France. This was conveniently the week prior to the World's Poultry Congress in Amsterdam. Upon my arrival in France, Geoff Fairhurst met me off the plane and drove me, first for a weekend at home and then to St. Malo. It was good to see him and Marcela again, now established in their French dwelling.

The IEC was mostly about politics and marketing with very little attention to science and technology. The social aspects and food, however, were outstanding! Alex Craig, who was one of the Egg Board Directors, was also representing CEMA at the IEC, gave Geoff and me, and several others some outstanding meals at a nearby restaurant.

One of the tours was to Mont. St. Michel, which must celebrate the same saint as St. Michael's Mount off the Cornwall coast but I never learned the origin of either.

The World' Poultry Congress in Amsterdam in 1992 was outstanding in many respects and a good model for us. However, it was held at the RAI, a conference centre a long way from downtown Amsterdam where most of the hotels were located. In addition, the exhibition was run by VIV, the Dutch exhibition giant, in Utrecht, 50 km away. Those factors notwithstanding, the Congress ran very smoothly and the social events were superb. The organization was led by Piet Simons, who was given a year's leave from his job at the government research station, Het Spelderholt, specifically to run the Congress. The venue provided all the necessary facilities, the program of invited speakers and submitted papers, and posters was excellent, and everyone was well satisfied.

The inaugural session with the usual speeches, was followed by a fantastic laser show and a splendid reception, where, of course, I met dozens of old friends and had a great time. There was another reception after the first day's scientific sessions, held at the Amsterdam Zoo, which I noted had "many drinks but little food". Seems you can't have everything! The Indian WPSA held a fine reception to encourage attendance in 1996, complete with good spicy food.

But the *pièce de resistance* of the social events was the farewell party at the ConcertGebouw. This was a huge concert hall built in the 19th century. They had all kinds of exhibits (nothing to do with poultry), a jazz band, a steel band, a plethora of food and endless beer.

The WPSA Executive meeting for 1993 was in Seoul, South Korea. By this time I had secured preferred status with Canadian Airlines and was able to get a Business Class ticket for the long flight to Tokyo. At this time,

Canadian was the main choice for Asian destinations, with daily DC10 flights to Tokyo and some other cities. When I boarded, they upgraded me to First! Also in the cabin was Albert Reichmann, at that time a big shot in Toronto real estate, but I bet he paid for his seat! On the way home, I had to spend the night in a hotel near Tokyo's Narita airport, but then got upgraded to First again for the Toronto flight.

The WPSA Korean Branch treated us royally. The meeting coincided with the Asia-Pacific Federation regional Conference and Exhibition and we attended this, as well as a guided tour to a poultry farm, a feed mill and a Korean Folk Village. This last was about 100 years old. I began to get to know my colleagues on the WPSA Executive a lot better during this meeting. This included Bruce Sheldon from Australia, who was President of the Asia-Pacific Federation, as well as a Vice President of WPSA. He and his wife Joan loved to travel, and I met them almost everywhere I went. Chris Hann, Journal Editor, Secretary Rose Marie Wegner, and Treasurer Wade Brant were all good company. B.V Rao, representing the 1996 Congress, attended and reported on its progress.

The Executive meeting was fine and we had begun to recruit sponsors for the Journal to alleviate the financial situation. This had been a challenge for several years. Piet Simons was a great one for arm-twisting companies into paying up. Of course, the Dutch industry was huge in terms of suppliers; feed microingredients, processing equipment, layer cages and feeders, etc. etc. and Piet did a fine job. The Exhibition company VIV bought the back cover of the Journal almost in perpetuity.

The European Federation Symposia were valuable too. I went to Tours, France in October 1993 for the meetings on the Quality of Eggs and Egg Products. I gave one of the papers but the meeting was most valuable for the contacts made. Dr. Sally Solomon, who was Chair of the Symposium and a world authority on the egg shell, had received some support from the Egg Board for part of her research program. Another attendee, Max Hincke from the University of Ottawa had also had support for a summer student. After talking to them, as detailed in Chapter 7, they combined with Yves Nys in France to submit a joint proposal that the Egg Board supported for several years, greatly extending knowledge of egg shell structure and physiology.

Of course, being in France, they fed us exceptionally well. We had one dinner composed entirely of products bearing the *label rouge* quality symbol. The final banquet was presented in a lovely *Chateau* a few km out of town, and accompanied by a choral interlude.

After the meeting, David Martin, Editor of *Poultry International,* gave me a ride to Lysieux, where I met up with my old flame Carole Chassagnard (née Shepherd), whom I had courted long ago in Kent. She was by now a *Chatelaine* in a huge 400 year old dwelling, but only the rooms they were living in were habitable. They had 5 children at school so the place was hopping when they began coming home. They were gradually fixing up the rest of the place. I stayed one night in a nearby hotel but enjoyed a splendid dinner with them, and the next day Carole's husband Pierre drove me to the local train station to start the next phase of my journey. This was to England, to visit with Chris Hann, who had now become the Editor of the *World's Poultry Science Journal.* We discussed WPSA affairs and also visited Cliveden, a National Trust property on the bank of the Thames.

The 1994 WPSA Executive meeting was held in Glasgow, Scotland, in conjunction with the European Poultry Conference. Their hospitality was outstanding, as was the Conference. Glasgow was at the time transforming itself from a fairly grimy industrial city into a tourist and conference destination. Their use of some of the old historic buildings was very well done. One reception was held in City Hall and another at the University. Of course, there was also beer; meeting with David Martin, Norrie Semple and numerous others involved many pints. At the opening reception I was dragooned into the position of "stooge" in a version of the Ode to the Haggis, and drank the first Scotch I'd had in forty years. I sampled much better Scotch at a tasting and tour arranged by David Martin and Sally Solomon at the Glengoyne Distillery.

The Indian Branch was much in evidence promoting the 1996 World's Congress, and a few of the Canadian Steering Committee gently talking about Congress 2000.

I went to the 1995 Executive meeting in Katowice, Poland. Poland had a long history in poultry science and in fact was awarded a Worlds Congress in the 1980s but was unable to proceed.

In Katovice, we stayed at the Palace Hotel, which my diary states was "a fine misnomer". It was the ancestral seat of the Radziwill family, long neglected but at the time under restoration (like much of Poland). My room could be politely described as Spartan, but the surroundings were excellent. Our meeting was successful in the sense that no major controversies arose. There was a move by Piet Simons to discontinue paying expenses for Vice Presidents to attend the meeting but it was quickly squashed. The Journal publication was very late, due to a variety of quite solvable problems. There had been changes in publication arrangements that had not helped the situation.

After the meeting in Poland, I flew to Paris and spent a day at the INRA in Tours, hosted by Yves Nys. I met most of the poultry group there and was duly impressed with the variety and quality of their work. Following this, I visited Geoff and Marcela Fairhurst and enjoyed their hospitality once more. I also met with old friends in the Shaver (now ISA) office, J.L. Gac and J.L Salaun.

The Indian World's Poultry Congress was very successful, despite the death of President B.V. Rao only a few months before opening. Rao was the CEO of Venkateshwara Hatcheries, a major player in the Indian industry. They had distribution rights for Cobb meat chickens and Babcock layers and were extremely important in the commercial industry. From what I was told, they also pretty well owned the WPSA Branch! The Congress was held in New Delhi, and was efficiently conducted at a good hotel, the Taj Palace, with an associated Exhibition at a remote location. Although I succumbed to Delhi belly for about 24 hours, I participated in the Congress and thought it was well run. I chaired a session on Egg and Poultry Marketing which was well attended and the audience, enthusiastic.

At the WPSA Executive meeting, the 2004 Congress was awarded to Turkey (majority of 1 vote, after a recount).

Mrs. Anuradha Desai, B.V. Rao's daughter, and now President of Venkateshwara Hatcheries, took over as President of the Congress and subsequently as President of WPSA. She attended and Chaired the annual Executive meetings, but WPSA affairs were essentially managed by Piet Simons in The Netherlands during her term of office.

I visited India several times and personally enjoyed the occasional meeting with Mrs. Desai after I became WPSA President in 2000.

The Post-Congress tour of India and Nepal (literally a Cook's Tour), was excellent and is described in detail in Chapter 16.

In February 1997, I made the first of several visits to Australia. This one was to present a scientific paper to the Australian Poultry Science Symposium, and of course to pitch WPC2000. Poultry science in Australia had some similarities to Canada. It is a huge country, and production and research is scattered widely around the country. The distribution of production may not have been quite as wide as in Canada, where there was production in all 10 Provinces and sometimes one Territory, but nevertheless took place in most of the Australian States. The WPSA Branch was well supported and in fact the scientists had essentially established sub-branches in several locations. The Symposium in Sydney was an annual affair and well worth attending. This was especially so for

Canadians, as it was held in February and it was good to feel some warmth!

In this case, Nita and I flew in on February 10th. At this time, one had to fly from Toronto to Honolulu (almost 10 hours, with a 3 hour layover) and then on to Sydney (9 hours). The only bad thing we experienced in the whole trip was finding a piece of luggage identical to ours, but not ours, on the luggage carousel. The owners had already left with ours and it took most of the day to sort it out. But we had a pleasant day anyway. We were met by Ray Leach of Field Fresh, and he gave us a little tour of Sydney before dropping us at the hotel. We managed to relax for a few hours before an evening dinner tour of Sydney Harbour, courtesy of Novo-Nordisk, an enzyme company.

The following day I gave the WPC2000 pitch to a meeting of the WPSA Branch. We attended the Symposium Banquet in an imposing old dining room in St. John's College. I gave my paper on the final day, and also spent an hour with Hugh McMaster of the Australian Egg Industry Council, comparing notes. Australia had quite recently abandoned supply management and the outcomes were still being analyzed.

I had an interesting tour of a company called The Egg Basket. Three partners were involved in production and marketing, and I visited these operations as well as three retail stores. Interestingly, none of the stores had refrigeration for their egg displays. I then attended the WPSA sub-branch meeting at Seven Hills, and again gave an impromptu pitch for WPC2000. Most of the rest of this trip was holiday and is described in Chapter 16.

We had a quick trip to Melbourne, and I spent most of a day with Greg Parkinson, who worked on poultry at the Victoria Institute of Animal research. It was very hot, 38-40°C, when we visited Kinross Poultry Farm. This was in transition; they had one new building completely enclosed, with pad and fan ventilation, stacked cages and full environmental control. The old buildings were what they called saw-tooth design, with open sides and stair step cages. Even at close to 40°C, the Australorp crosses in this building did not seem unduly stressed; they were panting and a few had wings outstretched, but mortality was not increased. To achieve some degree of cooling, they sprayed water on the metal roofs; humidity was so low that the water evaporated before reaching the eaves. I gave another impromptu talk to the Victoria sub branch of WPSA.

In Brisbane, we were met by Bob Pym whom I had known during the time he worked with Rob Gowe at the Animal Research Institute in Ottawa. We toured the Poultry Research Station before lunch with him and David

Farrell, Paul Mannion and David Robinson. (David Robinson had been a M.Sc. student at Wye before I left). After the tour and more talk, Nita left to explore the city, while I gave a short talk on Egg Shell Quality to the Queensland sub branch of WPSA.

I also had a full day in the field; Graeme Bell of Sunny Queen collected me and I toured their egg processing and quality assurance departments. I then switched to Geoff Stuart, who drove me to Ipswich, where I met Ralph Hohl and his colleagues at Home On the Range Eggs. They gave me a superb lunch at an old (1887) pub, called Hotel Cecil. The egg industry was surviving the transformation from supply management to a free market. Of course, unlike Canada, they didn't have a huge industry next door waiting to flood their market!

The WPSA Executive meeting in 1997 was in Nyborg in Denmark, some 135 km west of Copenhagen. I had a short visit to the UK prior to the meeting, spending time with Eric Wainwright and visiting his daughter Pam in the Scottish border country. Pam was widowed a short while previously, and had sold their B&B. She was then in a rental cottage while deciding on a permanent home. I also visited David and Angela Bourn in Sussex – I was best man at their wedding 39 years ago – how time flies!

On arrival in Nyborg, I had dinner with some of the WPSA Executive.
I spent quite a while talking to people from Turkey, where the WPSA Branch would host WPC2004. We didn't know much about the Branch. The President was Prof. Ruveyde Akbay, who seemed to run the Branch but nobody outside of Turkey knew much about her. She had spent some time at Cornell but little was known about this either. Piet Simons suspected that the Congress and subsequent Presidency of WPSA was a power trip for Mrs. Akbay! It subsequently turned out that she was very capable, ran a good Congress and was a competent President.

I stopped again in England on the way home, hosted by Pete and Val Halliwell in Upper Clatford. Lots of beer in the Crook and Shears, a good day out in Portsmouth at the Historic Ships exhibit and a day sailing. Pete had a yacht for many years (Val never sailed) and although the weather was quite rough, we made it to the Isle of Wight and back, with, of course, several pints and lunch in a pub.

The same evening in the Crook and Shears, Jim and Liz Parlour came to have a drink with us. Liz was formerly Liz Lepper, (I rented a room in her parents' place in Wye, known as the Lepper colony) and Jim was one of the Wye M.Sc. graduates. A small world! Jim was no longer in poultry, but teaching part time at a community college and running an antique store.

The morning I left, while having breakfast with Pete and Val, we heard on the radio the news of the death of Princess Diana, former wife of Prince Charles, in a horrific auto accident in Paris.

In June, I went to Israel for the WPSA's Executive meeting. Nita joined me and did some tourist things while I worked, but I also saw some of the sights after the meeting. I had always felt a strange connection with Israel, which intensified after my mother told me that in fact I was Jewish. I read Michener's book, *The Source*, for the second time before visiting. Details of our touring experiences are in Chapter 16.

The Executive meeting ran very late and on this occasion, President Mrs. Desai did not arrive until 4.00 pm (the meeting began at 10.00 am). The event coincided with the European Poultry Conference, which attracted more than 500 people, and the Israel Branch, a very strong and active one, ran an excellent meeting. WPC2000 had a small booth at the Exhibition and sponsored a breakfast to promote our Congress,

The program included a guided visit to the Israel Museum, which helped us understand the country's 8,000 year history (and confirmed a lot of what Michener wrote!) and we also had a full day tour including one of the equipment manufacturers. We visited a kibbutz, Tel Aviv to see Yitzatch Rabin Square, and the ongoing excavations at Caesarea. Finally a brief stop in Jaffa overlooking the Mediterranean.

I left Israel and flew to Portugal for a meeting with the WPSA Branch, and was royally entertained by Manuel Soares Costa and his family. The Portuguese branch was very active and I already knew several of their members, from the time I travelled with the Shaver distributor, Granja Barca Nova. I gave one of my talks on the Egg Shell; it was simultaneously translated, but all of the discussion was in Portuguese, so I was unable to take part.

The European Poultry Conference in 1999 was held in Bologna, Italy. This turned out to be an excellent meeting. I chaired one of the sessions during the Egg symposium. But the highlight for me was a visit to the University Library, arranged by Sally Solomon from Glasgow. Here was saw one of Ulisse Aldrovandi's (1522-1605) original text books, *"Ornithologia"* containing beautiful, original paintings, and as a special privilege, were actually permitted to handle it. I suppose now that Aldrovandi was really the first ever Poultry Scientist. (And not just poultry: I recently read a book in which he was referred to as an authority on botany.) Bologna had an amazing history and we enjoyed our time there. Branch President at the time was Prof. Achile Franchini and the hospitality was outstanding!

The editorship of the *World's Poultry Science Journal* was an important post. In the 1990's it was held by Chris Hann, then retired from the UK Ministry of Agriculture, and an excellent Editor. Late in the decade, he announced his retirement from the post, and advised us to appoint Jim MacNab in his place. Jim was a nutritionist working at the Roslyn Institute (formerly Poultry Research Centre) in Edinburgh. At the time, the WPSA was publishing the Journal itself, and it was produced in The Netherlands on the advice of Piet Simons, who negotiated an unbeatable price for printing. So Piet was very much involved in the process. During my visit to The Netherlands for the VIV show in November, 1999, Piet began to express doubts about Jim's effectiveness. I dismissed this at the time, but not entirely. I knew that David Martin, co-Editor of Watt's *Poultry International*, had expressed some interest in the position. It was likely, when I became President of WPSA in August 2000, that either Piet and Jim would have "come to terms" or I would be faced with making the change in some way. As it turned out Piet and Jim could not find common ground, and in June 2001, I asked Jim to resign. He took a couple of days but then agreed. So David Martin, by this time retired from Watt, took the job and did it very well for approximately 5 years.

As President of WPSA from 2000 – 2004, I was expected to attend the international exhibitions where we had a presence. This included the European events that alternated each November between VIV in Utrecht and Eurotier in Hanover. In 2000 it was in Hanover. I flew to Amsterdam and took the train to Apeldoorn where Piet Simons lived. He gave me a brief tour of the Spelderholt research institute where he had worked for many years, before driving us to Hanover. We also had a meeting with Ken Plaxton of Elsevier who told us about their web-based scientific journals, obviously hoping to attract the *World's Poultry Science Journal*. The show was quite busy and I got some feedback, mostly positive, regarding WPC2000. I managed to get taken to dinner by the Watt crowd, who spent a lot of time criticizing *World Poultry* for which I was then writing exclusively! I later caught up with Wiebe van der Sluis and his colleagues from Misset/Elsevier, including Sarah Mellor, and got their side of the story, so balance was restored.

The show was busy, with the Turkish people actively promoting their 2004 Congress, and the Germans, the 2002 European Conference planned for Bremen. In the evening, a big group of us were invited to dine at the home of Rose-Marie Wegner, former WPSA Secretary. This included Piet and me, Arnold Elson and his wife Kathy (Arnold was the housing and environmental expert from the UK), Ragnar Tauson, poultry welfare specialist from Sweden, and a couple of others I didn't know. Rose-Marie was an excellent host and we had a very good evening.

January 2001 saw us in Atlanta for the poultry show. I spent some time at the scientific meetings the two days prior to the show.

I had decided that we should have an Executive meeting by conference call, and after a lot of running around in circles, someone from the Conference Center Communications Office put it together for us and we had a successful meeting. Piet, Francine and I were in a small glass booth in Atlanta, and everyone else at home, in six different countries, and likely as many time zones.

The show was busy as always. The Turkish people used our old WPC2000 exhibit, suitably modified, which was gratifying, as we clearly had no use for it and it had cost a significant amount.

As had become a "tradition", Piet Simons, David Martin and I had lunch at Max Lager's pub for the WPSA Awards Committee annual meeting; this to plan for the awards in 2004, so not a long affair.

We attended the Watt reception the evening before the show opened, and I had dinner with Wiebe van der Sluis and the Elsevier people just to keep things in balance. I spent most of my time at the WPC2004 booth, but managed to see most of the rest of the exhibits that interested me. And, as always, lots of old friends to meet, and a few new ones made.

Starting on February 1st, I began my only round-the-world trip for WPSA. I flew west to Los Angeles and thence to Sydney, Australia, which at the time was my longest flight ever, 14 h, 40 min. I met WPSA Vice Pres. Colin Fisher on the plane and we shared a cab to our hotel. As usual our arrival was 8.00 am after crossing the date line, which for me was always disorienting. However, I did my best, and had a very nice pub lunch with an old school-friend, Mike Bertram and his wife Patti. Then I met Wiebe van der Sluis, my Editor at *World Poultry* and we spent time discussing this year's writing program. All of this prior to the opening of the Poultry Science Symposium organized by the Australian Branch of WPSA. They ran very good meetings, attracting an audience from all over the South Pacific. I attended and said a few words at the Branch Annual General Meeting and enjoyed the subsequent Banquet at St. Andrew's College.

On the last night in Sydney, I had dinner with my friends Graham and Robin Donaldson, here on holiday from Maryland. They had a beautiful apartment overlooking Sydney Harbour, with a view of both the Bridge and the Opera House, and while we were sitting with drinks on their balcony, we watched as the huge liner Queen Elizabeth II left the docks.

For the weekend, I flew to Brisbane, where I was entertained by Ralph Hohl and his girl-friend Carol. Ralph was in egg production in a big way and his wife had recently died; Carol was "retired" from some career in Melbourne – I never quite understood what she did. It turned out that neither of them cooked much, but they both drank enough for a regiment, so it was quite a liquid weekend. They showed me the Sunshine Coast and the Gold Coast, which were both extraordinarily beautiful. I stayed the first night in Carol's spare room in her flat in Caloundra. Ralph really showed me the sights! We went to Surfers' Paradise, where the Asia-Pacific WPSA Federation Conference would be held in 2002. The second night we were in one of Ralph's many houses, where we had a barbecue and of course copious wine.

The following day, Bob Pym, who was then President of the Australian Branch, picked me up and we went to look at the Brisbane Convention Centre, where they plan to hold WPC2008. It was quite like the Montreal Palais but newer. We later met with other people on the Congress planning team and I answered a lot of questions about our experience in 2000, which might help them later. I was staying in the Hilton, which was clearly angling to be the Conference Hotel, and they gave me a very superior room! I enjoyed Brisbane; not only the weather but the whole environment. A river meandered through the city and the City Cat, a water taxi, was a standard way of getting around. I had a day to spare in Brisbane before the next leg of the trip, and went on a bus tour. However, I had seen most of the sights with Ralph!

My next destination was Dhaka, Bangladesh, reached by way of Singapore. Bangladesh was certainly a poor country, but they went out of their way to show me hospitality. I stayed in a nice hotel and was taken everywhere by car. But the streets of Dhaka were astonishingly chaotic, with rickshaws (both human and motor powered) everywhere, exhaust fumes from ill-maintained two-cycle engines, and noise, noise, noise.

The Bangladesh Branch of WPSA was an outstanding example of how valuable the Association could be. There was not a lot of scientific infrastructure in Bangladesh, but the Branch also functioned as an industry organization; all the CEO's and technical staff of the production companies were members. The event I was to attend, along with Piet Simons and Mrs. Godwin, President of the Sri Lanka Branch, was their annual Poultry Show and Seminar. This was well organized and interesting, particularly a paper by Dr. G.L Jain who worked as a geneticist for the Venkateshwara Group in India. I made a short speech at the opening ceremony. This was also where I made the first presentation of my paper, "100 Years of Poultry Genetics", subsequently published in the *World's Poultry Science Journal*. Piet and I were presented with beautiful carved, multi-coloured roosters. They were hard to carry and mine lost a few feathers on the way home, but I still have it in my office!

The commercial poultry industry in Bangladesh was growing fast, with all of the pain that sometimes entails. There was also a huge number of small flocks, and this was one of the places where the International Network for Family Poultry Development was extremely active. I really enjoyed this first visit to Bangladesh. Its only challenge was it was 100% dry with no exceptions for foreign guests!

I left Dhaka with Dr. Davedhkar of the India Branch and he guided me to our next destination, Pune, with stops in Kolkata and Mumbai. We actually stayed overnight in Mumbai in a palatial hotel where I was able to get a beer!

In Pune I had a VIP welcome from the Venky Group; a garland and photographs. The first day I visited the Dr. B.V. Rao Institute of Poultry Management, named for the late President of the Venky Group, and prime mover for the 1996 Congress. This was a remarkable place where hands-on training was provided to Venky staff and indeed many others, to raise standards of knowledge of poultry science, technology and management. Its Director, Dr. Bhagwat was a true enthusiast and did a very fine job. Bhagwat had trained with Prof. Jim Craig at Kansas State. He spent an hour describing the Institute and what it did, and I was greatly impressed. I also went to the Veterinary Research Laboratory, where research and diagnostic work was performed. Later in the day, several of the Venky people took me for a drink and dinner at the Blue Diamond Hotel. When we arrived, they were surprised to find it "dry" – one of three days in the year when this happens. Nothing daunted, somebody booked a room and we got drinks by room service! And we had a very good dinner too.

I found Pune different from the other Eastern cities I had visited; less poverty, less pollution and more civility. The people all seemed industrious and proud of their place in the world. I had a free day here and Dr. Dhavedkar took me on a short sight-seeing tour, including the local reservoir.

The next day, Dr. D. took me by train to Hyderabad to see the Venky Egg Further Processing plant. The train journey was dreadful; although we were in a second class, air-conditioned sleeper, we shared it with two strangers. Sleep was an illusion. We took packed meals from the hotel as there were no catering facilities on the train. We arrived in Hyderabad at 5.30 am and had about an hour of sleep before dawn. The view from this hotel was awesome; a gorgeous lake with slight mist over it when we first saw it. We had a short walk before breakfast, and then the visit to the egg plant. This was state-of-the-art technology, and billed as a benefit to the egg industry. I was not quite sure about this, as in many cases, further processing was a last resort when shell egg prices declined. However, it would perhaps be useful in the long term when the market for egg components matured.

We flew from Hyderabad to Mumbai to connect with my flight to the next destination; Rome by way of Frankfurt. The flying time from Mumbai to Rome was 11 h, with a 2 h layover in Frankfurt, and I got there, having slept very little, at noon, with no commitments until the next day. So I found my hotel and gratefully slept for about 6 h, then walked until I found a local Trattoria for dinner. I ate very well for the equivalent of CDN$30.00, and will always remember that 1 l of mineral water cost the same as 0.5 l of excellent red wine!

The reason for my trip to Rome was to visit the United Nations Food and Agriculture Organization (FAO) and to meet their genetics and gene conservation staff. Keith Hammond, a whirlwind of a man from Australia, was very informative about FAO's activity in the field of animal genetics. I also met two veterinarians who were working in the area of small poultry flocks and their contribution to alleviating poverty in rural communities. Finally, I spent some time with Beata Scherf, who ran the FAO program for conservation of animal genetic resources. I was becoming interested in this field at the urging of D.Mc.Q. Shaver, who was spearheading this activity, or rather loudly lamenting the lack of it, in Canada. It was a very full day, after which I enjoyed another excellent dinner – even better than the previous night – for almost the same price. The following day, I flew back to Toronto. My total flying time around the world was 60 h. I was glad to be home.

European Federation Symposia
The European Federation of branches established a number of Working Groups that held Symposia, usually in the years when there was no Congress or regional conference. They were hosted by national Branches. In 2001, I attended two of these, one in Switzerland and the other in Turkey. The Swiss meeting was on Poultry Welfare. This was the first occasion I experienced serious discussion on production of organic chicken and eggs. At this point in my career, I just wasn't able or willing to give this much time or attention. Subsequent developments have, of course, proved me to be out on a limb! I was still unconvinced of the added value of organic food, but a significant minority of consumers obviously disagreed, and were prepared to back their preference with money. The Symposium had other interesting aspects, including my presentation on the Canadian Codes of Practice. There was also a tour which included some free range and organic production units.

After leaving this meeting, which was held at Zollikofen, near Bern, I took the train to Zurich and flew to Izmir, on the west coast of Turkey, for the Symposia on the Quality of Eggs and Poultry Products. These were two excellent events, organized by Servet Yaltsin, who was also Scientific Chair for the forthcoming World's Poultry Congress in 2004. The venue was in Kusadasi, in a beautiful resort with rooms overlooking the Aegean Sea. It was quite close to Ephesus, the ancient city that was also part of one of the tours. I had my picture taken making a speech from the steps of the "Library" ruin.

My arrival was two days early, so I was able to spend a relaxing day on the beach, in the sun and in and out of the water, and make preparations for my formal appearances as President. The WPSA executive meeting occupied most of one day prior to the opening of the Symposia. We had a very full agenda, but this was an excellent Board; everyone was well prepared and we got through in good time. It was at this meeting that David Martin was officially appointed Editor of the World's Poultry Science Journal, although he had been functioning in the position for several months.

The Symposia were very good; I spent most of my time in the Egg Quality sessions, which I had committed to cover for World Poultry, while my Editor, Wiebe, covered the Poultry Meat section. Egg shell quality, one of my long term interests, was widely covered in and out of the formal sessions; Julie Roberts, Sally Solomon, and Yves Nys, all world authorities, gave me lots of ideas.

The social side of the event was also very successful; my diary records "dancing" with some of the voluptuous girls imported for the occasion. Dancing is not my thing so there must have been a lot of persuasion involved!

On the penultimate day, (September 11) after the scientific sessions were over, I was returning to my room, and saw Paul Siegel; he said "Turn on your TV" which was something I seldom did. But I turned it on anyway, to watch the terrorist attacks on the World Trade Centre in New York. At first, it was just a loop showing a plane approaching and colliding with the building, but later the details came out and, as they say, the rest is history. The meetings went off very well but of course all of the conversations were about the terrorist attacks, and the very practical challenges faced by those of us resident in North America, since all airports were closed and transatlantic travel had ceased.

My scheduled departure from Izmir was September 14, but nobody would confirm anything, except the hotel bus to the airport. We got there at 5.00

am. American airports were still closed but apparently flights to Canada were being re-started, and I was very fortunate to fly as expected from Izmir to Zurich, and on to Toronto. What was really miraculous was that Nita, who had spent time in the UK and expected to meet me off her flight from Heathrow a few minutes after mine from Zurich, actually did so!

In October, I flew to Guatemala City for the ALA meeting. WPSA was not active in Guatemala but we had high hopes. The Directors of ALA were known locally as the "millionaires club" and I pitched WPSA as a way to improve their technical competence and scientific abilities. Nobody argued and I thought good might come from the visit. Latin America was fertile ground for WPSA; I talked with people from several countries in the region, many of whom had trained in the US, who might be able to help. One challenge was the large number of veterinarians (I don't think their training was as thorough or took as long as a North American vet. degree) and the poultry vets had their own professional associations in several countries.

After leaving Guatemala, I flew to Santiago, Chile. Here I met Soledad Urrutia, Editor of Misset's Spanish language magazine, *Avicultura Profesional,* and Jose Luis Arias, a scientist at the University, another egg shell specialist. As my arrival was on Sunday, Jose showed me around Santiago, which was a fascinating city, very European in some ways. He told me the old Fish Market, a 100 year old structure made of wrought iron, was imported from London, England. After lunch, we took a trip on the cable car to the summit of Mt. Cristobel for really fabulous views of the city, whose population was then about 5 million. I spent some time with Soledad, giving a formal interview for the magazine about WPSA, how it worked and what a national branch could contribute to a country. She was just the person to start a branch in Chile. I spent the rest of the day, which was a holiday, with Jose Arias and his family. They drove me up a huge canyon alongside the Colorado River, and we had lunch in Casa Bosque, a remarkable building constructed of whole pine tree trunks, and the walls packed with recycled tires.

The following day was hard work; my host was Hector Hildalgo, who I think was "Dr. Poultry Science" in Chile at the time, He introduced me to the head of the national Egg Producers Association, whose first words to me were "Do you know Brian Ellsworth?" They knew one another from the International Egg Commission. This was a good start and we got along well. I had a similarly friendly welcome at the Poultry Meat Association, but still didn't identify a volunteer to help start a WPSA branch. I spent some time with Jose in his laboratory at the Vet School. I also met with the Poultry Veterinarians, about 15 of them, and gave a short version of my talk on 100 Years of Poultry Genetics – just some of the history and a bit about egg shell quality and structure.

I left Chile with high hopes of a new branch there and flew to Buenos Aires for a similar campaign. The first night I was given dinner by two veterinarians, at a wonderful steak house. My steak was nearly 4 cm thick, and even with their very good Cabernet Sauvignon, I couldn't finish it. The next day I met with the heads of the Egg Producers Association, and their nutrition consultant. We talked a lot about WPSA and also our supply management system in Canada. I found many people around the world were interested, but the prospect of any country voluntarily starting such a system was daunting, especially in the absence of a predatory competitor like the US next door to Canada.

I was then passed to Marcelo Schang, a government employee, for the rest of my stay. Marcelo would become a key instigator for the WPSA Argentine Branch. We spent time with a group called GTA, for Groupo Trabaca Avicola and I gave my 100 Years speech in its entirety, with Marcelo translating. I had a lot of good questions and the whole experience was very positive. Many of the people here had very good English, and were friendly and welcoming. Someone's last piece of advice when I was leaving: "Don't drink the Brazilian wine". That turned out to be right – the wine on the otherwise very pleasant VARIG flight to Sao Paulo was awful.

My host in Brazil was Edir da Silva. Edir was the President of the WPSA branch and a very enthusiastic promoter of the Association. He worked at UNICAMP, the University of Campinas, teaching food safety and microbiology. My arrival was on a Saturday so we had a social weekend with Edir's family. This included his daughter Sylvia who was about the same age as my daughter Carole. They lived in a beautiful house in a gated community, with a big pool and associated rec room, kitchen and barbecue.

My first day of "work" in Brazil was spent with Luis Sesti, Secretary of WPSA Brazil, who worked as Veterinary Director for Agroceres Ross, a joint venture with my old firm. But what a contrast! When I left Ross in 1977, we were contemplating, but had not achieved, a shift from mass selection for body weight and conformation to some form of pedigree population and attention to reproductive traits. Here in Brazil in 2001, they had fully pedigreed flocks of all the lines, full electronic data collection and satellite transmission to the HQ in Newbridge, Scotland. We visited several farms, but only to look over the fence – Biosecurity was a fact of life and "No Visitors!" meant no visitors at all, not even the President of WPSA! As well as showing me the breeding program, Luis and his team gave me a snapshot of the Brazilian chicken meat industry, which of course was huge and growing at the time. Ross claimed a 49% share, and Hubbard, a former strong competitor, had slid from 40% to 0 in 3 years because of a congenital disease problem.

Edir then took me by plane to Brasilia for meetings with the main poultry trade organization. It was my first (and only) visit to Brasilia. The modern (post 1960) buildings were all extremely modern, while the older structures, according to Edir, were built by the communists. They reminded me of pictures from communist era Russia. However, the new architecture was quite stunning. Not always to my taste, but interesting.

We attended the opening of the 17th Brazilian Poultry Conference, which took place in the Department of Foreign Affairs building. The opening speeches were loud, passionate and all in Portuguese, with no translation, so I got very little from it. Later, we went with Andrea Gessuli for a quiet drink, to discuss Andrea's magazine, and the regional Poultry Show she would be running in South Brazil in May 2002. WPSA would have a presence at the show. We also learned that the VIV show in Sao Paulo, which had greatly annoyed the local industry, would not be repeated. Brazilians were very proud of their independence and big enough to do most things themselves!

Late in October I went to Brazil again, for the exhibition in Porto Alegre. But before going there, Edir booked me in to a beach hotel in Cuaragua on the east coast. I spent quite a bit of time writing various pieces for the *Ovum* and *World Poultry*, but I also walked the beach several times. I saw some of the largest beach houses I've seen anywhere, and the smallest bikinis.

The meeting in Porto Alegre was the World Conference on Animal Production, and I met its Dutch President Akke van der Zipp, who was actually a poultry scientist. I presented my paper, "100 Years of Poultry Research", although I thought it was not a suitable venue. It was reasonably well received.

One very interesting paper here was by John Hodges. He talked in a philosophical way about European attitudes to animal production. I had lunch with him afterwards; we had never met before but it turned out his career path was very similar to mine. He left the UK in 1970 to teach at the University of British Columbia, but also worked for FAO in Rome, and for the dairy industry in the UK. He retired to live in Austria, with his wife, who I think was a Canadian Mennonite. A very interesting person.

My other commitment at the Conference was to co-Chair a session called Poultry Nutrition and Production. This turned out to be a fiasco. Only one of the five speakers showed up; we had two Chairs and an audience of 17 in a hall capable of seating 1500!

They presented me with a bottle of Brazilian red wine; I had to admit it was better than my previous experience with Brazilian wine, but no better than I was making at home! I am sure that today, they will have caught up with the rest of the wine world!

By this time, I was travelling so much that I often got upgrades to Business Class on Air Canada, and this happened on my way home. I had also begun to recognize some of the staff, and had a nice chat with Monica Tsumo at check-in. She lived in Sao Paulo but was originally from Canada and still wore a Canadian Airlines band holding her ID!

This was the end what became an annual venture to South America, and looking back, I think it was well worth the effort. And best of all, I really enjoyed it!

My first flight on the way home was from Brasilia to Manaus, over some spectacular scenery – rural views and lots of jungle, and the huge Amazon as we approached Manaus. I only had 40 minutes there and have always wanted to go back, as the city had an amazing history. I flew from Manaus to Miami, with no problem, but then stood on the ground 90 minutes waiting for a gate. After the now expected and protracted customs and immigration into the US, I arrived at the gate for my 7.15 pm flight to Toronto at 7.30. However, that flight was delayed and I made it, but not my luggage. I finally arrived home just after midnight, more than 12 h after leaving Brasilia.

In November, Nita and I did a tour by car of some of the US Universities with a strong poultry interest, to encourage student membership in WPSA. We had decided to give students free membership for at least a year. My first stop was Blacksburg, where Virginia Tech. had a very strong poultry program led by Paul Siegel. I met with a group of about 15 students and gave an abbreviated version of "100 Years of Poultry Genetics" and we had a very good evening. Paul also gave us a tour of the campus, including the recently restored Smithfield Plantation House, built in 1775. We met the head of the Dramatic Arts Department and talked theatre!

On the way to the University of Georgia, Athens, Nita and I stayed in Charleston for the first time and enjoyed it, especially the seafood at Hyman's. The history of the city was amazing, and we learned a lot about it on a carriage tour of the old town.

At the Poultry Department at Athens, I had a good meeting with the staff, and Linda Lacy, wife of Department head Mike, took Nita on a tour of the town. I had a tour of the poultry farm and poultry meat processing plant prior to the student meeting. My pitch was the same; about 30 were in attendance and as always, enthusiasm was high. Most of these students would have jobs waiting for them when they graduated, or assured graduate work if that was their goal.

We drove from Athens, through Atlanta, towards Auburn AL, but stopped in Madison GA to admire some beautiful old Victorian houses. In Auburn, we met with David Roland and his wife, Linda, who took us to dinner and then to the community of Opelika, to admire a great display of Christmas lights on some of the houses. I again spoke to about 30 students, and had lunch with Sarge Bilgili. Sarge was a migrant from Turkey and becoming marginally involved with WPC2004.

Next stop was Raleigh NC, where I spoke to about 20 students. Department Chair Gerry Havenstein showed me around while Nita took time with his wife Joyce, and we spent the night at their home, a pleasant change from motels.

This was our last commitment and we drove from Raleigh heading North, to visit Bill and Madelyn Weaver. Bill was not long retired from the Chair of Poultry Science at Penn State. Nita and Madelyn had met many times at Poultry Science meetings, and I knew Bill from many encounters there and elsewhere. Bill had just completed publication of his and Don Bell's book, *Poultry Production*, a huge task and probably the last hard cover book on the subject before everything went online. I got an advance copy and reviewed it for *World Poultry*.

How many students ever signed up for WPSA as a result of these sessions, I never knew, but it was good exposure for the association and I very much enjoyed it.

Piet Simons, Francine Bradley (respectively Secretary and Treasurer of WPSA) and I met in Atlanta in January 2002 and we again held a conference call with all the Vice Presidents. I found this a useful way to keep in touch. We also went to the International Poultry Scientific Forum (a highfalutin name for the former Southern Poultry Science), and I met at length with Wiebe van der Sluis, Editor of *World Poultry*. We also attended what was always the best social event of the year, the Watt Reception the night before the poultry show opened. We mostly worked with the Turkish group promoting WPC2004, but I took some time out to see the show and do some work for Elsevier, for whom I was a consultant at the time.

My pre-flight check-in on the way home was my first experience of the enhanced security in North American airports resulting from the terrorist attacks in September. It took an hour from arrival at the airport train station to reaching the departure gate.

In June of 2002 I made another trip to Brazil with an excellent visit to the EMBRAPA (federal research organization) Swine and Poultry Unit in Concordia. Unfortunately I arrived at the airport in Chapeco at midnight, and missed what must have been a beautiful drive in daylight, 1½ h through massive forests and mountains. However, I did get to see it on the way back and it did not disappoint. The Research Centre was doing excellent work, though some of the genetic projects (supervised by a Guelph Ph.D. graduate) seemed to me a bit out of touch with the current state of commercial breeding. I was able to meet with and talk to many of the scientists and promote WPSA.

From here I flew back to Sao Paulo and was driven to Campinas, where the annual FACTA/WPSA Conference began the following day. This was a huge event, probably comparable to Poultry Science in the US, but with more commercial people there. Edir da Silva and Luis Sesti were my hosts and I made a short speech on behalf of WPSA at the opening ceremony. I also met for the first time, Fabio Nunes, who was a very active consultant to the Brazilian industry. He was influential and a good person to have on side. Before leaving Brazil, I was hosted by HyLine to visit their new hatchery in San Jose de Rio Petro, 450 km from Sao Paulo. This was very high tech and fully biosecure, with shower-in and no compromises.

The European Poultry Conference, organized by the German Branch, was held in Bremen in September 2002. It was preceded by a long meeting of the Scientific Committee for WPC 2004, which I attended. We also had the annual meeting of the WPSA Executive, and the Journal's Editorial Board, arranged by Editor David Martin.

The Conference was a big success with some innovative aspects; they held a Poster party with beer on tap, which got many people to see the posters and interact with the presenters.

I presented a paper but unfortunately have no record of what it was about! Dietmar Flock, President of the German Branch, entertained the WPSA Executive for a very good dinner after the Conference ended, and he must have been very pleased with the way everything worked so well.

At the end of September, I went to Cuba, which was hosting the Latin American Poultry Congress, with the hope of starting a WPSA Branch there. My host was Myriam Perez Pla, who was the first President of the Branch that was eventually formed. She and her husband were great hosts and showed me a lot of the old city of Havana, which I might not have seen without them. I also spent time with Geoff and Marcela Fairhurst, who were there for the Congress, along with other friends from Shaver, including Donald McQ. Shaver; he had sent breeding stock to Cuba a number of years ago and was quite revered. He gave a talk at the Conference, which was not very appropriate; no visual aids and a rambling presentation about conservation and sustainability which, while all very important, was a bit out of the scope of this Congress. I gave a brief (and illustrated) presentation about WPSA which I think was instrumental in starting the Branch. The main challenge they had was paying dues to WPSA; this had to be in hard currency, and I think we eventually circumvented the Cuban regulations by having someone from Watt Publications smuggle the money out!

I was home only a day after this before leaving, with Nita, for the Asia-Pacific Federation Conference in Gold Coast, Queensland, just South of Brisbane. The meeting was held in the Conrad Jupiter's Hotel, Casino and Conference Centre, an amazing complex. The journey there was long and tiresome, and we didn't arrive until mid afternoon local time, when we both needed a rest. However, duty called and after a very brief nap, we had to go to the opening reception. Nita said it was like sleepwalking!

The Conference was well organized and well attended; there were many Branches in this Federation, all eager to participate. And at the Federation Executive meeting, there was strong competition between India and Thailand for the privilege of hosting the next meeting. It eventually went to Thailand, probably because India had not long ago hosted a World Congress. I spoke briefly at the closing ceremony.

Shortly after returning from Australia, I went to Spain for the annual FIRA exposition in Barcelona. and the launch of Jose Antonio Castello's new book. Jose, who made his living writing, had long been a big supporter of WPSA. He seemed to be everywhere I went and we were good friends. It turned out to be his 31st book! There was Champagne and much hand-shaking, and in the evening, a recognition dinner, at which I made a short speech of appreciation. Meanwhile I listened to some of the scientific papers and toured the exhibition. There were a lot of old Shaver people around and the ISA exhibit was a popular one. I spent quite a while talking to Jean-Louis Gac, who had been the General Manager of Shaver France during my second spell at Shaver.

In total for 2002, I made six trips on behalf of WPSA, spending about 40 days away from home, not counting about 20 more in Australia on vacation. Although I was still doing significant writing and consulting as well, I made WPSA the priority; I gave up some of the committee work I had been involved in while working for the Egg Board in order to do this. In my "spare time", I still did a lot of work for Galt Little Theatre, as well as working at home on the house and garden. These were busy years.

January 2003 saw us again in Atlanta for the show, meetings with WPSA, with Wiebe, my Editor at *World Poultry*, and all the other regular activities. We went to some of the papers at the Scientific Forum, but by now, I was losing the urge to keep right up to date, and I did a lot of socializing! However, at their closing session, I gave a short pitch on WPSA and introduced Ruveyde Akbay, who was there to promote WPC2004, by then about 18 months away.

We had our annual mid-year WPSA Board meeting by telephone, and of course we all went to the Watt Publishing reception the evening before the show opened. I met up with Sigrid Boersma, former co-op student now working for Cuddy Farms and took her to the Watt party.

The show was its usual busy time; I spent most of it at the WPC2004 booth, but of course managed to see quite a bit of the exhibition as well. I also spent some time, and had dinner with Frank Holik, a Canadian entrepreneur who was considering purchasing the rights to make Cagemaster plastic cages for laying hens. He did the purchase and I kept in touch with him for several years, but he never put the cages back in production.

At the end of March, I went to England to visit the UK Branch and to speak at their annual meeting. I also met my daughter Carole there (she flew from Halifax, where she was living at the time) and we spent a very good holiday before and after the WPSA meeting, which took place in York. The night prior to the meeting, I spent time with David Martin discussing the Journal, and this being England, we enjoyed several pints and a very good Italian dinner!

The papers I heard and saw were excellent; the UK had a very active poultry research program, with the Universities of Reading, Bristol, Nottingham and Edinburgh all providing input, as well as the Roslyn Institute. Following the first days papers, we had the Gordon Memorial Lecture, given this year by Grahame Bullfield, a geneticist from Roslyn. This was interesting to me, as Bullfield studied molecular genetics, of which I knew next to nothing, but he did show how some of his work might be applied to poultry breeding as I remembered it. This lecture was followed by a reception and dinner, at which I made my first real "after dinner" speech. I had prepared this quite thoroughly, including jokes, and it seemed to go over well. I attended the final days papers and the Branch Annual Meeting and then left for my holiday with Carole. (see Chapter 16)

I made another visit to South America in early May, 2003. I flew to Buenos Aires by way of Sao Paulo, and the total elapsed time was 24 h! They (Marcelo Schang *et al)* had arranged very nice accommodation at the Recoleta Guest House, which was very informal, run by a family and a bit like an English B&B. So I was able to catch up on some decent rest before starting on my formal work. Buenos Aires impressed me with its calm and civility; it was hard to believe that a year previously, the streets were full of people beating on pots and pans. Later in the day, Julian Melo and one of his graduate students, showed me a little more of the city, confirming my very positive feelings about it. We also toured outside of the Colon Theatre, a 100 year old Opera House. As I had quite recently experienced the relatively new one in Sydney, I planned to go to a performance there later in my trip, and did so to see *Giselle.* The interior of the building was astounding and quite beautiful. Ballet not being my favourite artistic medium, and my Spanish minimal, enjoyment of the show was limited!

It was while checking my email the first night that I learned of the death of Bruce Sheldon, Senior Vice President of WPSA. I had been alerted to his declining health, following hip replacement surgery, but his death was still a shock. Bruce worked long and hard at WPSA affairs, especially the Asia-Pacific Federation, and he was also a good friend.

I was taken from Buenos Aires to Concepcion del Uruguay to a meeting of AMAVEA, the association of local poultry veterinarians. I gave them one of my scientific presentations and also a pitch for them to join WPSA with which they had many interests in common. It was a good meeting and I left with the feeling that we could expect quite a few to join the Branch. We also discussed the possibility of the two organizations holding a joint meeting the following year.

I had some free time before leaving and continued my touring of the city, consumption of the world's best steaks, and some really excellent wine. If I learned Spanish, I felt I could live very nicely in Buenos Aires!

As I did the previous year, I flew from there to Brazil, to attend the annual FACTA meeting in Campinas. It was here I first made the acquaintance of Malcolm Mitchell, from the Roslyn Institute. I had seen him around but now got to know him over a bottle of Argentinian wine during a dead time before the meeting. We later changed to gin-and-tonics; he was a very good drinking companion!

The meeting was excellent and I spent quite a bit of time with Avigdor Cahaner from Israel, another WPSA Vice President. Several of the more important papers were given in English, including one by Heidi Scharr of Lohmann Animal Health on the use of live vaccines to control Salmonella.

Following the meeting Edir da Silva took me to visit some friends who were involved in breeding beef cattle. The place was an old coffee plantation, beautifully located and modernized in superb taste. They were breeding the Caracul, formerly almost extinct, but now several generations on, it was doing well and adapted to the local conditions. We had a sumptuous lunch in a wonderful, high ceiling room with a beautiful chandelier; these people knew how to live!

At the beginning of June, I went to Cuba for the inaugural meeting of the new WPSA Branch there. As well as some tourist activities, I had a good run down of the Cuban industry. There were about 35 people at the meeting including a Deputy Minister of Agriculture. The Constitution was approved by acclamation, the officers elected, then the VIPs, myself included, went to a splendid lunch in the Ministry of Education. This lasted about two hours, after which they delivered me back to the hotel and an afternoon by and in the pool – very good as the temperature was ~35°C.

The following day the new Branch President, Myriam Perez Pla and a group of her colleagues took me on a full day trip including a 62,000 bird layer farm in Pinar del Rio. Because of the "system", i.e. high level of education but few opportunities, 33 people were employed at the farm, including an economist (maybe he was an accountant), a veterinarian and several other important sounding people. The flock was descended from breeding stock that Donald Shaver had supplied back in the 1960s. The birds looked very good and they told me the previous flock laid 292 eggs; not sure how long they took to do this. The rest of the day we were tourists: we saw some very beautiful scenery and enjoyed an excellent lunch, lots of rum and beer, and altogether a very good day out.

Before leaving, I met more of the scientific and veterinary community. They were encouraging small family owned poultry flocks along the lines promoted by the International Network that was cooperating with WPSA, so I was able to provide some contacts. That night I was on my own for dinner, so walked to the Restaurante Floridita, of Hemingway fame. The experience was interesting, but the food, very ordinary! Because of flight scheduling, I had most of a day to kill before flying home, so I went on a city tour by taxi. I had an exceedingly knowledgeable driver, who took me all over Havana, including statues and buildings dating back to the 15th century. It seemed a pity the country was so politically isolated, and relatively poor. Many of the older buildings, especially those on the sea front, were deteriorating badly, and with no prospect of restoration.

In July, I travelled to Bristol in the UK for the European Symposium on Poultry Welfare. The trip was partly funded by CEMA, for whom I wrote a report. This was the usual excellent meeting and a very, good social program, including several informal pub-crawls. I was not as good at these as in my early days, but I survived. I also spent some time with David Martin, and we reviewed some difficult correspondence from the Turkish Branch, with respect to alleged libel of their President, Mrs. Akbay. As world President, I had to compose a conciliatory letter, which I duly did.

I spent a couple of days with ex-Geordie Don Legg, and his second wife, Wanda, before leaving England. Don had embraced philosophy in his old age and I got in terrible trouble with one of his friends at a dinner party, when I told him how much I enjoyed reading Ayn Rand's books! I was motivated to re-read some of them later.

The 2003 WPSA Executive meeting was held in Lillehammer, Norway, in conjunction with one of the European Working Group Symposia. This had been the site for the Winter Olympic Games. It was a long way from anywhere but we still managed full attendance. Plans for the 2004 Congress were provided by Prof. Akbay and seemed to be going well. As always, there was a lively social scene, although it was somewhat constrained by the astronomical price of beer, wine and liquor. However, I had fortunately brought some duty free gin, so all we had to do for a while was buy the tonic! But even that was expensive. A beer in an ordinary bar cost the equivalent of US$7.50, which was about double the price anywhere else we knew about! Those with generous expense accounts were very popular! Among the media people who helped here was Jackie Linden, David Martin's successor at *Poultry International*. Lots of old friends, including Sarah Mellor, who had by now left *World Poultry* for new pastures, and many new ones, were there. One big party included both Jackie and Sarah, plus people from France, Poland, Israel, Germany, and Rob Renema from Alberta with one of his students.

WPSA went on a recruiting drive after a very generous donation of US$300 from UK Branch member Gordon Rosen to pay the first year's dues for new members.

David Martin held an Editorial Board meeting for the *Worlds Poultry Science Journal* that was well attended.

On my return to Toronto from this trip, I was met by one of the largest power outages in North American history. It involved, at the least, all of

Ontario and six Northern States. So the ramps for deplaning did not work, and the airport was on emergency power, so baggage transfer was delayed and slow, and on and on. My baggage turned out to have missed the plane anyway – I had a very quick transfer at Heathrow. It took me several hours to get home and of course everything there was dark and our refrigerator and freezer gradually warming. For us, the power came back in about 16 hours but many had a much longer wait, with huge losses of perishable food both at homes and in the stores.

In September, I spent four days in Turkey, this time in Ankara. I met with a variety of people; politicians, industry and the Consortium which would administer the Congress in 2004. It was at this time that I began to feel much more comfortable about the prospects for the Congress. Prof. Akbay had all the right contacts. She and her husband, who was President of the University of Ankara at the time, lived in a very posh apartment across the street from the Prime Minister. She could call on all kinds of influential people and knew them well. Although Turkey was noted for corrupt business practices, it seemed to me that we could have a successful Congress in spite of that.

I spent a day visiting one of the major chicken operations. They had Ross Grandparent stock in a joint venture similar to the one I saw in Brazil, and also processed 10,000 birds/h in a very modern plant said to exceed EU standards, The growing farms were all highly automated, using an environmental monitoring system developed in Israel. (Nova Scotia's Farmax system would have done it too if it had been properly developed and promoted!)

I went from Turkey to France, to another of the European Symposia, this one on Poultry Welfare in St. Brieuc. I had a very good dinner there with David Martin, Ragnar Tauson, Achille Franchini and Sally Solomon, the night before the meeting began. As always, the meeting was well organized and some good papers were presented.

Before leaving France, I was invited to spend a day at the ISA facility close by St. Brieuc. This was a brand new office and lab complex along with laying houses. The lab dealt with egg quality. I looked into the layer house through a window; everything was bar coded now and records made and retrieved electronically. The office was so new that the staff were celebrating with champagne as I left!

In January, 2004, I went to Atlanta for the science meetings and the show, and of course to work at the WPC2004 Exhibit. The Congress was then only 7 months away and we had a lot of visitors at the booth. Plans for the Congress were well in hand and we were all pretty happy with the progress being made. Ruveyde Akbay and her group worked hard; we also managed some good visits to a variety of hospitality suites including major Congress Sponsors.

We had our annual conference call for the WPSA Board. Six of us were in Atlanta and the remainder on the phone.

In April, Secretary Piet Simons came to visit Canada. We met in Calgary and drove to Edmonton for a series of meetings, including an excellent session with Frank Robinson and the Poultry Research group at the University. I presented an updated version of my "100 Years of Poultry Research" and Piet talked about the WPSA. We had a very good tour of the Research and Teaching facilities and met with their most enthusiastic staff. Apart from Frank, they included Rob Renema and Doug Korver, as well as some graduate students and support staff.

We did some sightseeing on the way to Banff, including Lake Louise, which was still frozen over. We stayed in the Banff Centre and attended a series of meetings, including the Expert Committee on Eggs and Egg Products.

The main event was a Symposium on Eggs and Egg Products and there were quite a lot of international visitors, including Julie Roberts from Australia and Robert Elkin, now the Head of the Poultry Science Department at Penn State University.. The papers were very good and everyone enjoyed the mountain environment before and after.

In early May, I made my final visit to Brazil as WPSA President. Nita came along for the trip, her first to South America. The occasion combined the annual FACTA meeting, held this year in the coastal city of Santos, near Sao Paulo, with the official "inspection" of the proposed 2008 Congress site in Salvador, 2000 km further up the coast. The FACTA meeting was its usual success, and I gave my paper on Egg Shell Research. Piet Simons, and another WPSA Vice President, Colin Fisher from the UK, were also with us. Salvador was chosen as less expensive and possibly safer than Rio de Janeiro or Sao Paulo. The Congress Centre was adequate, although quite old, and unfortunately in a different part of the city from most of the hotels. It was downtown while the hotels were mostly close to the beach. However, we were assured that there would be free shuttle buses to ferry people back and forth. These occasions were a bit like a very miniature "Olympic bid" and so we were treated like royalty! No other Branch had bid for the Congress, so the choice of site was basically a foregone conclusion.

The Congress in Istanbul took place June 8-12, 2004. It went very smoothly; good papers and well attended. I presented a paper jointly authored by me, Francine Bradley, Dietmar Flock and Piet Simons dealing with how the WPSA contributes to poultry education. There was a good session on my special interest area, egg shell quality and structure, and one of the outstanding papers was by Dr. Maureen Bain, formerly a student of Sally Solomon's.

The Congress was most successful; all of the ceremonial affairs went well including my passing of the WPSA flag to the new President. The closing Banquet was yet another demonstration of Prof. Akbay's wide influence. It was held in the Dolmabahçe Palace grounds, which were not normally available for such events, and the entertainment was by the Turkish National Ballet.

We had the annual WPSA Board meeting the day prior to the Congress, and the Asia-Pacific Federation also held its annual meeting. Newly elected President Ruveyde Akbay chaired a short meeting of the new Board on the final day.

I had a long session with Soledad Urrutia and Thomas MacAuliffe from Chile to discuss the Constitution for their new Branch, which seemed to be emerging after many years of persuasion from me and others.

Nita and I very much enjoyed the entire time we spent in Turkey, and she became good friends with Ruveyde.

As Past President, I retained a seat on the WPSA Board and continued to attend the annual meetings. I made some strategic trips when needed.

In August 2004, two months after the Turkish Congress, I spent 2 days attending a Seminar organized by the new Branch in Columbia. The political situation in Columbia at that time was much improved – for several years it had been a no-go destination but was by then more or less stable. (I remember Ron Jones from Shaver going there regularly and reporting that he was taken everywhere with an armed escort).

I spent most of the day following my arrival in the hotel, but met with the local Branch officers and the late John Brake, from NC State Univ. who was another speaker at the Seminar. He helped with setting up the audio-visual system and actually loaded my talk (100 Years of Poultry Research) onto his laptop. The Seminar was very good, with 120 people in attendance and full translation. I also talked a bit about WPSA, but most of the program was John Brake, who seemed to have a big connection in Columbia. This became even clearer when we returned to the hotel, where he was accompanied by a quite gorgeous woman and we had drinks in the hotel bar. Later at a very opulent and quite formal dinner celebrating the Seminar, I was seated opposite to her, and noted she had more cleavage than Elizabeth Taylor! I wondered whether John's wife in NC knew about this.

I went to the Atlanta show in January 2005. Australia had not yet begun to promote the XXIII Congress, so we did not have an official exhibit. I cruised the show and met old friends. Notable was a splendid dinner at the Pleasant Peasant with Sigrid Boersma, now well established with the Cuddy hatchery in Ohio. A very good return on the Egg Board's investment in a co-op student.

At the end of January, there was a huge tsunami in the Indian Ocean, which did enormous damage to countries surrounding the Ocean, particularly India and Sri Lanka. After discussion with the WPSA Board, I made a special trip to India, Sri Lanka and Bangladesh. Most memorable were the sights in southern Sri Lanka, where huge waves had penetrated far inland with devastating consequences. I was also a guest of the local WPSA Branch at a meeting at the University in Kandy. This was far from the action of the tsunami, but a very pleasant experience. The University retained a lot of its British-ness, with its Senior Common Room, etc. I gave a short talk about WPSA.

Subsequently, it was decided that in remembrance of the tsunami, WPSA would award several scholarships for students to attend the B.V. Rao Institute of Poultry Management in Pune, India.

In October 2005, I travelled to Europe, accompanied by Nita. I had commitments for WPSA, but this seemed quite like a holiday! First stop was Frankfurt, where we had a 7 hour layover. Someone in the lounge suggested we take the train downtown for the day, and this proved to be an excellent idea. We walked along the river for a while and had a beer in a very nice 15th century pub. We were in the old part of the city, what must have been the town square, where we had lunch.

Next stop was Dubrovnik, for the Genetics symposium, organized by Working Group 3 of the Federation of European Branches.

Nita did tours while I attended papers on the first day. This confirmed my suspicion that genetics had changed a great deal in the 25 years since I was last employed in the field, and that I no longer understood a lot of what went on especially in the research field. The following day I presented my paper "100 Years of Poultry Genetics" to general acclaim. As 2005 was the centenary of the rediscovery of Mendel's pioneering work, it was an opportune moment for the review. I tipped my hat to the modern geneticists by asking one of them, Michele Tixier Boichard, to write a few paragraphs at the end of the paper. The text was subsequently peer-reviewed and published in the *Worlds Poultry Science Journal.*

Nita and I both went on an organized tour the following day, and we enjoyed a trip up the coast, visits to an Arboretum, and 400 year old plane trees in Trsteno. On our last day, before leaving, we walked the walls of the City of Dubrovnik, one of its main tourist attractions that Nita had done the first day. She had no problem repeating the walk, as vistas over roofs were among her favourite tourist sights!

Our next destination was Beirut, Lebanon, but in order to get there, we had to backtrack; a short flight to Zagreb where we stayed overnight, then a flight to Milan and finally from there to Beirut. Here, Nuhad Daghir, formerly with Shaver and now a Professor at the American University of Beirut, had arranged for us to be picked up and taken to our hotel, the Rotana. This was a splendid place with a rooftop swimming pool, and our room on the 11th floor overlooked the Mediterranean.

At this time, Lebanon was stable after several turbulent years; the streets were safe and we had time to walk around. A huge amount of reconstruction was under way.

Our visit coincided with Ramadan. They arranged for us to eat lunches with the Christians and dinner with the Muslims. Both meals were massive feasts, particularly the evening meal, where everyone waited until the bell rang indicating the OK to eat, drink and in many cases, smoke!

We had a tour of the University farm in the Beqa Valley, but it was preceded by a visit to the historical site at Baalbek, which went back ~ 5000 years to the time of the Phoenicians. It reminded us of some of the places we visited in Turkey the previous year. The surrounding mountains were rugged, and a lot of the valley, although it looked fertile, devoid of crops for lack of irrigation.

Nuhad, who was President of the Lebanon Branch of WPSA, arranged for me to give a talk about the Canadian system of Supply Management to a meeting of members. After this we were hosted for a post-Ramadan feast by Dr. Nada Usayran and her husband Bassim. Nada had recently spent a sabbatical year in Australia. Nita and Nada became great friends; Bassim told me when they go shopping for his clothes, he waits outside the shop while Nada buys! While I acknowledged that we shared the same reluctance for "shopping" I at least bought my own clothes!

Nita was unwell with stomach disorders the following day, and I was taken on an industry tour. The company I visited was processing 0.5 million broilers/week and had 0.5 million laying hens. They had breeders and a hatchery to supply both segments, and a chain of retail stores selling both chicken and eggs. The production buildings were old but in good shape with full environmental control in most cases.

The next day, Nuhad took me on a trip to a huge chicken processing plant in the Beqa valley, run by Musa Freiji, who had at one time been the Shaver distributor in Lebanon. We saw the whole plant including further processing, and the product of last resort, mechanically deboned meat. Naturally, part of the processing line worked according to Muslim requirements.

Not far away was a very old egg production complex run by Musa's cousin; open houses, some floor managed and quite labour intensive.

The afternoon was spent visiting a winery called Domaine de Tourelles. Actually, they told us that the wines were a sideline; the main business was the production of Arak. The wines we tasted, especially the reds, were excellent and I took two bottles of Cabernet Sauvignon back to the hotel. We had no host for dinner that night and having been consistently overfed, stayed in the room with just the wine and some fruit provided by the hotel.

I spent some time in Nuhad's office downloading my copious emails, before another WPSA Branch meeting, where I gave a presentation on egg shell research.

Our final tourist activity was with Nuhad and Monah, first to the Jeita Grotto, said to be the finest natural grotto in the world. It was certainly spectacular; photography was forbidden but they sold CD's! We then drove out to the coast, north to Byblos, where we had a wonderful fish lunch at Bab el Mina, reputed to be one of the best fish restaurants in the country.

Out last day was free and we did some walking in the city, and used the rooftop pool. Dinner was at the home of Musa Freiji and his wife. Their apartment overlooked the sea and was quite magnificent. Nuhad and Monah, and another Lebanese couple now resident in Bakersfield CA made up the dinner party. Conversation ranged widely, but it was here that we learned that 25% of Lebanese citizens lived abroad. This had resulted from successive political crises and upheavals, and subsequent events have only continued the trend. A sad commentary on a potentially prosperous people, living in a very beautiful part of the world.

Our flight home was *via* Frankfurt; the flight from Beirut left at 2.30 am so we went straight from the dinner party to the airport. Not much sleep that night, but we were able to rest a little on the long flight from Frankfurt to Toronto.

Chapter 11

The XXI Worlds Poultry Congress: Montreal, August, 2000

After an informal meeting of some of the WPSA Canada Branch members in 1988, Branch Secretary Alan Grunder and I made a bid at the Congress held in Nagoya, Japan for the 1996 Congress to be held in Canada. We lost by two votes in 116 to the India Branch, led by its President, B.V. Rao. I asked a few people, including the UK's Trevor Morris, why we lost and the answer was "Well, everybody has been to Canada but nobody has been to India!" It was in fact the first Congress to be awarded to a developing country.

Alan and I vowed never to attempt such a bid again, but it was not long after I returned from Japan that I had a call from Louise Beer at the Palais des Congrés (Convention Centre) de Montreal, suggesting we bid for the 2000 Congress and hold it there. We eventually made the bid during the 1992 Congress in Amsterdam, where it was not contested.

In November 1990, I made the first of many trips to Montreal to begin planning the 2000 Worlds Poultry Congress. The first one was just to get to know a little about the city and tour the Palais des Congrés. At this stage, everything was "on the house" including nice hotel accommodation and excellent food. The Congress Centre would handily accommodate the meeting with the huge benefit of the exhibition being in the same building. We had already seen in Japan, and would be reminded in India, how important that would be.

I later checked out the Toronto Convention Centre and the one in Vancouver, just so that we would have choices, although Montreal was clearly the leader. One potential disadvantage was the festering separatist movement in Quebec; we had been told in no uncertain terms by members in Western Canada that they would not participate in the Worlds Congress in Montreal if the province voted to separate from Canada.

At the 1992 Amsterdam World's Poultry Congress, there was no competition for the 2000 Congress but the Canadians behaved as though one might suddenly emerge. Most of the arrangements were made by Louise Beer. We hosted a lunch for 120 invited guests, and the Canadian Ambassador came from Den Hague to address it, along with myself. At the subsequent WPSA Council meeting, Montreal was acclaimed as the venue for Congress 2000. At that same meeting, I was elected Senior Vice President of WPSA, which was also gratifying.

In 1993, the Montreal Palais dés Congrès made me an Accredited Ambassador, even though we had not yet signed a contract. The ceremony was very formal and I had to rent a tuxedo! Everything was in French so I understood very little, but the food was good. Probably the most enjoyable part of the trip was that following the event in Montreal, Nita and I visited Mike and Margaret Crossling at their farm near Huntingdon in south western Quebec. They were both from my home village of Ponteland, near Newcastle on Tyne, in England. Following the close result of the Quebec secession vote in 1985, Mike, who worked in the financial sector, was let go and for several years, they were unable to sell their house. Margaret was a physiotherapist but had quit working to raise their two girls and her license had lapsed. They eventually sold the house and bought the small farm where we visited them.

Meanwhile, Margaret had qualified to be a Customs Officer at one of the local border crossings from the US. We had a very nice visit, with dinner, talk and far too much brandy.

In October 1993 I made another trip to Montreal for the first of many meetings of the Congress Steering Committee. Thirteen people attended and we made a lot of progress. Primarily, we elected a Secretary, Alan Bentley, who worked for Agriculture and Agri-Food Canada (AAFC). The contact with the Federal Government was important because they were a prime candidate for sponsorship, and also had to "approve" the Congress to satisfy one of the WPSA requirements.

The next Steering Committee meeting was in May 1994, and we found a new recruit as Treasurer, Pierre Bergeron, who had taken early retirement as President of Merck Canada. Others in attendance included Robert Gauthier, a nutritionist with wide experience in the Quebec industry and Rock Laroche, who had worked for many of the breeding companies and was well known across Canada. Piet Simons was also there on the official WPSA site inspection mission. On this occasion we also signed the documents to create the corporation, World's Poultry Congress 2000 Inc. which would be the official company running the Congress. Its officers were the same as those of the Congress but this structure limited our liability in the event of unforeseen legal issues.

At the October 1994 meeting, we had Rob Etches from Guelph in attendance and he agreed to be Chair of the Scientific Program Committee.

On each visit, I stayed at a different high-end hotel. We would need an official Congress hotel where the WPSA Executive would stay, along with some of the invited speakers. So far I had been in the Meridian and the Queen Elizabeth.

221

In January 1995, I met with Alan and Pierre to begin working on a budget. On this occasion, we met in Ottawa. I drove there. At this time I was learning the lines for my part in *The Crucible*. I had a tape recording of the other actors and spoke my lines when needed. I was so concentrating on this that I drove 50 km past my exit for Ottawa and was late for the meeting!

We had by this time secured the promise of significant funding for the Congress from several agencies including the Canadian Egg Marketing Agency (CEMA) and this provided us the money necessary to continue our planning process. At a long meeting in Montreal in April 1995, we interviewed five different Professional Conference Organizers (PCOs) as we had determined that this was far superior to trying to do it ourselves. The Dutch had not used a PCO, but they had Piet Simons full time and probably significant help from the Conference Centre.

We decided, after much discussion, on Events International Meeting Planners (EIMP). Their office was very close to the Palais des Congrés, and they offered full service for all our needs, which some of the others lacked. The CEO was Albert Barbusci, but our principal contact was Eddie Polak. He was hugely enthusiastic and had lots of experience. He also had very expensive tastes, which we had to control if we were to have a financially secure Congress.

On this occasion, I stayed at the Intercontinental Hotel, which eventually became our HQ property. It was comparatively small, but close to the Palais (easy walking distance) and with excellent facilities. As by this time I knew I would be spending significant time in Montreal, I determined to get to know the city a little better. The Congress location was on the border of Old Montreal, which had an abundance of excellent, small, independent restaurants. It was also where Montreal's only English speaking professional theatre, the Centaur, was situated, and I saw an excellent play there, *The Substance of Fire.*

I ate at Restaurant Pêre St. Vincent, and this became my default eating place when I was staying downtown. It was quite small and friendly, bilingual staff, French food and a good wine list. What more could one ask?

We had several one day or half day meetings in the fall of 1995, mainly just Alan Bentley, Pierre Bergeron and me, along with Ed Polak from EIMP. One challenge at this time was the impending referendum on Quebec separation; we knew that if they seceded, we could not hold the meeting in Montreal. The referendum to permit Quebec to separate was lost by less than a percentage point, much to the chagrin of the then Separatist government.

Just before Christmas 1995, Alan, Pierre and I had a meeting in the Egg Board office, with Albert Barbusci and Anne-Louise Bertucco from EIMP, to discuss plans for industry sponsorship. Haydn Jones, representing the feed industry, and Jean Skotnicki, the Canadian animal health companies, heard our plans and promised to inform their respective industries.

In January 1996, Ed Polak and Martine Coutu from EIMP attended the Atlanta show to learn what the poultry industry was all about. I made sure they met with the people from Watt Publications, and of course the Indians were promoting their Congress, so it was a good opportunity for them to see how things were being done. It was at this point we learned they had both flown Business Class from Montreal, and we had to put a stop to that extravagance. I think we said any flight less than 6 hours would be Economy from then on.

In February, we finally signed the contract with EIMP.

Because of the close result of the Quebec referendum, Ed Polak wanted a second look at Vancouver and I joined him there in early 1996. He had good contacts at Tourism Vancouver and they entertained us like royalty. Eddie also got tickets (very good ones) to a hockey game at GM Place; Vancouver *vs* St. Louis, and this was when Wayne Gretzky played for St. Louis! I had to admit I enjoyed the experience, but I would still rather have been in a theatre! One of the problems with Vancouver was the price of hotels. Even conference rates were about double those quoted in Montreal, in round figures (1996) $200/night *vs* $100. So although that might not directly affect the conference finances, it would in all likelihood reduce attendance. We also looked again at Toronto; their facility was excellent, but the rent, higher than Montreal. Hotels were competitive. I think it was a foregone conclusion that Montreal would be our choice and so it was. Frankly, for an international meeting, Montreal was at the time a truly cosmopolitan and welcoming city.

We rented space at the 1996 London Poultry Show, primarily to let people know that Canada would be hosting the Congress, and of course, to look for sponsors. So I had to divide my presence between the Egg Board, OPC and WPC2000 booths. Fortunately the Egg Board had stopped having the Egg Quality contest, which had previously taken up much of my time.

Shortly thereafter, WPC 2000 Inc. held its first Annual General Meeting in Montreal. We had a good turn out of our growing group of volunteers, plus representatives from the feed and animal health sectors, and three of the four Federal "feather agencies", Chicken, Egg, and Turkey. We worked hard to secure advance funding, as we needed to have good representation at the Indian Congress later in the year.

I attended the Indian Congress, along with Pierre Bergeron and Robert Gauthier. Ed Polak came, and Rob Etches, Scientific Program Chair was there as well. The WPSA Executive meeting also took place ahead of the Congress. We had the ceremonial passing of the WPSA flag from India to Canada at the end of the Congress.

There was a booth for WPC2000 in the Congress hotel and it was gratifyingly busy most of the time. We talked to Dr. Ton Schat, from Cornell University about the possibility of holding the International Symposium on Marek's Disease at the same time as the Montreal Congress, and he agreed to consider this.

We had previously approached the Poultry Science Association to encourage them to hold their Annual Meeting back-to-back with our Congress, and this had been agreed.

We hosted a reception to announce WPC2000 and between 70 and 90 people showed up, which we deemed satisfactory. Of course every Canadian delegate was there so we had a lot of promoters to help us. I gave what I described as "the shortest speech of my life" and I think we did the best possible job in making sure everyone knew about our Congress.

Back in Canada, our planning proceeded, and after a short preliminary meeting earlier in the month, at the end of October the Executive Committee approved a budget for $4.5 million. EIMP got $245,000. At this time, we also confirmed that the International Symposium on Marek's Disease would be held concurrent with the Congress. So we now had potentially three meetings scheduled: PSA, WPC2000 and Mareks, all within 6 days. A Poultry Science Summit!

Once the Indian Congress was past, we could promote exclusively and we took space at the Atlanta show in January 1997. Even before the show opened, we had our first big success with sponsorship. I had previously worked with Olivier Behagel, who was heading Shaver in Canada, and he had agreed they would be a Premiere sponsor at the $100,000 level. But a few days before Atlanta, a merger had been announced that placed ISA in the hands of Merial, so the sponsorship arrangement had to be approved by the new management. Fortunately, this was accomplished and we were able to make it public at the show. Once this was done, we were able to convince Jamesway Incubator Company, also based in Cambridge, to come in at the same level. Congress Secretary Alan Bentley had made sure that

Agriculture and AgriFood Canada was already committed as a Premiere sponsor. We worked other prospects for two days. By the second evening my conservative estimate was that we could count on $3.3 million in sponsorships and exhibit space sales. A great start to the year for WPC2000. Ed Polak and I also spent time with VIV and Watt Publishing. While neither would be a financial sponsor, both could be extremely helpful by providing exhibit and advertising space for us in the period leading up to the Congress. VIV would have liked to run the exhibition at the Congress, but as it was held in our facility it was regarded as an important revenue stream for the Congress. Watt had a big interest in the Congress as always, and of course with my new agreement with Misset (see Chapter 9), their main competitor, we had the print media well covered.

Shaver celebrated 50 years in the breeding business at the show, so it was a notable time for them and for WPC2000.

We kept working on sponsorships. In June Louise Beer and I met with the new President of Intervet Canada, Jorgen Jorgenson, along with Rock Laroche, to recruit them as major sponsors. At the time Intervet was one of the major suppliers of vaccines to the Canadian poultry industry.

In August, at the PSA meeting in Athens GA, we held a meeting of the Scientific Program Committee and did a lot of advance planning, securing people to help with reviewing abstracts, suggestions for Plenary Speakers, etc.

The International Egg Commission met in Toronto in September. I had always hoped that some synergy might develop between them, WPSA, and the Congress, but it never did. I was able to give a pitch for the WPC2000 at the end of their Film Festival, to an audience of about 75 people, and I hoped that some of them might attend. And some of their corporate members might be exhibitors. After all, we had many interests in common!

We had regular meetings of the Executive and Scientific committees in Montreal. Sometimes Nita came with me – the hotel was paid for and we enjoyed eating out and also the Centaur Theatre. The October meeting in 1997 was such an occasion. We always had good attendance; Hank Classen from Saskatoon came regularly even though it took 3 days of his time for a half-day meeting. We were planning our First Announcement at this time. Prior to appointing EIMP we had developed a corporate logo that included chicken, turkey and egg. It was a clumsy affair, which EIMP quite rightly thought could be improved on, and they did a fine job! Their image was definitely avian, but quite abstract and most attractive. The old logo appeared on some letterhead and envelopes (the remainder of which I am still using 24 years later) but the new one graced all of the important publications.

In January, 1998, I went on a "junket" to Turkey. This really had nothing to do with WPC2000 except that Ed Polak from EIMP got the tickets from Turkish Airlines, and thought it would be good to see Istanbul and the site of the 2004 Congress. Doris MacMillan from the EIMP office also travelled on the same basis. Interesting background here was Doris's son David was just getting started in the Montreal restaurant business; he now runs Joe Beef and several other high end spots. Doris left Montreal in the aftermath of the great ice storm of December 1997. We met at Kennedy airport, waiting for the Turkish Airlines non-stop Airbus 340 flight to Istanbul. We both got upgrades to Business Class, which lessened the pain of the long flight, over the Atlantic and most of Central Europe. We were met by Walter Hostmaster of International Destinations Inc., the promoter of the junket. We had great rooms at the Ceylan Intercontinental – rack rate US$255/night!

They treated us royally, but frankly I didn't need the presentations from hotels and restaurants. The venue for the Congress was a bit of a let-down; it was not nearly as good as Montreal. However, the sightseeing part was very good and I probably wouldn't have time for this when attending the Congress. We visited the Dohlmabaçe Palace, an amazing home of former Sultans but now a museum. We also, naturally, saw the Blue Mosque and the Grand Bazaar on the sightseeing trip. And on another trip, we spent a half day at the Topkapi Palace and museum. The highlight there was the exhibit of 2 candlesticks, solid gold, weighing 48 kg and encrusted with diamonds.

We met the PCO that would run the Congress and gave them some helpful (we hope) information.

On our return to North America, I went straight to Atlanta for the annual Poultry Show and Southern Poultry Science. However, I had a weekend to readjust to Eastern time, and enjoyed a great theatrical performance as well: *Counsellor At Law*, at the 14th Street Playhouse. I had seen this done at the Shaw Festival some years ago but it was very well done here too.

We of course promoted the Congress at the show, did lots of hospitality suites, talked to a million people, and generally tired ourselves out. EIMP had four people there, so we made quite an impact.

Piet Simons was there as he always was, and he, David Martin and I had our annual meeting to discuss the WPSA awards, for which we were the

Committee. Lots of drinking, food of an amazing variety and price, and I went home on the Friday evening thoroughly exhausted.

A few days later, we had another meeting in Montreal; Scientific Program and general affairs, and Mike Lilburn from Poultry Science also came to check out the facilities. The Scientific Program looked fine but we had some difficulties with sponsorships. However, these were not long term and were soon resolved.

Although internet use was still not universal, Albert Barbucci and his team easily persuaded me that we should have a website and showed how it would work. By 2000, of course it was absolutely essential.

Valerie McLeod, one of EIMP's marketing people, stayed in Cambridge for a few nights in July 1998 and we visited Shaver and Jamesway (now both major sponsors) to keep them up to speed with how the Congress was evolving, and how they might best exploit their sponsorship. We also visited a potential sponsor, Ford Dickison Industries, in Stratford. At this point in time, FDI was owned by Tony Francolini, and he was most enthusiastic, promising to be a sponsor at some yet-to-be-determined level. In the event, FDI changed hands again prior to the Congress and they were not represented. We also spoke to Maple Lodge Farms, but although they expressed interest, they did not participate as sponsors.

The Poultry Science meeting in 1998 was at Penn. State Univ. at State College, and we held a meeting of the WPC2000 Scientific Program Committee there on the first night. This worked very well as most of the scientific team were there. Rob Etches, at the time a senior faculty member at the Univ. Of Guelph, was Chair of this Committee and was highly effective. However, a few months later he announced his resignation from Guelph to take up a position with a genetics company in California. While he retained the Chairmanship of the Committee, we had to ask Steve Leeson, another Guelph faculty member, to be our local contact. This worked well for the rest of the pre-Congress period.

I made frequent trips to Montreal, often combining these with visits to egg producers in eastern Ontario. Usually, Alan Bentley and one or two other Committee members would join me and Ed Polak for planning meetings and progress reports. I always stayed at the Intercontinental Hotel now; as a VIP, I got an upgraded room. All their rooms were wonderful but the upgrades were on corners with added views.

Late in 1998, we added Misset Publications as a Premiere Sponsor and had to increase the size of our First Announcement to accommodate their advertisement.

We had a full meeting of the Executive Committee and the Organizing Committee in October 1998. The revenue from sponsors was now sufficient that we were able to help to pay expenses, as people like Hank Classen had to travel from as far away as Saskatoon. On this occasion, several of us went to the Centaur Theatre, where we saw one of my favourite Canadian actors, Nicola Cavendish, in a Michel Tremblay play (translated of course) called *For The Pleasure Of Seeing Her Again*. By this time, the Palais was gearing up its publicity and I was part of a video that they spliced into their regular promotional product.

We had a significant presence in Atlanta for the January 1999 Poultry Show. Ed and I attended the PSA Board meeting at which the decision to hold the PSA Annual Meeting in conjunction with WPC2000 was confirmed. By this time Ed Polak had begun his campaign for EIMP to become involved in future Worlds Poultry Congresses after Montreal; I knew Piet Simons opposed the idea, but I was, at this stage ambivalent. We promoted the Congress and the Association from the WPSA booth.

I had a meeting with Jim Arthur, then President of HyLine, one of the major egg type breeders, and Al Corneil, who ran their Ontario distributor, McKinley Hatchery. The meeting was ostensibly to discuss the possibility of their obtaining some research quota from the Egg Board. I was discouraging, because I knew most of the Directors would be hesitant, but of course it was not my decision to make. However we also talked about HyLine as a possible WPC2000 Sponsor, about which I could be much more positive. In the event, HyLine became an exhibitor at the Congress, but I don't think they ever got any research quota.

To promote the Congress in Canada, we took space at the London Poultry Show in April 1999, and Alan Bentley and I ran the exhibit. By this time we had a pop-up booth for WPC2000 that was very useful. Of course, I also had to spend time at the Egg Board exhibit, so it was a busy show.

The full Organizing Committee met in May 1999 and we toured the Palais again, this time with the logistics person, to begin allocating space for the various activities. Greg Martin, the Business Manager from PSA was also in attendance. By now we were beginning to see how things were progressing and on the whole we were pleased. As always, more sponsors and advertisers would be welcome but we looked like meeting the budget, and the Exhibition space was being picked up quite well. As we generally did in Montreal, we ate very well during the visit. These expenses all came out of the Congress budget, but as nobody was being paid (except the EIMP people), it seemed reasonable compensation.

In June, I went to Turkey for the VIV Exhibition, at which WPC2000 had a booth. This also gave Piet Simons and me the opportunity to spend time with some of the Turkish people, led by Prof. Akbay, who would be running WPC2004. Although Piet had expressed doubts about their ability to run the Congress, it was becoming apparent that they could, and likely would be successful. The downtown Congress Centre was very good for the meeting but unfortunately could not accommodate an exhibition. We worked hard encouraging people to consider WPC2000, now only 14 months distant. Of course several of their organizing committee did attend, to see first hand how we would run our Congress.

Even with the event a year away, we still spent quite a lot of time chasing potential sponsors and exhibitors. I talked with Cuddy, Hybrid Turkeys and Pfizer repeatedly in the summer of 1999. We had many conference calls with Ed Polak and others from EIMP to coordinate these efforts.

In July, Weibe van der Sluis, Editor of *World Poultry*, visited Montreal for a preview visit, and I was able to show him round. By this time, I was writing exclusively for his publisher, Misset, so this was a useful opportunity to show him the future WPC2000 site and our developing plans. He also got to meet the staff at the Palais and EIMP.

The PSA Annual Meeting was held in August in Fayetteville, Arkansas, and I took our booth there, and worked it some of the time, but we had one of the EIMP staff, Carol Laflamme to help, as well as Sherman Touchburn, another member of the Scientific Program Committee.

From this point until close to the opening of WPC2000, I would spend at least one day in Montreal each month. I worked closely with the EIMP staff and with any of the Organizing or other Committees that were needed at the time. With each visit, I became more enamoured of Montreal; in August 1999, I ate outside at a restaurant called Homard Fou. I ate smoked salmon and scallops, drank white wine and espresso, and listened to the jazz duo at the next door restaurant play some of my favourite pieces! What could possibly be better?

The WPC2000 Second Announcement was published and circulated at this time.

In November, I headed to The Netherlands for the VIV show in Utrecht, to promote the Congress. Piet Simons had a more or less permanent space at the show, and we used it to promote WPC2000. On the first morning, who should show up but Sigrid Boersma, who had been our summer co-op student at the Egg Board, working on the HACCP program. So I recruited her to help us with the Congress promotion. We didn't actually pay her but bought her a nice lunch and dinner. The show was good for us and we had lots of interest. The Turkish delegation was also there, and they negotiated a deal with Jaarbeurs, the operators of the VIV shows, to run an exhibition in conjunction with the 2004 World's Poultry Congress, and to pay the Congress US$150,000. We had lots of meals and drinks around Utrecht, with Wiebe, my Editor at *World Poultry*, and David Martin and lots of the folks from Watt Publishing, who also had a strong presence in The Netherlands. I spent the weekend with Wiebe in Doetinchem before flying home.

We had our own booth at the 2000 Atlanta show and I spent a lot of time there. I attended part of the PSA Directors meeting, to answer their questions and get answers to some of my own. Al Bentley came from Ottawa to help with our exhibit. EIMP sent three people, including two from their Exhibition Department. They worked hard and sold a significant amount of exhibit space for Montreal. On the Thursday evening, I took them to dinner and then to the Alliance Theatre to see *Shadowlands*, a play about British author C.S. Lewis. This was a terrific play but with a seriously sad ending, maybe not the best for the occasion, but nevertheless worth seeing.

The Turkish people were in Atlanta working on WPC2004, and I again met their Scientific Program Chair, Servet Yalcin. Servet was a no-nonsense scientist and although firmly in the shadow of Prof. Akbay, was a huge asset to the organization of WPC2004. In the course of the six or seven years I interacted with the Turkish group, I never saw her make a false move. I also learned that Prof. Akbay had more to her than any of us originally suspected and we became good friends. At the various venues we both attended, I as President and she as President-elect, we enjoyed each other's company. Nita also found her a great shopping companion, especially where hard bargaining was required!

For the month preceding the Congress, I had decided to spend most of my time in Montreal and so we rented a suite in a long stay hotel. We looked at several, and I remember each one bragging about its hair dryer; I had by then lost 90% of my hair, so what was the point? Maybe they thought I would have company!

Papers, abstracts and posters began to arrive for review in April. I produced a poster jointly with Sigrid Boersma describing the Egg Board's HACCP program. All of the submissions were peer-reviewed, the posters mainly by Sherman Touchburn and a graduate student at Macdonald College.

To help us encourage young scientists from developing countries to attend the Congress, we applied to the Canadian International Development Agency for funding. We had numerous applications from young scientists and narrowed it down to 34 who would be eligible if the funding became available, which it eventually did.

Another challenge was language and translation. At some of the previous Congresses I had attended, there was often simultaneous translation into several languages, always Spanish, frequently French and German. The Russian delegation often brought their own translators. More recently, however, Congresses had tended to work only in English. This would not be acceptable in Canada, an officially bi-lingual country, particularly when the Federal Government was a major sponsor. But the cost of simultaneous translation at the time of the Congress was approximately $1000/h for each language. In the end, we decided to have translation only for the opening ceremony and a limited number of papers on what we had designated as "Producers' day" when we expected attendance from producers, mostly from Quebec, which was predominantly French speaking.

We had almost 700 posters submitted, probably a record at the time. So with the help of Steve Leeson and Shai Barbut (another faculty person at Guelph), we divided them into 3 daily sessions.

VIV held an exhibition in Turkey in June 2000, and I went there to work the WPC2000 booth. It also gave me the opportunity to meet more of the people who were planning WPC2004. When I arrived, the WPC 2000 literature which was shipped from Montreal had not been delivered. Fortunately I had carried some with me, we had a hired "hostess" at the booth and so we were able to work well until the shipment eventually came. The show was only three days, but afterwards, Piet Simons and I were driven to Mudurnu for a consultation with a large poultry company that was introducing their new "Free Range chicken" with a big publicity promotion. I thought the real target of this product would be Western Europe; Turkey was at the time hoping to join the EU. The promotion consisted of loud music and models in bikinis! The models were quite gorgeous, but not a chicken is sight.

The object of the visit, I now discovered, was for Piet and I to somehow audit the production system and confirm that the "Free Range" designation was genuine. We were assisted by a company called SGS, who had done this before. We visited several production units and verified that indeed, the birds were allowed access to pasture as required. We also toured the processing plant, state-of-the-art equipment from Dutch company Stork, working at 8,500 birds/h and a range of 100 end products.

Later in June, I attended the Cornell Poultry Conference and was able to promote the Congress, but it was getting late; most people would already have plans for August.

Starting the third week in July, I began working several days each week at the EIMP offices. The long stay suite at L'Appartement worked very well. It was on Sherbrooke Street, about a twenty minute walk from the office. There was a liquor store and a bank machine on the way. I made my own breakfasts and sometimes dinner, but if anyone else from the organizing committee was around we usually ate out. The place had a rooftop pool that I used frequently. I watched TV only occasionally, but was glad to be able to see Queen Elizabeth the Queen Mother's 100th birthday parade on August 4th!

I was always concerned at the paucity of early registrations, and even in July, we had less than I hoped. It seemed that the discount for early registration did not attract as many people as we expected. This was good financially, but not for peace of mind.

At that time, airline fares were greatly discounted if a return schedule involved a weekend away. So Pat Attridge, still my travel agent, booked four round trip tickets, two originating in Toronto and two in Montreal, and I was able to fly at the cheap rate without staying away weekends!

On one of these weekly trips, I got to meet a look-alike Colonel Sanders (he of the Kentucky Fried Chicken restaurant chain) The real colonel was several years dead, but this one did promotional work and we decided to "display" him at the Congress. He really looked the part with white formal suit, beard etc and identical glasses to those in KFC advertisements.

I found my presence at the EIMP office worked well – they were sometimes inclined to leave things when they should have worked on them, and I forestalled such events. And I was able to do last minute checks on and proof-read the Final Program, which if not done would have resulted in an inferior presentation. I was surprised at how much of the work they actually contracted out, mostly to people unfamiliar with the big picture.

One of the good things Ed Polak brought to the table was serious negotiating skills. When we had an idea of numbers, he was able to talk suppliers down from budgeted figures and also reduce the cost of the Proceedings. We had already decided not to print these; very few registrants had taken up the offer at extra cost, and those who did had the money refunded. This was the first Congress to provide Proceedings only in electronic format, on a CD rom. EIMP had told us that the majority of printed Proceedings at other Congresses they managed were left in hotel rooms! I had two vigorous complaints about not getting hard copy Proceedings, but with this out of about 1000 registrants, I felt we did the right thing. Certainly it saved us thousands of dollars. Interestingly, few computers sold in 2020 have CD drives. I have no idea how many people would want to access WPC2000 proceedings now, but they might find it hard!

The Poultry Science meeting started registration at the Palais on Thursday August 17th and their meeting started on the 18th. I spent most of the day meeting and greeting, while also keeping in touch with EIMP; they loaned me a cell phone for the week.

At this time I moved from L'Appartement to the President's suite at the Intercontinental Hotel.

We had some fun waiting for the Indian delegation. Nobody knew how or when they would arrive. The WPSA India Branch Secretary arrived first. Then late on Friday, Mrs Desai and her entourage came. This was important, as she was expected to Chair the WPSA Executive meeting.

On Saturday, the PSA meeting was in full swing, and preparations for the Marek's Symposium and the Congress nearing completion. Nita arrived from Cambridge and moved in to the President's suite with me.

The Marek's Symposium held a reception in their hotel and Mrs. Desai and the Indian Branch hosted a very good dinner party. I wrote in my diary afterwards that Mrs. Desai was "really rather a sweetheart".

The WPSA Executive meeting lasted from 9.00 until 3.15 on Sunday. In the evening, we hosted them for dinner at my favourite restaurant, Pêre St. Vincent. One of the nice things about this was the walk from the Palais, though the old city. We had a private room and while it was impossible to use their regular menu for such a group, they did a special one for us that was just as good. The manager gave us a brief history of the place and then took our orders. I put in my diary that we ate and drank like kings; 24 of us at a cost of $1,700, which was good for the year 2000.

The Congress opened on Monday August 21, but the day began with the Annual General Meeting of the WPSA Canada Branch, held for once, in Canada.

The Poultry Science Association finished its meeting in the morning and we had a transitional session as a bridge between the meetings. The first paper was the WPSA Lecture, usually presented at the PSA meeting. It was given by Gerald Havenstein, Chair of Poultry Science at NC State

Univ. and the topic was: *From Chicken Coops to Genome Maps*. This was followed by a presentation from British journalist Gwynne Dyer on *The Politics of Food*. The topic was inspired by Rob Etches, our Scientific Chair, and was excellent. This was followed by the presentation of Awards by the Dutch Branch. Deborah Whale gave a very good speech on behalf of the Poultry Industry Council, which won the Organization Award. My good friend and world egg shell specialist, Sally Solomon from the Univ. of Glasgow, won the Education Award.

In the mid afternoon all of the main players for the Opening Ceremony assembled for "mingling" in a specially created Green Room with drinks and canapés. Mrs. Desai and several of her Indian delegation were there, along with the Canadian Minister of Agriculture and Agri-Food, Lyle Vanclief, and several senior civil servants. Also included were members of the organizing committee and the WPSA Executive,

As a lover of theatre I could not help being seriously impressed with the Opening Ceremony. This was one of the high points of EIMP's creative skills. A TV personality, Dorothée Berryman, was MC and first appeared dressed in a costume of the 1920's. Canada had hosted the third World's Poultry Congress in 1927. She eventually found her way to 2000, and introduced the various speakers. I gave the welcoming address, followed by Lyle Vanclief on behalf of the Canadian government. Piet Simons and Mrs. Desai spoke on behalf of WPSA. And Donald Mc.Q. Shaver, now the elder statesman of poultry in Canada, gave one of his inspirational speeches about feeding the world. But these speeches were liberally interspersed with "entertainment"; we had a group of Indigenous dancers, a school choir from Quebec and a native singer. And the sound and lighting effects were quite flawless.

From this major event, we all moved to the Exhibition Hall for the ribbon cutting ceremony, and I toured some of the exhibits with the Minister. He left shortly after, and I continued my tour, meeting old friends, and receiving congratulations on the opening ceremony. This was gratifying, but of course it was very much a team effort, and we finally left the Palais around 8.00pm. Nita and I dined at Chèz Bernard with Pierre Bergeron and his wife Elaine.

Several of us from the Organizing Committee met with Eddie Polak each morning to receive progress reports, and any challenges that needed dealing with. One of these was a protest by People for the Ethical Treatment of Animals (PETA), who dumped a load of (cow) manure on the plaza outside the Palais, but failed to enter the building. We were warned that they would come back with more protests, but they never did.

I met with a group from the WPSA Australian Branch who were bidding for the 2008 Congress to be held in Brisbane. I also attended the meeting of WPSA Branch Secretaries. This was a very good idea, originally started by Piet Simons; Branch Secretaries were often the hardest working, and least recognized, among Branch members. At the time, the Canada Branch Secretary was Karen Schwean Lardner from U. Sask. Karen was a huge asset to the Branch, and also to her College. She was then nominally assisting Hank Classen and managing the poultry research unit, but she went on to become an excellent researcher and teacher in her own right, eventually President of the Branch and most recently, President of the PSA.

Later in the morning the Bart Rispens Memorial Lecture, an important part of the Marek's Symposium, took place and was open to everyone: about 600 people showed up.

The Congress, in addition to the more than 700 submitted posters, hosted over 150 invited speakers, 31 Symposia and 20 specialist workshops.

The Australian Branch hosted a reception to introduce their bid for the 2008 Congress; we attended and of course would support them. Nita and I took Bob Pym and Julie Roberts for a quick meal before heading off to the Molson Centre for the Ice Show. This was a free event for WPC2000 delegates, and we got to meet the skaters afterwards.

Tuesday was also the Producer Day and we had quite a few farmers attend special sessions.

When you have spent four years planning an event that lasts for four days, it's amazing how quickly it happens!

We had spent a lot of time at the WPSA Executive, working for the first time ever with the International Network for Family Poultry Development (INFPD). The United Nations Food and Agriculture Organization had put them in touch with us and we gladly cooperated. The Network helped small farmers in developing countries improve both their diet and their income by establishing poultry flocks, often just 5 or 10 birds, usually running loose and fed minimal diets. All of their communication beyond the actual farmer was electronic. We arranged a Symposium for them and it was well attended. I became personally quite enthusiastic about this program, and it has grown and prospered in the ensuing years.

Wednesday saw the WPSA Council meeting, at which decisions were made regarding future Congresses, and a new slate of Vice Presidents was elected. We used an electronic system of voting, which created some controversy; however I always felt it was better than the paper ballots we had used previously, leading to recounts on several occasions. Brisbane won the right to host the 2008 Congress, in a close competition with Salvador, Brazil. (Salvador eventually hosted the 2012 Congress). Bruce Sheldon (Australia) was elected as Senior Vice President and the other VP's were Dietmar Flock (Germany), Avigdor Cahaner (Israel), Colin Fisher (UK) and Rob Gous (South Africa). WPSA had always prided itself on the wide geographical distribution of its Executive and this was no exception. The Officers, Treasurer Francine Bradley (US) and Secretary Piet Simons (Netherlands) were re-elected, and as was traditional, the President's position went to me as President of the Congress. We did the ceremonial handing of the WPSA flag and Presidential medal to me from Mrs. Desai.

The cultural event on Wednesday was a concert of classical music held in the Notre Dame Basilica, featuring I Musici de Montreal. They were quite wonderful. The Basilica was noted for its acoustics; no microphones were needed, and when I made the introductory announcement in that huge space, everyone could hear me.

The final day, Friday August 24, included a Symposium on Egg Shell Quality, attended and addressed by all of the world authorities on that important topic. In the afternoon, I chaired a session on Egg Further Processing, which almost ran into the Closing Ceremony. But everything worked out in the end, and the Organizing Committee met in our hotel suite to celebrate a successful Congress. They presented me with a very impressive Inuit soapstone carving as a memento of the event.

Our closing Banquet was held in the old Windsor Station and was supposed to have four food stations representing four regions of Canadian food. They were suitably decorated but all had the same food! However, everyone enjoyed the event, and nobody except a few on the Organizing Committee seemed to notice the food situation.

The following day, was time for tidying up loose ends, but first, I went to the Holiday Inn to see off our Congress Youth Tour: 26 young people from 20 countries off on a five day tour of Ontario and Quebec.

All told, I was happy with the Congress. I felt that Canada had made everyone welcome, and we provided an excellent blend of science and culture to our very international audience.

We had a *post mortem* meeting in December mainly to discuss finance and the split of any residual funds between WPC2000 and PSA. I am not sure how this was resolved because shortly after this, EIMP essentially took over the bank account and did not take our calls. It left a sour taste in the mouth but also demonstrated the wisdom of not agreeing to EIMP becoming the permanent organizer for World Congresses, as they had ardently wished to be. In March 2001, I learned that EIMP had billed WPC2000 twice for the same services in the amount of $200,000. At a subsequent meeting to discuss this matter, Eddie massaged the accounts to show that from an expected loss of $90,000, he could now show a break-even, taking into account a GST/TVQ refund of about $200,000. It seemed we were completely in their hands; we left unsatisfied but powerless.

In May 2001, we had the Annual General Meeting of WPC2000. We had to "Table" the financial report, as the dispute over GST/TVQ rebates was still not resolved. In November, EIMP reported a large loss apparently due to overcharging sponsorship expenses. However, by this time it was their loss as they had taken over the bank account! We met in Montreal and Pierre, the treasurer summed it up: "We have been screwed without being kissed!". A disappointing end to a very successful event.

Chapter 12
Life at Home after 1980

Change of Plan on the Housing Front

When I got back from the Breeders' Roundtable in St. Louis in May, 1980, I was confronted with a startling development. Nita had seen a house at 251 West River Road in West Galt for sale, and really wanted us to buy it. This was a very pleasant area. The house was about 60 years old, on a lot that went from the road, 250 m to the river, It was frame construction but the siding on the ground floor was river stone and mortar, with stucco on the second floor. It was spacious (or seemed so to us – it was later referred to by someone as a "cute little house") with a smallish kitchen, a spacious separate dining room and a beautiful living room (with a fireplace). There was also an addition to the living room that we called the sun room, which overlooked the view to the river, all on the ground floor. Upstairs were four bedrooms, a bathroom and a sleeping porch.

We first of all thought about buying this house and keeping the St. George building lot for future development. We talked at length about it: it was a complete contrast to the proposed building in the country, but it had the advantage of being close to town. I think Nita loved it more than I did at that stage. We arranged for Joe Somfay, architect for the proposed St. George property, to look at the West River Road house (which we had already decided, if we bought it, to call "The Folly"). He didn't like the house, said it would be high maintenance, and would need $2000 to $3000 spent on it immediately. All of this turned out to be correct.

We haggled a bit over the price and eventually signed an offer with closing at the end of July. The vendors were the son and daughter of the original owner, Walter Cross, a local businessman. They had grown up in the house. The daughter married and moved away. The son, Tom, married and built a home on a five acre property across the road that grew raspberries. It subsequently became an upscale subdivision called "Berry Patch Lane". Our house had been empty for several years after Walter's widow, who had lived there alone, died. For many years after we moved in, anyone local called it "the Cross house".

We still hadn't sold the house on Dakin Crescent, so we changed realtors. Our new agent, Hugh Priest almost immediately brought an offer, which we accepted, even though after the commission of 5%, it would mean a loss overall.

We soon got a mortgage on The Folly, and some bridging finance while we owned two houses. When out on another errand, Nita saw a trailer for sale and easily negotiated its purchase for $125 in cash. This enabled us to move ourselves to The Folly and have the trailer for future use. It was an old tent trailer lacking the tent, quite rusty but the chassis was largely OK. In the end, I replaced the floor and sides twice with plywood before selling it in 2013 for $50!

Tom Cross allowed us access to The Folly before closing and we began re-decorating. The house had wallpaper everywhere and of course none of it was to our taste. I rented a steamer most weekends; in some places there were seven layers to remove! By the time I finished, I had much rather have bought the steamer and then sold it again.

We took possession on August 4th but did not move in until the 14th. By this time most of the wallpaper was gone, some of the rooms had cracks in the plaster filled and were painted. The internal walls were lath and plaster, not drywall. We moved most of our stuff in the trailer. Nita did a lot while I was at work; she could not back up the trailer but fortunately The Folly had a circular driveway so she could drive right round and out again! I have a hard time now realizing how hard we both worked, as well as raising children aged 5 and 3 years. I had a full time job plus consultancy; Nita worked the livelong day and cooked most meals (although I did barbecue quite a lot in summer) and somehow we made The Folly just fit to live in. But there was still a lot to do.

Priority was the kitchen. It had a sink and power outlets for the stove, fridge etc and a broom closet in one corner, but very little counter space or storage for pots and pans or anything else. We dismantled the broom closet, built "temporary" counters including the existing sink, and shelves below to create a workable kitchen that in fact lasted for several years. In 1988, we had a nice professionally designed and installed set of cupboards, counter tops and drawers that were still there when we left in 2013.

We broke the workload with social events. The day after moving in, we scrambled to Stratford with Henry and Christa Bayley to see *The Seagull*, and on the weekend had dinner and lots of good Portuguese wine with Manuel and Luis Costa. Manuel's wife had returned to Portugal by this time.

The same weekend we again went to Stratford, picnicked (by the river, including champagne) with Cliff and Hazel Luce before seeing *Much Ado About Nothing*. This had a stellar cast, including Maggie Smith, Brian Bedford and William Hutt. (The last was an understudy for an ailing actor).

We later went to the Shaw Festival and saw Shaw's *The Philanderer* at the Court House Theatre.

My mother came a few days after the move, on a CP charter flight direct from Newcastle. She loved the house and yard, and the children enjoyed her visit. It took some of the pressure off Nita and me.

Nita, PJ and I applied for Canadian citizenship in December 1980 and officially became citizens on April 28 1981 at a ceremony in Waterloo. Of course Carole was born in Canada, but at the age of only 2 could not understand why she was not involved in this ceremony and did not receive a bible!

In September 1982, we listed the building lot on Conc. 5 for sale with a Brantford realtor, as we now had too much invested in 251, West River Road to move, and it would be better for the kids. The realtor did not have any luck, but Olive Fowler eventually sold it for us for $38,500, so we came out a little bit ahead after fees and financing costs

At home, we continued to make The Folly into our dream house. We both agreed that the house had its nightmare aspects but we gradually eliminated or worked around them. Quite early on, we installed a fireplace insert that was very heat-productive, compared with the old open fire that sucked the heat up the flue. After the St. George lot was sold, each year we bought a truckload of 12 foot logs, and I chainsawed and split them myself. The first time we did this our neighbour, Hazel Detlor, complained to the police about the noise. The cops duly arrived, usually while I was taking a breather, and asked if I was using a chainsaw, and I said of course I was. The police were uniformly friendly! Eventually, I was charged with breaking the local noise by-law, had to hire a lawyer for about $500, duly went to court and the case was dismissed. Much to Mrs. Detlor's annoyance, our neighbours Betty Graham and Vera Waite appeared as witnesses on my behalf. I thought it was unfair to pay my own lawyer and, indirectly by way of property taxes, the City's so I complained to the City Manager and got $250 back!

In 1982 I installed white lapboard siding on the second storey of the house, covering the stucco which was beginning to look old and the paint flaking off. It was was hard to install, since it was entirely above head height, but I eventually got the hang of it and it looked very good. The siding was guaranteed for twenty-five years and was still in decent shape when we sold the house in 2013.

In an area in the back of the basement, that had originally been part of a former garage, I created a workshop and space for making beer and wine. I built an insulated dividing wall to make the workshop a little warmer, and room outside for the lawn tractor that we needed to cut the back 40. The workshop in the basement proved useful. I added insulation to the outside wall and built a very sturdy work bench from a drawing in the Readers Digest Do-It-Yourself Manual. This was still in good shape when we moved in 2013, but we left it behind as there was a decent work bench in the new place, and we could not get the old one through the door to the outside! In the early days, the workshop would regularly flood when snow on the lawn outside melted and flowed in through the garage where we kept the garden tractor.. After spending a lot of time several years in a row baling it out, I eventually dug a small sump hole near the outside and diverted the water into it, to be pumped out with a sump pump before it could flow into the workshop.

The basement also contained the cistern, into which rainwater from the roof was directed. Water was pumped from this to flush toilets and provide cold water to the shower. This was not quite the most hygienic system. Looking in to the cistern when it was relatively full we could see leaves in various stages of decomposition, and the occasional dead squirrel similarly decaying. When the pump quit, the service man said he could replace it, but it wouldn't last long because of the acid rain! So we decided to convert to 100% use of water from our own well for everything. This worked very well until a prolonged drought one summer a few years later caused the well to run dry. At this point, we were able, at considerable expense, to connect with City water, using the well only for outside use like watering the lawn.

When we demolished the old cistern, we gave this space over to our son PJ for a workshop and he eventually used it for bicycle maintenance.

Throughout the late summer and fall of 1980, we continued work on the house. The bedrooms all had built in closets, but no permanent shelves or clothes racks. I remember one that had an old broom handle held up by two bent nails for hanging clothes! So I designed and built shelves with proper doweling underneath for all four bedrooms. The basement of the house was strictly functional; when we moved in, it was relatively empty except for the giant furnace and associated 400 gallon oil tank. We installed a washer and drier, a second fridge, and a lot of shelving for storage.

When we bought The Folly, neither public water supply nor sewage disposal were available. We found out later that our sewage disposal system consisted of a large concrete pipe about 8 feet across and 12 feet deep dug into the ground just below the formal garden. This may have been adequate back in the days before washing machines, but we found that it soon filled up and seeped over on to the lawn. So we arranged for Davy Smith (Mary and Elgin's son) to come with his backhoe and dig a tile bed. This was strictly illegal but did the job. He started early one morning and was finished, with gravel and tile installed and covered, by noon. Our neighbours saw what was happening but, surprisingly, did nothing. The system worked perfectly for as long as we needed it. When City services became available in 1997, we connected to the sewage system and, then as detailed above, to the water supply.

Another major project: we decided to re-insulate the attic. It had minimal fibreglass over newspapers when we moved in but the fibreglass had settled and likely was ineffective. Removing it and replacing with new 10 cm batts was an awful, dusty and uncomfortable job but I managed it over a couple of weekends. Before we sold the house in 2013, this too was considered inadequate and we had a large quantity of insulating material blown in to a depth of over 50 cm.

The heating system when we bought the house was an oil fired furnace and hot air duct work to each room. This was a retrofit after the house was built and the air supply to the top floor was not really efficient. This was not too bad for heating, as hot air tends to rise anyway, but when we put in air conditioning we had real problems getting cool air upstairs. In 1985 we changed to a natural gas furnace, which lasted about 25 years! Removal of the 400 gallon oil tank also gave us more storage space in the basement.

The outer walls of the house were of conventional frame construction with no insulation. Around this time, there were government subsidies for adding insulation to older homes, and urea-formaldehyde foam was especially popular. It was ideally suited to our house since the siding outside was stone and inside, lath and plaster. To install the urea-formaldehyde, the operators drilled holes of about 1" diameter, 16" apart in all the inside walls and then pumped in the foam. This was hard on us, having recently moved in and redecorated, but we did it anyway. It was just like moving again, as all contents and furniture had to be 3 feet from the walls. The holes were filled with the blue insulation and had to be smoothed out, filled with polyfilla and then the walls repainted. Within a few weeks of this, it was learned that some of the installers of the urea-formaldehyde foam had not done it correctly and there was a potential for formaldehyde, a known carcinogen, to infiltrate the dwelling. A huge cottage industry developed to test for formaldehyde, remove the insulation if needed, and undertake all kinds of very expensive remedial work. We got as far as testing, with negative results. However there were government grants to install a heat exchanger that would create positive pressure inside the house as well as recovering some heat from the exhaust air. We had one installed.

The final major development was the old sleeping porch. When we took over the house, this room was full of dust and garbage. It was unheated and uninsulated. It was accessed by a door from the upstairs of the house down a large step. The floor formed the roof over the balcony below. It ran pretty much the length of the main structure, about 20 feet long and 6 feet wide. There were windows (some that opened) on three sides, all old fashioned wooden frames with six or eight panes of glass, some cracked and broken. We decided to make this "the office". Over a period of several months, we removed in turn, each window, removed all the glass and repainted the frames, and replaced the glass and putty. I removed the interior walls and ceiling, put in some insulation and covered it with some nice tongue-and-groove cedar boards. We put in two electric baseboard heaters. Even with these improvements it was still cold in winter. For several years we added temporary clear plastic sheeting over the windows. Eventually, we replaced them with modern double-glazed windows. We put bookshelves all along the walls opposite the windows, and on the outside wall not occupied with desk and filing cabinets. It was very practical as an office although the view (~ 250 m to the river and beyond) could be distracting. But for my writing and private work before and after retirement, it was invaluable.

The Folly had a great back yard for the kids. Below the terraced garden there was a great slope for tobogganing, rolling huge snowballs and all manner of fun. PJ taught himself to ski on little red plastic skis when he was quite young. Along with some formal lessons and a lot of time at Chicopee, the local ski hill, he eventually became very proficient, changed to snowboarding when it became fashionable, and then back to skiing in the 2000's. Although I tried hard to enjoy skiing, it was never my thing, and Nita did not enjoy it at all. We got cross country skis when we returned from Scotland but seldom used them and as the winters became milder, the opportunities diminished and we eventually put them in a garage sale without regret.

For about five, sometimes six months of the year, the back yard grew some grass and many weeds, but it still required cutting. I had a series of second hand garden tractors for mowing this, and eventually, in 1996, a new one purchased at Canadian Tire. It was still almost functional when we left in 2013. At first, I cut all of the grass on our patch, plus neighbour Betty Graham's, and the City's road allowance. When Betty died in 1997, I stopped cutting that part, and also the City's footpath. By this time, the row of maples I planted along our northern boundary were nice mature trees and grass beneath them hardly grew. The reduced commitment still took about 1½ hours to cut, and the lawn surrounding the house, another hour, so this was a significant allocation of time. For a while, PJ, then Carole, did part of this but when they had both left home, it reverted to me.

1982 was a bad year financially. Our mortgage came due at the end of July and the best we could do with interest rates pushing 20% involved monthly payments of almost $1000. I can't remember what my salary was at the time but we had to delay things like clothes and holidays, and any capital expenses. This arrangement was only for one year. By August 1983, interest rates came down and we re-negotiated for payments of $650/month and the mortgage would be paid off in 3 years!

In the late 1980's we were seeing lots of cracks in the plaster ceilings on the ground floor, so we had them professionally re-plastered, and then re-painted the three main rooms ourselves. At this time we also replaced and improved all of the lighting, and installed a ceiling fan in the living room.

When we bought the house, it had green asphalt shingles on the roof. When these wore out, we found there were multiple layers, so had all those removed before replacing them. When these in turn wore out in 1996, I found someone who exhibited aluminum shingles at the Poultry Show who would put these on our house for $6,770, about double the price of asphalt shingles. They were guaranteed for life. It took one man about a week to install the aluminum shingles but they looked excellent and were still good when the house was sold in 2013.

In October, 1985 we finally bought a TV. We had resisted this, as we preferred the kids not become addicted, and also felt that N. American TV programming was far inferior to what we had in Britain. But we ended up with a small dish like a frying pan in the attic (cable TV was not yet a factor and the traditional antenna got fewer channels) and a Sony TV set plus a Video Cassette Recorder in the fourth bedroom, then called the TV room. The kids watched it most. I started to watch the news when I got back from work but soon gave up as I had already heard it on the radio in the car, without the constant advertising. I have never become much of a TV watcher. The kids were quite selective and as adults don't watch much at all. Of course now they all have smart phones and other sources of information. Nita enjoys TV but mainly imported British series and dramas she can record and watch later, fast-forwarding the advertisements if necessary. The total cost of the set-up in 1985 was close to $2,000! Our latest TV, purchased in 2018 was less than $500 for a flat screen about 4 times the size of the old Sony. But of course we pay $160/month for the cable and Personal Video Recorder (and home phone and internet) so I guess it all works out to the benefit of the technology industry.

Our neighbour and good friend Betty Graham died of cancer in 1997. Her house was eventually sold and the new neighbours moved in, a couple with a daughter and two sons, all teenagers. They turned out to be the neighbours from hell. The parents ran a pub on Beverley Street called the Rose and Crown, and of course they were there at all hours, and the kids left to themselves. They seemed to live on take-out food and dumped the wrappers in their driveway, from where they blew into ours. One of them began growing marijuana in the basement and dealing on our driveway at night. He also did other nefarious things and did jail time. The daughter dressed like street-walker and may have been one! The adults eventually gave up the pub, and separated, but they must have lived there at least a decade. We were happy when they moved!

Loss of my Mother
While my mother was with us in June of 1982, we hosted a "Queen's Birthday Party" for her. (her actual birthday was December 24th) Everyone came in red, white and blue, we served homemade beer, red and white wine and hamburgers. Guests included most of our friends from St. George, Henry and Christa Bayley, the Shavers and the Malcolms.

The following year she came in mid August for three weeks. This time I was working a lot but took a few days off and we took the whole family to Canada's Wonderland. The kids loved it! We got a lovely picture of my mother with Carole in a "Swan boat". I took her on a short trip to the near North: Orillia, Muskoka, Algonquin Park, French River, and then home by way of the Ferry from South Bay Mouth to Tobermory.

On February 10th, 1984, my godfather, Eric Wainwright phoned to say my mother had collapsed and been admitted to the Royal Victoria Infirmary in Newcastle. Her doctors were saying she was "Not critical" and not to worry, but of course we did worry, and I began to tentatively plan a trip to see her. Nita, with whom my mother had established a very fond relationship, was as devastated, maybe even more so, than I was. Mother improved enough to be discharged from the RVI, and went to stay with Eric. She continued to improve until Friday, February 24th at which point she collapsed again, Eric and a friend who had been a nurse put her to bed and she died quietly in her sleep. I learned of this when Nita phoned me at the office and quickly booked a night flight to Heathrow. I arrived at 7.45 am, Saturday had to wait a couple of hours for a flight to Newcastle, where Eric met me and took me to his home in Gosforth. We later went to the house in Ponteland and did some tidying up, and again the following day, when I found and reviewed all the "papers", but the bulk of this work was to come later. My mother had been very fond of house plants and we were able to give all of these to the family next door.

However, we had to deal with the Bank, and with our lawyer, Iain Nicholson, who was a contemporary of mine. He did all of the legal stuff and also took care of the sale of the house. Eric had done all of the arrangements with the undertaker and the Crematorium. I obtained the death certificate from the Doctor's office.

We managed some nice pub lunches at the Highlander Inn, and, with my great friend Elizabeth Henderson (née Dobson) at The Wagon. By this time I had rented a car to release Eric from all the transport obligations. Elizabeth, who had also been very fond of my mother, joined me for dinner at the George Hotel in Chollerford. She had marriage problems; she was not well, drank a lot. Her husband, Alastair was having an affair. They had a son, James, and I kept in touch with him for a while after Elizabeth died in April 2000. James, as I remember, did very well, joined one of the professions and ended up in the far East.

The Cremation service was hard. By Elizabeth's count there were 29 present. A eulogy by Alan Dunstone (very well done but I had no idea who he was) was followed by a reception, where I spoke to everyone, known and unknown, and finally Eric, Elizabeth and I had a good lunch at the Imperial Grill in Newcastle.

Once the official duties were completed, I was able to make some professional use of the trip, and renew contact with my old and trusted friend, Geoff Fairhurst. I took the train to Birmingham and Geoff met me and drove us to the Buckatree Hotel in Wellington, Shropshire. We had dinner, followed by a pint or two, and talked until 1.00 am. The following day we met with Chris Belyavin and Dick Wells from Harper Adams College. Dick was a year behind me in the Poultry M.Sc. at Wye, and Chris ran an egg layer testing station. After that we visited Sun Valley Turkeys in Shobdon. This was another Cargill subsidiary and there was talk of me consulting with them, but nothing came of it; maybe I had been too long out of touch with turkeys!

The following day, Geoff drove me to the Post House Hotel near Heathrow. I stayed there overnight and Don and Joan Legg (more expatriate Geordies) came for dinner and a long chat, and I flew home the next day, met by Nita as arranged by phone.

At the end of March, 1984, we all four of us flew to England. Nita's mother Flo and husband Mick looked after the kids while Nita and I went, using a rented car, to Ponteland to clear out my mothers place prior to its sale. We stayed with Eric Wainwiright. Since my mother had bought a car (they never had one while my father was alive) we thought we would be OK for transportation, so left the Avis car in Newcastle. Her Honda promptly "died" so we had to rent again while it was fixed. Elizabeth Henderson took the living room suite, but everything else, we had to separate; going to Canada or for what we called the "rag and bone man". We were fairly ruthless as our house was pretty much furnished but there were a few items, either valuable or attractive, or both, that we decided to ship home. Of particular note was the Cuckoo Clock, which I had requested be saved when my Great Uncle John's house was being dismantled back in the 1970's. My mother had endless trouble with it (it was then about 100 years old) and had the motion replaced by an electric motor, which drove the hands but not the cuckoo and chime. The clock, of course, was in the dining room but we only found the motion (in a box labeled "cuckoo clock innards") when we looked in the attic after we had done with all the other house contents. There wasn't that much, but it cost us £600 to ship back to Canada everything we picked out.

A few months after we got back, we were visiting Brenda Purvis and her partner Gerhard, and met one John Hopkins, who said he knew about cuckoo clocks, so we asked him to put ours back together. He agreed and in February 1985, we had it going in our house. But I think he consulted with a real expert, Harry Kramins, who lived in London, and who serviced and maintained it for the next 30 years. By this time Harry was in his 90's and no longer able to work on the clock. After a serious false start with a so-called expert in Guelph, we found John Shantz, who had a business called Antiques in Time in Stratford. By this time (2018), the clock was about 140 years old and needed rebuilding (again!) John charged $1,024 but the clock ran well for a couple of years. Then the chime and the hands went out of sync, and I spent another $250 to have him fix it.

We found that the UK real estate business was not as cut and dried as it was in Canada, or at least not what we expected. We'd had apparently "firm" offers for the house in Ponteland, but none was consummated. It was finally sold in July and after paying off Iain Nicholson and sundry other charges, I think we got about £50,000, and quickly paid off the mortgage on The Folly.

As a bit of self-indulgence while we were doing all the work in Ponteland, we drove over the Roman Road to Cumbria and had dinner, bed and breakfast at the Crosby Lodge, the old haunt from my Ross days. We also had a drink at the Queens Arms, Warwick Bridge, another Ross Breeders haunt.

When the stuff from Ponteland arrived in Canada, we again sorted through it and a lot of antiques were sold. With the exception of the silver, most of it, almost $1,000 worth, went to Peter Volmer, a retired teacher turned antique dealer we had met through our friends in St. George. We eventually sold the sterling silver in 2020, but it was basically sold by weight – nobody wanted antique spoons any more.

One of mother's minor bequests was £200 to the National Trust. I thought this was too little (the will had been written several years earlier) so I decided to take out a life membership for myself for £300. In retrospect it was a poor deal for the National Trust, as they have had to provide service to me for over 35 years! However, it was very nice for Nita and me to get free admission whenever we traveled to the UK and visited Trust properties!

Donald Shaver's 90th Birthday Party
Following my retirement, I saw quite a bit of DMcQ, especially with regard to germplasm conservation, but we also met socially from time to time. As his 90th birthday approached we thought it would be a good idea to host a party for the Shaver Old Boys (impolitely known as SOBs) and Girls to celebrate the event. So in early August, 2010, we sent out invitations to everyone we could think of, also soliciting food, and had a small tent set up near the house. In the event, it was a perfect day, we didn't need the tent, and just under 50 people showed up for very good food, lots of my homemade wine and beer and great company. Don was thrilled, as nobody else had considered such a reunion. His family likely arranged some smaller events, but I am sure they expected him to pay for them!

Our Health
My health during this whole time was generally robust, except for occasional coughs and colds. But in 1987, I began to experience quite severe lower back pain. Our long time family doctor, Philip Trudel, prescribed pain relievers and muscle relaxants, which did not help. I then had several sessions of physiotherapy that were similarly ineffective. I finally went to see a chiropractor, Hugh Hendry. When I left his office after the first session I felt considerably worse, but after 24 hours, much better. I went back several times a week, then less and less, until he told me he was done! By that time, I felt better than I had in months, and attributed this entirely to Hendry's adjustments. Soon after that, he retired but sent all his patient information to a much younger chiropractor, Todd Walker. When I next had back problems, I saw Todd, who persuaded me to have regular "maintenance adjustments" every three weeks, and I have continued this indefinitely. I rarely feel any back pain now.

In 2002, our family doctor of many years, Phil Trudel, thought my cholesterol level was on the high side and put me on statin pills. I was never convinced these were useful; the dose increased from 20 mg to 40 mg as I became older. I think my cholesterol level was stable but the arithmetic involving my age raised the risk factor! Much later, in about 2018 after Dr. Trudel had retired, his replacement, Dr. Sefin, said there was no evidence that statins had any value in patients over 80, and so I ceased to take them.

The only other medical item of note followed my first colonoscopy, which was recommended due to age, shortly after I retired. Following the procedure, Dr. Donna Kolyn informed me that she had identified a large polyp, too large for her to deal with, and so she referred me to Dr. Ron Markon at St. Michael's Hospital in Toronto. I duly saw Dr. Markon, who repeated the colonoscopy and reached the same conclusion, and he said that they would have to remove the polyp. But, he said, "The timing is interesting. In two weeks time, St. Michael's will host the 20th International Symposium on Therapeutic Endoscopy. We would like to perform the operation as part of this Symposium". I made no comment, and he continued to tell me that a closed circuit television version of the procedure would be transmitted live to an audience of experts in the Harbour Castle Hilton Hotel in Toronto, and another group at an hotel in Vancouver! "But they won't see your face!", he added. This duly took place; I remember only the crowd in the operating room before I was sedated, and the opportunity to view the polyp, described as "the size of a plum", afterwards. They kept me in St, Michael's overnight, but I went home the next day and had no further problems. Those who have endured a colonoscopy will no doubt agree that the procedure is easy and painless; it is the preparation that is completely disgusting, and after my 80th birthday, Dr. Kolyn and I agreed that I would no longer have these procedures every five years.

Nita's health was relatively good in general. She had several fractures and a few other problems, but In May, 2004, when we returned from a trip to Brazil, she began to notice bleeding in her bowel movements. She went to see the same surgeon who had done my first colonoscopy, Dr. Donna Kolyn, was put on the waiting list, and had the procedure in late June. In a July appointment with the surgeon, she was told she had colon cancer and would require major surgery to deal with it. We had planned to visit PJ in British Columbia in September, so this would definitely be put "on hold".

Nita's surgery was scheduled for Wednesday August 4th. We had previously booked a two-day trip to Toronto, including a harbour cruise, dinner, overnight stay at the Royal York Hotel, and seats to see *Mama Mia* at the Royal Alexandra Theatre. We went on the tour and saw the show, but Nita had to fast, so I had dinner alone. The room at the Royal York was microscopic! We were up at 4.30 am so as to deliver Nita to the Cambridge hospital at 6.00. The surgeon phoned later to tell me the operation was successful – no complications – and I actually visited Nita later in the afternoon. She was still pretty groggy and I didn't stay long. The surgery was indeed major; the incision ran from her navel to close to her vagina. She stayed in the hospital for 10 days.

Soon after coming home, she began to see fecal material leaking into her urine and she went back to the hospital, *via* Emergency, where she was quickly re-admitted and scheduled for more surgery the same evening. It subsequently transpired that the original "no complications" report was not true; there had been challenges in the later stages of the surgery that we were not told about. In the end, they had to give her an ileostomy, which was later reversed.

Recovery was slow, and we were still scheduled to visit PJ in his new house in Bralorne, BC in September. In the event, we made the trip and although the travel was stressful, the change of scenery and the ability to relax were surely beneficial. We got a wheelchair for Nita in both Toronto and Vancouver airports, which worked OK.

PJ's location was amazing! We did shopping in Squamish, Whistler and Pemberton on the way to Bralorne, because there was literally nothing in the way of retail there. There was a general store in Gold Bridge, about 10 km away, but it had limited stock and was, of course, expensive. The house looked very empty! But they had moved from a basement apartment, in a pickup truck with a small trailer, and had only the bare essentials. But it was very comfortable, and the silence in the neighbourhood, breathtaking. We ate and drank very well; PJ and his girlfriend Melanie did a fine job with hospitality.

Nita was able to take short walks, and we visited the local Museum, where Melanie volunteered as Curator; in the land of the blind, the one-eyed man is king! PJ and I also went on a float plane ride from Tyak Mountain Resort with the pilot who took him and his friends for their mountain bike expeditions. PJ took us on several trips in the truck into the mountains, and I could see how he just **had** to live there.

I was able to do a little walking on my own, including right behind his house, a 300 m climb with amazing views of the town and surroundings. Bralorne started as a gold mining town. In fact there was still a mine in operation, although it seemed to be somewhat precarious. Nearby was the totally abandoned town of Pioneer, with lines of prefab houses (apparently supplied by Eatons Department Store). The Bridge River, which flowed through Bralorne was also visible from our walk. All around were lakes and rivers, and of course, forestry. No shortage of tree planting!

At the end of our stay, PJ took us to Vancouver, where we spent a couple of days with Sandy and Eva Cairns. They were both retired doctors; Nita had met Sandy in Ontario and they had become friends. By this time, Nita was able to walk for a reasonable distance and we did some local sightseeing. From Vancouver, Nita flew back to Toronto, while I had to go to Quebec City for a meeting concerning farm animal genetic resource conservation.

Soon after we returned from BC, Nita began her chemotherapy and radiation treatments. Side effects were minimal at first but at the end, immediately before Christmas, she was in very poor shape. The radiation took place in Hamilton; for the first few sessions, I drove her to the hospital. We then discovered that there was a lodge run by the Cancer Society where she could stay free for a week at a time. She eventually spent two separate weeks there, which took the pressure off me, as I was still doing a lot of consulting and writing. Just to complicate life further, I had a small part in Galt Little Theatre's production of *Oliver!*, which also took up considerable time.

Nita's recovery was long and hard. The combination of chemotherapy and radiation took a huge toll of her strength; it continued until just prior to Christmas, and the chemotherapy several weeks into the new year. But she eventually became cancer-free for 15 years, before another similar event in 2020. This required more surgery, followed by prolonged chemotherapy but no radiation.

Christmas Time
Our Christmases at The Folly tended to follow a similar pattern year after year. Bob and Beth Huntington had a Christmas tree farm that was mostly overgrown (i.e the trees were 15-20 feet high) but a few smaller trees that would fit in a house. We would go there a week or two before Christmas and trudge through the snow looking for the "perfect tree", then chop it down and retreat to their house. We would join them and other guests for drinks and buffet lunch before returning home with the tree on the car roof. The sun room at The Folly was perfect for a real tree and we always erected it in the same place, and decorated it with an ever-growing collection of ornaments. When Carole was about 10, she persuaded us that cutting down the tree and then tossing it in landfill was bad for nature. So we bought a fake tree from White Rose (now long gone from the retail scene). This tree began to seriously fall apart in 2020, and we had to replace it!

For many years when PJ and Carole were growing up, our friend Gill Teiman would come for Christmas and it became a tradition for her to read them *The Night Before Christmas* before bed on Christmas Eve.

Christmas mornings also followed a pattern. Kids would be up early but all they did was open stockings hung in front of the fire. Neighbour Betty Graham, and often other friends of Nita's would join us for a full breakfast and then everyone went in the sun room for the gifts beneath the tree. One of these would be a massive rawhide stick for the dog, who knew it was there and made straight for it.

Opening gifts would occupy several hours, with coffee and snacks, interspersed with collection of wrappers and fixing of toys.

Apart from 1985, when we had a goose, turkey was the fowl of choice and I always cooked it. I made the stuffing (dressing) using a recipe from the Chatelaine Cookbook called Grandma's Stuffing, basically celery, onions, seasoning and breadcrumbs. And I made bread sauce. Everything else was done by Nita: roasted potatoes, Brussels sprouts, corn pudding, wild rice casserole and copious gravy.

We would have wine and snacks on and off during the day and eat turkey dinner late afternoon. It was a great way to spend a family Christmas.

We also had the occasional Big Party for friends and neighbours. For one of these, in 1996, we figured on 36 people, and served the following: Tourtières (Canadian pork pies) with mushy peas, carrots and cole slaw; cheesecakes, fruit salad and a cake platter; all the beer and wine you could drink.

Once PJ and Carole had left home, Christmas, and possibly Thanksgiving were the only times we were all together. 1999 was such an occasion, when PJ was still working in Toronto and Carole still at University. PJ cooked dinner of steaks with peppercorn sauce for dinner on Christmas Eve (he learned a lot about cooking while working at various restaurants) and we all watched "White Christmas" on TV, with Danny Kaye, Bing Crosby and Rosemary Clooney.

Bridge

My maternal grandfather and my mother were both Bridge players, and so was Nita, in her University days. Nita continued to play quite regularly in different clubs from the time we were married. I had played Solo at home with my parents but never learned Bridge until 1986. The reason for the delay was primarily because while I worked for Shaver and Ross, my job involved significant travel, and it would not be fair to a partner to be so often absent. However, by 1986, travel was somewhat diminished and I thought it was time to start. Playing Solo had provided me with "card sense", the concept of tricks and trumps, but Contract Bridge bidding was quite a novelty. Nita and our friends from St. George, David and Ann

Bachelor began the teaching process in March 1986. I think I learned the basics quite quickly and in a few months was able to make up a table and not embarrass myself or my partner too badly.

I partnered with Nita at a two-table club that met on weekends. Most of the players were from Kitchener. However, as is inevitable, people died and were not replaced and the club eventually folded.

Then there was another club of two tables that had originally been all women. However, at one point someone moved and they couldn't immediately find a replacement, so a male spouse took her place. The next time someone quit, I moved in, and now (2020), there are 3 men and five women.

We would often have one and sometimes two tables at home or in others' places. We recruited a variety of neighbours and friends to make up a table at home. It wasn't deliberate but these people were often seniors and sometimes very senior! Ruth Collyer, who hailed originally from Newfoundland, was in her 90's. When her daughter insisted on her moving to a seniors' residence, she complained that it was "full of old people"! Hazel Brown was a close neighbour 3 doors away, living in a basement flat below her daughter, and was also in her 90's. Both played a good game by our standards.

This continued on and off indefinitely. Once I was retired, we tended to play more Bridge and some time in the 2000's we began to go to Bridge sessions in one of the Senior Centres, where a professional teacher, Joy Dundas, was the Director. I think this led to both of us improving our game and learning a few new conventions that made the game more interesting, and us more competitive. Joy was a wonderful teacher; she was patient to a fault, nothing seemed to faze her and no question was too basic, or complex, to get an answer.

The most we ever did as hosts was for three tables, 3-course dinner and Bridge in late 2003. I noted the superiority of the food (Awesome Country Paté, Burt's Beef Stew with mashed potatoes, desserts, veggies and dip, and all the wine we could drink, which turned out to be six bottles) and the very ordinary Bridge!

I think by this time, I had become addicted to the game and played more than Nita, although we still played in our regular Tuesday night two-table club and some Saturday evening sessions. I played each Friday at the Seniors Centre in Hespeler, with Lucinda D'Oliveira for a partner. We were encouraged to try Duplicate Bridge, but after a couple of afternoons, we decided it was not for us.

I began to play online, still in a relaxed style with similar minded people, and from 2018 on, spent any uncommitted evenings sitting on front of the computer screen that looked like a Bridge table! This is now most nights, while Nita watches TV. Once the COVID19 pandemic began, all in-contact Bridge games ceased. I now have a regular partner who lives in Fresno CA!

We once tried to teach Carole and Dan how to play Bridge. Carole had been quite keen on Euchre at one time so knew about tricks and trumps. Dan was about the same. After one session we reluctantly gave up! Dan was prepared for the long haul but Carole wanted to learn it all in one night!

Flo and Mick
Nita's mother, Flo Atkins and step-father Mick visited us one winter when we lived in the St. George house. We saw quite a bit of them when we lived in Scotland, and when we returned to Canada in 1977, Flo visited us most years until the late 80s. She was, of course very different from my mother, having been a single parent since Nita was born, raising her and her brother Noel. She worked as a pub manager/cook and various other cooking-related jobs until she married Mick, who was a retired electrical worker. Together, they moved a small bungalow in the Nottingham area. She had few interests outside family and needed constant "entertaining" during her visits. Also, she favoured Noel above all else and treated Nita shamefully in many ways, leading to considerable resentment. She and Mick had a small mortgage on their bungalow, which Nita and I paid off for them, but all her few assets went to Noel after she and Mick both died.

One benefit from Flo's visits was the opportunity it provided for Nita and I to leave her in charge of PJ and Carole for a few days. In September 1987, for example, we spent 3 nights at Killarney Lodge in Algonquin Provincial Park. This was a full service, high end Lodge and provided the ultimate in luxury: comfortable, separate cabins all on the lake shore and mostly invisible from each other, three sumptuous meals daily, with a packed lunch if you needed it, canoes available and so on. We did some nice hikes in the Park, went to Witney (just outside the East Park Gate) for beer and gifts, and generally had a wonderful time. After this, we drove to Niagara-on-the-Lake and spent a night in a B&B, seeing Noël Coward's *Hay Fever* and Bernard Shaw's *Fanny's First Play*. I think this was the heyday for the Shaw Festival; they stuck to their mandate and had superlative acting and productions.

Flo's last visit was in 1996. She was at the house when I returned from the World's Poultry Congress in India. Nita was very stressed with the visit and also the fact that her brother Noel kept phoning from England. He had moved house and clearly did not know how to deal with a lot of things. I had never had any time for him; I thought he was basically a wastrel. Flo worshiped him, much to the detriment of her relationship with Nita. At the time of Flo's visit, Nita was planning to go to England to help Noel decorate his new house (by this time he was divorced from his second wife). The day she left, I came home to find Flo quite drunk, and Carole and I had a difficult time getting her ready to go to the airport. Meanwhile, the same day, I had a telephone call from Nita, telling me that Noel had physically assaulted her; she left his house with a black eye and a lot of bruises and went to stay with a friend for the rest of the trip. So much for brotherly love!

Cats and Dogs

I was the cat person; Nita liked dogs, particularly and exclusively the Jack Russell Terrier. Nita's former husband provided our first Jack Russell, Tess (of the d'Urbevilles), and someone brought us Solomon, the black cat, so that he wouldn't be taken to the pound, soon after we moved in to the house near St. George. Solomon must have had Siamese blood as he had the voice and the kinky tail, but was otherwise jet black. He was intact when we got him, and used to leave for "trips" until he came back almost minus an eye, after which he was quickly fixed. Tess was a great dog and loved car trips as well as walks in the bush around our house. We had to leave them both behind when we went to Scotland, but they had a great home with Mary and Elgin Smith. Tess quickly learned to round up the sheep, and the hens!

In Scotland, we acquired a real Siamese, Simon (with actual pedigree papers!) from one of the secretaries at Ross, Avril. She live by herself in a house with innumerable Siamese, which basically owned the place. She had a lock on the fridge, as the cats had learned how to open the door. We bought a Jack Russell, Maggie (Tulliver, from *The Mill on the Floss*) from the Linlithgow and Stirlingshire Hunt. They were great friends and both went for walks along the street in Pattiesmuir and into the Bell Hills, although Simon would not go the whole way, just wait for us and join us as we came back into the village. They both came back to Canada with us and lived first in Dakin Crescent and then The Folly. On one of her first outings in Canada, Maggie encountered a groundhog. She eventually killed it and came home covered in blood, almost all of it from the victim.

Our dogs and cats seemed to live for only ten years or so. Simon developed what was probably a brain tumour and had to be put to sleep in the spring of 1984. Following this, we discovered one of the columnists in the local paper, Sheila White, was looking for homes for a litter of Siamese. No papers this time, but we eventually decided to take two of them, Samson

255

and Delilah, Sam and Deli for short, and these arrived at The Folly in late August at the age of 6 weeks. The dog, Maggie, was not amused but was desperate to "play" with them. The little cats growled and spit at her, but this was quite temporary, and they ended up good friends. When they were grown, these cats joined the dog on her local walks. We would walk down our property, then south along the river bank. The cats didn't go very far; when they felt it was far enough they would go up a tree and wait for us to come back. We got some really good pictures of them gamboling in the snow in our back yard.

After Maggie, we got Flossie, probably our least favourite jack Russell. She was obsessed with balls and retrieved then from far and wide, even half way across the river. She was unfortunately run over on West River Road right in front of the house. The last Jack Russell was a great one – called Woogle, after somebody's baby talk. She took over Sudden Tract, our standard walk. Nita would take her there almost every day. Weekends it might be me and Carole, or sometimes just me. Her second name was Sweet Time, after the habit of vanishing just before the parking lot was reached. On one occasion, she was picked up by some well-meaning man who thought she was lost, and he called her a "Jack Daniels"! But she was a splendid friend and a good house dog as long as she had her exercise. Like several of her predecessors, she could detect another dog outside at 100 paces, and barked her head off, but never bothered about other people. She overlapped with Sam and Deli. Sam very sadly disappeared when we took him on holiday to Frank Hurnik's cottage at Bradley's Harbour on the Bruce Peninsular. He had been sick and we should have left him in the cottage while we went for a walk. Deli lived to a ripe old age, in spite of having a hind leg amputated after (I am not inventing this) falling out of a tree!

The final two cats, again Siamese, James and Jessica, came to us as adults. Their previous owner was hospitalized and they lived alone in her apartment for several months before we got them. They spent most of the first two months at The Folly behind the chesterfield beside a hot air outlet, but once they emerged they became great friends, no problem with the dog, and altogether a great credit to their race! Both succumbed to kidney failure. The veterinarians told us that kidney disease in cats progresses until the kidney function is beyond treatment before symptoms appear.

Woogle died (or rather, was euthanized) in 2000 after developing lung cancer. We decided that, since we intended to travel more after my retirement, that we wouldn't have any more companion animals after the last two cats finally died.

Reading

As well as writing, I have always enjoyed reading. When we got TV, I of course began watching it and enjoyed some of the programs. And when traveling, turning on the motel TV was almost a reflex action. However, I found myself falling asleep in front of it and at some point in the late 1990's I wrote in my diary that I finally decided I did not like TV any more. The exceptions were some of the CBC's comedy programs – This Hour Has 22 Minutes, The Royal Canadian Air Farce and, best of all, The Red Green Show. The last was for rednecks and I enjoyed it right until it ended, being too politically incorrect for the CBC. But my reading time increased a great deal. In the early days, I tended to read non-fiction, especially biographies and memoirs. But later, I broadened the field to include a great deal of fiction. When we lived in The Folly, we belonged to the Book of the Month Club and accumulated a huge collection of books, but we had lots of room to keep them.

One of our favourite authors was James Michener, whose historical fiction was wonderful; we learned about the places we knew, and many that we didn't. His book "The Source" was for me the most memorable and I read it twice, the second time just prior to visiting Israel. We owned most of the books by Canadian author Pierre Berton and enjoyed those too. When we downsized in 2013, we had to dispose of almost all of our books, and discovered to our dismay that nobody wanted them! Most were either sold at the yard sale for 50 cents each, or donated to Goodwill.

My reading now is exclusively from borrowed books, mostly from the Cambridge Public Library (mysteriously now called the Idea Exchange). And reading is a compulsion; it is very disturbing to finish a book and not to have another waiting. This has made the Download Library another feature of my reading, as in "emergencies" I can always download something onto the iPad.

Since I began keeping a list of the books I read, I have read well over 1000.

Canoeing

We owned canoes most of the time we lived at The Folly. We could put in to the Grand River at the bottom of our backyard and be in Paris in 3 hours, or more if we delayed, picnicked, or the wind was from the south.

I think our first canoe was a cheap fibreglass affair which was quite unsuitable for the rocky Grand River. Fortunately, it was stolen not long after the first set of repairs were completed. We eventually bought a used 16 foot Old Town canoe from Camp Wanapitei, where PJ went to summer camp. This canoe was almost indestructible, but very heavy. This was fine for us and we continued to use it until we joined the Ancient Mariners'

Canoe Club. We could borrow Club canoes and, if needed, trailers, so having our own was no longer necessary, and we sold it for about the same as we paid.

We knew nothing about canoeing but just learned as we floated. One of the few "accidents" resulting from our ignorance happened in April 1986, when PJ and I decided to paddle from Breslau home. It took us 6 hours and we took no food or water! This would be 3 separate trips for the Ancient Mariners!

But most of our trips were quite successful and uneventful. Paris was the best destination because we could leave one car there and drive ourselves home. Taking a picnic in fine weather was a really splendid way to spend a summer day, and all of us enjoyed the experience. The Grand River, once one gets downstream from Glenmorris, may not have changed much since the Indians owned it back in the 19th century.

Nita joined the Ancient Mariners Canoe Club in 2003, having met with them during her volunteer job in the snack bar at the Ted Wake Lounge (one of the City of Cambridge 50-plus Centres), where the club had its meetings. This was shortly before her diagnosis of colon cancer, so she did very little other than a few winter hikes that year. I joined a year or so later; I was still working part time but arranged to be available most Tuesdays, the day the Mariners met. We learned more in the first day of training with the Mariners than we had in the previous 20 years. We had to re-learn some important things, such as the forward power is supposed to come from the bow paddler (in our case, Nita) while the stern person is in charge of the overall steering and strategy.

We paddled with the Mariners most weeks from May to September, on the Grand, the Speed, the Eramosa and the Nith. In the winter, the Club arranged weekly hikes on local trails. We attended most of the Club's social events. We also took advantage of the regular week long outings to Chesley Lake and Bondi.

Chesley Lake was a large complex owned by a religious group, with forty or so cottages, a golf course and dining room. The Mariners had been going there the second week in June for a long time. We went Monday to Friday, and the idea was that we would be guinea pigs to allow their seasonal staff time to train for the ensuing summer. When Nita and I first attended, we took 3 trailers (each with 6 canoes) and with a few privately owned canoes, this would make about 40 people on the river, which was the Saugeen. Most of the put-in points were a half hour to an hour's drive from Chesley Lake, so the trips would last most of the day.

We would have Happy Hours before and sometimes after the evening meal, although drinking was frowned upon by management! When we first attended, we found it was the best way to meet and get to know a variety of members and we really enjoyed it. Later, we found it becoming a bit tedious, and the canoe numbers much reduced. More people brought bicycles and golfed, and so we stopped going.

Bondi Village is near the town of Dwight, adjacent to Algonquin Provincial Park. It has an 8 bedroom Lodge and a number of cottages on Lake of Bays. There were no meals provided but there was a full kitchen in the Lodge and the Mariners cooked their own meals for up to about 24 people. Timing was the end of September, when the fall colours were expected to peak. The numbers were limited by the size of the dining room and the capability of volunteers to cook for large numbers. It was very popular and the organizer hardly needed to promote the event: he just contacted the regulars and it filled up!

In 2017, Nita and I volunteered to organize a second week (first week of October) targeted at new members who would not have the opportunity to get in on the first week. It was quite a lot of work especially the purchase of food for in our case, 16 people for a total of 16 meals each. Budgeting was also a challenge. But we slightly overestimated, and on the final morning, we gave everyone a $10 refund. It was a great group of people and everyone enjoyed the experience.

Members of the Ancient Mariners were expected to participate in the Club's management. After a couple of years, I became Chair of the Program Committee, and Nita, of the Social Committee. The Program committee was responsible for the canoeing and hiking programs, and finding leaders, tow drivers etc. for every event. The Social Committee arranged barbecues, river clean-ups and subsequent lunches, and a semi-formal Christmas Lunch, among other activities. I became Vice President in 2010 and then President for the years 2011 and 2012. The President usually held the post for one year. In my case, the day before nominations closed, the then Vice President telephoned me and said he had decided not to stand for President. So I continued for a second term. Nita was President for 2014. I think we were the only married couple who have both held the Presidency!

I found being President of this Club an enjoyable task, because of general enthusiasm and the ease of getting people to volunteer for almost anything! We had hard working department Chairs and just about everything rolled out according to plan. Nita had some challenges, mostly due to a misogynistic attitude of one former officer who thought he could still run

259

the show, and some knee-capping by the previous President that was totally unnecessary.

Other Real Estate

It has often been said that real estate investments are the best way to make money! We have never been quite convinced about this, but we surely tried.

In early 1987, I was made aware of a "never-to-be-repeated" real estate opportunity in Mississauga, near Square One, a major shopping and commercial centre. This was Anaheim Investments' Chelsea Towers Condominiums. The deal was $12,000 down, a $70,000 mortgage, and the unit would be rented out with the rent covering the mortgage payments. And mortgage interest would be tax deductible. Nobody said anything about Condo fees. Or property taxes. Anyway, in we went. We held this property until the time I was looking to retire from full time work. We eventually sold it $115,000 after fees.

We went in for a similar deal in Woodstock in 1990, though this was a much more modest affair. But it was poorly managed and I eventually joined the Board of the Condo Corporation. We changed the management company and achieved some kind of order, but it was never a huge success. In all these places, most of the units were not owner occupied; they were investments like ours. So the rents were pooled and this made life simpler, at least when one's unit was empty. In 2001, after I retired, we decided to sell our unit. I inspected it and had it spruced up by the tenant, and listed it for sale. The offers came while I was on a long tour of South America, and I had to fax signed documents from Chile and Brazil. In the end, it did not sell and we took it off the market and rented it again, with management by one of the members of the Condo Corp. Board with whom I had become friendly. We eventually sold it for a very modest profit.

Our timing with real estate has mostly been off by several years. We sold the Scottish house for pretty much what we paid; three years later it doubled in price. The Mississauga Condo was sold shortly before I retired: held a few more years it would have increased 50%. A year after we sold the Woodstock Condo, Toyota built a factory there and property values went through the roof!

With some of the equity from the sale of the Mississauga condo we bought one in London in 1998. It was roughly 1500 sq. ft. It had three bedrooms and a finished basement. This would provide a home for PJ and Carole, with enough rooms to rent out to cover most of the mortgage, taxes and condo fees. We fixed it up, with paint and some simple window coverings, before anyone moved in, but after that, we hardly spent anything on it. In the event, PJ only lived there for one year, but Carole stayed for a total of four. During the year PJ lived in the condo, we had the only tenant who gave us trouble: he was three months in arrears with rent and stole money from PJ's room. We managed to replace him and all was well. Neither PJ nor Carole payed us any rent, but Carole loved the place, managed the tenants and generally oversaw it. As her University career approached its end in 2002, we decided to sell the condo. I was approached by two realtors, who agreed to a shared listing. The day after listing there was an offer. We bickered a bit and eventually signed the offer I later found that one of the realtors already had a buyer lined up, so they got their commission without doing anything other than the paperwork. But we were significantly better off when all was settled, after owning it for 4 years, and it made a great home for Carole.

Postscript

We sold the house (The Folly, although we had ceased using that name some time previously) in 2013 because we wanted to downsize. The original cost to us in 1980 was $74,500. We poured a lot of money into the house for both maintenance and enhancement. The listing price in 2013 was $480,000. The sale was prolonged because an early conditional offer stretched on and on, long after we began paying rent on our new place and then moved there. We eventually withdrew from the conditional offer. When we then sold to a different buyer, it was under a lot of price pressure. We got $435,000 minus the realty charge. The new owner did some renovations but lived there only for about 3 years, before selling it for a $693,000. That purchaser never lived in it, but after a little over a year, demolished it and built an enormous mansion that literally stretches from one lot line to the other. Our only permanent legacy is the line of maples which we planted on the north boundary of the property. They are now fully mature, beautiful trees.

SCUBA Diving

Some time in the fall of 1996, I watched a TV program about the Great Barrier Reef. As we were already scheduled for a trip to Australia the following February, I was inspired to get a SCUBA license. I found a PADI (Professional Institute of Diving Instructors) group in Brantford that would get me as far as is possible in winter in Canada, and they told me I should be able to find someone to complete the process in Port Douglas, Queensland, Australia. One factor not in my favour was my age; most of the people both in Brantford and Port Douglas could have been my kids! The Brantford people were very thorough and did everything they could in the Wayne Gretzky pool, including one-on-one instruction. There were also video tapes and homework.

The group in Port Douglas was OK but the instructor declined to give me the license, mainly due to time constraints. So the following summer, having again contacted the folks in Brantford, I met them in Tobermory, near where we were on holiday. Tobermory was a popular venue for SCUBA divers because of the number of wrecks around the coast of the Bruce Peninsular, some right in the harbour. So I did my dive on to one of the wrecks, did all of the things one does, and was awarded my license. It was a very hot day, and I can still remember coming out of the cold water in a black wetsuit, and having to walk some distance before taking it off. I staggered in to a nearby pub to meet Nita, and drank two pints one after the other.

The things I will always remember have to do with safety, and although I never used the license, this has remained with me: Never SCUBA alone!

Chapter 13

My 50th Birthday and Retirement Parties

I'm writing this chapter not so much in celebration of my half-century and retirement, but to recognize the many friends who helped celebrate it and who have not otherwise been part of this story. Associated with my 50th, we had a great safari to James Bay, which was somewhat unique.

I am fortunate to have been born in June, when celebrations can involve, or happen in, the great outdoors! Nita's birthday, on January 30th, lacks this advantage, so we have to be somewhere else if we want to be outside.

For my 50th, we planned dinner in a large tent erected in the back yard, with a catered buffet. This was preceded by local tours for out-of-town visitors and followed by the safari to Moosonee on James Bay. Because the Polar Bear Express to Moosonee did not start operating until after my birthday, the whole celebration was delayed a week.

The actual day, June 12th, was a frantic affair. I had a board meeting and gave my monthly report to Directors at the office, there was an interview meeting for the Egg Board sponsored Chair at the University and Nita came home from a brief spell in hospital. We did manage a good dinner, and Henry and Christa Bayley came for champagne and treats later in the evening.

I invited anybody and everybody who had ever been part of my life to the party and the safari, and a surprising and gratifying group took up the offer. I took two full weeks off work to be with our guests and lead the Northern Ontario trip, which had been long planned and most of the reservations made in advance.

The tent was erected, tables and chairs set up, and everything made ready for the big day on Saturday June 21st.

As they arrived, we showed the guests downtown Galt (now very much Cambridge but the locals still retained the old names) and we brought in submarines for lunch.

Geoff and Chris Fairhurst were the first to arrive. I have dealt extensively with Geoff and our professional life in earlier chapters. Chris was a wonderful person. Geoff was her second husband, and she brought 3 children from her first marriage. They then produced one of their own. But by the time of my party, all their kids were grown and they were able to spend holidays abroad. Geoff and Chris stayed with us in the spare bedroom, before it was used for TV. Other overseas guests were billeted with Betty Graham, our neighbour, and Doug and Ivy Brown in St. George. Geoff was by now firmly established in management at Shaver Great Britain. When he left Wye, he worked for a while for the UK's largest (then) hatchery, Thornbers, but when that company imploded, he went to Sweden to manage an egg operation for one of their customers. The family all learned Swedish and used it at home. While at Shaver, Geoff also spent time in Yemen, establishing a layer farm in the desert for one of their customers. So we had a lot of catching up to do, and plenty of beer to assist memory.

One day I took Geoff and Chris, PJ and Carole to a picnic at Pinehurst Lake, just a few km from home, and met Alix Malcolm and her sister Flo, our old neighbours from St. George, there. The kids took our inflatable dinghy and had a great time on the lake while we talked and enjoyed the picnic.

Another day we rented canoes and paddled to Paris. We had three canoes. Geoff and Chris in one, Ian Drysdale and June Hibbert in another, and Bob Huntington and his nephew Richard Merritt in the third. I did not paddle the first stretch but met the group at Glenmorris, about one third of the way, where we all ate submarines. Then Richard drove my car home and I paddled the rest of the way with Bob. We went to Bob's place after reaching Paris, for beers.

Lawry Keene and his brother David, and their two wives, had run the Queens Arms in Warwick Bridge, one of my haunts near Wreay in Cumbria, while I was working for Ross. Lawry and his wife Jean arrived early and took Geoff and Chris to Niagara Falls, while I worked on details for the party. Later that day, I collected Norrie and Ada Semple from the airport, and later still, David and Angela Bourn. Norrie, as described in Chapter 5, was Ross Poultry's King of Scotland and a great friend.

The evening of their arrival, I barbecued steaks for 8 for a very late dinner. A busy day for a fifty year old, but at the time it was quite doable!

Ted and Janet Jones

Ted and Janet were friends from Toronto. They were real city people in the sense that they did not own property but lived in a very nice apartment in Don Mills. Janet was a teaching friend of Nita's whom she met while teaching at an inner city school in Toronto. She later married Ted, who sold insurance and benefit packages to companies. Ted and I would often lunch together if he was in the area. We saw them often at our home and theirs. They enjoyed both live theatre and movies (Ted especially the

264

latter) and we often attended these together. Janet retired early, and they then bought a cottage on Crego Lake in the Kawarthas, where we also visited along with our children when they were young. The cottage was right on the lake, which was private, and so not crowded, and everyone knew each other. PJ and Carole loved it, the company was always congenial and the sunsets, magnificent.

Ted's family had a history of early death from heart problems. His twin brother died quite young and Ted was accordingly very careful. Unfortunately, he was diagnosed with Parkinson's disease quite soon after they bought the country property, and then died from a heart attack. Janet kept on with the cottage, but then got breast cancer, recovered briefly, but not long after, we visited her in a retirement home in north Toronto, where she appeared to have the beginnings of dementia, and she died not long after. A sad story.

David and Angela Bourn
David Bourn was a school friend, and close neighbour of John and Corrie Hume (my Great Uncle and Aunt) on Jesmond Dene Road in Newcastle. He had originally planned a career in the Fleet Air Arm. But when he married Angela (née Taylor, sister of my friend Michael) she persuaded him that this was not a long term career and he resigned. After an unlikely, and mostly unloved stint as a representative for the Shell oil company, he returned to flying, but this time in the more sedate commercial airline industry. By the time of the party, he was flying Lockheed TriStars for British Airways. He eventually retired from BA (compulsory at age 55 I think) and worked for a few years for Air Lanka based in Sri Lanka. He operated a flight to Toronto before the party, and another one to take them home, so his cost was zero, and Angela's not much more.

I was Best Man at their wedding in Newcastle in 1958. In 1998, after a business trip to The Netherlands, I spent a few days with them at their home in Slinfold, Sussex, and helped celebrate their Ruby Wedding. This was a splendid affair and they managed to have 33 people there, all of whom (except, of course their children and grandchildren) had attended the original wedding. This included the Bridesmaids; naturally, all of us being 40 years older made identification difficult!

(When I got home from this party, I had a letter from Don Legg, at whose wedding I was Best Man for the first time, also in 1958. He was writing to tell me he and his wife Joan had separated after 40 years. I later discovered he had an affair with a neighbour while Joan was at work, and they eventually married.)

The Attridges

Patricia Attridge, known to most of us as Pat, but Tricia in her family, first emigrated from her native London, England in the early 1960's. When I first got to know her in 1967, she was DMcQ's secretary and/or personal assistant. Her parents Arthur and Flo also emigrated and bought a house in Galt. Arthur and Flo had managed a pub in London. While they must have made a great pair in the pub, they were physically a big contrast. Arthur was stick thin, while Flo was short and stout. This did not prevent her from living to the ripe old age of 92, while Arthur died much younger, some time in the 1970's. Flora died in 2003.

Pat continued to work for DMcQ until he retired. She did not relish working for anyone else and left to buy a travel agency business in town, which she ran successfully until the beginning of the 21st century, when internet bookings began to cut into the travel agency business. So Pat closed up shop and spent a few years with a desk in another agency until she retired. For many years, she dated Dave Roberts, another Shaver employee from the 60's. Dave moved around quite a bit but continued the relationship with Pat and they eventually married.

Pat's sister Pam, and husband Malcolm Gee emigrated in 1967, and Malcolm got a job with Shaver, working in the hatchery. They all had recognizable London accents which stayed with them indefinitely. Our Englishness made us natural friends, although we made lots of Canadian friends as well.

Pam and Malcolm adopted 2 children, David and Sarah, and seemed to enjoy life, but quite suddenly in the early 1970's, Malcolm left the family for another woman. This did not work and Malcolm died in the 1980's alone and in poverty. So Pam raised the children herself, living in a small bungalow that the family had bought for them. After the kids left home, Pam, who had always been on the same scale as her mother, became quite obese, as well as being diabetic, and died quietly in 2018.

David Gee developed a career as an artist, and designed the cover for this memoir.

Both Pat and Pam were at my 50th birthday party.

Lyris Tracey

Lyris features frequently in my story. She was born in Trinidad, and qualified as a physiotherapist in London, England. She moved to Toronto and worked there until she retired. Lyris was very tall, coffee coloured and extremely attractive. When we first met her in Toronto, she had a companion, Binky, who was equally tall and they made a great couple.

One weekend, they came to stay with us when we were living in the house in St. George. Nita and Binky took a walk along the concession road and our red-neck neighbours were outraged that we would invite "coloured people" to stay with us. We had some splendid parties at Lyris's place on Sherbourne Street, where she lived permanently until her death in 2019. She had friends from all over, with perhaps a majority from Trinidad and the UK.

Lyris had four brothers, three of whom, all professionals, lived in Canada or the US, along with nieces and nephews. Lyris never owned a car, although I think she had a drivers' license. When Binky was around, she always had transportation but after he left to return to Trinidad to marry and start a family, she relied on friends and buses. I would often stay over with Lyris if I needed to be in Toronto; she had only one bedroom but two convertible couches! We would often eat out and then I would drop her off at work after breakfast the next morning. She at one time played Bridge and Nita and I would make a four with one of her friends. After she retired, we saw less and less of each other; she did not enjoy the bus trips to Cambridge, and we became reluctant to face Toronto traffic. When we last saw her, some time in 2018, she was in poor health, almost confined to the apartment, and literally a shadow compared to what we remembered. It was a sad day when one of her nieces phoned early in 2020 to say she had passed away. One thing Lyris always concealed was her age! We should have asked her niece.

Henry and Christa Bayley

I first met Henry when he joined the faculty at Wye College in 1963. Henry was single at the time and chose to live in Withersdane Hall, rather than, as I did, seek independent accommodation outside the College. But we became good friends and spent a good deal of time together. Henry left Wye in 1965 to joint the Department of Nutrition at the University of Guelph. So when I moved to join Shaver in Galt a little over a year later, he met me off the plane and ferried me around while I got settled. By this time, he had met Christa, a German emigrant, and they were married in May 1967. I was unable to be at their wedding because of a business trip for Shaver. They moved into a nice apartment in Guelph but a couple of years later, soon after their daughter Anya was born, they moved a few blocks to a house on Bellevue Avenue, where they still reside.

Henry and Christa were witnesses at our wedding in Toronto City Hall in December 1972. It wasn't until the 50th anniversary of my landing in Canada that I realized that the anniversary of my wedding to Nita falls on the same day, so in 2016, we celebrated both events.

We remained close friends, as our families grew. They had three offspring spanning the same years as our two. Henry continued to work in the Department of Nutrition until he retired, including a spell as Department Chair. His interests were peripheral to those of the Egg Board, and this I used to justify quite frequent lunch expenses for the two of us.

Chris and Olive Fowler

Chris was already employed by Shaver when I joined in 1967, but he tended to be posted overseas a great deal of the time. In fact several of his four children were born in different countries. Chris was born in England and had a Diploma in Poultry Husbandry from Harper Adams College. He spent time starting up and managing Shaver GMBH in Dusseldorf, and also helping to establish a joint venture in India, and another in New Zealand. But at some point he became based in Cambridge and was the Technical Manager. He left for a while to open a greenhouse business in Owen Sound, but then returned to Shaver and bought a house quite close to us on West River Road. They had a magnificent garden, and we often exchanged hospitality. After retirement, Chris and Olive moved to Brantford and we saw much less of them. Chris died in 2020, well into his '90s, and Olive I 2022.

Frank and Gertraude Hurnik

Frank was a refugee from Hungary, and Gertraude was originally German. They met when Frank was a prisoner of war in Germany and Gertraude worked in the prison! Frank moved to the University of Guelph during the 1970s, one of the first in the field of poultry welfare, and Gertraude managed the University's poultry research farm at Arkell, just south of Guelph. I worked occasionally with Frank and gave one or two lectures to some of his classes. They built a summer cottage near Bradley's Harbour on the Lake Huron side of the Bruce Peninsula, and Nita and I spent several week-long holidays there by ourselves. It was originally quite isolated and thus perfect for nude sunbathing which we both enjoyed. The chance of unexpected visitors was always present but we thought it was worth the risk! They also owned a farm north of Guelph and retired there. Frank later died from Alzheimer's.

Ron Jones

Ron was Production Manager for Shaver. He was self-taught in hatchery management but extremely skilled, and was responsible for expanding Shaver's hatchery capacity during the period of rapid growth in the 1960s and 70s. I am not aware of Ron's history beyond the fact that he was born in Wales and spent time in the Welsh Guards. Army discipline followed him into business and he was very strict. On one occasion, he suspected that a hatchery manager was by-passing the shower-in procedure on his way in to work. Ron sat in the dark, waiting, and when the employee indeed showed up having not showered, he was fired on the spot. Ron retired from Shaver in early 1996 and we went to a splendid retirement party for him at the Galt Country Club. He continued to work as a consultant on hatchery affairs for some of Shaver's customers for several years. The major tragedy of Ron's life was when his wife Nancy suffered a stroke and went into a coma. Ron visited every day. She never emerged from the coma but lived for at least a decade. Ron died in 2020 from Alzheimer's disease.

Peter and Patricia Quail
Peter worked in Marketing for Shaver. He was a British emigrant, graduating from the Royal Agricultural College at Cirencester. He always sounded as though he had just stepped off the boat, with an extremely cultured British accent. This was doubly surprising because his wife Patricia was American! Peter worked for Shaver for a number of years, but I think became increasingly frustrated. After leaving Shaver, he created The St. George Company (he lived on a farm in St. George) which was quite successful and employed at least one of their 5 kids.

Roy and Marlyn Hurnanen
Roy joined Shaver in the 1970s in Marketing and was one of the victims when the ISA takeover occurred. Both he and Marlyn were from Alberta, but they stayed in Ontario and after leaving Shaver, Roy bought an auto-detailing franchise. He ran this for many years until retirement. We lost touch with them until some time in the late 2010's, when we met at a birthday party. We found that they both played Bridge and so we began exchanging Bridge nights. This came to an abrupt halt with the 2020 COVID pandemic

 Joe and June Hibbert
The Hibberts were friends in St. George. June worked for the local library and Joe was a teacher at Mohawk College. Joe knew by heart several of Robert Service's poems – the Cremation of Sam McGee, etc. and recited them at many of our parties. The Hibberts were also Bridge players. Over the years, they also attended Galt Little Theatre and while I was building sets there Joe often helped. We joined them and others from St. George in a group attending Theatre Aquarius in Hamilton. We had season subscriptions there for at least ten years, and saw some great theatre. More recently, Joe has suffered from a progressive disease that limits him in many ways, and has also had both legs amputated, so was wheelchair bound. Joe died in 2022.

Ian and Clara Drysdale
The Drysdales also lived in St. George. Ian qualified in Medicine at Kings College, Newcastle, at the same time I was studying Agriculture, although

we did not know each other at that time. Clara is Italian, married Ian while in England, and they both came to Canada shortly after Ian graduated. Ian practiced medicine in Brantford. He learned to play the guitar while we knew them and we would sometimes sing together, but he had an unique repertoire of his own too. They had two kids, Alex and Sylvie, who had both left home when we got to know them.

Ian was at one time very keen on sailing, and PJ and I once spent a very pleasant weekend with him on Lake Ontario. He eventually gave up after a near-disaster in the Pacific Ocean. He was sailing with a group and their boat was hit by a cyclone. It was severely damaged and they were very lucky to survive.

Ian and Clara seemed never to be satisfied with where they lived. When we first knew them they had a beautiful country property a few km west of St. George. I think they have moved at least five times since then; a realtor's dream client! Their son, Alex moved to BC early in his career, but died quite young from cancer in the early 21st century.

Bob and Beth Huntington
Bob was a retired teacher and Canadian naval officer. Beth was Assistant Medical Officer of Health for Waterloo Region. They lived about 2 km south of us in a log house up a long driveway. They had about 50 acres, mostly planted with (now overgrown) Christmas trees. They had a huge vegetable garden. Bob had many "toys" including a tractor driven sawmill. We met them through Doug and Ivy Brown and got to know them well. We exchanged hospitality and they once took care of PJ when he got back from Summer Camp a few days before we returned from the Poultry Science meetings. Bob kept up with a lot of reading of science and technology – I think he had a subscription to Scientific American. So we often talked genetics! Beth died from cancer in the early 2000s, but Bob continued living in the same house. While in his late 80s, he tapped a large number of Maple trees on the property and established a top-of-the-line evaporating system to make Maple syrup. He did not have a license to sell it but bottled it and gave it to all and sundry visitors.

The Party
So that I could spend time with guests, we had Richard Merritt and one of his friends Carolyn to tend the bar. We began with drinks promptly at 7.00. The total attendance was about 70 people. The meal was catered as a buffet with a huge beef roast as the centre piece, plus all the fixings and sundry desserts. I made a prepared speech around 10.00 pm, sang a few songs and then circulated until we wound up about 2.30 am Sunday morning. There were a lot of good pictures and these served to remind me of the many friends who joined in the celebration. As to gifts, there were many; some

frivolous, a number of bottles, and a tee shirt saying: "The First 50 Years are the Hardest". But probably the most memorable was a brass sculpture of two chickens mating, given me by Dr. Otto Weninger, Shaver's veterinarian. Of course I had to say, when I opened it, "Would you look at those fucking chickens!", even though PJ and Carole were there. I still have the sculpture.

The Safari to Moose Factory

First the name: Moose Factory is an island on the Moose River and is where the Factor, an employee of the Hudson's Bay Company (HBC), lived. The reason for going there was that it was among the first European settlements in Canada, established by the HBC in 1673. Much more recent, established in 1903, was the town of Moosonee. This was on the bank of the Moose River, not far from where it empties into James Bay. Moose Factory was served by river ferries from Moosonee in summer and an ice road in winter. Moosonee was the northern terminus of the Ontario Northland Railway, and the Polar Bear Express ran from Cochrane as a tourist train for a few months each summer. Moosonee cannot be reached by road.

The participants on the safari were: the Hunton family of four, Geoff and Chris Fairhurst, David and Angela Bourn, Norrie and Ada Semple and Lawry and Jean Keene.

We rented an eight-seater van, and this along with my car, just accommodated us and our luggage. We left Cambridge at noon on Monday and headed for the Bruce Peninsula. Since we weren't in a hurry and had motel reservations, we diverted in Wiarton to see the cottages at Colpoy's Bay and also met our old landlady, Betty Siegrist. Betty showed the group the quite rare Lady's Slippers in the bush across the road from the cottages. We stayed the night in Tobermory, in order to be on time for the first ferry of the day to South Bay Mouth on Manitoulin Island.

The ferry, the Chi Cheemaun was very efficient and loaded and left promptly. The weather for the ferry trip was poor but it brightened up as we toured around Manitoulin Island, with a stop in Gore Bay and lunch in Little Current. To make life easier and less complicated, Geoff collected $100 from everyone for gas, coffee, lunches etc. and when it ran out, just collected more. This worked very well. We spent the second night at the Trade Winds hotel in Lively, near Sudbury.

The following day we spent several hours, including an excellent lunch, at Science North in Sudbury. This was a provincial museum, in some way comparable with the Ontario Science Centre in Toronto but with a Northern flavour. It proved an excellent way to spend the day, and hard to leave. PJ and Carole enjoyed it as much as the older folk.

The drive from Sudbury to Timmins, our next stop, was quite monotonous, being mostly through bush, but interrupted by the Watershed Exhibit. It is where all subsequent rivers flow north into the Arctic, while rivers to the south flow to the Atlantic.

We were up at 5.45 am the next day for the 105 km drive to Cochrane, where we joined the Polar Bear Express, which left on time at 8.30 for the trip to Moosonee. This 300 km trip was not spectacular, but there were occasional glimpses of the Moose River, and the odd stop at an outpost.

Moosonee turned out to be a dusty frontier town, with the majority of the population Indigenous. We stayed at the Moosonee Lodge, which had its own restaurant, and was OK. Nothing fancy though! After lunch, we took one of the tourist boats to Fossil Island, where the guide cooked bannock, and told us some of the history. The folks in Moosonee, mostly indigenous, made part of their living from tourists and were good at it. They seemed to despise the natives who lived on the Reservation at Moose Factory, who just lined up for their government cheque every month and spent it on liquor at the Hudson's Bay Store

We had drinks and dinner in the hotel and a short walk along the river bank before going to bed. Everyone seemed to be enjoying the trip so far.

The next day we went on a cruise down the Moose River on the MV Polar Princess. The scenery was not great because the surrounding land was so flat. Quite by chance, we discovered that the Captain of the ship was born in Sunderland, a few miles from Newcastle where I was born. Small world! On the way back, we spent time on Moose Factory Island, notable particularly for the old Anglican Church. We also visited the HBC Store. We got back to the hotel mid-afternoon and most of us had a brief siesta. Then we partied for the rest of the day with an intermission for dinner.

On our last morning, we took a trip in a float plane to see a bit more of the geography. This was a good way to see the surroundings and appreciate where we were and the places we had seen the previous two days. David Bourn, the airline pilot, viewed this trip with some trepidation as the float plane was not in its first youth. We didn't actually see any baler wire holding it together but there may have been some! David was quite relieved to be back on *terra firma*. In order to be in place for his flight home, David and Angela had to leave us in Moosonee and they flew back to Toronto. The rest of us left on the Polar Bear Express in the late afternoon and stayed the night in Cochrane.

It's 783 km from Cochrane to Cambridge but we decided to make that trip in one day as everyone wanted to be home. We left at 6.30 am and drove an hour before breakfast in a truck stop in Iroquois Falls. We had lunch just south of North Bay and a coffee break near Orillia, then non-stop to the Constellation Hotel near Toronto airport, where we said goodbye to Norrie and Ada. They were going on elsewhere in North America before going home. We got back to The Folly at 6.00 pm and had KFC for dinner. A great trip all round and well worth the money and effort we put in to it. However, I think everyone agreed that while Moosonee was definitely worth visiting, nobody would ever want to go back there. Someone, I think it was David Bourn, later visited some even more remote place, which was said to make Moosonee seem like Paris, France!

Retirement Party, July 1st, 2001
This party was a good deal less formal, with none of the pre- and post-party events. And it was largely done in-house, with PJ, Carole, PJ's then girl-friend Melanie and I doing most of the work. We hired a big barbecue to cook a 30 pound beef roast, rented tables and chairs, and a 3 m x 3 m gazebo to serve as a bar, and prepared all the other food ourselves. And of course unlimited home-made beer and wine. We did all the shopping and as much prep as we could the day before. Carole picked two 6 quart baskets of strawberries, we made deviled eggs, and many vegetables.

On the day, we started the beef quite early on a rotating spit, but we eventually had to move it to the grill surfaces and turn it often, just to get it hot right through.

Although held on July 1st, we had poorish weather and had to spend part of the time indoors. But we had to eat at the tables outside. I think the temperature was about 15°C, cold for July, and everyone moved indoors once they had eaten. About 50 people came. PJ and Melanie, Carole and her friend Alison Plantz did a lot of the hosting, bar tending and serving, allowing me to circulate. It was a good party and I enjoyed it, although as at all functions like this, I felt I would have liked more time with everybody I spoke to!

Although I was retired in the sense of not having to go to work every day, I was still intending to write and do consulting work for an unspecified period. So it wasn't a goodbye party at all as far as most of the guests were concerned.

Chapter 14

My life In and Around Theatre

My first experience of live theatre was probably at Ponteland's Memorial Hall, where the local amateur dramatic group performed. The shows I remember were *Quiet Wedding* and *Quiet Weekend*, both farces by local playwright Esther McCracken. We would occasionally go as a family to shows at Newcastle's Theatre Royal and the Jesmond Playhouse.

When I moved to Kent, I occasionally took the trip to London for live theatre but this was infrequent. I did see Agatha Christie's *The Mousetrap* near the beginning of its record run, *West Side Story*, and a few other now forgotten shows. But then I found The Marlowe, a lovely old theatre in Canterbury, just a short drive from Wye, where I was working, and this provided many pleasant experiences.

On moving to Canada, I soon realized that professional theatre was relatively scarce, but rapidly growing. Toronto had its Royal Alexandra and the newly opened O'Keefe Centre (it subsequently became the Hummingbird Centre, the Sony Centre and is now the Meridian Centre) which had a huge capacity. I remember seeing *Fiddler On The Roof* there at least twice, and one or two other productions.

But the main attractions were the Stratford Shakespeare Festival (established in 1953), and the Shaw Festival at Niagara-on-the-Lake (established in 1962).

Stratford began, naturally enough, performing exclusively Shakespeare plays, but has since expanded and essentially now does almost anything the Artistic Director wishes, within the confines of financial expediency.

The Shaw's mandate when it opened was to perform the plays of George Bernard Shaw and any others written in his lifetime; since he lived for 94 years, from 1856 to 1950, this provided a great deal of scope. However, successive Artistic Directors have strayed from the original mandate and the Shaw now, like Stratford, is performing whatever can be combined with economic reality. Both Festivals now perform large scale musicals, because they almost guarantee BIS (bums in seats), a fact discovered by many professional theatres at some point in their history. I began to visit both Festivals on a regular basis soon after I arrived in Canada.

When I met and then married Nita, I found that she too was a theatre goer and we both enjoyed a wide variety of experiences in Toronto, the Festivals and indeed elsewhere.

Galt Little Theatre. (GLT) later. Cambridge Community Players

It was in 1985 that we became seriously involved with community theatre, but once we discovered Galt Little Theatre, we were quickly hooked. The group was started by some of the staff at Galt Collegiate Institute in 1933 and they performed on the school stage, named Tassie Hall. Over the years, they moved in and out of many different places. We saw one show in a converted grocery store! However, they eventually secured a permanent home in a beautifully converted church on Water Street in downtown Galt. The building was purchased by the City, and the renovations and conversion funded by various governments, plus a huge fundraising effort by members of the theatre. The theatre had a large proscenium stage, seated 200 people, and had an upstairs hall used for rehearsals and social affairs. There was a licensed Green Room, dressing room, and excellent technical facilities. The deal with the City relative to the building was that they owned it and GLT rented it for $1.00/year. The City was responsible for the exterior maintenance, while GLT covered all interior maintenance, heating, etc. GLT was also able to rent out the premises between their productions.

At the time we joined, there was a disproportionate number of expatriate Britons, so of course we fitted in very well. This changed over time, and the mix became much more a reflection of current Canadian society, although it has to be said that visible minorities are much under-represented.

When we joined, several of the existing members stood out. Joan Howell, a fellow Geordie was acting, directing and generally extremely busy. Her husband, Roger, was a stage manager and administrator – I don't ever remember seeing him on stage. Martin Stinton had been a prime mover and shaker in persuading the City to purchase the building and the associated fundraising to convert it to a theatre. He was also an accomplished actor. His wife K was very active as an actor also ran social activities and the theatre box office. Harry and Jean Wood (yet more Geordies) were actors and directors, and also close neighbours of ours on West River Road. However, they resigned from the theatre soon after we joined and eventually moved away. Jim Bath, another Brit, was an actor and director. Kay Mattear, an exiled Glaswegian, with the accent to match, was a director and her husband Jimmie a wonderful singer.

Nita had always enjoyed theatre work, having done a lot at various schools. She spent many days at GLT in October and November, 1986, on our friend Harry Wood's production of *Snow White and the Seven Dwarfs*, in which PJ performed. She also worked on props for the production of *Crystal Clear*.

In February 1987, after one of the not infrequent Board revolutions, I became Vice-Chair, Business, with John Lewington as Chair of GLT. At this time we had monthly Board meetings, usually in someone's home, and monthly General Meetings in the Green Room that were well attended and could last for 2 hours!

I helped marginally with Jack Etherton's production of *I'll Be Back Before Midnight*. The play involved a murder scene in which an axe appeared to be struck into a character's back. Obviously this was faked; the lights went out momentarily, and when they came back up, the actor was face-down on the stage, with another axe seen protruding from his back – I created the axes! Jack was a long time member of Galt Little Theatre, as actor, producers, director, in fact literally Jack of all trades. His day job was as a radio announcer for the local AM radio station. Sadly, a year after after *Midnight* Jack suffered a fatal heart attack in the Green Room. His name was remembered for many years as an in-house set of awards for GLT's productions was named for him. (The Jack-E awards).

By late 1987, Nita was running the Box Office, having taken over from K Stinton. She did props for Joan Howell's production of *There Goes The Bride*, and was also prompt. I helped with the set, beginning a long career in set construction. For the Christmas show that year, we had Jim Bath's production of *The Sleeping Beauty*, and both PJ and Carole had parts – a real family affair.

We began to invite casts and crew home for wine and food the nights we saw the shows. Harold Mahaffey's *The Canadian Connection*, a fun review involving Newfoundlanders poking fun at Canadians, was probably the first of these, and we had about 25 people back. Fortunately, the combined living room and sun room at The Folly could easily accommodate this number.

This period, while I was Chair, was exceptionally busy, and for part of the time, while Martin Stinton, who had become the Facility Manager, was on a prolonged absence, I did most of the work associated with rentals, set-up, opening up, closing down and so on. I was also heavily involved with set construction. There was generally significant tension between me and Martin Stinton. Based on his leadership in getting the building for the theatre, he continued to feel a sense of ownership that made it difficult for those of us who had been elected to do our jobs.

Nita and I both spent a huge amount of time at the theatre. I was building sets, Nita painting them. I chaired both the Executive Board and General meetings, and of course faithfully attended pub nights every Thursday. Set building, painting, rehearsals and any other activities that could be scheduled for Thursdays, always were, and there were often 25-30 people in the Green Room by 10.00 pm. It was definitely a fun time at GLT, and bar sales were a significant revenue source. In late 1988, I was "recruited" by Director Kay Mattear to audition for what I was assured would be a small part in her play *Who's Life Is It Anyway?* Small or not, I got the part! Here was an illustration of a constant challenge: any call for auditions would attract three women for every man who showed up. This play had two female and five male characters. So the female parts were easily cast, and the male leads, but for the other men, they had to scour the Green Room on pub night! Along with me, another set builder, Joe Hibbert was also cast. The main character in the play was a paraplegic as the result of a road accident. The part was played by an accomplished actor, Rob Judd. He spent the entire play on a gurney, centre stage. Rob told me during rehearsals that he normally used his position on stage to help remember his lines: In this case he had to use the presence of other characters. My part was a psychiatrist who was trying to persuade him that life might actually be worth living. I had two scenes and tried to make the most of them. I have never had any trouble being in front of an audience, but acting was different from speech making! I have to thank Director Kay Mattear for her efforts to make me an actor; while I don't see myself as one, I certainly enjoyed the experience, and was quite eager to take other small roles as they emerged.

Play polishing for the show was by John Snowdon. This was my first close-up with John, whom I got to know much better as time went on. A fellow Geordie, but a theatre man to his fingertips. He taught theatre at high school, he acted and directed at Guelph Little Theatre, and later, for many years, managed Theatre In The Trees, a dinner/theatre held in the University Arboretum.

My other acting roles included the King in *The Sleeping Beauty*, a Christmas show later in my career.. This was really a vehicle for the many children who wanted to be on stage, and it was great fun. At the time, Sue Bottrill's dance group used the theatre for their productions and we had about ten tiny girls dancing as part of *Sleeping Beauty*. I remember saying to the Queen, how it looked as though someone was winding them up and pushing them on to the stage, they were so well disciplined!

I later played the Policeman in Anne Morison's production of *Our Town*, one of my favourite plays, in 1994. In 1995, I played the Magistrate's Clerk in Joan Howell's production of *The Crucible*, by Arthur Miller. This had a large cast and was a stunning production. Two events stood out: first on one night one of the cast, an experienced actor, missed a line and froze. A young actor with a relatively small part knew the script, threw him his line, and the audience was none the wiser. The second event was one of my most memorable. One of the characters (Mary) was being interrogated right downstage in the centre. All eyes were on her. The tension was absolute. You could literally hear a pin drop. Great theatre! The actor was Sarah Quantrell.

Tragedy is part of theatre but we endured a real tragedy in late 1994, when we learned that the Guelph Little Theatre building had caught fire and burned to the ground. They performed in various locations for a few years, but eventually purchased an industrial building and converted it into a splendid theatre space that they still (2021) use.

Another tragedy closer to home was the death of actor/director/all time theatre person Mike Butcher in November, 1999. Mike and his mother Christine had been with us several years and Mike had done all kinds of things on, off and behind the stage. He was quite young, maybe in his 40's and died suddenly as a result of a minor mistake while he was in hospital.

My Fair Lady, directed by Joan Howell, was a huge production in 1989. Two volunteers sewed all the costumes, it had an enormous set including a retractable stair way connecting the mezzanine with the stage. Some of the furniture was borrowed from the Preston Springs Hotel, which at the time was still a retirement home. (It was finally demolished in 2020) When we went to collect the furniture, Joan pointed to a large chesterfield, and said "We'll take that". I got hold of one end and couldn't lift it, so I said to Joan, "It's screwed to the floor", to which she replied, "No, it's just heavy". She was right! We moved it to the stage and it was on and off 8 times each show. I know because I was a stagehand! This was a fabulous job though, and being back stage for almost the entire show, by the time it closed, I knew the script by heart. As most theatre people know, *My Fair Lady* is based on Shaw's *Pygmalion*. When we later saw *Pygmalion* at the Shaw Festival, I was able to follow it perfectly, except when the songs were absent, which was a bit disappointing. PJ helped with the lighting for *My Fair Lady*, operating the spot light.

The production sold out some nights before it opened and they had to schedule extra performances. On opening night, one of our set changes got a round of applause, and the crew were part of the Curtain Call. The show eventually ran for 11 performances. Those were definitely heady days for GLT!

I have lost count of the times I have seen *My Fair Lady* and *Pygmalion*, but the Galt Little Theatre production was notable for its Eliza, played by Hilary Spence (now Hilary Ledingham). Born a Geordie, like me, she nailed both the cockney accent and the "posh" one perfectly. And she sang like an angel. Of the other Elizas I have seen, only one comes close: a Texas born actor who played the part in a dinner theatre production in Lancaster PA in 2018. Also noted was an actor of Indian descent who took the part in the Shaw Festival's 2015 production of *Pygmalion*. This production was set in 2015, had a few changes in the script and I thoroughly enjoyed it. Nita and several others absolutely detested it. The actor who played Eliza is said to have responded to Shaw Artistic Director Jackie Maxwell, when told of her casting, "You're fucking kidding me!"

A few weeks after *My Fair Lady* at GLT, we started the set for *Death Of A Salesman*. This was directed by Ted Phythian, an extremely talented individual who played a small part in *My Fair Lady*. I recall sitting through the first read-through after the play was cast, prior to set construction. Ted made the point that every word of the script should be studied for its obvious, and hidden meanings. He was an excellent director. He had decided against realism for the set and it consisted of three hexagonal risers of different heights. Each one represented a different room in Willy Loman's house. We had to get an engineer to show us how to make hexagons from 4 x 8 ft plywood sheets!

I read many scripts with the hope that I could help continue the success of Galt Little Theatre's productions. One I came across in 1990, after seeing the play at a theatre in Regina, was a set-in-Canada version of Ibsen's *An Enemy Of The People*, written by Betty Jane Wylie, who lived in Mactier, Ontario. We never did get to produce it but I thought it was very timely.

One year I also took a break from set construction to learn about lighting from our resident genius, Roy Schrieber. Roy's entire life, apart from a very routine job at a local garment factory, was theatre and especially lighting. He had no formal training but was acknowledged as an expert by anyone who knew him. I learned to hang and focus lighting fixtures, and briefly how to operate the lighting control board. I agreed to design and run lights for Anne Holding's 1992 show that was entered for Festival. Roy did not like Festivals because it involved him taking time off work and he didn't agree with the Festival anyway! The play was J.B. Priestly's *When We Are Married*, which was a wonderful show and she got an excellent cast. I got lots of help hanging and focusing lights and it went really well. The show was great and adjudicator complimentary, so off we went to the Festival in Sarnia! Here I ran into trouble; the set took a long time to erect and had no time to set light levels, so we had a very bright wash over the back wall which nobody, including the adjudicator, liked.

In 1994, with Roy and my daughter Carole, I helped design and run the lights for Marion Smith's production of *Dirty Work At The Crossroads*, an old fashioned melodrama. This was fun and the show, very well received. Standing ovations were rare in community theatre, but this show got one on its last night.

I worked one show as Assistant Stage Manager in 1991, so by then, I had done most of the backstage stuff with the exception of sound, costumes and make-up!

1991 was the year when John Snowdon gave a workshop in our theatre to teach us the use of Styrofoam in set decor. We were building the set for *The Passion of Dracula* and it required multiple wood beams. Joe Hibbert and I mass produced these using the method John had demonstrated, to the point that we had too many.

In June 1992, after a large exodus, I was again elected to GLT Board, along with Jim Bath, Jeanette Chippindale and K Stinton. We were later joined by Gilberta (Bert) Patrick, who served as treasurer. I was Chairman. In many ways, Martin Stinton still ran the show: with K on the Board and himself Business Manager, he could essentially bypass the Board whenever he wanted.

In September 1993, I received a formal complaint from Shannon Markle, a hugely talented girl who led the theatre's Youth Group, that Martin Stinton had effectively kicked her out of the rehearsal hall, where she and the Youth Group worked, because the activity had not been correctly scheduled. The theatre by-law included the procedure for a formal complaint and the response required. This was to be a formal hearing including both the complainer and the person complained against. Martin refused to participate and instead consulted his lawyer.

They both attended an Executive meeting later in the month, but Martin tried to persuade her to back off, and he surely picked the wrong girl! After they left the meeting it was decided to "censure" Martin by requesting a formal apology. Shannon said she would accept this, but of course, it was not to be. One Director changed her mind. My support as Chair began to wane. Then K Stinton resigned from all her theatre responsibilities (Board member and Box Office Chair). At a general meeting in October 1993, a motion was made to request my resignation, and in spite of good support for my position, was carried by 18 votes to 12, with 2 abstentions. Seeing that I had significant support, and knowing better than most of the opponents the actual facts of the case, I decided not to resign immediately. The motion that was approved had to be ratified at a subsequent general meeting, which allowed time for people to change their minds if they wanted to. And I could do some gentle canvassing!

Meanwhile, I received a formal letter from Martin, resigning his position as Business Manager, and everything else he was involved with. When the meeting arrived at which the motion to ratify my expulsion came around, it was defeated 28 – 10 with two abstentions, so I was OK. Just to make sure of the voting, Shannon encouraged all of the youth group members to attend the meeting and vote!

An outstanding production in 1993 was *Waiting For The Parade* by John Murrell, directed by Jim Bath. Ann Morison, who had worked for several years at the Stratford Festival, designed the set and supervised costumes and decor. The set was hugely imaginative. The play involved four different women waiting for their husbands to return from World War II, so they each had a "station" on stage. But to indicate how close they really were, three roof trusses (made of styrofoam) were suspended above the stage. The backdrop consisted of an ethereal Union Jack flag; superimposed on it were images of soldiers with rifles and other elements of warfare. Nita led the painting crew and they did an outstanding job with a very complex theme. The show went to the Western Ontario Drama Festival and the painting received special mention by the adjudicator. This is not to diminish the acting, which was also to an exceptional standard.

While Nita spent most of her time at the theatre painting, she also did many other things as well as running the Box Office for several years. She was Producer for Ann Morison's production of Ibsen's *Hedda Gabler*, in 1995 and also did an extraordinary job painting the set. The wood paneling was so realistic that people went onstage after the show to see that it was, in fact painted on our regular flats.

In May 1993, Nita and I spent a week in Peterborough at the Theatre Ontario Festival. Galt was to host it in 1994 so we went to see how it was done. We enjoyed the plays and picked up enough information to ensure we could successfully host the Festival in our theatre. We had difficulty finding someone to Chair this Festival. The Stintons (Martin and K) volunteered, then withdrew, volunteered again and then finally withdrew during the brouhaha over Shannon Markle's complaint. Roger and Joan Howell eventually stepped up and ran it very successfully.

Galt Little Theatre prospered mightily in the 1990s. We had mostly full houses, lots of competition for the privilege of directing, and numerous skilled (and some less skilled) volunteers in every department. In one single season, the theatre made a profit of $19,000, and accumulated a large surplus over the decade, enabling it to undertake a major renovation of the building in 2000. This involved raking the auditorium floor, and creating a large workshop beneath the stage. Planning of this took a long time because the City of Cambridge owned the building and thus we had to go through more hoops than we expected. Eventually they hired an architect, and it turned out to be Joe Somfay, the same person who designed a solar house for us in the late 1970's, that was never built. The work took place in 2001.

Another piece of excitement for GLT was the Western Ontario Drama League (WODL) Minifest. This was scheduled for one of the WODL theatres and involved as many as 6 different productions of the same one-act play by different member theatre groups. In 1997, Minifest took place in Ingersoll. The play was *Master of the House*. GLT's production was directed by Marion Smith, and I played the part of Dr. Jellicoe. It was great fun.

We did our show and watched all of the others. Minifest went out of its way to be non competitive, but there was a critique and each group got a fun award. Ours was the *Coronation Street* Award!

One of my all-time favourite plays was *On Golden Pond,* and GLT produced it in 2000. It was Directed by Kath Judd and Henry North played the lead. I led the set crew and we built an outstanding, and quite complex structure, made more complex by the fact that the play was entered in the WODL Festival, so the set had to be portable. Nita led the set painting crew. The nature of the play also dictated very complex decor; everything that might be found in a summer cottage had to be on stage. The set got compliments from the adjudicator and the play went to Festival, held that year in the Palace Theatre in London.

In 2001, GLT produced the musical *Grease*. Musicals took up more time, more energy and resources than dramas, and this one was huge with a large and talented cast, live band and all the right trimmings. Many of the cast came from the theatre's Youth Group, both past and present. It amazed me that such a relatively small group could succeed with such a production.

The building renovations were completed just prior to *Grease*, and we moved what little equipment we had into the workshop below the stage and began to use it. One of our volunteers, Art Hewitt, constructed a large work table in the middle of the space and we made shelves, cupboards and racks for paint, lumber and tools. It seemed a miracle we could ever have functioned without it. These changes took place while we were building the set for *The Nerd*, directed by Steve Gregg, with his wife, Kate as Stage Manager. Steve worked at Stratford, in set design and construction and Kate was a theatre person from 'way back, so they made a good team. But the set was designed, and frequently re-designed, as we built it, not the way I was accustomed to working. However, it was OK on the night!

I went to Sarnia for the Western Ontario Drama Festival in March, 2002. J.B. Priestley's *An Inspector Calls* (Kincardine Theatre Guild) and *The Diary Of Ann Frank* (Theatre Woodstock) were highlights of the week, from my perspective.

Also in 2002, Shannon Markle Directed *Little Women* and she asked me to design and build the set. The plot was quite complex and my first and only foray into set design was not without challenges. My first attempt created blind spots on stage, but we finally reached a compromise and the set and the play were both successful. Nita again did an exceptional job of set painting. Shannon was a perfectionist; actors and technical staff were all affected by this, but the end result justified the turmoil.

Galt Little Theatre hosted the Western Ontario Drama Festival in 2003, and I was joint Chair with Marion Smith. Marion was a long time member, director, actor etc. and also knew everything about Festival. It was a lot of work for both of us, but well worth it; our theatre made money, our audience had the opportunity to see five different plays in one week, and experience the adjudication process if they wished.

We were planning and recruiting sponsors and volunteers during the latter part of 2002, and then really intensive work began in earnest in 2003. We held frequent meetings, and of course Marion and I reported to the WODL Board on a regular basis. Just before the plays were announced, we hosted all those groups who were entered to tour our theatre and determine how their plays might fit on our stage.

The five plays selected were:
- *Vigil*, by Morris Panych (Theatre Sarnia)
- *COSI* by Louis Nowra (Guelph Little Theatre)
- *Everything in the Garden*, by Edward Albee (Theatre Kent)
- *A Year in Edna's Kitchen*, by Sandy Conrad (Kincardine Theatre Guild)
- *The Drawer Boy* by Michael Healey (Theatre Burlington)

I did an interview on CKCO television the week before Festival opened to encourage attendance but we had excellent sales even before that.

The Guelph show *COSI* took many of the awards including Best Production. Guelph Little Theatre was always (and remains) an excellent community theatre group.

The Festival ran smoothly with no major problems and we were all very pleased with the outcome. Of course, Nita and I attended all of the events, the opening reception, plays, afterglow parties and the final Banquet and awards ceremonies.

At the GLT Annual Meeting in June 2003, I had a pleasant surprise when they made me an Honorary Life Member.

For a very brief period in the early 2000's, a professional group calling itself Theatre Cambridge rented the Cambridge Arts Theatre for a summer season. It was somebody's brain-child and lasted only two seasons. The two shows that I saw, *Over The River and Through The Woods*, and *Six Dance Steps In Six Weeks* were well done but the audiences were very small and production costs astronomical. The group was unable to pay the rent to Galt Little Theatre, so the City of Cambridge, which had insisted we rent to them, had to pay instead.

After paying a small part in the second of Joan Howell's productions of *Oliver!* in 2004, I moved directly to Marion Rogers' production of Shaw's *The Devil's Disciple*. I had "performed" in this at the Royal Grammar School back in 1953, with the non-speaking part of Aunt Titus. This time I auditioned and got two parts: Uncle Titus, who had a short dialogue in Act I, and the executioner, who had a non-speaking but very important part in Act III. I also headed the set construction crew, and this was a major task, as there were a number of set changes during the show. We were still reconstructing part of the set at the time of the Dress Rehearsal, but as always, it was all right on the night! An unexpected diversion during this show was the Director's insistence that while the crew was changing the set between two of the scenes, the actors, including me, performed the *Cotillion*. Dancing had never been my forté, and according to Henry Bayley, who saw the show, this was quite obvious!

Nita painted her last set at Galt Little Theatre in 2007. It was not a happy retirement, but provoked by the Director's failure to properly thank her for her work. Henry North had been divorced for many years, and lived with much younger, and usually quite attractive women. To him, Nita at 63 was just another theatre volunteer. At his request, she repainted the set (he disagreed with her choice of colours) and did everything he asked, and that was it. Everyone else got personal cards and lots of praise, but for Nita, hardly a mention.

I continued to lead the set building crew for a few years but eventually gave it over to a somewhat younger person.

We of course continued as audience members. The group, with the best of intentions, changed its name to Cambridge Community Players to be more inclusive, but this did nothing to halt a slow decline in the quality of the productions, and simultaneously, audience numbers. I was no longer involved with the management group, so I have no idea of the political goings on. A number of talented actors left and began to work at other community theatres. In general the quality of the productions declined. One exception was *Doubt*, by John Patrick Stanley, Directed by Lori Distel and starring Kath Judd and Steve Robinson in 2014. This was quite an outstanding production, but still attracted poor audiences.

To try to fill a void when two of its members left together in 2019, I returned to the Board as Chair. I found we were short of everything; Directors, Board members, actors, tech staff. We had a playbill of sorts and those of us on the Board worked overtime to try to recover the lost glory. We thought things were going well when we got an audience of 100 in our 200 seat theatre. I only stayed a year, and by that time the COVID pandemic had closed live theatres down for an indeterminate time.

Other Theatre Experiences
Of course, outside of Galt Little Theatre, we attended quite a lot of professional theatre. We became members ("Friends") of the Shaw Festival at Niagara-on-the-Lake in 1988. We always preferred Shaw to Shakespeare although we did go to Stratford from time to time. But Shaw was definitely our favourite.

We attended our first "Friends Day" in June 1988. At this time Christopher Newton was at the height of his power and success as the Shaw's Artistic Director. He gave a warm welcome, followed by a fascinating talk by Cameron Porteous, who was head of Design. For us amateurs, this provided an eye-opening experience! Then we saw a performance of Shaw's *You Never Can Tell* on the main stage, followed by wine and cheese, and a splendid dinner with some of the cast. We went to these "Friends Days" for several years, until we became so familiar that we stopped going! We did, however, remain members until early in the 21st century.

After staying in a variety of hotels (extremely expensive, but nice) and some B&Bs with more or less success, we finally "found" Richard and Monica Taylor's Carnochan House, right across the street from the Festival Theatre.

We stayed there many times, starting in 1991, when we saw Nicola Cavendish in a brilliant performance in *The Millionairess*. This was the

285

first time we saw Nicola; she spent just one season at The Shaw, before returning to her native Vancouver. But we saw her a year or two later, when she toured the country performing the one-woman show *Shirley Valentine*, a very British play by Willy Russell. We later discovered that she was desperately trying to master the British regional dialect, when she met a recent immigrant at her hair salon, who spoke with exactly the right accent. Nicola hired her for a month and ended up word perfect. Her depiction of Shirley was outstanding.

At the Shaw Festival Friends Day in 1994, Carole was with me. We had a talk about Design, and then a fascinating seminar with Goldie Semple, Simon Bradbury and David Schurmann, entitled "Approaching the Script". All very relevant to what we should be doing in community theatre but often do not. We saw *Arms and the Man*, Shaw's famous anti-war and anti-capitalism play, and went to a reception with the cast afterwards. A wonderful day for both of us.

I think the '90s were the Shaw's heyday. They stuck to their original mandate. In 1995 we saw Shaw's *You Never Can Tell* and Noël Coward's *Cavalcade*, the latter directed by and starring Artistic Director Christopher Newton. Two wonderful productions!

Richard and Monica eventually retired from the B&B business. After a couple of false starts, we "found" Lorraine and Dennis Stapleton, who were a little out of town but very comfortable, and reasonable, and we kept going there until we pretty much gave up on the Shaw in the 2010s.

We occasionally went to Stratford, where they did work equal to Niagara-on-the-Lake. An outstanding production that I attended with Roy Schreiber in 1996 was *The Merchant of Venice*, with Douglas Rain as Shylock. Rain was a wonderful actor; we had seen him at the Shaw Festival and he did a great job of Shylock.

Another Stratford show with great memories for me was *Death of a Salesman* produced in 1997 at the Avon Theatre, with Al Waxman as Willy and Martha Henry as his wife. Their set was totally realistic (in contrast with the Galt Little Theatre production) and absolutely breathtaking. I went with Carole and we had to go up to the balcony during intermission to see a different perspective on the house and the black and white terrazzo floor.

This year too, I watched a movie of the 1984 Stratford production of *The Mikado*, which we also saw on stage. That was when they regularly did Gilbert and Sullivan, but the memorable part for me was Richard MacMillan as Pooh Bah. I am sure no Japanese is as tall as Richard, but artistic license in this case allowed him to dominate the stage and secure more than his rightful share of laughs. By the time of this production the original rights on G&S productions had expired and they introduced contemporary political jokes at the expense of Pierre Trudeau among others.

In 2003, Nita and I joined with a group of friends from St. George to buy season subscriptions at Theatre Aquarius in Hamilton. Over the ensuing fifteen years, we saw some excellent theatre there. It was also a social occasion; we went to the Saturday matinée and then had drinks and dinner, sometimes in friends' houses and sometimes restaurants. When they changed their curtain time from 2.00 pm to 1.00 pm we stopped going, as that timing for our social events did not work.

Among the most memorable shows were *Doubt*, by John Patrick Stanley, *The 39 Steps*, adapted from the John Buchan novel, and *Playing With Fire*, by Kirsty McClellan Day. The last was a one man play about a hockey player's descent into substance abuse, and his subsequent recovery.

Drayton Entertainment
Finally, a real local success story. In 1991, a few people in the community of Drayton, ON (pop. <2,000) were wondering how to utilize an old 1902 building, of which the ground floor was municipal offices and the second floor a long unused Opera House. They hired a recent theatre management graduate, Alex Mustakas to advise them. He proposed summer live theatre. After a massive local fundraising campaign, one show running for 44 performances with a budget of $99,000 was mounted. Fourteen thousand people showed up to see it.

Fast forward to 2019. Drayton Entertainment Inc. with Mustakas as Artistic Director and CEO was operating seven theatres across Ontario, had a budget of $33 million and sold 250,000 seats (12 of them to Nita and me!). They built a headquarters theatre in Cambridge including 500 seats, a production centre where all their sets are constructed and painted, two rehearsal stages and accommodation for actors.

Some folks thought that such a development in Cambridge would lead to the demise of community theatre. I never agreed with that, believing that anything that encouraged people to attend live theatre would benefit everyone. Of course in 2020, they like all other live theatres, shut down due to the COVID pandemic.

Chapter 15

Holiday Times

Some of our earlier holidays are incorporated into Chapters 2-5. However, as the topic became quite large, I have created this separate Chapter. Holiday time while I worked for Shaver was limited to two weeks. With the Egg Board, it gradually increased, and of course some holidays were tacked on to business travel of one kind or another. Following my retirement on 2001, our flexibility was greatly enhanced.

Trinidad and Tobago, May 1976
This took place while I was working for Ross Poultry. I spent a week working my way south from Edinburgh and ended up with a weekend in Wye visiting old friends and pubs. Following this I met up with Nita at Heathrow Airport for our flight to Port Of Spain, Trinidad. Our arrival there was auspicious; once the customs and immigration people found we were staying with Mrs. Tracey (whom they referred to as "Lady Tracey") we got VIP treatment and straight through the system. We were met by Binky, who drove us to Tacarigua, where Mrs. Tracey lived as the Principal of a large orphanage. She knew every child by name. We had a nice bedroom downstairs and enjoyed the very relaxed atmosphere. Lyris arrived four days later. (In 1981, Lyris brought her mother to see us in our house on West River Road in Cambridge [see chapter 6]. I noted that our children were "eating out of her hand within 5 minutes". She was a memorable woman in every way.)

All kinds of friends and relatives made sure we saw much of Trinidad as well as spending time on some lovely beaches. We saw cocoa and coffee, the views from Mount St. Benedict, and the bird sanctuary in the Caroni Swamp. Here in the evening we saw the Scarlet Ibis and Egrets coming home to roost. Of course the boat we were on was well supplied with beer, and we had a great time.

In Port Of Spain, we saw the Botanic Gardens and the Governor General's residence, and had a beer in the upside down Hilton. One evening we went with Mrs. Tracey to the Venezuelan Embassy for a charity party celebrating "Women of the World". Many wore national costumes and there was music and entertainment. Mrs. Tracey was extremely well known and liked, and staying with her was much more of a privilege than we had expected. She was a remarkable and cultured lady, and lived well into her 90's.

Lyris had four brothers; only one remained in Trinidad; Knolly. The others had all moved to either Canada or the US. All were professionals. Knolly was the odd man out; he was still studying, but was also known for occasional bouts of heavy drinking, when he would vanish for several days. But he was otherwise charming like his siblings.

The day after Lyris arrived we all, including Mrs. Tracey, flew to Tobago and stayed at the Sunset Inn. At the time Tobago was a quiet little island with some lovely beaches and also old fortifications from the colonial era. Pigeon Point was a short walk from the hotel and a great place for sun and swimming. Store Bay was another venue for relaxations and we spent a day there, with lunch at a local bar. Binky and Lyris' friend Jean arrived a couple of days after us and made a great group for conversations; all active, intelligent, interesting people. Jean worked at the United Nations for much of her career.

All of us took a boat trip to Buccoo Reef, known locally, and rightly, as the Eighth Wonder of the World. It lay off the southwest corner of the island. This was one of our first snorkeling experiences; the coral and fish life were awesome, the coral gardens exquisite, and the nylon pool the best place we ever swam in.

Another day Binky, Nita and I went water-skiing. As always, we kept going too long and were exhausted afterwards! We had a special fish lunch arranged by Mrs. Tracey, cooked in the hotel kitchen, and later, a local delicacy; crab curry. Eating and drinking were both superb.

The last couple of days we were on our own in the hotel; everyone else went back to Trinidad. We had lots of sun and swimming and discovered and confirmed the joys of sex in the water! Following our return to Tacarigua, we were driven through the bush and forest to Toco on Trinidad's northeast coast where we stayed in a holiday cottage called Sea Mist. It was quite isolated, had a lighthouse and lovely, mostly deserted beaches. The Atlantic was as ferocious here as elsewhere, and seclusion was needed if one intended to swim, but there were some nice places. The whole holiday was relaxed and a great break from the intensive work environment I was experiencing.

The Bruce Peninsula and Other Cottages
Shortly after we returned to Canada in 1977, I managed a week's holiday with the family. I had checked through the Ontario Holiday Guide looking at rentals and found Cedar Haven Cottages at Oxenden, near Wiarton on the Bruce Peninsula. This turned out to be a stroke of genius! The cottage was right on Colpoys Bay, but the water was cold and the beach, rocky. PJ (22 months old) enjoyed the beach, as he knew nothing better, along with the iron rowboat provided. The cottage was built of cedar logs and was a thoroughly practical, old fashioned beach holiday residence. It had three

bedrooms, tiny kitchen with stove and fridge, bathroom and living room with a wood-burning stove. It was one of four, all built as rentals by the owners, Charles and Betty Siegrist. We roamed about the Bruce Peninsula, finding a nice sandy beach and warm water at Oliphant, which became a favourite. Nights were for barbecues and reading back at Cedar Haven, once PJ was safely in bed.

We loved this place! We kept on returning after Carole was born in 1978, and took Nita's mother when she visited. After we stopped renting there we stayed in touch with Charles and Betty. Charles died in the early 80's, and Betty eventually sold the cottages to four families who used them as summer residences. As time moved on, two of the families left, and the remaining two families each owned two. When we visited Betty, as we did most years, in 2015, we met the owners of the cottages we rented back in the 70's. They had renovated one and called it "Almost Heaven" and now rented it out while they spent weekends in the other. We took it for two weeks in July in 2016 and 2017, and one week in 2018.

We spent a week at the end of August in 1980 at a cottage on the beach at Port Elgin, on Lake Huron. This became another annual event as well as Cedar Haven on the Bruce Peninsula. The cottage was a bit larger, with room for my mother and the kids to have separate bedrooms. The beach at Port Elgin was sandy and the water, much more inviting. And the sunsets were legendary.

I had to interrupt the first holiday there for an overnight trip to Strathroy, to attend the Maple Lynn Foods annual barbecue. Nita came with me and we stayed at the Golden Pheasant motel. She took in the tour of the Egg Grading Station, and I gave my standard speech on Egg Quality.

In July 1989, we had the first of several really nice holidays at Frank Hurnik's cottage near Bradley's Harbour on the Bruce Peninsula. Frank built it himself, using pine logs cut on the property. It was very remote and private, and quite basic. An A-Frame structure with one large room downstairs and a spiral staircase leading to the second floor where we slept. The was no beach but it was right on the water and swimming was possible. However, the water was usually very cold. The 1989 trip involved all four of us.

The privacy being almost 100% here, clothing was optional when appropriate. Nita tanned beautifully and totally so this was an added bonus. Although we mostly ate at the cottage, we found an old pub a half hour away by car, Colonel Clark's Tavern, where we occasionally ate out. It was informal, decent food and beer, so a nice change of scenery.

We continued to spend one or two weeks at Frank's place for several years. It was such a nice centre; Tobermory was a half hour drive, and Cypress Lake, Dorcas Bay and several access points to the Bruce Trail were within easy driving distance. This was before Tobermory and Cypress Lake (now the Bruce Peninsula National Park) became go-to destinations for the crowds from Toronto and elsewhere. It is now necessary to book a parking spot at the Cypress Lake location.

We had another cottage holiday in July, 1990, this time near Bracebridge in a cottage "borrowed" from Teresa Miller at the Egg Board, or rather from her close friend Bill. Carole was already at Camp CanAqua, so we took PJ and his friend John, plus Geoff Fairhurst. It was a gorgeous place, right on the lake, quite private and altogether impeccable. We took the trailer with bicycles, windsurfer, and our inflatable dinghy, so we were good for anything. There was a canoe at the cottage. Geoff and the boys spent time fishing and occasionally watching baseball on TV; Nita and I canoed, Nita sunbathed in the dinghy a few metres off the beach, we all spent time reading. A fine four days of relaxation for us all. Geoff drove the boys, cat and dog home on the Friday morning, while Nita and I went to Crego Lake to spend the weekend with our friends Ted and Janet Jones. We collected Carole from camp, which was not far away, and brought her home.

In 1992, we spent a week at Frank Hurnik's cottage without children. PJ had bicycle races and Carole was at Camp CanAqua. This was a real opportunity to fully relax and we welcomed it. We walked the dog every morning and did lots of sunbathing. I was reviewing chapters for my book, *Poultry Production* but lots of other reading too. We had gourmet meals at the cottage and a couple at restaurants.   Colonel Clark's Tavern had degenerated into a beer hall but we discovered Tamarack Island Inn not far away. This was mostly residential but non residents could have the set menu, fixed price dinner and it was very good. The Hurnik cottage was truly relaxing, especially in the later years when we were without the kids. No time constraints and apart from exercising the dog and ourselves, no real obligations.

We never wanted to own a cottage: renting, borrowing or visiting was much better for us, as we had enough to do maintaining our one old house. A cottage would have been a huge commitment in time as well as money, and both were quite restricted in our case.

Later in 1993, we spent a week at Port Elgin in our neighbour Betty Graham's cottage. PJ didn't go but Carole and her friend Allison did. It was a nice relaxing week. And in July that year, we rented a small cottage in Wellington in Prince Edward County, for a week, taking Carole and another friend, Nadine. This was right on the water, and also very close to

Sandbanks Provincial Park, which had the most wonderful sand dunes and beaches. We also spent one day on a cruise out of Gananoque, through some of the Thousand Islands to Boldt Castle. This we had visited several times; it was started by a very rich American as a gift to his wife, but when she unexpectedly died, all work ceased. The place deteriorated for many years but has since been restored to approximately the state it was in when work ceased. Subsequently, (in the 21st century) some aspects have been even further developed.

Following the World's Poultry Congress in August 2000, I had long planned a holiday! I took two weeks to clear the backlog at the office and catch up, Then I had two weeks of vacation. The first week I worked at home and we had two days of theatre at Niagara-on-the-Lake. We then spent a week at a really remote cottage on Bear Lake. The closest town was Dorset but it was a good half hour drive.

The cottage was down a very steep and rugged driveway and at one point in the week I had to have the car towed up to the entrance. The owners visited us by float-plane the day we arrived! Although still warm during the days, evenings were chilly and we were glad of the wood stove in the kitchen.

The cottage came with a small aluminum boat but no motor, so we rented an outboard for 3 days. We spent quite a bit of time exploring the lake; it was a bit frustrating because every place that looked nice to land and explore had a cottage on it. We could get through a channel into Kawagama Lake, which was much larger and also ringed with cottages. Even where there was no cottage, there would be a "No Trespassing" sign. But the weather was mostly fine and we enjoyed the freedom to just relax. We were able to sunbathe at the cottage until about 3.30 pm, when the sun vanished behind the trees. We barbecued most of our dinners and as always, ate well.

We went to Dorset one day to meet and have lunch with our friends Ted and Janet Jones. It turned out to be our last meeting with Ted, who died suddenly not long after. We toured Robinson's, Canada's largest country store, and bought moccasins. Interestingly, we visited the store again in 2020 and it hadn't changed a bit.

Another day, we drove to Algonquin Provincial Park and walked two of the trails, as well as touring the Logging Museum. This was quite an intriguing story of an important part of Ontario's history. We came back *via* Dorset, where Nita managed to spend $288 on clothing in Robinson's store! All on sale of course.

Great Exuma

In 1985, we decided to spend some of the inheritance from my Mother on a winter family holiday. Many years previously, I had bought, on installments, a ¼ acre home-site on the island of Great Exuma in the Bahamas, so we decided to visit it. This was long before the package-holiday system began, so we made all the arrangements through a travel agency. We flew from Toronto to Miami, and thence to Nassau for our connection to Georgetown, Great Exuma. Arriving in Nassau on Sunday, we were told the Georgetown flight operated only on Wednesdays! So we had to stay overnight in Nassau and <u>charter</u> a small plane to fly to Georgetown the following day. It took all of our cash to pay for this, but fortunately we were able to replenish the cash supply later. The flight in a small plane was spectacular as we flew low over many small islands. We stayed at the Out Island Inn, quite a luxurious affair, and very comfortable. After the challenges of getting there, Great Exuma turned out to be just what we expected. We had lots of beach time, PJ and I went on a beautiful boat trip to the reef where were able to snorkel and see the outstanding tropical fish. One day we rented a power boat with water skis, and explored the tranquil waters around the island, had a picnic on a deserted beach, and all of us except Carole (who was still a bit young) got up on skis.

We made an appointment to see the home-site, which was one of many thousands sold. It indeed existed, on a dirt road a kilometre or so from the beach. It had a few feeble palm trees, but the soil was sparse.

Apparently, the natives used these places for gardening, but only for a couple of years, after which they moved on.

The holiday was a real success and we eventually got compensation from the airline that booked the non-existent flight.

In 2016, Nita and I decided to re-visit the island for a winter holiday and look again at the home-site. This time we booked our own flights online, and rented part of a house near the beach on airbnb. There was a grocery store close by and we ended up sharing a rental car with the people renting the upstairs of the house, an American couple. When we tried to locate the developer of the home-sites, we found he had skipped town after selling some 17,000 lots. This on an island with a population of just over 10,000! We drove out to where we thought the site was, but by now all the side roads were overgrown with tropical jungle and the only way to see the place would be by helicopter! So we checked with the local government. The deal had been that no property taxes were levied until the site was developed. Now they wanted $100/year regardless. But they were unlikely to collect, so we decided to abandon the project. Only if someone wants to develop the whole area as a large holiday complex would a sale be remotely possible.

The couple upstairs went lobster fishing and shared their catch with us. The weather was fine and I went swimming most days on a deserted beach 5 minutes walk from the house. We had a good holiday, except for the insects. Tiny little critters that came through screens; you couldn't feel them bite but they left a rash covering most of our bodies! Nita suffered more than I did, and didn't go outside the house the last two days.

Expo '86 in Vancouver
We decided to take the family to Vancouver for Expo '86. We thought PJ and Carole, now respectively 11 and 9 years old, would enjoy it. This turned out to be a mistake, primarily due to the huge crowds and line-ups for everything. So they ended up playing in the kids' play area while Nita and I lined up to see the various pavilions. And PJ was quite sick for a couple of days.

The show itself was very well done and the location, False Creek, spectacular. The pavilions we managed to see were excellent and a lot of the water based activities well worth seeing. On our last night there was a very good fireworks display which everyone liked. And the weather, for Vancouver, was amazing – four days of perfect sunshine! It rained buckets the morning we left, but by that time, who cared?

St. Lucia
We always enjoyed a break from the Ontario winter, and the year following my mother's death, we took the whole family to St. Lucia. We got non-stop flights both ways, but the St. Lucian Hotel, where we stayed, was a 1½ hour drive from the airport, which was a bit of a challenge. However, it was an excellent choice – in my journal I describe it as "suave"! No meals were included and after a horrendously expensive "*a la carte*" dinner in the hotel's restaurant, we found they offered a deal for breakfasts and dinners that was quite reasonable.

The relaxation was wonderful after the stresses of work and home. We did swimming, water skiing, snorkeling and several very nice cruises on a catamaran to Anse Castanet and other sightseeing areas. This included the world's only drive-in Sulphur Spring! The coral reefs and fish were endlessly fascinating (to me at any rate) and we saw many wonderful examples.

One curiosity here was that when we got some drinks to have in the room, we found endless rum but no mix (the boat came without mix!). So I discovered that provided the rum is decent quality, it was very drinkable with just ice. Like most of the islands, St. Lucia made its own rum, and some of it was very good.

Back to the UK

The Egg Farmers were not averse to foreign travel, and I think they paid the fare for me to attend the Symposium on Egg Quality at Harper Adams College in England in September 1985. But I extended the trip for a prolonged stay in Britain to catch up with old friends. I spent a couple of days in Wye, staying with Ann Pearce, but most of the things I enjoyed during my time there had changed. I knew very few people in the pubs and nobody in the College, which was about to close for good, after the University merged it with Imperial College in London. I visited Dan and Margaret Durrant in Norfolk, and spent a few days staying with Eric Wainwright in Newcastle.   There I also caught up with Elizabeth Henderson and we had a good dinner together at an Italian restaurant in Newcastle.   I rented a car and drove Eric over the Military Road into Cumbria, for a drink at the Queens Arms in Warwick Bridge and lunch at the Crosby Lodge, a splendid day out.

Then I headed North to Scotland, stopping for lunch with Pam Boyd (née Wainwright) in Newton St. Boswells. I stayed in Edinburgh and stopped in at the Ross Breeders office. Many people I knew were still there and it was a pleasant visit. After this, it was on to Pattiesmuir to renew acquaintance with Olive Booth, Pam and Bill Elford, our former neighbours. I had dinner at the Sealscraig in South Queensferry, where Nita and I often dined when we lived there.

I went to the former Poultry Research Centre (it now had a new name – the Roslyn Institute) and found everyone worried about its future, but otherwise a splendid resource for the poultry industry.

I continued North and spent a very boozy night with Norrie and Ada Semple. The next morning, which counted as work, I spent with the Ross commercial hatchery manager, Robin Johnson, seeing layers in action. Also work-related was my visit to the West of Scotland Agriculture College, where I spent the night with Tom and Mary Whittle. Tom was Principal of the College, a very hard-working teacher and a great promoter for the industry. I left their place in the morning for the short drive to Prestwick airport and an uneventful flight home.

June 1990 saw me on a short trip to the UK before a WPSA meeting in Spain. I went by train to Newcastle and much enjoyed the scenery. Two splendid days with Eric Wainwright gave me a recap of some of Northumbria; Belsay Castle, very close to Ponteland, and Cragside, a

National Trust property famous for its hydro power supply and rhododendrons, which were close to their peak when I visited.

Then I took another sightseeing train trip to Norwich, to visit my old friend, Dan Durrant and his wife Margaret. Dan was in retirement (but available for consulting) while Margaret still had a job at Lotus Cars. We did a lot of nice pubs and talked over old times and new. Dan was in fact redundant, not retired but he seemed OK.

From Norwich, I traveled to London, and more friends, Don and Joan Legg. Don was another ex Geordie and truly retired following a curious career after which he was paid to stop working – I never really understood this. They had bought and essentially rebuilt a house in Hanwell, into which his daughter, son in law, two grandchildren and themselves, were now planning to move. I stayed one night and enjoyed Don's music – he was self taught on the piano and now had an electronic keyboard.

Finally I spent a day with Pete and Val Halliwell in Upper Clatford near Andover. This was a really cute village in which almost all of the houses had thatched roofs, and it had a superb, and very old pub, The Crook and Shears, where Pete was one of the regulars.. We visited the Danesbury ring (similar to but not on the scale of Stonehenge) and had Indian food in Winchester.

In October 1993, following the Symposium on Quality of Eggs in Tours, France, I spent several days in England. After visiting Chris Hann in Berkhamstead, I rented a car and drove to the Lake District. I stayed in a nice B&B in Grayrigg, near Kendal and the next day, I drove to Langdale and had myself a wonderful hike right near where I had camped with the Royal Grammar School back in the '50s. I walked up The Band, around the shoulder of the valley, and ended up in Ye Olde Dungeon Ghyll about 3.30 in the afternoon. They served me 2 pints of excellent bitter but the kitchen was closed! I had not called ahead to my cousin Barry, but when I phoned, he invited me for dinner. Still in my hiking clothes, I joined in a formal dinner party for some of his friends. The following day, I met up with Alan Sykes, formerly from Wye but now much retired, although he looked much the same as I remembered from 1967, the last time I met him. We had lunch, and by this time the weather (as was prone to happen in the Lake District) had turned for the worse, with wind and rain. So I visited Wordsworth's birthplace in Cockermouth.

After the European Poultry Conference in Glasgow, in 1994, I spent a few days holiday in Scotland. I visited Pam Boyd near Dalkieth at the same time as her father, Eric Wainwright. We did some nice walks in the Border country. Then after a night with Sally Solomon and her husband, Roger, I drove to Ardnamurchan (on their advice) to see some rugged Scottish country and coastline. It was quite beautiful, but the weather was cool. I was told the Scots think it's great as long as it doesn't rain!

Following my trip to Turkey in June 2000, Nita and I spent a few days in England. She had already had a week with her friends Liz and Brian in Bath. We got a rental car and went first to see David and Angela Bourn in Slinfold, Sussex. David was not well so although we stayed two nights, we spent a whole day in Kent. Of course we had to go to Wye; by this time the College was long closed but the environs were still enchanting. We walked on to the hills above the village, where the Crown was cut into the chalk, and on to Canterbury with lunch in the Thomas Becket.

Then we drove North *via* Grantham and Scotch Corner to Newcastle and visited my godfather Eric Wainwright. He treated us to dinner in the recently refurbished Wagon Inn, near Ponteland and we enjoyed a long chat. And we took a circuitous route home *via* Walton and Morpeth, haunts from my early days. This turned out to be the last time we saw Eric; he died peacefully in 2002, aged 92.

From Newcastle, we headed for my cousin Barry's 70th birthday party at his home in the Lake District. We stopped in Ponteland, at the Blackbird Inn, and then headed West on a beautiful drive through Haydon Bridge, Alston and Penrith, ending up in Ambleside. By now the weather had deteriorated to a common feature of the Lake District: torrential rain. Barry and Ann's house, Pool Foot, was full but he booked us a B&B in Skelwith Bridge. Miraculously, when we awoke the next morning, the rain had stopped, the sun was shining and sheep grazed peacefully outside our window!

Barry's birthday was a really big affair. They had a marquee set up for food, we had drinks outside on the lawn and a great party. The outstanding thing was that for the first time ever, all seven Hunton cousins were present: Tony and Pam Shadforth, Barry, Heather and Tina Colville, and Basil Scofield. An historic picture was, of course essential. The guests varied in age from Ann's mother down to tiny children. The main meal was lunch, and afterwards, Barry had arranged a cruise on Coniston Water for the whole party. After this we all came back to Pool Foot for soup and leftovers. It was a really memorable day.

The following day, Nita and I left for home, but not before a little diversion into Langdale and an hour walking the fells. We drove south along Lake Windermere before heading for the motorway and Heathrow Airport.

In the Spring of 2003, I went to the UK for the annual meeting of the WPSA Branch. Our daughter Carole, who was living in Halifax at the time, joined me in London, and we rented a car for two weeks. Our first stop was with my former colleague and good friend Dan Durrant and his wife Margaret. They lived in Wacton, near Norwich; this was a good place to head for after a transatlantic flight – just over 170 miles. We did some walking and Dan and I watched part of a rugby match on TV! It was the Calcutta Cup, England *vs* Scotland, that my father had always attended. On this occasion, England won convincingly. We did some local walking and Dan took us through Wroxham and Horning to see part of the Norfolk Broads. They invited Ross and Christine Houghton for Sunday lunch. Ross had worked for Buxted Chicken after quite a career involving overseas work, but was now retired. I had known him in his Buxted days.

After the WPSA meetings in York, during which Carole did the tourist things and found lots of great pubs, we drove to and toured Fountains Abbey, a very large, and mostly ruined structure owned by the National Trust. I had a life membership of the Trust so all their places were "free" for us. We stayed in an old hotel, The Unicorn in Ripon and ate a good pub meal in the Black Bull. By this time we had decided that Black Sheep Bitter was our beer of choice.

We had a wonderful drive through the Yorkshire Dales the next day; Leyburn, Reeth, Muker and over the Buttertubs Pass to Hawes, where we had lunch at The Fountain. We then drove through Dentdale and explored the village of Dent, which I had first visited when at Camp with the Royal Grammar School in the early 1950s. It had not changed at all – still cobble stone streets winding through solid stone houses and shops. Then through Sedbergh, Kendal and Ambleside in the Lake District, to stay with my cousin Barry in his and Ann's lovely house in Clappersgate. We had a fine day's walk and climbed Skiddaw (931 m), which I had not done before. Of course, we had to have a pint in the first pub we saw after descending! The next day, Carole and I went on a boat trip on Lake Windermere, had lunch at The Sun in Hawkshead and visited both National Trust properties devoted to Beatrix Potter. In the evening, Barry and Ann took us to a concert in Kendal given by Lakeland Sinfonia. We enjoyed the music and had a surprise meeting with Alan and Margaret Sykes – Alan was my senior colleague at Wye College for the years prior to my emigration.

Our last day in the Lake District we spent on our own, and I drove into the Langdale valley, past the Dungeon Ghyll pubs and over both Wrynose and Hardknott passes. Of course we kept stopping to take in the scenery, and from the Three Shires Stone, we walked to Red Tarn We had lunch at the Woolpack Inn before driving through Eskdale, Ennerdale, Cockermouth and Keswick. We took Barry and Ann for a meal at the Outgate Inn, a full roast beef dinner with all the trimmings including dessert. When they offered dessert, Carole asked for another pint instead!

From the Lake District, we drove North and East to Newcastle. We stopped for a look at Housesteads on Hadrian's Wall and in Ponteland, we drove past 14 Darras Road, where I grew up, and the Blackbird Inn, which was closed at the time. We looked unsuccessfully for my father's and grandparents' grave in the churchyard. In Newcastle we stayed in a hotel in Jesmond, and, the time being mid-afternoon, walked to the Royal Grammar School just as the kids were coming out. They looked exactly the same as ever, grey jackets and shorts, blue caps, but now, every one had a cell phone clamped on his ear. We walked around the University campus and looked at the new Agriculture building, and in the evening took a taxi to the old Quayside area. There was no sign of all the old docks and buildings, but a very beautiful new pedestrian bridge over the Tyne. We ate at a very upscale, and expensive Italian Restaurant, our first dinner not at home or in a pub on the whole trip.

From Newcastle, we headed South, all the way to Sussex where we stayed with David and Angela Bourn. David was a school friend. They took us to some local pubs and fed us a splendid dinner, and the next day, David drove us to Chartwell, Winston Churchill's country house in Kent, now a National Trust property. I'm not sure how much Carole enjoyed it but I know I did, although I had been here before. I have always been a great Churchill fan (as was my father).

Our final stop was with Peter and Val Halliwell, in Upper Clatford, near Andover. Peter was another Wye M.Sc. poultry graduate. He was also a fixture at his local pub, The Crook and Shears, where we had lunch on arrival. They then took us to Stonehenge, which was the first time Carole had seen it, and Avebury, actually a much larger stone circle but not nearly as well known.

It was only just over an hour's drive to Heathrow from Peter's place and we left early the next day, as Carole's flight was at 11.00 and mine, 12.30. A great holiday for both of us!

Texas

Following PSA at Texas A&M in 1990, Carole, Nita and I had a brief holiday in Texas. We rented a luxury condo near Padre Island for 3 nights and spent much time on the beach. August was not really the time to be on the Gulf beaches – temperatures were close to 40°C which even for us sun-lovers, was a bit much. But the condo had a nice pool to which we could retreat for the afternoons. We drove from there to San Antonio and stayed there two nights. We did the tourist things; city and riverside tour, and the

IMAX movie of *The Alamo*, and of course absorbed quite a bit of American history along the way. We drove home by the scenic route, taking almost 3 days, but it was a nice relaxing drive. We always shared the driving so even one day with 800 km was not too stressful.

California

In Janaury 1993 we flew to Los Angeles to celebrate Nita's 50th birthday in the sun. We had no reservations except a rental car which turned out to be a very smooth Chrysler New Yorker. We spent two nights in Laguna Beach, where we did beach things and got some sun, and then, with a brief stop in La Jolla, to Lemon Grove, where a friend on Nita's lived. She was originally from Cleethorpes, and sounded as though she was just off the boat, in spite of being in the US for ~ 30 years. We did some tourist things in and around San Diego, and then left and ended up in Palm Springs for the birthday celebration. We had a very nice dinner and stayed two nights. We took the tramway to the peak of Mount Jacinto, where there was snow! But, this apart, the weather was much as we expected and we became nicely tanned before returning to the Canadian winter.

We went back to California in March, 1994, but this time the northern part of the state, after flying in to San Francisco. We had no reservations, but found decent places to stay. We stayed several nights in Monterey, spending time on Cannery Row, of Steinbeck fame, and eating quite splendidly on local seafood. Another landmark, Fisherman's Wharf, had lots of interesting places to visit and we saw a great production of *Pirates Of Penzance* at the Wharf Theatre. One of the nice things they did was to have the cast meet and greet the audience as we left the theatre.

We stopped in Carmel for shopping (mostly window-shopping as this place was the home of the rich and famous) and drove along the spectacular coastline including Big Sur. The weather was very capricious and as soon as we got on a beach, it started to rain. We eventually decided on a scenic drive, and toured *via* Hollister and Bitterwater, over the hills into the Salinas Valley. We had a coffee in King City and drove back to Monterey, passing through Salinas on the way. There were more memories of Steinbeck there.

On the way back towards San Francisco, we eventually found the perfect beach, and sunshine to go with it. It was called Gray Whale Cove. It cost $5.00 admission, and "clothing optional!" We really enjoyed it, although the water was cold. We eventually left when a thick mist came in. Next day we went to Point Reyes Seashore, but it was misty, and we headed across the peninsular to an even more perfect beach called Heart's Desire, part of Tomales Bay State Park. Here clothing was required but it was a gorgeous beach, and we spent most of the day there. We stayed in Santa

Rosa and did a beautiful drive from there through Clear Lake Park and into the Napa Valley. We stopped in Calistoga and St. Helena, and ended up in San Francisco for the final two nights. Here we met Pam Boyd (née Wainwright) who just arrived from Scotland to stay with her son, Martin. So we did tourist things in San Francisco: Lombard Street for a hilly walk, Chinatown, the Italian section, and Fisherman's Wharf for a splendid dinner. And of course, we went and saw the Golden Gate Bridge.

Following our 1998 visit to Whistler, we couldn't take the rented Ford Explorer to the US, so we checked it in before flying to Los Angeles, where we got a much more modest Chev Cavalier for our California adventure. The weather was not promising and we ran through very heavy rain before spending the night in Solvang. I had stayed in this unusual Danish community before, on a business trip, and it was still the same; very Danish except for the background of mountains.

It kept on raining while we drove through the mountains to Tehachipi, where we met and stayed with Bill Jasper, a former WPSA President and long time poultry person. By the time we got there, the rain had turned to sleet. Bill and his wife Dee lived in the wilds, but they were most hospitable, gave us a great dinner and overnight stay. Bill was a great talker and one night was quite enough! From here we drove (still in the rain) through the Yucca Valley, and spent the afternoon in Joshua Tree National Park. Here it largely stopped raining and we enjoyed the wild flowers, wonderful views and rock formations. Also, of course, the Joshua Trees, which were quite unique.

Then we headed for Desert Hot Springs, where we stayed at the Miracle Springs Hotel and Spa, and went in the pool and hot spring before dinner. By the next morning it was sunny but with a gale! We managed to find a sheltered spot for a bit of sunbathing. They couldn't house us another night so we moved to a cheap motel nearby called Stardust, which included a basic kitchen, so we went grocery shopping, including wine and beer, for the night. We dined on salmon steaks with shrimp, and crab salad. The weather was still not tropical and the next motel had to give us a portable heater to bring our room up to 63°F. Still not much sign of warmth, so we decided to head for the coast. To get there, we passed through Palm Springs and Rancho Mirage, before crossing the coastal range of mountains, where there appeared to have been about 30 cm of snow! We stayed in Oceanside and had a wonderful seafood dinner at the Monterey Fresh Fish Restaurant. Heading back towards Los Angeles, we found a little beach and some sunshine, but that was all we got for warmth!

So we flew back to Vancouver, and got the "red-eye" flight back to Toronto, arriving at 7.20 am. I called at the office on the way home to pick up mail, and it included a cheque from Elsevier for US$497, being royalties on my book for 1997. Nice surprise! The date was March 31st and when we got home the temperature was 25°C, higher than we had all week in S. California.

Nova Scotia

We drove to Nova Scotia in 1994 for a holiday, but also to present my report on a consulting mission I had undertaken for the provincial government. This only took a day, in Truro, and then we spent a very pleasant time based in Baddeck. We drove the circular route around Cape Breton, and also visited Louisburg, a reconstructed fort on the coast. In Baddeck there was a dinner place providing a decent sized lobster, plus all-you-can-eat mussels, coleslaw and dessert. We each ate 3 plates of mussels; no dessert. The lobsters were great. The drives to and from Nova Scotia were good too: we drove east through Quebec including the Gaspé coast. On the return trip, we passed through Maine and Vermont, visiting a friend of Nita's in Burlington before heading into New York state and crossing the border into Cornwall ON.

Beautiful British Columbia

In 1995, we visited PJ in British Columbia before going to Poultry Science in Edmonton. We drove west through the US; Michigan, Wisconsin, Minnesota, North Dakota and Montana, and then southern Alberta and into BC. We spent our last night "on the road" at a place called Spences Bridge. It was on the Thompson River, also the trans Canada highway and the main Canadian National rail line. It was still 200 km to Whistler, where we met PJ the following day after a total drive of 4,400 km. We had lunch at La Rúa, the very upscale restaurant where he worked. Although this was summer time, we found everywhere busy. Primarily developed as a winter resort, Whistler was doing its best to be a year-round destination. Mountain biking works on ski slopes! We stayed in a B&B called Golden Dreams, the first we ever knew with a Jacuzzi!

The following day, PJ took us up 3 chairlifts to the top of Blackcomb Mountain, and showed us the ski slopes where they do their thing in winter. But the views were fantastic, and he knew every visible mountaintop by name, the full 360°! A real Mountain Man. I was truly impressed. We ate dinner at La Rúa, and I noted that in 36 hours, we spent $350 on food for three people!

After leaving Whistler, we visited Frank Born near Abbotsford. Frank was marketing Born-3 eggs, omega-3 enhanced, in BC and hoped to expand across the country. We had lunch and spent time enough to secure information for an article in *World Poultry*. They actually sold Born-3 eggs in Ontario for a few months, after which the distributor was taken over by a competitor with its own brand of omega-3 enhanced product.

We left Whistler with few regrets; it was not our kind of place and the developments had destroyed a lot of the natural beauty for material gain. We had a very nice drive from there to Edmonton, passing through the Mount Robson Park and with a brief stop in Jasper.

The drive home from Edmonton, across the prairies and the Ontario bush was enjoyable as ever. We have never thought the prairies boring; huge sky, colourful landscape and enough places to stop for coffee, gas, meals etc or for picnics, as we carried our Koolatron portable fridge with us on all trips. We took four days to get home, staying overnight in Wynyard SK, Falcon Lake, MB, Thunder Bay and Wawa ON.

In July, 2005, after Nita had crossed the country with Barb Craig in her RV (which I once described as a condo on wheels), we rented a car in Vancouver and had a holiday, first on Vancouver Island and then the mainland to see PJ. We stayed with Nita's friend Kate McQuillan and husband Lee, who were retired and lived in Comox. We had a wonderful drive from there, including through the Pacific Rim National Park, to Tofino, Long Beach and Uclulet. We saw the old Douglas Firs in Cathedral Grove, a magnificent sight. Just a day trip but well worth the effort.

After leaving Comox, we toured more of the island including Campbell River where we saw and heard, at top volume, a chain-saw carving contest in progress. Had a good fish and chip lunch in Deep Bay. We enjoyed a good walk on Qualicum Beach and spent the next night in Victoria. The following day we went to Butchart Gardens, another amazing experience, before taking the ferry from Swartz Bay to Tsawasen. We stayed the night in Hope, before driving the Trans-Canada Highway through the Fraser Valley *en route* to PJ's place in Bralorne. We shopped for groceries and motorcycle parts for him on the way. It was a marvelous drive; canyons and mountains, then finally along Carpenter Lake before coming to Gold Bridge, just 10 km from Bralorne. As always, PJ and Melanie fed us well; barbecued salmon the first night, and steaks the next one. We did some walking around his place including what we called The Pimple, a steep hill behind his house. I had done it a couple of times the previous year, but now Nita was able to do it as well.

We left Bralorne after breakfast and drove back to Vancouver, where we spent the night with Sandy and Eva Cairns before flying home.

As though we didn't have enough holiday choices, somehow we got sucked in to a hard-sell presentation in Kitchener offering resort experiences. They wanted $14,000 down and then we would get (for ever) 3 weeks in their resorts for $37/night. I have always been thankful that we didn't bite.

India and Nepal, Including a Flight over Mt. Everest
One big trip that I did on my own was the Post-Congress tour of North India and Nepal following the 1996 World's Poultry Congress in New Delhi. Nita had decided long ago that she did not want to be exposed to the stray dogs, poverty and squalor in India she had heard about. These did exist, although they did not spoil my enjoyment of the trip. This was literally a Cook's Tour: Thomas Cook was well established in India in the tourism business and did an excellent job.

We traveled by bus, except for a couple of short flights. Some of the buses were air conditioned, others not. Indian roads were busy, noisy, and in many cases not very good. Pot holes abounded. Every truck had a sign on the back saying "Please horn" and they all did!

Our first destination was Jaipur, the pink city. On the way, we saw some of the poverty, with many people apparently living virtually out of doors. But the climate was kind, and we did not see anything that suggested the people we saw were unhappy. Children going to school were in uniforms, obviously a holdover from the British influence prior to independence. The streets of Jaipur were fascinating; pedestrians galore, plus water buffalo, camels, the occasional elephant, and every conveyance known to man – bikes, mopeds, rickshaws, etc.

Our tour included the Wind Palace, really just a facade, and the Amber Fort, built in the 16th century and still in remarkably good shape. Of course our bus, identified as a tourist vehicle, was besieged at every stop by beggars, hawkers, snake charmers, and anyone else who thought he could make a few cents from the rich folks. I found the way to avoid them was not to make eye contact, but it was hard.

The next destination was Agra, reached, my diary says, after another bone shaking trip. We changed guides at Fatepur Sikri, and encountered huge traffic jams and long diversions before reaching Agra at 4.00 in the afternoon (having left Jaipur at 7.15 am). It was only about 250 km! We visited the Taj Mahal the same afternoon. Of course it was world famous, but even its reputation didn't do it justice. The whole story, the structure and surroundings were just breathtaking. I paid a guide to take me around and got some excellent photographs. It was quite unforgettable. One of the facts of life on guided tours is sales pitches. At this, Indians were world class! I expect the tour guides got a kickback from the commercial places we visited, and they certainly did OK with the poultry scientists. One couple bought a $2,000 carpet. In Agra, I think everyone bought some mementos; I certainly did, and I was generally not much given to this. But I brought home a small piece of marble with insets alleged to be similar to those in the Taj Mahal. It was very attractive and we still have it in spite of downsizing all our "stuff" when we moved to a smaller residence in 2013.

Like the other towns we visited, Agra demonstrated again why it was a good choice for Nita not to come. As well as poverty, there was massive garbage; when outdoor markets closed everything was just left behind. And the animals on the streets boggled the mind; dogs, cats, cows, donkeys, ponies and pigs, as well as the aforementioned camels and elephants, and even the occasional chicken. Of course, they scavenge among the copious garbage, so perhaps there was some innate balancing at work.

We flew from Agra to our next stop, Kajuraho. This was a small town famous for its Hindu temples and the stone carvings on them. These included many erotic sculptures that of course attracted much photography. Following the obligatory stop at a craft store, we had lunch and then a trip to Raneh Falls, a conservation area with multiple, and very beautiful waterfalls. On the way back to the hotel, we stopped in a small country village to see rural life. The beggars were more subdued than in the city, but it was an interesting day, all told. With a little spare time, quite a lot of us spent time in the hotel pool, lukewarm, entirely from solar radiation. Hydration could be a problem in India, but fortunately there was an abundance of very good beer, and we indulged at length. Also, at some point, I had acquired a bottle of Crown Royal, and we had this for nightcaps.

Our next stop was Varanasi, on the Ganges, a short flight from Kajuraho. Varanasi was a large city and our hotel was right downtown. A power outage on arrival killed the air conditioning. We visited several temples including one which was lit by neon lights (power obviously back on) for some kind of   Festival. But the main point of the visit was to observe the cremations that regularly took place on the river banks. We saw one in progress. The objective was for the ashes to be distributed on the River Ganges, which was holy water, even though grossly polluted. Transport in the city was by rickshaw.

Early the next morning, we went on a short "river cruise". We walked from the bus through narrow streets, past lepers, beggars, and a few ordinary people, to a small boat that was pulled upstream about 0.5 km and then drifted back. People washed, bathed in and even drank from the river.

Most of the dead were cremated but the poor and the very young bypass the flames and were just tossed into the water. You had to see this to believe it, and realize that the Indians were quite sincere in their reverence for the river and found quite acceptable all of the activities that surrounded it.

We were not sorry to leave Varanasi and take the short flight to Kathmandu, the capital of Nepal. It took us 2½ hours to clear the airport; long lineups for security, visa purchase, money exchange, but we finally made it to the Hotel Cross Country Kathmandu for a very late lunch. Then a tour, first to the Tibetan refugee centre, where the community made all kinds of goods, including carpets, for sale, with the proceeds helping to bring in more refugees. After this, we went to Patan, which was in the old part of the city dating back to the 9th century. It contained several temples and a Royal Palace.

There was a strike in progress, so there were no buses. But our guide arranged a rickshaw tour of the city, the Palace and the Market. Being pretty well tired of temples and palaces, I retreated to a rooftop garden/bar and quite by chance witnessed a political demonstration. There was a lot of shouting, then people running with hammer and sickle flags, followed by a paddy wagon full of soldiers in riot gear.

The big event for me in Kathmandu, however, was the flight over Mount Everest. At the time of his death, I think my father owned every book so far written about Everest. This was before it became just another expensive tourist destination. So it was in his memory that I shelled out US$120 for the trip with Nepal Airways. They guaranteed you would see Mt. Everest; this was because the cloud cover never exceeded 6,500 m and the mountain was 9,000 m. I traveled with Colin Whitehead, from the PRC in Edinburgh. There was fog at the Kathmandu airport that delayed departure, but we eventually left at 8.15 am in a 48 seater turbo-jet. It was a fantastic flight, first over the foothills and valleys approaching the Himalayas, and then the great mountain itself, with the peak glistening in the morning sun. It was mostly cloudy but on the return flight, we saw many more beautiful, rugged, snow covered peaks. I think I shot three rolls of film during the flight! Then we went back to the hotel for a very late breakfast.

This was the end of the Cook's Tour, but my flight out of New Delhi was not for another 3 days, so I had been booked for two nights in a hotel in Nagarkot, about one hour's drive east of Kathmandu. After the pollution and bustle of the capital, this was a most welcome change. The air was clear, and the silence, almost overwhelming. Each room in the hotel was named for one of the mountains; mine was Mt. Nilgiri, 7,061 m. It was quite a long way from the Himalayas, but when the clouds cleared, I could see parts of some of the mountains. It was said that Everest should be visible at sunrise; I did get up and look but I was not sure I saw it. However, the experience was worth the early alarm call.

Later, the hotel receptionist became my walking guide and we strolled for more than 3 hours. The high point here was about 2,200 m, so ¼ the height of Everest, but more than double the highest point in Great Britain. This break was so peaceful it was almost unreal. But all good things must come to an end, and I eventually was driven back to Kathmandu, stopping to take photographs along the route. All of this travel, and the transfer and hotel in Delhi, was part of the Thomas Cook service. I arrived in New Delhi around 4.00 pm. My wake -up the following morning 5.00 am so the fact that I described the hotel room as "battered" didn't matter much. That night, I ate at an ethnic Indian restaurant, accompanied by cloud of insects. The food was excellent; obviously the insects had good taste. I also finished the Crown Royal. I flew from New Delhi to London, and thence to Toronto, and for both flights I was upgraded to Business or first Class, which made life very pleasant indeed.

Australia

Early in 1997, we made our first trip to Australia. The first few days were spent in Sydney and the surrounding area, while I was on WPSA business, but then we stayed almost three weeks more for a holiday.

While I was working and visiting, Nita had a wonderful day in Sydney, meeting quite by chance, someone she had taught with in the 1960s at O'Connor Drive School in Toronto.

Next day we had a great tour of the Sydney Harbour area with Joe Vella and Rowley Horne. Joe had visited us in Canada not long before. Rowley was an extension specialist working with poultry. They knew the place inside out and took us everywhere! This included climbing to the top of one of the towers at the end of the Bridge. The Sydney Harbour Bridge had always fascinated me because it so resembled the Tyne Bridge, where I grew up. The resemblance should not be surprising: When Sydney called for tenders to build the Harbour Bridge, the Tyne Bridge had not long been completed, and the contractor clearly had an inside edge in the bidding. The Sydney bridge was quite a bit longer than the Tyne Bridge but the design was identical. I now have photographs of both of them, one of the Tyne Bridge purchased from a local newspaper by my father, and one I took myself during this day's tour. In one of the towers at the Bridge end, there was a museum, and one of the exhibits was the original contract, in pounds, shillings and pence; apparently the bridge was completed on schedule and with no cost overrun.

We ate a tremendous lunch with Joe and Rowley in the revolving restaurant atop the Victoria Square office tower, and later visited the Queen Victoria Building, which was almost demolished in the 1970s, but now wonderfully restored. We finished with a drink in the Marble Bar in the basement of the Hilton Hotel, which evoked the atmosphere of early 20th century London.

Joe and Rowley then drove us to the home of Mike and Patti Bertram, in Woolahra. Mike and I were born 3 days apart in Newcastle-on-Tyne and met at the Royal Grammar School. He joined the merchant navy after leaving school, and now had a shore job in Sydney. We had a fine evening and slept in what had been their kids' room in the basement. Mike went to work the following day and Patti took us on a tour of the local beaches, including the world famous Bondi and finally to Clovelly, where she left us for the day. It was a gorgeous little bay, with rocky outcrops protecting it from the Pacific waves. Lovely fine sand, and optionally topless, which suited us just fine. We had lunch in a local pub, and Mike and Patti picked us up and took us back for a barbecue dinner at their place. Later, Nita and I went to the Wharf Theatre to see the Sydney Theatre Company's production of *The Herbal Bed*; a beautiful space and a good play.

Next day, a Sunday, they drove us into the Blue Mountains, a splendid trip. We saw Echo Point and the Three Sisters, and had a good walk to view Katoomba Falls and the old mines. Finally we went to Sublime Point for yet more terrific views of these unusual mountains. On the way home we called to pick up AUS$1,500 in cash, being my travel grant from WPSA Australia, plus a one-day consulting fee. We took Mike and Patti for dinner to the Flavour of India.

We spent another relaxing day at Clovelly; I did some snorkeling and swimming, and we walked up onto the adjacent cliffs for super views of the ocean and the surrounding area. In the evening we took the Harbour Ferry to McMahon's Point, and walked to a high rise where our friends Graham and Robin Donaldson were on holiday. Great to see them in their home country! We got take-out Thai food, and as always, Graham had a fine wine selection.

We were sad to leave Sydney, but happy to spend two days in Melbourne, which was another great city. I mostly worked around Melbourne but we had enough time to enjoy the sights, and a great meal at Il Gamberi, which served Italian style seafood.

I also spent time working in Brisbane, which gave Nita the chance to spend a day on the beach at Surfers' Paradise. When I returned from my day on the egg farms, we were officially on holiday. We had dinner at Bob and

Sally Pym's, made somewhat chaotic by Sal's absence until about 9.30 at their son's school debate, but we enjoyed it nonetheless, especially after she returned.

Our next stop was Alice Springs. To get there, we flew from Brisbane via Cairns, and had great views of the Great Barrier Reef on the first leg of the flight. From Cairns to Alice Springs, we flew across desert; more than an hour passed without us seeing a single sign of human life. We rented a car in Alice, and drove (**very carefully, on the left side of the road)** to the Alice Motor Inn, where we stayed three nights.

One of the reasons to go to Alice Springs (there can't be many) is that it is the closest town to Ayers Rock (now officially Uluru). Close is a relative term – in this case 400 km. But there was no speed limit and hardly any traffic, so we drove there and back in 13 hours and saw what was to be seen. The temperature at the Rock was 40°C; there had recently been rain, and the whole place was besieged with flies. This must be a regular feature, as many people had face coverings. We spent time in the Cultural Centre and learned a bit about the history of the rock and the aboriginals, for whom it was sacred.

We found that there was more to Alice than the road to Uluru! We toured The Residence, formerly for government officials but now a heritage exhibit, the Museum, and the Old School (now the National Trust boutique). We climbed Anzac Hill to watch the sunset, and bought a pizza for dinner.

On our last day, we drove to the old Telegraph Station, and the original Alice Springs water hole. We spent time at the Royal Flying Doctor Service and learned how important it was to the far-flung community. The Ross River Homestead, we found to be a bit of a disappointment but the drive there was spectacular. We thoroughly enjoyed our time in "the middle of nowhere" but it's not a place to visit twice!

Our last destination in Australia was Port Douglas, where I planned to complete my SCUBA license and see the Great Barrier Reef at close quarters. Due to flight delays we arrived at the Lazy Lizard Motel at 20 minutes after midnight, but our room was waiting with the key inside.

I contacted a dive school and joined a class that had been doing what I did in Brantford. As was the case there, I could have been a father to any of the other four students. The instructor was not too happy with the situation, but I had paid and so he had to deal with me. We did work in the pool and the next stage was open water on the reef. We traveled there on a very sleek boat called Quicksilver, We eventually did three dives. The instructor wouldn't give me the SCUBA license but I got to see the reef anyway and it was quite spectacular. But I think Nita saw almost as much from the floating platform in a viewing room with a glass bottom.

We enjoyed Port Douglas; Nita bought some very nice clothes and a beautiful silk scarf that we had framed at home. We spent time on the beach and ate very well.

We did a full day guided tour including Cape Tribulation and the Daintree Rainforest. Cape Tribulation was named, apparently, for a bad time during Captain Cook's voyage. The trip also included Mossman Gorge and the Dinosaur Falls. At the Falls, the men of the group were encouraged to swim in the muddy, swollen river beneath the falls, while the women took pictures!

And one night we went to the Clink Theatre to see a community production of *The Odd Couple – Female Version* which we really enjoyed. The theatre was in an old Courthouse and the jail cells were the toilets! I have often wondered how Neil Simon would react to hearing his play in Australian dialect, compared to the original New York accent for which it was written.

We found Australia quite wonderful and couldn't wait to go back. We both felt very much at home and everyone seemed so friendly.

We had another very interesting holiday there following the WPSA Asia-Pacific Federation Conference in 2002. I had already contacted Ray Evans, another M.Sc. graduate from Wye, before the meeting. At the time, he was living at his late in-laws farm near Wooloorin, a 320 km drive from the Gold Coast. So we rented a car and drove there. The farm was quite small, with a mixture of bush, paddocks, some swamp and dams, and quite different from anything we had seen before. We had a good time reviewing what had happened to our various mutual friends since leaving Wye. Ray had spent most of the time in Australia and married there. He worked for the South Australia government, and lived in Adelaide. We only stayed one night before heading back to the coast at Noosa Heads on the Sunshine Coast. We stayed at Peregian Beach for a couple of nights. Unfortunately, the weather was mostly cool and cloudy, but we still managed to walk on the enormous beach, and even lay on it in one brief period of sunshine. One day we visited the ginger factory at Yandina and much against my instinct, bought a huge jar of preserved (in liquid) ginger which I insisted Nita carry home!

We arrived in Armidale as planned and stayed with Julie Roberts. Julie was a faculty member at the University of New England, and another student of the egg shell. She lived in a small house with many dogs and cats, but they got used to us very quickly and I even had a cat on my knee while reading when Nita and Julie went to explore the town. Julie's partner Tim came for a splendid dinner of roast leg of lamb and all the trimmings. Tim was a retired animal scientist and we found we had some mutual friends, as he had spent some time in Scotland. We had part of a day on campus and I met some of the faculty interested in poultry, especially Mingan Choct, who told me about a proposal to establish a Cooperative Research Centre for Poultry. This was intended not as a physical facility, but more of a formal way of scientists in different centres cooperating on joint projects. Australia's poultry scientists were spread about the country in the same way as Canada's.

After two nights in Armidale, we headed first East towards the coast, This proved to be the most spectacular scenery we had seen so far, through the Dorrigo Rainforest Preserve and the Skywalk, where we stopped for several hours. We stayed the night in Coff's Harbour, before heading for Sydney, to stay with Mike, my old school friend, and his wife Patti. The first day there we took the train into town for shopping and to book tickets for the Sydney Opera House, where we saw Gilbert and Sullivan's *Iolanthe*. This was one of the less famous operettas but we really enjoyed it, as well as experiencing the amazing acoustics. We had one day in the sun on Clovelly Beach before returning to Canada. Another great time in Australia!

Diversions
Driving to the Poultry Science meetings often gave us a chance for off-the-beaten-track-travel. The 1997 meeting was in Athens GA, and we drove almost the whole way there on I-75. On the return trip, however, we headed northeast towards Asheville, NC and picked up the Blue Ridge Parkway for over 100 miles. We stayed overnight in Spruce Pine, a tiny village in the mountains. It had a motel and a nice Golf Club where we ate dinner. We continued on non-major roads through part of Virginia and Kentucky, finally staying the next night in South Point, OH. Here we had time to spend by the pool and it really felt like a holiday! We spent the whole of the next day driving through Ohio and ended up in a motel in Toledo. The motel was very average but we had a terrific dinner in Stinger's Café. When we got home the following day, we had traveled 1850 km, compared with 1550 on the interstate on the way down. But well worth the extra time!

The 2005 PSA meeting was in Auburn AL. Piet and Therese Simons came over to attend the WPSA Board meeting also in Auburn, and Nita and I arranged some holiday experiences before and after. We drove our car from home, visiting Bill and Madelyn Weaver in Gloucester VA and spent a day in Williamsburg. We met Piet and Therese off their flight in Atlanta, and spent the first day in Savannah, GA. We did a tour on the trolley system and saw a lot of the town. Being August, it was very hot and we had to retreat to a pub to cool off! Some more walking brought us to the Civic Square market area. We had lunch in another pub, but while there, the most ferocious thunderstorm took place, lasting about 2 hours. We drove mostly country roads from Savannah to Auburn, slower but much more to see than on the interstates. We passed through Vidalia, GA, famous for its sweet onions.

After the PSA meeting, we drove back and around Atlanta, through Chatanooga and Knoxville TN and eventually to Gatlinburg, home of Dolly Parton's Dollywood, which we passed but did not visit. We had booked a condo at Deer Ridge, about 20 km out of town, which turned out to have the most spectacular mountain views, fully equipped kitchen etc. etc. We had to drive back to Gatlinburg for dinner and some food supplies. The following day, we drove through the Great Smoky Mountain National Park, gorgeous scenery, and stopped for a walk at Clingman's Dome, a high point off the main highway. Thunderstorms were in evidence and we had to abandon more walks until the afternoon. We ate our picnic lunch in the car. Later, we were able to walk for a while in the Cherokee Indian Reservation, along the Cherokee river.

We did some sightseeing in Gatlinburg the next day, including the Artisan's circuit, and then drove 40 minutes to Hartford, for a Whitewater rafting trip on the Pigeon River. There was a long safety talk, mostly about what to do if one fell out of the raft! A short bus ride took us to the river. We told the guide "Minimal risk, please, we are old people!", but we encountered several Grade 4 and many Grade 3 rapids along the way, (Grade 6 is the most dangerous) and we were all pretty well soaked when a Grade 1 thunderstorm hit. So when we finally got back to the start, we basically wrung out our clothes and sat on garbage bags for the ride back to the condo, showers, dry clothes and a comfortable drink before dinner.

On our journey the next day, we happened to pass the spot where we rafted; the river was obviously controlled by a dam, as on this occasion, we could have walked across it. We ended up in Asheville NC where we visited the Biltmore Estate, former home of the Vanderbilt family. This was an excellent visit, also partly shortened by thunderstorms.

From here we drove back to Atlanta, for Piet and Therese to catch their plane home, and Nita and I headed home on I-75 all the way to Detroit, with overnight stops in Athens TN and Lima OH.

Israel

In June 1997, we both went to Israel for the first, and, lamentably, only time. Nita did some tours while I attended WPSA meetings, but we both went on the Conference tours and then, later, a post conference trip to the Dead Sea.

We stopped to see the caves where the famous scrolls were discovered, and stayed at the palatial Crowne Plaza right on the beach of the Dead Sea. Of course we both went in and it was quite amazing: I actually read a newspaper while floating, and the paper did not get wet! It was extremely hot; 37°C in the shade and the water, almost the same. We had an afternoon trip to Masada, a mountain fortress built by King Herod. This was, I think, the first time ever we were almost forced to carry water, and it was good advice – we each drank about 3 l in the course of the trip, as well as, in my case, a couple of beers!

We returned to Jerusalem so that I could see some of the city, Nita having already had the grand tour. We were "befriended" by a guy called David who offered to show us around and we could "pay from the heart". He certainly showed us a lot of history over about 2 hours, and then said he thought US$120 would be about right! We gave him CAN$40 and fled back to our hotel. But we certainly saw a lot of Jerusalem and it was hard to forget. We spent the rest of the day by the hotel pool with friends, before packing in anticipation of our 4.30 am wake-up call. Nita flew directly to London and then home, while I went on to a WPSA meeting in Portugal.

Barbados

By early 1999 I had accumulated enough frequent flyer points for a flight to the Caribbean, so we decided on a winter holiday in Barbados in January. We found a hotel through our friend and now travel agent Pat Attridge, a place where we could do our own catering if we wished. It was called the Sandridge Beach Hotel. The hotel was on the west coast, about 50 km from the airport. We got there late, about 9.00 pm, when it was pitch dark, but found in daylight it was beautiful! We had 2 balconies where we could have our meals as long as we didn't mind sharing with the birds. The first day was cloudy but, of course delightfully warm. It was a ten minute walk to Speightstown (pronounced Spitestown) where we bought groceries for breakfasts and lunches, as we had decided to eat dinner in restaurants. The groceries were expensive (by our Canadian standards) but then so were the restaurant meals they replaced. When the sun came out later, we went to the nearest beach, which was gorgeous as only Caribbean beaches can be. We had to be careful in the sun our first day.

We took the bus to Bridgetown, the capital, the next day, and looked around. It was a bustling town, but we didn't particularly like it. We found the shops either tourist traps or cheap native stores selling things we didn't want or need. That evening we ate dinner at Fathoms, a very upscale restaurant overlooking, and 5 m from, the sea. It was very expensive but very good.

In order to see the island on our own, we rented a mini-moke for a couple of days. This was a very basic, tiny car with no doors or windows (most likely illegal now in these days of mega safety rules) but there were lots of them around. We really saw a lot of the island: Holetown, where we got the vehicle, Welshmans Gully, Harrison's Cave, the Flower Forest, and we ventured to the east (Atlantic) coast near Bathsheba. The second day we returned to the east coast and explored from Bathsheba south and the south coast, where we stopped and picnicked at Dover Beach on beautiful white sand. We bought some fresh fish in Oistins on the way home for a splendid dinner which Nita prepared.

I contacted Devere Cole, co-owner of Shaver Barbados and he and his wife Vera gave us dinner at Fathoms. We had a good chat about the old days with Shaver, and I told him about my work with the Egg Board. I found that many people, including him, were surprised when they learned that we promoted and advertised eggs. Since they were regarded as a staple, why advertise? I could point out the huge competition for breakfast as well as the discouragement from cholesterol and Salmonella.

All in all, it was a great holiday. We returned to Barbados quite recently on one of our Travelzoo specials, but we mainly stayed in the hotel (the trip was all inclusive) and enjoyed the warm February weather.

Italy
Many of our holidays were in conjunction with WPSA events; I mostly got my flight and hotel paid, so all we paid for was Nita's plane ticket and a few meals. Such a trip was our 1999 visit to Italy. The European Poultry conference was held in Bologna, and we spent time in Florence before, and Rome after the meeting. All this was arranged by our friend and travel agent, Pat Attridge. Florence was spectacular and we saw as much as we could in two days. Bologna itself was a wonderful place for holidays, and although I spent most of the time in meetings, Nita saw lots of the sights, and I got to see original copies of Aldrovandi's "Ornithologia" as part of a private tour in the University Library.

In Rome, we had a modest hotel (3 stars, but still modest) but we enjoyed the sightseeing. Like many tourist cities, Rome had a "stop and go" tour bus and we got tickets for two days. At this point, I was 63 and Nita, 56, both reasonably fit, so we did a lot of jumping on and off the bus! We spent a good deal of time in the Vatican (I noted one could spend a year if one studied it all) and saw the Sistine Chapel and the Museum. Lunch and back on the bus, and stopped to see Piazza Navonna and the Pantheon. On our final day we again used the bus and visited Piazza Venezia, where we climbed to the basilica and around the ruins. We didn't have the time to study this either. We walked to the Colosseum and had a short guided tour where we learned a bit more than we would on our own. Even **we** were exhausted after these two days, so it was good to have the upgrades for our flights home, and the associated lounge in Rome's Leonardo da Vinci airport.

At this stage in my life, I still used a film camera, and I had the pictures developed and printed in town. Today, I cannot imagine this but still have the prints to prove it happened. After a few years, however, I switched to a digital camera, so now all the pictures are stored in my computer and we hardly print any of them.

Mexico

The first holiday in Mexico was a package deal on Mexico's Riviera at Akumal, near Tulum. All inclusive, guaranteed sunshine, and a fairly simple flight all contributed to an enjoyable week. Buffet meals and unlimited beer and wine were welcome, and we did some long beach walks to compensate. We went on one of the optional tours to the Mayan ruins at Tulum, followed by time at a water-park called Xel Ha, where we snorkeled among the fish and coral reefs.

When I was visiting Geoff Fairhurst in France, he invited us to use his house in Nuevo Vallarta for a holiday before he moved there, which he expected to do late in 2004. So we planned the trip and also invited PJ's then girlfriend Melanie, and her mother Annie to join us for part of the time. This took place in February, 2004. We flew via Mexico City (with an overnight stay) to Puerta Vallarta, and were met by Enrique, the real estate agent who had found Geoff and Marcela the house, now named Villa Marcela. He helped us get a good rental car for US$150/week, and showed us the house and the nearby plaza for shopping and restaurants. This was all in Nueva Vallarta, about a half hour drive from Puerta Vallarta. We unpacked and went back to the plaza for groceries and a restaurant dinner. Coming back, we got hopelessly lost! We didn't know the street address and we must have driven 50 km before we found it by accident. A frightening experience indeed. Shopping was easy; there was a Wallmart in Puerta Vallarta and a good store in the local plaza. Eating out was fairly cheap and good. We had agreed to buy Geoff a barbecue, as he hadn't yet acquired one. We got it at Costco, and I assembled it; the instructions were in Spanish only but I had no parts left over and it seemed to work.

We spent several days exploring local beaches as well as sunbathing in the very secluded back yard. I wrote that there was nothing much more graceful than palm fronds in a slight breeze, and this was what greeted us every morning after breakfast. We would spend at least an hour sitting in and sometimes out of the sun before going anywhere, and clothing was always optional! We found one beach about an hour's drive away, where we could walk several km without seeing anyone, and an even more secluded bay. So we both got great all-over tans and generally avoided burns.

We were there for a week before Melanie and her mother, Annie arrived. We met them off the plane and took them back to the house. Melanie was on the lawn in her bikini almost immediately! I cooked us rib-eye steaks on the barbecue for the first dinner and they were pretty good. The barbecue used charcoal. I had become used to gas barbecues and all of the challenges of charcoal came back! Mainly the long wait before there was enough heat to cook anything!

We took them on a trip along the coast, headed towards Mazatlan (which Nita and I had visited on a rainy day earlier) but we got diverted, first to Suyalita, and then San Francisco, which turned out to be "the perfect beach" – one of many such places! We sat on the beach, went in the water, and eventually left in the early afternoon. We stopped in Ayala to buy some fruit and then drove home to Villa Marcela. I was always glad to get home; the driving was quite intense and everyone drove faster than I was accustomed to.

One thing we really enjoyed was the abundance of fresh fruit. We had a more or less continuous fruit salad bowl with pineapple, papaya, mango, orange and cantaloupe, with bananas on the side.

The three women spent a day shopping in Puerta Vallarta, while I did some writing work and checked email at a local internet café. This was of course, years before everywhere had wi-fi.

Another day, we drove through Puerta Vallarta, along a very spectacular coastline, and then into the mountains, to El Tuito (which I described as "the middle of nowhere") and then back to the coast at Mismaloya, where we did our usual beach thing and also went in the water. Melanie hosted dinner at Las Palomas, a restaurant in Puerta Vallarta Geoff had recommended.

Geoff had also told us about an all-day boat trip, and we did this with Melanie and Annie. One of the highlights for me was snorkeling with

Melanie around Los Arcos, a spectacular rock formation within the bay that includes Puerta Vallarta. We saw lots of fish even though the water was quite turbulent. We kept going along the coast, seeing communities with no road access, and stopped for a very good lunch with beer and shrimp at Las Animas.

After Melanie and Annie left, we had a few days on our own. We spent much of time sunning, and I did quite a lot of writing, for *World Poultry* and for the Egg Board newsletter. Nita had a couple of bad days with what we took to be Montezuma's revenge, which slowed her down, but all told it was a good trip. We always liked some sunshine to break up the Ontario winter, and Mexico had it in abundance.

Later in the year Geoff was diagnosed with lung cancer, and he never lived in Mexico. They had such plans; Geoff for fishing (they already had the boat) and Marcela for SCUBA diving. The place was quite perfect for them – a real tragedy they never got to use it. Geoff died late in 2005.

We went to Villa Marcela again in 2006, this time by ourselves. We did a lot of sunbathing and some swimming; there was a residents' club nearby that we could use for a day rate with a good beach for swimming. We went often to the almost deserted beach near Punta de Mita, where the few people who were there mostly disrobed completely, as were we. It was close to paradise.

Apart from sun and sea, we did another cruise in the bay, this time seeing lots of dolphins and whales, on the way to the Isles de Marietas. Here we had some beach time and also were able to do some snorkeling. However, the water was very turbulent and the fish, unexciting. Another boat trip took us to Yelapa, accessible only by sea, and noted for its waterfall. At this time it was barely a trickle!

Another activity at the local beach club was parasailing and Nita did this one sunny morning; she had a fantastic time and I captured it (partly) on video.

We also did one of the famed Canopy Tours in the rain-forest near Hacienda Palma Real. It was quite expensive but once in a lifetime was OK. And we were not getting any younger, so it seemed a good time to cross it off our bucket list. It was good fun and we enjoyed it, but once was surely enough.

On the day we were to leave, Marcela and her mother arrived from Cuernavaca to spend a few days at the Villa. It was our first meeting with her mother, a very gracious lady who unfortunately spoke not a word of

English. Marcela eventually settled the affairs in France and returned to live with her mother, who died in 2019.

Turkey

Immediately prior to the World's Poultry Congress in Istanbul, in June 2004, Nita and I had an amazing four day holiday arranged for us by the Congress organizers. We had a driver and a professional guide, Bulent, who had taken Bill, Hilary and Chelsea Clinton on a similar trip the previous year. They met us in Izmir, and we spent most of a day touring the local sights including of course, Ephesus. Nita hadn't seen this before and I didn't mind at all repeating the experience, with a much more informative guide than on the last occasion. I enjoyed seeing the Ephesus Library again, and mildly boasting that I once gave a speech from the steps; this was at the Egg symposium in 2001. We also saw the Virgin Mary's house and the ruins at Artemis.

In the afternoon we drove to Pamukkale, staying in the Colossae Hotel. We saw the old city of Heiropolis and were amazed at the "white cliffs" nearby, solid calcite as far as we could see. We spent time in the thermal pool and the jacuzzi before dinner, after which Nita insisted that we go to the belly-dancing demonstration. This was OK until the girl insisted I dance with her! My least favourite part of the trip so far.

The next day was mostly on the road, 600 km. We stopped *en* route at a carpet factory and were given a lot of information we really didn't need and, naturally, a very heavy sales pitch, easily resisted. The scenery was changeable; a very lush valley leaving Pamukkale, mountain ranges and steppe-like land, some agriculture, and a lot of scrub. We passed through Denisli, Cay, Konya and Aksry, ending up in Cappadocia.

We began to meet a few other poultry scientists here including Janet Fulton from HyLine. They were in a larger group while we were still in our private group of 2. It's hard to describe Cappadocia without pictures, of which I took many. The landscape was extraordinary, resulting from a combination of volcanic action, tectonic shift and erosion by wind, snow and rain. People had lived in cave-like structures in tall "tubes" of presumably clay left by the erosion but of course they were no longer inhabited. The following day we had a trip to Kaymakali, an abandoned city entirely underground with a former population of between seven and ten thousand. It was here that I acquired a very sore back, which was only resolved a couple of days later by a combination of a strong pain-killer pill and a $100 massage. We visited and onyx factory, where they created an egg from a cube of raw onyx (I still have the egg!). We also saw lots of turquoise and silver but didn't buy anything. One memorable activity was a walk in the Red Valley, and a short ride in a horse drawn buggy to a café where I had a much needed beer.

This was the end of our tour and we had a shuttle bus to take us to the airport at Kayseri, about 70 km, from which we flew to Istanbul for the Congress.

After the Congress, we went on one of the official post Congress tours, plus another short holiday to rest and relax, at a beach resort at Belek, east of Antalya.

The post-Congress tour was good, especially as we knew quite a few of the participants. We stayed at an hotel in Antalya and did tours by shuttle bus. Having had our own private tour, some of the Roman ruins we saw seemed somewhat familiar, and by the time we approached the fourth or fifth amphitheatre, my eyes were beginning to glaze over! But the guide was good and entertaining and we did not complain. We saw some wonderful coastal scenery as well. Two of the other participants were Dick and Jean Julian, from the Ontario Veterinary College in Guelph. I had known and worked with Dick a lot while I worked for the Egg Board, but it was nice to meet him away from work.

The tour lasted 3 days, and then we went to our beach resort for the final 3 days. This was part of the Turkish Riviera; lovely sand beach, endless food and drinks, and nothing to do! We spent the days on the beach, in and out of the water, which was beautiful. We found there were comparatively few English speaking people; lots of Russians and Germans. Some of the Russian women were extraordinary; huge breasts, tiny, sometimes one-piece bikinis and loud! One thing that bothered us was at the buffet meals; we took what we wanted and ate it all. They would take a plateful of, for example, fresh strawberries, eat very few and leave the rest which became garbage.

Turkey really gave us a wonderful time; the Congress was a big success, and our time before and after, extremely enjoyable.

Postscript
Of course we had many more holidays following my gradual slowdown of work and consulting, but this is not the place for them. Until 2008, we often had vacations along with the annual meetings of the WPSA Board. After the 2002 Asia-Pacific Conference, a post Congress tour of New Zealand was canceled for lack of support. So in 2003, we spent four weeks there with a rented car, and toured both islands. This was one of our best holidays ever!

We began to get regular emails from Travelzoo, which scoured the internet for special deals, and we had several trips essentially bought on impulse through them. These included 7-10 day all inclusive tours to Costa Rica, Ireland, China, Peru and the Dominican Republic.

We had always wanted to visit Alaska; after we had moved house in 2013, we got a mail shot from a local travel agent with a never-to-be-repeated offer from Holland America for a cruise to Alaska out of Vancouver. We did the cruise, and it put us off ocean cruises for life. Everything except the cruise itself was expensive; even a coffee one had to sign for. The land tours were good but they too were very costly. A few months after we got back, the agent invited us to a presentation by Viking Cruises, who offered river cruising in Europe and elsewhere. We got a bit of a discount and went first on their Grand European Cruise from Bucharest to Amsterdam. We were hooked! Viking included everything. A guided tour at each daily stop, endless coffee and snacks, and wine or beer with meals. Holland America did a body search on guests returning from shore to make sure we didn't bring any drink on board. Viking encouraged guests to buy local wine if we wanted a glass before dinner.

Best of all the optional extras with Viking was a concert in Vienna; music by Strauss and Mozart, with a glass of champagne in the intermission! We did their cruise from Moscow to St. Petersburg, and then the Eastern Europe cruise from Budapest to Bucharest. At the time of writing (late 2021) we hope to go on a river cruise in France, from Lyon to Avignon; it was canceled in 2020 due to the COVID-19 pandemic, but some day, we hope it goes! (Now, 2022, booked for 2023!)

Chapter 16

Our Son and Daughter

Peter Jon (PJ)

Our son, Peter Jon, was born in Dunfermline Maternity Hospital on September 24th, 1975. According to Nita, it was an immaculate birth, assisted by very efficient and professional midwives.

His name arose from a curious process. Every boy's name we could think of, except Peter, raised some memory from Nita of an objectionable brat she had encountered while teaching primary school. And we couldn't have two Peters in the house, so we added Jon. This was later abbreviated to PJ and sometimes Peege.

He was an easy baby to raise, as he slept most of the time! Interestingly, when he went to sleep in his crib in one of the upstairs bedrooms in our Scottish house, the cat would often join him and sleep on his feet (so as not, we surmised, to be bothered by his gurgling or crying). As soon as he awoke, however, the cat, sensing that quiet comfort had come to an end, would jump out and land with a thud on the floor, thus alerting Nita, who was downstairs, to his imminent need for attention.

He came to Canada at 22 months of age, quickly lost his Scottish accent, and grew up a proud Canadian. We opted to send him to French immersion school, which was newly offered in our region in an effort to produce more bilingual citizens. The system provided teaching in French in the mornings, English in the afternoons for the first few years of Public School. French as the teaching language continued into High School but at a reduced level. When he left school, he was comfortably bilingual, and could still, at 46, function in French if he had to, in spite of living all his life in English speaking environments. The only downside of the French immersion program was that it was not offered at the school closest to home, so Nita had to drive him.

PJ went to Southwood High School, about 2 km from the Folly. He was entitled to use the school bus but never did. However, when bad weather prevented the buses from running, he stayed home!

Team sports were never a factor in PJ's life. He learned to skate but never played hockey. He learned to ski in the back yard at home, on little plastic skis, and then took some lessons at the local ski hill called Chicopee. We ferried him and friends back and forth there on many cold winter nights.

PJ accompanied us on vacation while he was at school, and on the trips to Poultry Science mostly in the US. In 1988, he went to Camp Wanapitei for the first time. This was a wilderness camp on Lake Temagami in northern Ontario. The sessions lasted a month and were not cheap, but seemed to be a great way for young people to learn independence and leadership. He went there several times, and, as most summer camps do, they invited him to become a counselor. He wanted nothing to do with this! He said it would take all the enjoyment out of it, so that was the end of camp for him.

But his real athletic passion became mountain biking. This he began as a teenager and still continued at age 46. He financed his early bike by busing tables at a local restaurant, Café 13. He became very competitive, winning many local races and eventually, at age 17, became Ontario Junior Champion. This got him on to the Canadian National Mountain bike team. It was while he was on the Ontario Team in 1992 that he first visited Whistler BC. At that point, the die was cast, and his sole aim in life was to move there!

He did well enough in high school to be accepted into the Engineering program at the University of Western Ontario in London. (now called Western University). Engineering was considered the most intensive course after medicine, so the work was hard.

He spent a gap year in Whistler first, leaving home in September 1994, and traveling by bus through the US, stopping in Jackson MO to see friends, and Vail and Aspen CO for the World Mountain Bike Championships.

The first year he started living in a residence, but left after one semester saying there was too much distraction. At the end of his first year, he returned to Whistler for a year, and then lived for one year in the London condo we bought for him and our daughter Carole.

He had two or even three simultaneous jobs in Whistler. He bused tables at a high end restaurant, worked on one of the restaurants on the ski hill, and helped in a store selling mountain bikes. Work on the ski hill got him a free pass and space in the employees' dormitory. Before going to Whistler he had moved from skiing to snowboarding and became equally expert on the board. He spent another year in Whistler during the engineering course, and also an internship year with an auto parts company in Toronto, so his degree took six years from leaving high school. For his final year engineering project, he designed a novel suspension system for mountain bikes. When he made this presentation as part of the course, he received a mark of 98%! He graduated and got his Engineers' iron ring in March, 2001.

Following this, he got a job with another auto parts company in Toronto and enjoyed this immensely, as they had a contract engineering some components for a racing car. He got to travel to the Montreal Grand Prix among other events. The company also enabled him to take out a patent on his mountain bike suspension system, although it was never commercialized. The racing car was eventually completed, and PJ was then assigned to design components for the Ford Crown Victoria, This did not sit well at all. So, in 2003, he announced that he was quitting, buying a house in a remote village in BC, and making his living planting trees. He had experience tree planting from previous summer jobs. So off he went to Bralorne BC, pop. 39, for the next five years. We loaned him $20,000 as a second mortgage on the house. His system was to plant trees all summer until he had enough money to pay his mortgages, maintain his modest lifestyle plus keep a high-end snowmobile and his mountain bike in good shape. He also took with him his then girlfriend Melanie. She was trained as a glass artist, and PJ set up a small studio in the basement where she could produce her work. I don't think this was ever profitable, but Melanie did find whatever work was going in the village and helped as best she could. However, this relationship did not last, and she eventually moved to Vancouver with one of PJ's friends.

One of his favourite activities involved him and several others of like mind being taken with their bikes far into the mountains in a float plane, and cycling out. PJ got friendly with the float plane owner, and did some work for him in part payment for the trip. He also designed and built a rack attached to the plane to carry bicycles.

One of his friends on these trips developed serious and potentially fatal kidney disease, and after a lot of consultations, including with his loving parents, PJ donated one of his kidneys to his friend. This all worked out well and on his fortieth birthday, both of them did one of the trips with the float plane.

In 2010 PJ saw an advertisement in a magazine from a mountain bike company in Port Coquitlam BC, looking for a design engineer. The dream job! But he hadn't worked in engineering for the past five years, and did not have the P.Eng. designation that would allow him to sign working drawings. But he got the job, with Norco Bicycles, and moved south. However, he held on to the house in Bralorne as a retreat where he could practice the mountain biking and snowmobile activity he so enjoyed. On moving south, he reunited with Krystal Bodaly, whom he had met briefly in Bralorne. Krystal was a speech pathologist, worked full time, and had a condo in Maple Ridge BC, quite close to Port Coquitlam. So PJ. moved in with her and began his work designing mountain bikes. It was a feature of his life that regardless what happened, he always fell on his feet.

The relationship with Krystal quickly developed; she sold the condo and they bought a 3 bedroom house on the outskirts of Maple Ridge with a large garden. Krystal had a significant extended family, all in BC. At the time, her parents lived near Lilooet, on a small farm high up on the banks of the Fraser River, about four hours north of Maple Ridge. Her sister Alicia lived in Abbotsford, and they had numerous aunts, and her grandmother, all living within an hours drive. Nita and I spent two Christmases with them in Maple Ridge, but we didn't enjoy the weather (almost constant rain) and we sometimes felt a bit overwhelmed by the family!

PJ's job with Norco worked out very well; within a year, he got his P.Eng., and hired another engineer to work with him. Although the design work, marketing and sales took place in the Canadian office, all of the bicycles were manufactured in Asia, initially mostly in Taiwan. PJ traveled there once or twice a year and established good relations with their suppliers, often biking with the staff if he was there over a weekend. Later, most of the production was moved to mainland China and other Asian countries. By 2015, he had become Engineering Manager for Norco, with four subordinates.

In February, 2013, his son, Finlay Scott Hunton was born, and two years later, another son, Warner.

Kristal's sister moved to Kimberley, BC, and her parents were planning to re-locate there as well. She wanted to move along with them. So PJ negotiated a change with Norco; he resigned as Engineering Manager and was appointed Senior Design Engineer, and it was agreed he could work from home. He told me that the management part of the job was the least rewarding, and the reduction in salary, minimal.

So they sold the house in Maple Ridge, and were able to buy two houses in Kimberley, one to live in and one (with a small mortgage) to rent out. Their own house was quite beautiful, having been owned, and completely renovated, by a wealthy airline pilot prior to their purchasing it. Kimberley was ideal for them; you could see the local ski hill from their kitchen window, and mountain bike literally from their front door.

Carole Elizabeth
Carole was born on March 25, 1978, in Cambridge Memorial Hospital. Nita likes to tell this story: I for some reason had it in mind that Carole would be born at least a day later. So the night of the 24th, I cooked a

turkey dinner with all the trimmings, it being Easter weekend, and we duly ate at the usual time. About 3.00 am on the 25th, Nita woke me up as her contractions began, so up we got, and off to the Hospital. The on-call doctor was not her regular one, and the nurses were anxious to change shifts at 6.00 am. The birth was not immaculate; it was hurried and painful, but the baby was OK. Carole was named for my old friends, Carole Chassagnard (neé Shepherd) and Elizabeth Henderson (neé Dobson). Carole first lived at our Dakin Crescent house, but moved to The Folly when she was 2.

Like PJ, she went to French Immersion for her entire school career. Carole had no athletic ambitions but was very artistic from an early age. She became interested in theatre, maybe pushed a little by her parents, in her teens. She worked backstage and did a weekend workshop on Stage Management sponsored by the Western Ontario Drama League. Subsequently, she Stage Managed several shows at Galt Little Theatre. Once she went to University, she never seemed to have the time for this again, but she was an enthusiastic audience member, given the chance.

She began going to summer camp while she was at high school, but we thought there should be something a bit less athletic than PJ had done. We finally settled on Camp CanAqua, located on a small lake near Bancroft, ON. She learned kayaking and became an expert; also glass etching among other crafts. But the huge benefit Carole secured was lifelong friends. She eagerly became a counselor, stayed for several years and became Program Director. She still sees these friends regularly, even though some have scattered all over North America.

We had no idea what she might do in later life. When PJ went to University, she was adamant that she would do anything **except** Engineering. And yet, two years later, she followed PJ to Western, into the Engineering Department. Carole did not have a gap year, and lived the first year on campus. After that, we bought the condo on Summit Avenue and she lived there for four years. She actually managed the condo, collecting rent cheques and keeping the place full. It had three bedrooms plus a full basement, and while she paid no rent, the rent on the other rooms more or less covered the mortgage, condo fees and taxes.

Carole inherited part of my poor eyesight. She began to wear glasses in her teens, but in 2000 we gave her the gift of Laser treatment, at enormous expense! She was ecstatic. At the same time, I had my own eyesight assessed for the treatment, but the diagnosis showed that (in 2000 anyway) my vision was not susceptible to Laser treatment so I continued to wear glasses indefinitely.

Carole spent her summer vacation in 2000 planting trees in BC, again following in PJ's footsteps! He gave her the employment contacts, recommended work-boots and clothing, and was generally helpful. Carole enjoyed the camaraderie, the scenery and the paydays, but hated the job with a passion. She only worked a few contracts and then became a tourist for 3 weeks before returning home.

Between the third and final year, engineering students were encouraged to take internships, and Carole got a job at FAG Bearings in Stratford. We bought her a small car so that she could commute to work and still live in London. This worked out very well, and we sold the car at the end of the year at not too much of a loss. She enjoyed the work, and at the end of the year, the company offered to hire her after graduation. However, this would have involved her working in Sao Paulo, Brazil, at least at first, and she declined the offer.

Carole graduated in 2002, and at the traditional ceremony, where graduates received their engineer's ring, PJ presented it. This was, for us, very moving; they had their quarrels as children, but were close as adults. We were of course very proud of both of them. After the ceremony, we all ate dinner at the Veranda Café, one of our favourite places to eat in London for many years.

After graduating, Carole felt she needed some rest and a change of pace. So she decided to see the country by train. She bought a ticket that would take her to the west coast by any route, with multiple stopovers, and she was gone 3 months. She went everywhere, even Haida Gwai, met up with friends, made new ones, and altogether had a wonderful time. She kept a large illustrated log of her whole trip. When she returned she had no real plan. She stayed at home for a few weeks; no sign of job hunting! Then she decided to see the east coast. A camp friend invited her to stay in a house in Halifax with a bunch of college students, which she eagerly accepted, and got a job washing dishes at a high-end restaurant. There she met Dan Williams, who was training to become a chef. After a few months, she was no longer welcome in the student's house, and Dan was also moving, so what could be more convenient than moving in together? They rented the upstairs of a house in Halifax before discovering that the downstairs part was occupied by drug dealers. I never visited the house, but Nita saw it and was not impressed.

When Carole realized that washing dishes was not a long term career for an engineering graduate, she decided to take a teaching course, back at Western. So Dan, by this time qualified, got a job in London while Carole went back to being a student. They had a small apartment in the upstairs of a house not far from campus. Dan moved around quite a bit, as the chef business tended to be erratic. He actually spent a few months in Alberta, cooking for a mining camp.

Towards the end of the teaching course in early 2005, Carole was recruited to teach at an inner city school in Northampton, England. Of course by this time they were absolutely a couple, and Dan wanted to go with her to England. They had moved to Ottawa for a while and visited the UK Consulate to find out how Dan could get to go to England. (Carole had no problem, as with two British parents she was entitled to a British Passport). They were told Dan could go as a visitor, but would not be allowed to work. But if they were married, he could go as her husband and there would be no problem working. So they walked from the Consulate to the Ottawa Registry Office, got the necessary documents, and were married three days later, much to our surprise.

The job in Northampton was brutal. The kids were rude, undisciplined and uninterested in learning Math, which Carole was trying to teach. However, she survived the year with a lot of effort. Meanwhile, Dan got work in a pub, mainly microwaving frozen meals. But the leisure hours for a teacher were exactly opposite those for a chef, and they hardly saw each other. After a few months Dan was appointed "Chef in Residence" at another school in the same group as Carole's, and this worked very well. His students were there by choice and he had a great time. During the year, they were able to travel extensively in Europe, using discount airlines and cheap accommodation, and really made good use of their time. Nita and I visited them in the spring and we took them in a rented car to Cornwall, where we stayed in a B&B and toured the countryside and the coast, an altogether wonderful experience for all of us.

When they returned to Canada, Carole still had no job, and Dan had decided that the hours of a chef would never work while married to a teacher, and so he decided to change careers and study to become a photo-journalist. He enrolled at Loyalist College in Trenton, Ontario for the two-year course. Carole reverted to washing dishes, this time in a rather down-scale restaurant, and they were pretty hard up for a time. She eventually got a short term job teaching Math at the Sir James Whitney School For The Deaf in Belleville. Of course she needed an interpreter at the start, but quickly learned American Sign Language (ASL) and eventually became fully qualified and employed full time. She absolutely loved the work, although it was hard and sometimes frustrating. The school was residential. Many of the parents of the deaf kids had not learned ASL so when they returned home, the kids were unable to communicate.

Dan qualified in photo-journalism but instead of practicing, he decided to teach the course. He also taught some cooking related courses at Loyalist and Durham Colleges: although not full time faculty, he got enough contract work to keep him busy.

They decided shortly after they began living together that they would not have children. This was a surprise to us, as they both got along well with other people's kids.

They eventually bought an old farmhouse on the outskirts of Trenton with two acres.   The house was dilapidated and required much work, maintenance and upgrading. Nita never got to like the place, but they loved it and had no intention of moving.

While their wedding was attended only by Dan's brother and the necessary witnesses, they indulged in massive parties to celebrate their 5th and 10th anniversaries. (A 15th was planned for 2020 but rendered void by the COVID 19 pandemic.)   For the 5th they rented a huge barbecue and roasted a whole pig. Guests were from all over Canada and a few from the US.   Dan's chef friend Peter came from Vancouver to help with the cooking. There was endless beer and wine and everyone had a great time. Nita and I were the old fogies but we had a good time too, although we stayed in a nearby motel rather than camp on the grounds. The 10th anniversary was similar, but with roast lamb. There were people there from all over the place, and aged from a few months to me at 79 years.

Epilogue

I wrote my last paid article for a poultry magazine late in 2014, but I had been gradually reducing my output for a number of years prior to that.

I remained on the Board of the WPSA as Past President from 2004 until 2008, and helped with promotion of the twenty-third Congress in Brisbane, Australia. I prepared, with the Board's encouragement, a paper entitled "100 Years of WPSA" to celebrate the Centenary of the Association's founding, and presented it at the twenty-fourth Congress in Salvador, Brazil in 2012. I still scan the Journal contents page, but understand less and less of it!

I reduced my consulting and writing activities considerably after 2008 and eventually stopped seeking opportunities. This was partly because of inevitable aging, and a consequently lower level of ambition. But it was mainly lack of context; when was I last in a chicken house? What right did I have to pontificate about issues I no longer kept completely abreast of?

I was extremely proud to receive nomination, and subsequent election, to the International Poultry Hall of Fame at the Brisbane Congress. Thank you to the Canada Branch of WPSA and particularly Karen Schwean Lardner, for making the nomination. The citation says "contributions . . beyond the call of duty." That depends who was making the call; I enjoyed (almost) every minute of my time in various poultry occupations and never felt I was doing more than any other person would have done.

I hope I helped the Ontario Egg Farmers do things a little better for my being there. I know I was a significant part of the formation of the Canadian Poultry Research Council, and I am gratified to see what it is doing today, in 2022. As for my other activities, I always did what I thought would be best for the industry and those colleagues working in it.

Finally, if there are errors of fact contained in this memoir, I apologize; Nita read an early version and pointed out some mistakes, but any that remain are my sole responsibility.

Family life had its ups and downs, but in the end we have a comfortable home life and two successful, independent offspring of whom we are very proud. What more can I say?

With my mother and father   Near the Crown above Wye
in the garden, 1960   1960

Left, D.McQ Shaver with his military medals. Right, the author,
D.McQ. Shaver and Dr. George Ansah, geneticist with Hendrix
Genetics on the occasion of D.McQ's 90th birthday party

With Brian Ellsworth, General Manager, Ontario Egg Board

Examining Aldrovandi's original drawings at the University in Bologna.
L to r; myself, Julie Roberts, Dr. Benare, curator of the exhibit,
Kathleen, Univ. Glasgow, Sally Solomon and David Martin

Receiving the WPSA flag from Mrs. Anuradha Desai, at the 1996 World's Congress In New Delhi, India

With Dr. Bhargavi, Director of the B.V Rao Institute of Poultry Management in Pune, India

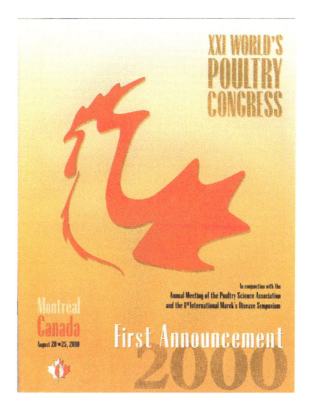

Cover of the First Announcement for World's Poultry Congress 2000 showing the abstract, but very avian logo, and the original one at bottom left.

With Nita and the "Colonel Sanders" lookalike at WPC 2000

With Mrs. Anuradha Desai, Nita (partly hidden) and Canadian Minister of Agriculture and AgriFood, Hon. Lyle Vanclief at WPC2000

Presenting the WPSA flag to Prof. Ruveyde Akbay, President of the Turkish Branch, WPSA, and the XXII Congress held in Istanbul.

Christmas time; the family including the Jack Russell, Woogle

The group just prior to leaving for Moosonee, June 22nd, 1986. Adults L-R David Bourn, Angela Bourn, Ada Semple, Chris Fairhurst, Geoff Fairhurst, me, Lawry Keene, Nita, Jean Keene and Norrie Semple. Carole and PJ seated on step.

Nita in Malta, 1976   Me in Trinidad, 1976

October 2008. L to R: Danny Williams,, Carole, Nita, me,
Kristal Bodaly and PJ at The Folly

GLOSSARY

Colour sexing   separating male from female newly hatched chicks based on the colour of the down. Can be easily done by unskilled people.

Feather sexing   separating male from female newly hatched chicks based on genetically determined length of pin feathers. Learning this method is relatively easy.

Fertility   Usually expressed as the percentage of eggs incubated that are fertile, i.e. contain a developing embryo

Four-way cross   A two-way cross male (A x B) crossed with a two-way cross female (C x D)

Hatchability   The percentage of viable chicks hatched from eggs incubated

Heritability   The degree to which a measurable trait (usually continuously variable) is influenced by genetic in contrast with environmental factors. Varies from 0 to 1.

Pedigree   describes the system whereby individuals in a flock are identifiable as to their ancestors. Achieved by mating one male to several females, identifying each female's eggs and incubating them in a separate container.

PSA   Poultry Science Association

Sexer   Skilled individual who can separate male from female newly hatched chicks. The Japanese method involved gently extruding sexual organs to make this distinction. Training for this method is laborious and may take several years.

Sexing errors   Male chicks incorrectly identified as females, or *vice versa*

Three-way cross.   Usually a pure male line (A) crossed with a two-way cross female (B x C)

Trapnest	A nesting box with a sliding door that closes automatically when a hen enters the nest, thus allowing for the egg to be identified to the hen that laid it.
Two-way cross	One pure line crossed with another (A x B)
Wingband	small metal identification tag attached to the wing, usually immediately after hatching
WPSA	World's Poultry Science Association